MANSFIELD AND DIRKSEN

Also by Marc C. Johnson

Political Hell-Raiser: The Life and Times of Senator
Burton K. Wheeler of Montana
Tuesday Night Massacre: Four Senate Elections and the Radicalization
of the Republican Party

MANZANITA, OREGON
JANUARY 15, 2024

MANSFIELD AND DIRKSEN

BIPARTISAN GIANTS OF THE SENATE

MARC C. JOHNSON

SCOTT:

THANKS FOR REACHING OUT. I
HOPE YOU ENJOY THIS POLITICAL HISTORY.

WARM REGARDS.

Marc C. J

Publication of this book is supported in part by the generosity of Edith Kinney Gaylord.

Library of Congress Cataloging-in-Publication Data

Names: Johnson, Marc C., 1953– author.
Title: Mansfield and Dirksen : bipartisan giants of the senate / Marc C. Johnson.
Description: Norman : University of Oklahoma Press, [2023] | Includes bibliographical
    references and index. | Summary: "The excavation of a cross-party political relationship
    that sheds light on the workings of the U.S. Senate during the 1960s. From divergent
    backgrounds and ideologies, Mike Mansfield of Montana and Everett Dirksen of Illinois were
    responsible for making the Senate work amid political upheaval. Their efforts resulted in a
    spate of surprisingly durable legislation around civil rights, voting rights, the environment,
    and social welfare"—Provided by publisher.
Identifiers: LCCN 2022061350 | ISBN 978-0-8061-9269-7 (hardcover)
Subjects: LCSH: Mansfield, Mike, 1903–2001. | Dirksen, Everett McKinley. | United States.
    Congress. Senate—History—20th century | United States. Congress. Senate—Majority
    leaders—History—20th century. | United States. Congress. Senate—Minority leaders—
    History—20th century. | Legislators—Montana—History—20th century. | Legislators—
    Montana—Illinois—20th century. | Civil rights—United States—History—20th century. |
    Suffrage—United States—History—20th century. | Environmental policy—United States—
    History—20th century.
Classification: LCC JK1161 .J64 2023 | DDC 328.73/071—dc23/eng/20230307
LC record available at https://lccn.loc.gov/2022061350

1 2 3 4 5 6 7 8 9 10

In memory of
three men who inspired and educated me about politics

Cecil D. "Cece" Andrus
governor of Idaho, secretary of the interior

Burdett "Bird" Loomis
scholar, mentor, citizen

Walter Nugent
intellectual, historian, gentleman

CONTENTS

INTRODUCTION

A DIFFERENT SENATE

> While I am about it, let me pay tribute to the humility and forbearance
> of the majority leader of this body. Believe me, Mr. President, I love him.
> I have been in his office many times. I know what a humble character he is
> and how he has tried to contrive an agreement, one way or the other.
>
> —EVERETT MCKINLEY DIRKSEN, 1962

This is the story of a United States Senate that no longer exists.

For nearly a decade, from 1961 to 1969, a Democratic and a Republican leader sat across the Senate aisle from each other. Competing, collaborating, and compromising, together they helped create some of the most important and enduring legislation in the history of the Republic.

The Senate of Mike Mansfield and Everett Dirksen in the 1960s now seems like an artifact of political history, a relic of an era when substantial elements of both political parties, and their leaders, considered it imperative to overcome their partisan inclinations in order to find common ground and advance progress on enormous national challenges. That it seems unthinkable for the Senate—and our politics—to work again as it did when Mansfield and Dirksen occupied the front-row seats of leadership is both a cautionary tale about Senate and democratic dysfunction and divide and, ultimately, evidence of a tragic failure of modern political leadership.

When pollsters from the Edward M. Kennedy Institute surveyed voters in 2018 regarding their attitudes about and knowledge of the Senate, fully 84 percent of respondents said that "most senators are unwilling to make compromises in order to get things done," and 80 percent indicated their belief that individual senators were too dependent on party leaders telling them what to do. Dissatisfaction with the Senate is a bipartisan issue among voters; in the same poll, only 28 percent of

1

those surveyed expressed satisfaction with the work of the institution that sits at the pinnacle of all American political institutions. The Gallup polling organization has been tracking congressional approval for decades, and its surveys broadly confirm a widespread belief that the Senate fails to live up to the expectations voiced by the Founders and by Alexis de Tocqueville who, as he observed the Senate in 1832, was impressed by the quality of its members. "Every word uttered in this assembly," Tocqueville wrote, "would add luster to the greatest parliamentary debates in Europe," while senators "represent only the lofty thoughts [of the nation] and the generous instincts animating it, not the petty passions." James Madison explained the necessity of the Senate by contrasting it to the unruly House of Representatives. Senators, Madison wrote, would be more experienced, serve longer terms, and possess a "greater extent of information and stability of character" than members of the House. Therefore, Madison believed, necessary balance and reflection would be maintained in the federal system: "The mutability in the public councils, arising from a rapid succession of new members, however qualified they may be, points out, in the strongest manner, the necessity of some stable institution in the government." That stable institution would be the United States Senate.[1]

The distinguished political scientist Ross K. Baker, a student of Congress and its history, has observed that "there is no institution in America that invites nostalgia more than the U.S. Senate," and on "no aspect of Senate life is the harsh light of nostalgia more scorching than in comparing today's leaders with those of the past."[2]

The journalist William S. White, a close confidant of fellow Texan Lyndon B. Johnson (LBJ), helped glamorize—and mythologize—the modern Senate in his popular 1956 book *The Citadel*. White's account helped cement the image of the Senate as a cozy club of (mostly) great (mostly male) statesmen where personal integrity was the only overarching rule. In White's frothy telling, the Senate "very often reflects the best instincts, and very infrequently the worst instincts, of the whole long political tradition with which the Anglo-American race . . . has endowed the world." But perhaps White got closer to the truth with this description: "the Senate is in a sense a high assembly but in a deeper sense it is a great and unique human consensus of individual men." Emphasis on *individual*. This study aims to analyze and explain one period in Senate history when the bipartisan leadership of the institution, as opposed to the influence of "individual men," allowed the Senate often to reflect the best intentions of a great democratic institution.[3]

Leading the Senate and the political parties that constitute it has always been an ill-defined, difficult business. Two of the more highly regarded Senate leaders of the recent past, the Democrat Robert C. Byrd and the Republican Bob Dole, used the same word—slave—to describe the job of Senate leader. Beyond what is called the "power of first recognition"—a powerful tradition allowing the leader to gain recognition before any other senator—a senator in majority leadership has few formal duties or real defined power.[4]

It has only been in the last one hundred years or so that the Senate has had a formal leadership structure, and Senate scholars Richard A. Baker and Roger H. Davidson have speculated that the Founders, who invented the Senate as part of a grand compromise to ensure the creation of a new nation, would be puzzled that the most individualized of political institutions needed such a position. Yet, from the beginning, Senate leadership has involved more than rules and institutional tradition. The personality of the leader has been an essential ingredient in whether the Senate can be made to work. Every subsequent Senate leader, whether or not they have known it, owes something to John Worth Kern, an Indiana Democrat who was among the earliest recognized majority leaders. Kern disdained an "iron fist" approach to the job in favor of "cajolery, humor, one-on-one bargaining, and personal rapport," yet as Walter J. Oleszek has written, Kern and every subsequent Senate leader had to confront "a continuing and perplexing condition: how to bridge the gulf between individual rights and collective action." Emphasis on *individual*.[5]

Thanks to Robert Caro's masterful study of Lyndon Johnson's Senate leadership in the 1950s, and William White's contemporary mythmaking about Johnson's elevated leadership status, all contemporary Senate leaders are measured against the LBJ legacy, even though Johnson's mastery of the Senate took place in a wholly different time when the ideological makeup of both parties was dramatically different than today and when bipartisanship was often a regular feature. Still, accounts of Johnson's obvious political skills—perhaps flavored with a measure of nostalgic mythology regarding his unrelenting, indeed often ruthless, passion for power— means no modern Senate leader seems able to measure up to the Texan. Yet, it is important to note that, beyond striving for cohesive party loyalty, no Senate leader since Johnson's time has claimed to emulate his "iron fist" approach to the job. In fact, the model Senate leader, his legacy invoked by partisans on both sides of the aisle, is not the overpowering, striving politician from the Texas Hill Country, but rather an unassuming college history professor from Montana.

Democrat Mike Mansfield amassed enormous influence and respect and remains the longest-serving majority leader in Senate history, not by accumulating personal power, but by giving power away. Mansfield's style of leadership made a virtue of the Senate's individualism—every senator, no matter how junior, no matter how powerless was the equal of every other senator. Mansfield's unfaltering sense of fair play and commitment to the Senate as the indispensable foundation of US government remains the legacy of his leadership. "Where Johnson was the Texas trail boss," Ross Baker wrote, "Mansfield was more like a Basque shepherd who ushered the Senate into the modern era, where the assertion of individual prerogatives trumped fealty to party leaders." Mansfield harbored, as the journalist Andrew J. Glass observed, "a somewhat mystic sense of the Senate's dignity and integrity," yet his benevolent style of leadership could not "abide behavior that tends to throw the Senate into disrepute."[6]

The Montanan was the anti-Johnson. "When Lyndon was the leader, he liked to play tricks on you," remembered John J. Williams, an iconoclastic Republican from Delaware. "The game was always trying to outfox Lyndon. But I would never try to pull anything like that on Mike. Why, he'd just turn around and say, 'The Senator is perfectly within his rights . . .'"[7]

While students of "the world's greatest deliberative body" can be forgiven for lamenting that we have not enjoyed better leaders throughout our history, in truth there has never truly been a golden age of the Senate. There simply have never been perfect politicians or Senate leaders; and Senate leadership, even when operating at a high level, has not always functioned in ways that have brought lasting credit to the institution. As onetime Senate staffer Ira Shapiro has noted, through good leaders and bad, "the painful truth is that the Senate has failed to measure up to the challenges of the times for long periods of American history." Yet, during the particularly contentious decade of the 1960s, Mansfield's Senate was as good as the Senate has ever been or is ever likely to be. This apex happened for reasons of personality, empathy, dignity, and candor, as well as a particularly unusual and effective type of political leadership.[8]

The senator who sat across the aisle from the majority leader, Republican leader Everett McKinley Dirksen of Illinois, was a perfect counterpoint to Mansfield in every important way. As different in personality and physical appearance as Butte, Montana, is different from Pekin, Illinois, Mansfield and Dirksen made the Senate function during tumultuous times. "You get more votes with an oil can than with a baseball bat," Dirksen was fond of saying, and his political oil lubricated, among other things, the historic Civil Rights Act and a host of other enduring and bipartisan legislative accomplishments. "We have an understanding that neither of us is caught flatfooted by the other," Mansfield said of his opposite number. "There's a fair exchange, scrupulously honored. If we can't work together, the Senate can't work."[9]

Dirksen reciprocated: "There has never been a time with a divisive spirit in the Senate," he said. "Mike could not come in that door and put all his cards on the table. 'All right,' he'll say, 'leadership is a two-way street—what do you think we should do?'" And Dirksen, operating always in the minority, time and again rejected partisanship when the Senate and the nation required progress.[10]

The two leaders were, of course, committed partisans. They certainly at times disagreed, most consequentially in their starkly different positions on America's tragic role in Vietnam, a divide they arguably might have done more to bridge. They advocated for, defended, and led politicians, and the business of doing so—like "trying to push a wet noodle," Dirksen's son-in-law Howard Baker, another Senate leader, called it—could be messy and contentious. Yet neither man was ever mean, small-minded, or politically petty. Each loved the Senate and its institutional importance, and each admired and genuinely liked the other.[11]

In a way rare before and unheard of since, the Mansfield-Dirksen Senate of the 1960s simply worked.

"What united America during those years, to the extent that it was united," the literary and social critic Bruce Bawer has written of the 1960s, "was not an elaborately articulated ideology but a broadly shared set of good intentions." But the promise of a New Frontier ushered in with John F. Kennedy's razor-thin presidential victory in 1960—113,000 votes would have changed the outcome, electing Richard Nixon— gave way to superpower rivalries, including the closest the world has yet come to nuclear war, social and racial strife, political assassinations, and a tragic war. Still, in this milieu, Mansfield and Dirksen assume their rightful places as architects of the political accomplishments of the decade: Congress defeated filibusters to pass landmark civil and voting rights legislation, created Medicare, and established a broader framework for conservation and environmental protection, while the Senate ratified the first treaty aimed at controlling nuclear weapons. Mansfield and Dirksen, amid much dissension, even chaos, in US culture and in politics—not to mention the divides between parties and among partisans—made the Senate function. How they did so is the subject of this book.[12]

The story that follows is not strictly chronological. The first chapter tells the story of a great Senate debate that took place against the backdrop of the still-developing Cold War and that serves in a way as a case study of the Mansfield-Dirksen approach to leadership and to the Senate. Two "Elements of Leadership" sketches explore the rhetorical styles of the leaders and how each interacted with the press. Chapters 2 and 3 detail the backgrounds and political coming-of-age of the two men who would lead the Senate in the 1960s. Chapter 4 charts the very nearly parallel paths Mansfield and Dirksen traveled to Senate leadership. Chapter 5 deals with how Mansfield and Dirksen each dealt with their former Senate colleague John F. Kennedy on foreign and domestic policy, and begins to probe the one great area where Mansfield and Dirksen arguably failed to bridge a partisan divide and, had they done so, might have avoided, or at least ameliorated, the calamity of war in Southeast Asia. Chapter 6 profiles the Senate leaders at the end of the Kennedy presidency. In chapter 7, Dirksen and Mansfield deal with another former Senate colleague who is determined to "out Kennedy Kennedy" on civil rights and create a Great Society. Chapter 8 traces Mansfield's persistent and prescient warnings about Lyndon Johnson's inability to extract the United States from its jungle war. Chapter 9 witnesses the last gasps of the Great Society, as Dirksen's influence declines leading up to his death in 1969 while a new Republican president—one Dirksen was not completely comfortable with—rises to dominate Washington. The epilogue considers the legacy of arguably the two most successful Senate leaders of the twentieth century and briefly touches on whether the type of leadership Mansfield and Dirksen embodied in the 1960s—friendship, candor, abiding respect for the institution of the Senate, and genuine belief in bipartisanship—could possibly work again.

1 THE MANSFIELD-DIRKSEN WAY

[The president] shall have Power, by and with the Advice and Consent
of the Senate, to make Treaties, provided two-thirds of the Senators
present concur.

—ARTICLE II, SECTION 2,
UNITED STATES CONSTITUTION

Prolonged contemplation of the nuclear effect could lead even the
most bellicose to the conclusion that mutual incineration was
of dubious benefit.

—ARTHUR M. SCHLESINGER JR., 1965

President Harry Truman once told J. Robert Oppenheimer, the theoretical physicist
and one of the creators of the first atomic bomb, that he simply could not envision
the Soviet Union ever possessing such a weapon. Nevertheless, on September 3,
1949, the United States lost what had been a four-year international monopoly on
the atomic bomb. Three weeks later, a still-disbelieving Truman told the world of
the development, carefully refusing to call the detonation in remote Kazakhstan a
bomb. "This probability has always been taken into account by us," Truman said,
attempting both to reassure Americans and downplay the significance of what most
policy makers knew to be a world-changing development. To cite just one example,
David Lilienthal, the head of the Atomic Energy Commission, called the existence
of a Soviet A-bomb a "whole box of trouble."[1]

Among other things, Soviet development of an atomic weapon gave the lie to
the American conceit that the United States held, and would forever maintain, an
insurmountable scientific advantage over the Russians, a technical superiority that
many believed would automatically translate to military dominance. The Soviet
atom bomb detonated the full-scale Cold War nuclear arms race. The United States

maintained a nuclear arsenal of about fifty bombs in 1948. By mid-1950 the number stood at some three hundred. With nuclear weapons development came the need, at least in the view of many in the scientific, political, and military community, to test those weapons. By 1963 the United States and the Soviet Union had conducted 434 nuclear tests in the atmosphere and more than 1,300 underground.[2] Those tests—others were conducted by the United Kingdom, France, and eventually China—spread enormous amounts of radioactive fallout across the globe. By one scientific estimate, they may have eventually contributed directly to nearly 2.5 million deaths and countless other cases of cancer of various types.[3]

With the nuclear genie fully out of the bottle, the decade of the 1950s saw both a steady expansion of nuclear weapons development and profound concern about how to begin to control those weapons. Both the United States and the Soviet Union advanced various schemes to limit and eventually eliminate nuclear testing, an effort that finally brought the issue of a limited test ban treaty to the floor of the US Senate in 1963. The issues were incredibly complex, often dividing scientific, military, and political leaders on goals and strategy. Negotiations were conducted against a backdrop of profound international distrust stoked by the intense anti-Communism of most congressional Republicans and many Democrats, particularly southern Democrats. Hawkish backers of absolute US military superiority existed in both political parties, most of whom believed that any deal with the Soviets would be a bad deal for national security. The Soviet Union was a suspicious, wary negotiating partner, and a host of Cold War tensions, from Cuba to Southeast Asia and the Congo to Berlin, hindered treaty-making efforts. US allies were often nervous, circumspect observers of the superpower rivalry. The outcome of the nuclear-testing debate held implications not only for preventing the unthinkable—a catastrophic nuclear war—but also for preserving and enhancing political power in Washington. President John F. Kennedy, despite facing a reelection campaign in 1964, pushed and prodded the negotiations forward, often in the face of both partisan resistance and opposition from his advisors and his own party.

Fortunately, Kennedy enjoyed a remarkably productive personal and political relationship with two men, the majority and minority leaders of the US Senate—Democrat Mike Mansfield of Montana and Republican Everett M. Dirksen of Illinois—who helped him navigate the tricky path to secure the advice and consent of the Senate. The ratification of the Limited Nuclear Test Ban Treaty in 1963, the foundation of every subsequent effort to control nuclear weapons, stands as Kennedy's major foreign policy accomplishment involving the Senate. At the same time, the episode is one of the best illustrations during the 1960s of how Mansfield

Senators Mike Mansfield and Everett Dirksen, photographed together in 1964, formed
the most effective bipartisan leadership team in modern Senate history. (*US Senate
Historical Office*)

and Dirksen, opposites in both personality and ideology, made the institution of
the Senate work. How and why this foundational treaty came to be during a contentious, indeed frightening time in world history, is, of course, a tale of political
skill, timing, and deal making. It is also a story of how cooperation by the most
successful bipartisan leadership team in the history of the modern Senate moved
the country—and the world—to a safer place.

Mike Mansfield was a remarkably self-effacing, laconic former history professor
who had once worked in the copper mines of his adopted hometown of Butte, Montana. Reporters frequently became exasperated with Mansfield's cryptic "yup" and
"nope" answers to their questions, but he came to command a level of respect,
indeed reverence, that has not been seen since his departure from the Senate in 1977.
Mansfield brought to the Senate his own version of Montana's progressive political

tradition along with an abiding interest in foreign policy, particularly regarding Asia, a subject that had been his focus as an academic. Mansfield was nothing if not a political pragmatist. As he told Neil MacNeil, Dirksen's biographer, "When it comes to parliamentary tricks, I have none. And if I had any, I wouldn't use them. An open-door policy is the only way I can operate. It's the only way I can hold the trust of my colleagues. I make no deals of any kind." A simple senatorial head count was enough to show him that to get big things done, the majority leader needed the help of the minority leader and, of course, the Republican votes Dirksen could influence. Mansfield's approach was simple but required constant, committed work. He would build trust and respect in ways large and small in order to draw against that reservoir of goodwill when he needed to do so. Mansfield described himself as "a conservative-liberal" who believed in "slow evolutionary change" that, while not always satisfying to everyone, would nevertheless be enduring.[4]

Everett Dirksen's mellifluous voice—he acted in and wrote plays as a young man—earned him the title "Wizard of Ooze" and made him a talented political showman, but he also became, particularly in the 1960s, a crafty legislative tactician. With an unruly mop of curly hair, Dirksen was never at a loss for words, which at least early in his congressional career, he offered in service of very conservative Republican policy. Yet his ideology could be as fluid as his vocabulary. In the 1950s, Dirksen was a devotee of conservative icon Robert Taft and strategized Republican efforts to head off a Senate censure resolution against Joseph McCarthy. Later, he found a way to lead his party to embrace civil rights legislation even while major spokesmen of his party—Barry Goldwater most prominently—rejected what Dirksen recognized as the inevitable arc of American history. During his nearly eighteen years in the Senate, Dirksen never once served in the majority, yet he became one of the most powerful, influential, and recognized figures in American politics.

⁓

The architects of the American Constitution were profoundly concerned about creating a system of government that would constrain the worst impulses of any of its separate parts. There would be checks on power and a balance among the three distinct branches. When it came to making treaties and ratifying them, even Alexander Hamilton, an advocate of a strong executive, applauded the constitutional checks on presidential power. Dividing treaty-making power between the executive, who could negotiate treaties with foreign governments, and the Senate, which required two-thirds of senators present to ratify the president's work, Hamilton wrote, "is one of the best digested and most unexceptionable parts of the [Constitution]."

The high bar required for Senate approval was, Gouverneur Morris observed, a desirable thing. "The more difficulty in making treaties, the more value will be set on them," he said. The Founders also sought to make treaty making rare. James Wilson, a delegate to the Pennsylvania ratifying convention, for example, said the power "should be very seldom exercised" and predicted "it will be but once in a number of years, that a single treaty will come before the senate."[5]

Even given the skill, passion, eloquence, and determination he brought to the effort to reach an agreement around nuclear testing, Kennedy still had to deal with the very real political reality that two-thirds of the Senate would have to approve any agreement he struck with Soviet leader Nikita Khrushchev. Luckily for the president, Senate leaders Everett Dirksen and Mike Mansfield seemed to embrace the sage advice of one-time Secretary of State Dean Acheson: "The central question is not whether Congress should be stronger than the Presidency, or vice versa; but, how the Congress and the Presidency can both be strengthened to do the pressing work that falls to each to do, and to both to do together."[6]

The 1950s saw a dramatic increase in the global nuclear arms race, often with frightening consequences. In March 1954, the United States denotated a powerful hydrogen bomb over Bikini Atoll in the Marshall Islands in the Pacific. The weapon was a thousand times more powerful than the bomb dropped on Hiroshima at the end of World War II. The political fallout from the massive atmospheric test equaled the radiation fallout, particularly after twenty-three Japanese fishermen working on a trawler near the detonation site suffered radiation sickness, with one dying. Voices as diverse as Pope Pius XII and Albert Schweitzer called for a ban on atmospheric tests to no avail; still, the tests continued and even increased with the United Kingdom detonating its own hydrogen bomb in 1956. Public concern over testing continued to grow in the United States with every new explosion. Democratic presidential candidate Adlai Stevenson, for example, called for a testing ban during his 1956 campaign against Dwight Eisenhower. Early in 1957, a Gallup poll found that 63 percent of the Americans surveyed favored some sort of test ban. Only 20 percent had held that view a year earlier. However, it was the Soviet government that first formally proposed a test ban in 1956.[7]

Mike Mansfield, at the time the Democratic whip and understudy to Majority Leader Lyndon Johnson, cited the poll results as well as the public statements from the pope, Dr. Schweitzer, and others in what he called his "H-Bomb" speech to the Senate in June 1957. By being the first to propose a limitation on nuclear testing,

Mansfield argued, the Soviet Union had captured a public relations advantage over the United States, and he endorsed negotiations to limit testing, a move that he claimed could eventually lead to reducing the number of weapons. "I am convinced," Mansfield said, "that a proposal to limit and restrict future nuclear tests on a multi-lateral basis would do the United States more moral and practical good in the eyes of the world than anything else we might do. Such a ban would re-establish a feeling of international confidence." He was correct in his prediction but fulfilling the goal would take seven more years.[8]

On October 31, 1958, three-party talks involving the United States, the United Kingdom, and the Soviet Union began in Geneva, aimed at crafting a test ban treaty. Eisenhower attempted to jump-start the talks by declaring a one-year halt in US testing effective from the day the negotiations commenced. Yet, hindered by complex issues surrounding verification and under a heavy cloud of distrust, the talks moved at a glacial pace, with many US officials warning repeatedly that "we cannot trust the Russians on this or anything else." Even after President Eisenhower called "an effective ban on nuclear testing . . . an essential preliminary to . . . attaining any worthwhile disarmament agreement," he faced skepticism and pushback from hawkish Republicans, conservative southern Democrats, and his own advisors. Many GOP leaders, having enjoyed the political advantage of bashing Democrats for what they contended were foreign policy failures related to the Soviet Union and China, also feared the loss of their political advantage if a Republican president seemed too eager to find common cause with the Communists in the Kremlin.[9]

The Geneva talks went totally off the rails in May 1960 when an unarmed high-altitude US reconnaissance aircraft—a U-2—was shot down over the Soviet Union and the pilot, Francis Gary Powers, was captured. With the 1960 election looming and the Geneva talks in a stalemate, Eisenhower contemplated lifting his own testing ban, fearing that it was disadvantageous to US national security. Eisenhower believed cancelling the test ban would be particularly compelling should his vice president, Richard Nixon, prevail in that year's election against Massachusetts Senator John F. Kennedy, but when Kennedy won the White House in November in one of the closest elections in American history, Eisenhower reluctantly concluded it would be imprudent to tie the hands of his successor. Nevertheless, as he wrote in his memoir, "I emphasized to President-elect Kennedy my conviction that our nation should resume tests without delay." Kennedy had other ideas.[10]

Most of the headlines from Kennedy's first speech to Congress in late January 1961 focused on his economic agenda—Dirksen said the new president was promising "more of everything for everybody, everywhere, all the time." Still, the president did say, "It is our intention to resume negotiations," toward a test ban treaty, "with any nation . . . willing to agree to an effective and enforceable treaty." Later in 1961, Kennedy told the Soviet newspaper *Isvestiya*, edited by Khrushchev's son-in-law, that a treaty limiting nuclear testing "would lessen the contamination of the air, it would be a first step towards disarmament, and I felt that if we could achieve an agreement in this area, we could then move on to the other areas of disarmament which required action." Still, the widespread skepticism in official Washington was underscored by a report that John A. McCone, the outgoing chairman of the Atomic Energy Commission, issued the same day Kennedy spoke to Congress. McCone, later head of the Central Intelligence Agency (CIA), called for the end to the "unpoliced moratorium" on testing. The moratorium was hampering development of new US weapons, McCone said, and absent speedy conclusion of an "effective and enforceable treaty," the situation presented a grave threat to national security.[11]

From the outset, Kennedy's goal of a test ban treaty was complicated by partisan politics as well as by widespread opposition from the powerful military and scientific nuclear community. It became even more problematic after a series of confrontations with the Soviets during the first two years of his presidency. The US-supported invasion of Cuba, a plan hatched during Eisenhower's presidency but implemented by Kennedy and backed by the CIA, ended in a fiasco in April 1961 when Cuban expatriates were routed by Fidel Castro's forces at the Bay of Pigs. A June 1961 US-Soviet summit in Vienna was generally perceived as a failure, highlighting Kennedy's foreign policy inexperience and igniting a new crisis after Khrushchev ended the summit by demanding that the United States withdraw from Berlin by the end of the year. Kennedy rejected the ultimatum; Russian troops then closed the border between East and West Berlin and began to erect a wall.[12]

Also during the summer of 1961, the Soviets announced their intention to resume atmospheric nuclear testing, a decision that profoundly disappointed Kennedy, and began a series of tests that culminated on the last day of October with the denotation over a remote area of Siberia of the largest nuclear device ever tested to that point. The Soviet decision to resume testing caused Kennedy to wonder whether future generations would conclude that he and Khrushchev had "brought the world to nuclear war." But he also knew that the United States needed to respond in kind to the Soviet move, even if doing so meant further complicating treaty negotiations. "What choice did we have?" Kennedy asked. "We couldn't possibly sit back and do nothing at all. We had to do this." Still, the decision to resume atmospheric testing seemed like a major step in the wrong direction, a rejection of the rational need to control the awesome weapons. As historian Arthur Schlesinger Jr. recounted, the decision involved "statesmen, generals and scientists" trying to reason through the reality that "irrational weapons could be put to rational use."[13]

Then Cuba once again took center stage in the tense US-Soviet rivalry. The new crisis arose after spy plane surveillance of Cuba confirmed the presence of Soviet nuclear missiles on the island, weapons that would be able to strike targets in the United States within a few minutes. The tense thirteen-day standoff that ensued, extending to a US naval "quarantine" of Cuba, seemingly took the world to the brink of nuclear war, but eventually Khrushchev backed down and removed the missiles. Ironically, once peacefully resolved, the Cuban Missile Crisis actually served to enhance trust between the two major nuclear powers. The "mutual fear of escalation," where a seemingly small confrontation could rapidly escalate out of control, suddenly looked to both Washington and Moscow as a situation to be avoided at all costs.[14]

"Perhaps now, as we step back from danger," Kennedy wrote to Khrushchev after the missile crisis ended, "we can make real progress in the field of disarmament." He pressed the Soviet premier for a renewed effort to negotiate a test ban treaty. Still, Kennedy faced conflicting and contradictory advice from his own political and military advisors, many of them convinced that no agreement with a Communist regime could possibly be enforced. His own Democratic Party was divided: southern hawks like Georgia's Richard Russell, the powerful chairman of the Armed Services Committee and the Senate's most influential voice on military affairs, was almost certain to oppose any treaty, while liberals, exemplified by Minnesota's Hubert Humphrey, were eager to find some avenue of détente with the Soviets. Republicans also held conflicting views, but a consensus seemed to be forming that a treaty was a bad idea. Conservative hawks like Arizona's Goldwater, an almost certain candidate for president in 1964, bitterly opposed any agreement with the Soviets, while liberal New York Governor Nelson Rockefeller, another potential presidential contender, also came out in opposition to a test ban. For his part Dirksen, safely reelected in 1962 and reflecting the dominant view of his Senate GOP colleagues, derided what he called a "parade of concessions" to the Soviets over nuclear testing. "This has become an exercise not in negotiation," Dirksen said, "but in give-away."[15]

Dirksen's comments underscored that even should Kennedy persist and be successful in negotiating an agreement with Khrushchev, he would still need to win over the Senate and somehow find a way to stitch together a supermajority in favor of any treaty. Treaty talks sputtered along through the rest of 1962 and into 1963 with little apparent progress, as the question of how to approach on-site inspections became a significant impediment to progress. Kennedy admitted that his hopes for a treaty were diminishing, but he kept returning to a fundamental belief: a test ban treaty was the key to slowing the nuclear arms race. "I am haunted by the feeling," Kennedy said in March 1963, "that by 1970, unless we are successful, there may be 10 nuclear powers instead of 4, and by 1975, 15 or 20. . . . I regard that as the greatest possible danger and hazard." In an attempt to break the stalemate, Kennedy decided to make a very public appeal to the American public—and the Senate—as well as the Kremlin leadership. He would use a June commencement address at American University in Washington to deliver a "peace speech" and announce a new round of three-party, US-UK-Soviet talks later in the year in Moscow. The speech became, in the words of Kennedy biographer Robert Dallek, "one of the great state papers of any twentieth century American presidency."[16]

Initially, however, the speech hardly created a ripple in the United States, in part perhaps because the headlines were dominated by southern Democrats' adamant rejection of the president's proposed civil rights bill and the repudiation by Republican National Committee Chairman William E. Miller of Kennedy's call for new test ban talks in Moscow. Kennedy was "playing a dangerous game," Miller said, and "should know that the complete record of the Russians ever since World War II is breaking every single promise they ever made." Dirksen also seemed unmoved by Kennedy's eloquence, complaining that the president was offering "concessions and more concessions to Khrushchev" and renouncing "the policy of strength." But if the American public was anything but attentive to questions of how to ensure that on-site inspections could hold the nuclear powers to account, leaders inside the Kremlin immediately took note of both the tone and substance of Kennedy's commencement speech.[17]

The tone was eloquent and heartfelt, with Kennedy saying the peace he desired was not a peace "enforced on the world by American weapons of war . . . not the peace of the grave or the security of a slave." Americans, Kennedy acknowledged, found "communism profoundly repugnant," but they also needed to understand the vast Russian suffering during World War II that informed much of the Kremlin's thinking about security considerations. Inability to bridge the superpower divide in the age of nuclear weapons could in a few hours, Kennedy warned, wreck "all we have built [and] all we have worked for." The substance of the speech also appealed to Khrushchev and his advisors. Kennedy called for establishment of a "hot line" between the US and Soviet leaders, a shared commitment to arms control, and a test ban treaty. And Kennedy clearly had Senate skeptics in mind as well when he stated, "No treaty, however much it may be to the advantage of all, however tightly it may be worded, can provide absolute security against the risks of deception and evasion. But it can—if it is sufficiently effective in its enforcement and if it is sufficiently in the interests of its signers—offer far more security and far fewer risks than an unabated, uncontrolled, unpredictable arms race." As Robert Dallek has written, "it was a tremendously bold address that carried substantial risk" since the profound distrust of the Soviet Union that became a fixture of American politics in the 1950s and 1960s "made it almost impossible for an American politician to make the sort of speech Kennedy gave."[18]

With resumption of Moscow talks imminent, Kennedy made a triumphant summertime visit to England, Germany, and Ireland to shore up European support for a treaty. British prime minister Harold Macmillan, increasingly a Kennedy confidante, was certainly hoping for a breakthrough as well, since a sex scandal had wracked his government. Three-fifths of West Berlin turned out to hear the president proclaim himself a Berliner—"Ich bin ein Berliner"—while presidential envoy Averill Harriman prepared to go to Moscow to reengage with the Soviets. But like a chess master playing several games at once, Kennedy never lost track of the imperative of getting an eventual treaty ratified by the Senate, telling Mansfield at one point that the credibility the military brass enjoyed among senators would be a powerful check on any political persuasion the president might muster. "The chiefs have always been our problem," Kennedy told the majority leader, warning that the opposition of the Joint Chiefs of Staff could torpedo the entire effort. Kennedy also worked the phone, explaining his views to senators, and even before the treaty was finalized, he dispatched Secretary of State Dean Rusk to brief the Foreign Relations, Armed Services, and Atomic Energy Committees.[19]

Although Khrushchev would make all the final decisions about a treaty, the American and British delegations, who arrived in Moscow on July 15, 1963, deemed it a positive sign that the Soviet leader had placed his dour but serious foreign minister, Andrei Gromyko, in charge of daily negotiations. Another good sign appeared at the first day's negotiating session. Khrushchev not only sat through the entire proceedings but joked with Harriman that he was ready to sign an agreement "and let the experts work out the details." Through ten days of talks the negotiators painstakingly hashed out treaty terms including, at Harriman's insistence, a clause allowing any country to withdraw from the agreement if another country exploded a weapon that was deemed a danger to its national security. This addition was no doubt informed by Kennedy's ongoing discussions with Mansfield about what the Senate would demand for ratification. Finally, on July 25, the detailed back-and-forth produced a document both sides could accept, and Harriman, Gromyko, and the British negotiator, Lord Hailsham, initialed it. The next day, Kennedy spoke to the nation—and effectively to the Senate. "No one can be certain what the future will bring," the president said from the White House in a televised address. "No one can say whether the time has come for an easing of the struggle. But history and our own conscience will judge us harsher if we do not now make every effort to test our hopes by action, and this is the place to begin." Kennedy expressed his hope that the Senate would quickly approve the treaty.[20]

A *New York Times* editorial opined that Kennedy's speech had reassured the public the treaty was in the nation's interest and predicted the Senate would decide "affirmatively and soon" to approve it. Mansfield and Dirksen however knew the Senate would take its time and that approval was not at all a sure thing; in fact, Dirksen had still not committed to support the treaty. "Every word and every line and every phase of the treaty must be carefully examined," Dirksen said, "for its present and future effect." Mansfield's public comments were consistent with what he had been saying privately to Kennedy and Dirksen: Republican votes would decide the fate of a test ban treaty. "It is my avowed hope," Mansfield said, "Senator Dirksen and I will be working shoulder-to-shoulder on this one when the chips are down." He continued, "I have every confidence in the fairness of the Republicans. I am certain that with them it will not be politics, but what will be good for their country." The statement was vintage Mansfield, downplaying partisanship and assuming the best intentions of the other party, particularly Dirksen.[21]

As attention shifted to the Senate, Dirksen's language became, in the words of historian Byron Hulsey, "more restrained and responsible." Some Republicans complained that Dirksen was merely waffling, straddling the moderate and very conservative wings of his party, while enjoying the attention of everyone guessing as to where he would eventually come down. "Dirksen loves theatrics," one senator complained. But the minority leader was also a legislative horse trader, a politician comfortable and skilled at balancing accounts, and he was certainly reading the political currents, which were shifting in the direction of ratifying the treaty. "Dirksen is not one to guess wrong about a thing of this kind," *Newsweek*'s Kenneth Crawford wrote in early August. "His associates, unlike some television viewers, never mistake his cultivated eccentricities—the gamin hair-do and the syrupy rhetoric—for clownishness. Nobody gauges the velocity of a political wind with a wetter finger." Dirksen also knew, as he demonstrated time and again during his career, when to jettison an old position and declare that "the time has come" to embrace a new one. By the time hearings on the treaty commenced before the Foreign Relations Committee on August 12, it was clear not only that Dirksen would support the treaty, but also that he would do so in a way that would bring along as many Republican senators as possible, an outcome Kennedy hoped for and Mansfield was determined to deliver.[22]

Foreign Relations Committee Chairman J. William Fulbright, an Arkansas Democrat, was a passionate supporter of the treaty and, with Mansfield's support and encouragement, he conducted ten days of hearings that included testimony from scientists, administration officials, and treaty supporters as well as opponents. Fulbright, like Mansfield, worried that Democratic hawks like Georgia's Russell and Mississippi's John Stennis—Fulbright's biographer termed them "permanent senatorial representatives of the military"—would find a way either to defeat the treaty outright or to attach damaging reservations that would render the agreement worthless or unworkable. For his part, Dirksen praised the testimony of the administration's leadoff witness, Secretary of State Rusk, who contended the agreement would enhance the nation's security. Rusk said there were no guarantees the Soviets would abide by the treaty but pointed out that, like many other world leaders, the Kremlin hierarchy "had a chance to peer into the pit of the inferno" that shook the world at the time of the Cuban Missile Crisis. "There are a number of things he clarified," Dirksen said of Rusk's testimony, "probably to the satisfaction of a good many persons." Not, however, to the satisfaction of one of the treaty's principal and perhaps most effective opponents, nuclear physicist Edward Teller, the Dr. Strangelove–like character widely credited with the American development of the hydrogen bomb. Teller, who had a wide following among the American right, insisted that, notwithstanding the dangers of radioactive contamination, atmospheric nuclear testing was critical to national security and particularly to the ultimate development of a missile defense system, a dream that would persist into the Reagan administration. "We could have and should have carried out more tests in the atmosphere," Teller testified, prompting Fulbright later to say of the refugee from communist Hungary, "Teller's an educated fool . . . I've never seen anybody quite as crazy as he is."[23]

The Foreign Relations Committee ultimately recommended approval of the treaty by a vote of sixteen to one, the lone dissenter being Democrat Russell Long of Louisiana, and attached only one reservation stipulating that the United States would not be barred from using its nuclear weapons in time of war. The committee's strong vote in favor was buttressed when former President Eisenhower endorsed the pact after calling for the stipulation permitting the use of nuclear weapons during wartime. Eisenhower's endorsement undoubtedly helped blunt the testimony of the Joint Chiefs of Staff, the military leaders Kennedy worried could stampede the Senate to opposition. The chiefs argued that the treaty was a net negative from a military standpoint, but that security concerns were balanced by the clear international political benefits to the United States of agreeing to the compact. Still, offsetting committee support for the treaty was a flow of constituent mail to senators that ran strongly opposed. Fulbright reported that in letters to his office, opponents of the treaty outnumbered supporters four to one. Dirksen's mail was also running heavily against the treaty, and the conservative editorial page of the *Chicago Tribune* was persistently critical of the accord, accusing Kennedy of "gaslighting" the nation, but opinion polls indicated something different: substantial public support, even in Dirksen's traditionally isolationist Midwest. It is not difficult to imagine that another politician, a different minority leader, would have hoped to deny a president of the opposing party a major legislative accomplishment heading into an election year and would have played his hand differently, seeking both to further divide the opposition and to enhance his own standing. But Dirksen did precisely the opposite, turning his efforts toward dispelling "the fears that have been so freely uttered and have found their way to the front pages."[24]

There was a pattern in what he was hearing from senators, Dirksen told Mansfield during a private huddle in the majority leader's office shortly before the Senate opened debate on the treaty, a "pattern of fear." He suggested to Mansfield that they tell Kennedy directly that he needed to understand what was creating the fear and take steps to address it. "You and I ought to get on our horses and go down to the White House," Dirksen said. Mansfield agreed immediately and placed a call to schedule a meeting. *Time* correspondent Neil MacNeil noted in off-the-record notes to his editor that Kennedy was initially reluctant to agree to the visit, not wanting to give Dirksen, who had not been all that helpful on the president's domestic agenda, including the administration's civil rights legislation, "the play" on such a high-profile issue. But Mansfield, always focused on how to move the Senate to ratification, pressed the White House, and the meeting was scheduled on the same day Senate floor debate began.[25]

"Now this is a little presumptuous on my part," Dirksen told Kennedy as he began reading aloud the draft of a letter he was hoping the president would agree to send to the Senate. The proposed letter offered "unqualified and unequivocal assurances" that the United States would pursue underground nuclear testing, maintain a posture of readiness to resume atmospheric testing, enhance detection capabilities to ensure the Russians were not cheating, and maintain a robust weapons development capability. Kennedy readily agreed to send the letter with Dirksen's proposed language, and Dirksen and Mansfield spent the remainder of the almost hourlong

meeting strategizing with the president about where the votes stood among senators of both parties. After the meeting, Dirksen immediately announced he would
support the treaty and would resist any efforts to amend or attach reservations to
the agreement. "Although Senator Dirksen's support was expected," the *New York
Times* reported, "the manner of his endorsement, without qualification and opposed
to reservations, was believed by observers to have supplied the bipartisan impetus
needed to keep the negatives to a hard-core minimum."[26]

As the president had promised, his letter—or more correctly Dirksen's letter
over Kennedy's signature—arrived two days later, in time to form the basis of the
minority leader's own Senate speech on the treaty. If the entire sequence of events—
the Mansfield-Dirksen meeting, the White House visit, and the Dirksen draft that
became the Kennedy letter—seems to have been skillfully orchestrated for maximum political effect, that is because it was. The Republican leader of the Senate,
disregarding partisanship, had decided to help the Democratic president accomplish
an objective that, as Kennedy told his staff, he would gladly forego reelection to
obtain. In reality, Dirksen's help would facilitate a huge Kennedy legislative victory
heading into the 1964 presidential campaign.[27]

Yet, even with Dirksen's promise of support, Kennedy remained pessimistic
about winning the necessary two-thirds vote in the Senate. "He was afraid," aide
Ted Sorensen recalled, "that the natural opposition of the Republicans, plus the
opposition of Southern Democrats led by Senators Russell and Stennis, whom he
knew had great influence, could easily put together one-third of the Senate plus
one and prevent consent to ratification altogether." Kennedy's dark pessimism,
perhaps stoked by less than full appreciation of the power of Mansfield and Dirksen
working in harness, as well as his underestimation of the theatrical impact of an
impassioned Dirksen speech, turned out to be ill-founded.[28]

Knowing that Dirksen was about to speak in the Senate on the afternoon of
September 11, Fulbright requested a quorum call to ensure that as many senators
as possible were in their seats for the minority leader's remarks. At 2:00 P.M., with
forty-one senators at their desks, many more than had typically participated in the
debate to that point, and with the gallery near capacity, Dirksen played the moment
for all it was worth. Uncharacteristically, Dirksen handed out copies of his speech
in advance. He had forty thousand letters in his office, Dirksen said, and a petition
signed by ten thousand of his constituents, all demanding he oppose the treaty.
Only three issues in his career—the debate over neutrality legislation in 1939, Harry
Truman's firing of General Douglas MacArthur in 1952, and the censure of Senator
Joseph McCarthy in 1954—had occasioned such public attention, Dirksen said.

New York Times correspondent E. W. Kenworthy noted that Dirksen "remarked with a grin" that most of the 250,000 letters received during the McCarthy censure "had remained unopened." Supporting the treaty was not an easy vote, Dirksen said, but he considered his responsibilities in the same way the British statesman and philosopher Edmund Burke had nearly two centuries earlier. "Your representative owes you, not his industry only," Dirksen quoted Burke as saying, "but his judgment; and he betrays instead of serving you if he sacrifices it to your opinion." The former actor, his gravelly baritone rumbling across the Senate chamber, was hitting all his marks.[29]

After reading Kennedy's letter and quoting from the 1960 Republican platform, which had supported exactly the kind of treaty the Senate was considering, Dirksen recalled the nuclear destruction of Hiroshima, less than twenty years earlier. "I want to take a first step, Mr. President. I am not a young man; I am almost as old as the oldest member of the Senate, certainly am older than a great many Senators. One of my age thinks about his destiny a little. I should not like to have written on my tombstone, 'He knew what happened at Hiroshima, but he did not take a first step.'"

"The longest journey begins with a first step," Dirksen said. "This may lead to steps that can spell a grander destiny for our country and the world. If there is a risk, this senator is willing to accept it." As Dirksen sat down, Mansfield was recognized immediately. He praised the minority leader for speaking "not on behalf of party but for the nation." How completely Dirksen had stepped away from the GOP's conservative wing became clear as the Senate debate continued. Barry Goldwater, already the front runner for the next Republican presidential nomination, took issue with Dirksen's admonition not to attach reservations to the treaty. "For every point of debate, for every argument, for every doubt," Goldwater said, "the answer is that we must look but not touch; we must consent, but not advise; we must approve, but not revise." Eventually, all the "killer amendments," including Goldwater's proposed one that would have tied implementation of the treaty to removal of Soviet military assets in Cuba, were defeated. At last, on September 24, the Senate consented by a vote of eighty to nineteen, fourteen more votes than the required two-thirds. Eight Republicans voted no, all western conservatives except for Maine's Margaret Chase Smith. In all, twenty-five Republicans followed Dirksen's lead and supported the treaty, and those who voted yes represented an impressive ideological cross section of the party, from Midwestern conservatives like Karl Mundt of South Dakota and Roman Hruska of Nebraska to northeastern liberals like New Jersey's Clifford Case and New York's Jacob Javits. All the Democratic dissenters were Southerners save for maverick Senator Frank Lausche of Ohio. Kennedy biographer Richard Reeves concluded that Dirksen's endorsement had effectively ended any suspense about the outcome of the treaty: "By the time Dirksen finished everyone in the chamber and in the country knew that the Limited Test Ban Treaty would be ratified as the first arms control agreement of the nuclear era." Across the Senate aisle, Mansfield stood, looked at the Republican leader, and said, "I salute a great American."[30]

Praise rained down on Dirksen, who had earlier seemed to waffle and waver over the treaty, perhaps in a strategic effort to maximize the impact of his support. Kennedy's letter, the *New York Times* editorialized, was "impressive for the assurances of military security it gave, but more impressive for its presentation by the leader of the Republican minority." This was an example of "bipartisanship where it counts" that the newspaper hoped might carry over to civil rights and other issues. "We doff our hat to Senator Dirksen," wrote the *Christian Science Monitor,* while the *Washington Post* said the Senate action "helped reshape American opinion in a way that can free this and subsequent administrations for further efforts toward peace." Richard Rovere, writing in *The New Yorker,* commented that the Senate had "proved itself a delicate and accurate instrument of representative government."[31]

Meanwhile, as the minority leader had predicted to Kennedy, the influential *Chicago Tribune* in Dirksen's home state "excoriated" him for supporting the initiative of a Democratic president. The newspaper's editorial after the Senate vote addressed Dirksen's position only obliquely, while lavishing praise on the nineteen senators who took a stand "against accommodation with soviet tyranny." On the same page as the editorial, the *Tribune* ran a scathing piece attributed to the *National Review Bulletin* that savaged Dirksen for "sabotaging" fellow Republican opponents of the treaty and declared, "The senator nowadays is much too warm in the Kennedy embrace."[32]

—

Dirksen also played a stealth hand by ensuring, even before his own public pledge of support for the treaty, that Eisenhower, who could well have been a decisive voice in opposition, would also support Kennedy's position. Dirksen's involvement with Eisenhower's endorsement of the treaty was not publicly known until years later, and it likely would have created a political firestorm had it became public during Senate consideration, since it essentially involved heavy presidential pressure on Eisenhower or, as some might suggest, leverage bordering on blackmail.

The story of how Eisenhower came to endorse the test ban treaty is complex and the provenance of the sources difficult to confirm, but it is clear that shortly after Robert Kennedy became his brother's attorney general in 1961, the Justice

Department was confronted with a case involving Eisenhower's one-time White House chief of staff, former New Hampshire governor Sherman Adams. Adams, perhaps Eisenhower's closest political confidante during his presidency, was forced to resign his White House position in 1958 when it became public that Adams had accepted various financial "favors" from a Boston industrialist, Bernard Goldfine. The two men had known each other for years, but the appearance of impropriety that attached to reports that Goldfine had paid hotel bills for the president's top aide, gifted him an expensive vicuña coat, and lent him a pricy Oriental rug created a major scandal for the largely scandal-free Eisenhower administration. Eisenhower initially offered a robust defense of Adams, calling him "an invaluable public servant doing a difficult job efficiently, honestly, and tirelessly." Besides, Eisenhower said, "a gift is not a bribe. One is evil, the other is a tangible expression of friendship." Adams denied any wrongdoing, claiming the gifts were merely the byproducts of his long association with Goldfine, but the chief of staff also admitted he had contacted at least two federal agencies on Goldfine's behalf. With support from congressional Republicans bleeding away and midterm elections looming, Eisenhower very reluctantly cut Adams loose in September 1958. That appeared to be the end of the Sherman Adams affair, but in 1961 and with a new administration in office, the case was still very much alive.[33]

As Robert Kennedy biographer Arthur Schlesinger wrote, "The favors [to Adams] went far beyond hotel rooms and the famous vicuña coat" and involved, as Goldfine was now asserting to the Justice Department, "more than $150,000 in cash over the period of about five years." The allegations seemed to be substantiated by "a series of cashier's checks Adams had given to his Washington landlady." The attorney general, a fierce defender of his elder brother, "could not have been displeased," Michael Beschloss has written, "by the prospect of using Adams to tarnish the record of Eisenhower, who so disapproved of his brother and who still commanded such influence on public opinion." Nonetheless, despite the opinion of the Internal Revenue Service (IRS) that a strong case could be mounted, Bobby Kennedy was conflicted about prosecuting Adams, in part because Goldfine's failing health and memory made him a less than reliable witness. In addition, bringing a case against the top aide of the previous occupant of the Oval Office then failing to secure a conviction would be widely seen, as Schlesinger wrote, as "a bungled attempt at political vengeance." Still, the opportunity to exercise White House political leverage on the former president clearly existed, and according to one version of the story the president quietly sent the evidence against Adams directly to Eisenhower who, in turn, sent a message back to Kennedy through an intermediary—the journalist

Joseph Alsop—that he fervently hoped his old friend Sherman Adams could "be spared further humiliation."[34]

Enter Dirksen. In his 1978 memoir, the disgraced but very much in-the-know former secretary of the Senate Bobby Baker—a less than credible witness due to his own ethical transgressions—claimed that Eisenhower, once he heard about the potential new charges against Adams, enlisted Dirksen to intercede with President Kennedy and, as "a personal favor to me," ask that the charges against his old friend be dropped. "He'll have a blank check in my bank if he will grant me this favor," Baker wrote of Eisenhower's pledge. Beschloss notes that "a cryptic exchange of letters between Eisenhower and Dirksen in January 1962 suggests that Baker's story may be accurate." In almost code-like language Dirksen told the former president that he had spoken with Kennedy "about one of your former staff members," adding, "I believe everything is in proper order." In a further exchange of letters in February, Eisenhower thanked Dirksen "for your efforts on behalf of an individual for whom we both have a high regard. I cannot tell you how delighted I am that, finally, he seems assured that the matter is indeed back on track."[35]

By Bobby Baker's account, Kennedy cashed his "blank check" with Eisenhower and also pressured Dirksen to support the treaty during a White House meeting that might have occurred on August 12, when according to the president's schedule, he met for nearly an hour "off the record" with Dirksen. "I want you to reverse yourself and come out for the treaty," Kennedy allegedly said, adding "I also want Ike's public endorsement of the treaty before the Senate votes." Baker's recounting of events seems plausible, but it also seems clear that Dirksen was already moving toward support for the treaty when he met with Kennedy in August, and he may not have needed much encouragement from the president to firm up his position. Whatever transpired and for whatever motive, Eisenhower's endorsement of the Limited Nuclear Test Ban Treaty came in a letter to the Foreign Relations Committee on August 26, and the former president's support for the treaty made front-page news across the country. Dirksen's own public endorsement happened two weeks later, after he and Mansfield talked with Kennedy on September 9. Dirksen, for a host of reasons, including high-level GOP cover for his own support for the treaty, may well have wanted the former president to offer an endorsement first. There was, of course, no prosecution of Sherman Adams, with Kennedy allegedly telling his attorney general if he did not agree with the decision he could resign. We also know, as Michael Beschloss has written, that Eisenhower would later complain to Lyndon Johnson about the "tactics" the IRS and Justice Department employed during Kennedy's tenure.[36]

When assessing how Dirksen came to his position on the treaty, as well as how Eisenhower arrived at his own endorsement, it seems fitting to recall Mansfield's frequent admonition that in politics it is never appropriate to question a person's motives because motives are frequently impossible to ascertain. A politician's judgment, Mansfield maintained, is another matter, and on this and many subsequent occasions in the 1960s, Dirksen's judgment was often aligned with what, one suspects, he saw as the right side of history.[37]

At a ceremony in the recently redecorated Treaty Room of the White House, President Kennedy formally signed the Limited Nuclear Test Ban Treaty on October 7, 1963. "This small step for safety," Kennedy said, "can be followed by others longer and less limited, if also harder in the taking. With our courage and understanding enlarged by this achievement, let us press on in quest of man's essential desire for peace." Kennedy used a fistful of pens to sign the treaty and handed them out to sixteen people, while Dirksen looked over this shoulder and Harriman, Fulbright, Humphrey, and Republican Senator George Aiken of Vermont, among others, looked on. Typically for Mansfield, he positioned himself so as not to appear in the photo that ran on the front page of the *New York Times* the next day.[38]

Mansfield's role in passing the historic treaty was barely noticed by newspapers in Montana, where news of a possible wheat sale to the Russians dominated the news in early October 1963. A lengthy Associated Press story on October 8, carried in virtually every Montana newspaper, did outline Mansfield's concerns about growing air pollution problems in Montana, while a press release from Mansfield on the same day announced the remodeling of the Petroleum County, Montana, post office. The *Chicago Tribune*, meanwhile, noted without comment Dirksen's attendance at the treaty-signing ceremony, but indicative of how his willingness to embrace bipartisanship left some conservatives fuming, the paper also prominently featured an article reporting on a campaign by a Republican group in New York that sought to remove Dirksen as minority leader. The Republican Committee of One Hundred cited Dirksen's "continual support" for Kennedy administration policies. Dirksen's leadership was deemed "disastrous to the United States and the Republican Party."[39]

Implacable foes of Kennedy's treaty, including Armed Service Committee chairman Richard Russell, sounded apocalyptic warnings about the dangers of reaching any accommodation with the Soviet Union and predicted the limited test ban agreement would more likely lead to war than prevent it. Russell confided to a friend that

President John Kennedy, surrounded by a bipartisan group of Senate leaders and arms control advisors, signs the Limited Nuclear Test Ban Treaty in the White House Treaty Room, October 7, 1963. Mansfield is at the far left; Dirksen is behind Kennedy. (*Kennedy Presidential Library*)

he hoped he would be proven wrong, but quickly added, "I greatly fear the future will prove the minority to have been right." Barry Goldwater's passionate opposition to the treaty helped further propel his presidential candidacy, and devoted Goldwater followers celebrated his bellicose threat that he would rather "lob" a nuclear weapon into the men's room of the Kremlin than make a deal with the Soviets. The *Chicago Tribune*, joining the chorus of naysayers who wrongly assessed what approval of the treaty would mean, predicted that opponents would be fondly remembered for their "logic and realism" in bucking Kennedy, Mansfield, and Dirksen.[40]

Historical assessments of Kennedy's effort to begin to control nuclear weapons, a foreign policy victory that aide Ted Sorensen said gave the president greater satisfaction than any other accomplishment of his presidency, tend to stress the limited nature of the agreement. The treaty did not, as Robert Dallek notes, "inhibit proliferation or slow the arms race," since China, France, India, Israel, and Pakistan all developed nuclear arsenals after 1963. Nevertheless, despite its limited scope, the treaty did cool US-Soviet tensions at a moment when all-out war between the superpowers seemed to many more likely than not. Even a limited test ban was, in the words of British prime minister Harold Macmillan's biographer, "a welcome and important change in fortune" that "paved the way for later developments such as the Non-Proliferation Treaty of 1968 and the Strategic Arms Limitation Treaties of the 1980s."[41]

Kennedy's success in working with Mansfield and Dirksen on a bipartisan basis to ratify the historic test ban treaty stands in stark contrast to the way the Senate has frequently dealt with treaties, ranging from the Senate's rejection of the Treaty of Versailles, President Woodrow Wilson's effort to recraft the world order after World War I, to President Bill Clinton's unsuccessful effort to gain ratification of a comprehensive test ban treaty in 1999. That ratification vote, much like Wilson's earlier effort, failed essentially along party lines, causing the then-Senate minority leader Tom Daschle to say, "This is a terrible, terrible mistake. If politics don't stop at the water's edge, nothing does." Senator Joseph Lieberman, a Connecticut Democrat (later Independent), captured how profoundly the institution of the Senate had changed, and not for the better, since the Mansfield-Dirksen era in the 1960s. "Something unusual and unsettling has happened to our politics when party lines divide us so clearly and totally on a matter such as this," Lieberman said of the Senate's failure to approve a comprehensive test ban. "That's not the way it used to be in the United States Senate and it's not the way it should be"[42]

It is tempting, particularly in our age of extreme partisan polarization, to feel nostalgic for a Senate where compromise once reigned, comity ruled, and bipartisanship frequently prevailed, but the Senate has always been a vastly complex and often very contentious place. Partisanship has always lurked just beneath the surface, disguised, softened even, by stilted senatorial courtesies and practiced rituals. Vying for individual and party advantage is as much a part of the Senate as are its standing rules, standing orders, unanimous consent agreements, and precedents. Yet, this book will make the case that the personal and political leadership styles of the Senate's leaders in the 1960s truly improved how effectively the Senate performed on the enormous issues that defined the decade: foreign policy, civil rights, the immense body of legislation that defined the Great Society, and the tragedy of Vietnam.

As majority leader, Mike Mansfield practiced a kind of leadership by deference, insisting that every senator without regard to party, position, or power was an equal to the other ninety-nine senators. His approach was a night-and-day difference from that of his immediate predecessor, Lyndon Johnson. As we will see, Mansfield's cooperative, low-key, consensus-building style initially brought considerable criticism before senators in both parties came to understand that his commitment to fairness in the operations of the Senate, combined with his obvious personal integrity and decency, actually made the Senate work in a way it rarely has since. Mansfield insisted on what Senate observers now call "regular order," the legislative practices where, among other things, committees conduct hearings and listen to and question witnesses. With "regular order," legislation—or a proposed treaty—is reviewed, often at length, in the germane committee, then debated on the Senate floor. Members of both parties offer and consider amendments. Committee chairs wield great discretion. The more recent congressional practice of often bypassing committees and their chairs in favor of decisions driven by the majority leadership would have found no favor with Mansfield. As his longtime aide Francis Valeo wrote of Mansfield's leadership of the Senate during the treaty consideration in 1963, "Mansfield deferred not only to the chairman of the Foreign Relations Committee, Senator Fulbright, but also to Senator Humphrey, to the minority leader, and to anyone else who wished to be in the spotlight. Mansfield's concentration was on obtaining the Senate's approval, and he praised all effusively for the achievement, while claiming none of the credit for himself." Mansfield held back any personal agenda, giving deference as leader to the Senate's institutional role, purposefully limiting his own power in order to make the process of creating legislation work, typically in a bipartisan manner. Ironically, by seeming to relinquish his own power as majority leader, in contrast to Lyndon Johnson's overbearing style of leadership, Mansfield quietly accumulated his own unique power and influence in the Senate. Dirksen was the perfect Senate partner who both appreciated and benefited from Mansfield's kind of leadership. Valeo observed that a good deal of Mansfield's strength as a leader followed from him being "the least pretentious of men" without "any inclination whatsoever to play dirty pool with such ideological splits and divisions that existed in the Republican minority." Dirksen, who "never lost the urge to stick a pin" that could deflate a pretentious colleague, never had such an urge with his counterpart across the Senate aisle. "Dirksen was satisfied," Valeo wrote, "that Mansfield was running the Senate for Republicans as well as Democrats and as closely in accord with the Golden Rule as was ever likely to be found in a legislative body." In turn, as we will see, Dirksen displayed genuine regard, indeed affection, for Mansfield, whom he came to trust completely, and Mansfield reciprocated fully. As a result, the minority leader sought to cooperate with the majority leader whenever he could, and vice versa.[43]

2 BUTTE AND PEKIN—POLITICAL ROOTS

Butte is not "the biggest mining camp on earth." It is not a mining camp
at all; it is a northwestern metropolis, center of state and regional industry,
metropolitan in aspect and influence. Nevertheless Butte thinks like
a mining camp.

—JOSEPH KINSEY HOWARD, 1959

The people [of Pekin] were Midwest Republicans, but there was
a special temper to the town's Republicanism, this was Lincoln country.

—NEIL MACNEIL, 1970

The political roads for two politicians from western Montana and central Illinois
eventually converged on the floor of the US Senate, but even after attaining national
prominence and the highest levels of Washington leadership, Mike Mansfield and
Ev Dirksen never strayed far from their roots: the mining and industrial center of
hard-edged Silver Bow County, Montana, and the Tazewell County farm country
of the Illinois River valley, respectively.

"All the major decisions of my life have been made here," Dirksen said of Pekin.
"This is my native city, where the family taproot goes deep, and it will ever be."
Mansfield said of his formative years, "My ten years in Butte as a mucker, miner
and sampler were ten years well spent and despite the heat, the copper water, and
the copper dust, Butte still holds the number one place in my heart."[1]

Mansfield, born in 1903, and Dirksen, born in 1896, were both products of first-
generation immigrants. Mansfield's mother and father met in the United States after
each entered Ellis Island from Ireland and settled in New York City, where Mansfield's father worked in construction. Dirksen's parents emigrated from Germany

and settled in central Illinois. While very young, each lost a parent, Dirksen's father dying of complications from a stroke when young Everett was nine, and Mansfield's mother dying of kidney disease when he was seven. The widowed Mrs. Dirksen settled on a small farm at the edge of Pekin and kept milk cows, chickens, and a large garden—the origin of Dirksen's love of gardening perhaps—that supplied the family table and provided produce to sell to neighbors. After Mansfield's mother's death and his father's workplace injury—Patrick Mansfield was seriously hurt when he fell from a thirty-five-foot brick wall while working construction—young Mike and two sisters were dispatched to Montana to live with an aunt and uncle who owned a small grocery store on the less desirable south side of Great Falls. His was not a particularly happy childhood. Economic times were difficult; Mansfield's aunt, particularly after her husband died, was "unacceptably stern and demanding"; and the lanky young Irishman carried a chip on his shoulder. "Mike's behavior may have contributed," as Mansfield's biographer notes, "to his grandaunt's decision in the fall of 1913 . . . to take him out of public school and place him in the stricter St. Mary's parochial school, where he was taught by nuns." Mike often skipped school and several times ran away from home, finally leaving for good in 1917, when he jumped a Northern Pacific freight train headed west.[2]

While Mansfield was an indifferent student, Dirksen excelled both in the classroom and before the footlights. Even though the buttoned-down conservatism of Pekin discouraged "anything smacking of art or culture or self-expression," Dirksen participated in oratorical contests, including one where he sought rhetorical tips from none other than William Jennings Bryan, the three-time Democratic presidential candidate. He also wrote and acted in plays. Between 1919 and 1926 Dirksen authored more than one hundred "plays, poems, short stories and five complete novels," none of them published. He was so enamored of performance that his mother forced him to promise that he would not pursue acting as a career. She hoped he might be a preacher.

In a place that revered Abraham Lincoln—Pekin had been in Lincoln's congressional district—it was natural that Dirksen embraced the Republican Party. Dirksen's father had encouraged the affiliation, naming his other sons Benjamin Harrison and Thomas Reed (after the powerful late nineteenth-century Speaker of the House). Ev was born while William McKinley was governor of Ohio and, thanks to his father, owed his middle name to the man who would become the twenty-fifth president. Afflicted, as his high school yearbook said, with "bigworditis," Dirksen mastered German and history and graduated as the class salutatorian.[3]

Mansfield lied his way into the US Navy in 1918 without finishing high school. Motivated by a desire for adventure and a hankering to see the world, he traveled surreptitiously from Washington state to the East Coast, smuggled along with a National Guard unit preparing to deploy to Europe as the United States poured troops into the fighting in France during World War I. In New York Mansfield reunited with his father, who refused to sanction a false age declaration that might have allowed the underage Mansfield to enlist. "Undaunted," as Don Oberdorfer has written, Mansfield "went to the Roman Catholic church where he had been baptized, obtained a copy of his birth certificate, and changed his actual birth date." A Navy recruiter accepted the altered paperwork, and Mansfield became an apprentice seaman in February 1918. He weighed barely 120 pounds, stood all of five feet four inches tall, and was a couple of weeks shy of his fifteenth birthday.

Mansfield's military career, all packed into the space of less than five years, is both astonishing and unprecedented for any member of Congress. He served in three branches of the military, all by the time he was twenty years old. After serving on a Navy cruiser on Atlantic convoy duty and after the Armistice ended World War I hostilities, Mansfield was mustered out of the Navy and returned to Montana. But work was hard to come by, the economy shaky, and an influenza pandemic raging. Three months after leaving the Navy, Mansfield enlisted in the Army, expecting to be assigned to occupation duty in Germany. Instead, he ended up in California, where he served out his one-year enlistment and the next day enlisted in the Marine Corps. Mansfield loved the corps, and his service took him to China and the Philippines, awakening what he called "an intense personal interest in China, in particular, and the Far East, in general." Leaving service as a private first class, Mansfield would proudly wear a Marine Corps lapel pin or tie clasp nearly every day of his political career.[4]

Dirksen also served in the military during World War I, his motive for enlisting apparently related to his German ancestry. Dirksen suspended his studies at the University of Minnesota—he was a junior—and enlisted in the army in 1917. The decision was prompted, at least in part, by the anti-German sentiment prevalent in central Illinois. Similar attitudes sparked widespread violations of civil liberties in Montana and elsewhere. As Byron Hulsey, a Dirksen biographer, has written, "Pekin's German-American bank was coerced into dropping the 'German' from its name, and the local Methodist church was implored to hold 'English-only' services.'" Local superpatriots threatened Dirksen's mother because she refused to remove a picture of the German kaiser from the family home. With both of his brothers exempt from service, Dirksen enlisted, at least in part, to preserve the family's good name. He eventually served in France with a balloon company assigned to an artillery unit, saw some minor action, and rose to the rank of second lieutenant. Mustered out of the army in 1919, Dirksen returned to Pekin and, by his own admission, floundered in a series of not very successful business ventures. He also returned to acting where, in 1924, he met Louella Carter, who would become his wife three years later and his lifelong political partner. "They shared," as one writer put it, "the idiom of unabashed sentimentality, piety, and openly professed patriotism." Dirksen referred to Louella as "the princess" and "my lady love."[5]

Out of the marines, Mansfield returned to Montana apparently ready to accept a life of hard labor in Butte's copper mines, a fairly typical calculation for a young man of no means and little education. A remarkable woman intervened and changed Mansfield's life. He would frequently say that meeting his future wife, Maureen Hayes, was the most important event in his life, since it proved to be the catalyst that got him out of the mines. Maureen, "confident, vivacious," and educated—she was teaching English at Butte High School when she and Mansfield met in 1928—persuaded the young miner that he had to finish his education, and she worked while he did so. "I had always been a loner who kept his thoughts to himself," Mansfield later said, "but Maureen brought out the talk in me . . . suddenly I had a new friend, perhaps the only genuinely close friend in my life." Like the Dirksen marriage, the Mansfields had what one friend called "a true love affair." Another said, "he always consulted her. He always worshiped her . . . he was her guardian and she was his consultant." Mansfield credited Maureen with every success that followed from their courtship, saying that "she literally remade me in her own mold." With Maureen's encouragement, he took courses at the College of Mines in Butte and in 1931 enrolled at what was then Montana State University (today the University of Montana) in Missoula. He was accepted as a "provisional student" since he had not completed high school, and the couple married in 1932. Mansfield earned an undergraduate degree in 1933 and a master's in history and political science in 1934. Maureen earned her own master's at the same time. In short order, Mansfield began his teaching career as an assistant professor of far eastern history. By all accounts he was an outstanding and popular teacher and, in what now seems like logical preparation for a political career that would see Mansfield become a recognized Senate expert on foreign policy, he also taught courses in Latin American and European history and the background of the French Revolution.[6]

While both Dirksen and Mansfield credited their wives with playing the central role in their political lives, Illinois and Montana ran a close second in terms of influence. The writer Dave Eggers, who grew up in Illinois, not surprisingly places Lincoln at the heart of the state's political tradition. "Illinois gave America Abraham Lincoln," Eggers wrote in a profile of the state. As an Illinois politician, Dirksen frequently invoked Lincoln as a political model, something that came naturally to him, much like his speechmaking. Like Lincoln, Dirksen styled himself a political storyteller, in the belief that most voters would soon forget a policy argument but would long remember a good story. Upon his return from army service in Europe, Dirksen became a member of the American Legion, ironically at the suggestion of future Illinois Democratic senator and majority leader Scott Lucas, whom Dirksen would later defeat. Thanks to his command of language and his skill in front of an audience, he was in demand as a speaker. As one newspaper reported of a Dirksen appearance, "there was no lack to his ability and the applause he received at the close of his address indicated the audience accepted his sentiments, though, as the toastmaster suggested, some of those present might differ with him."[7]

Dirksen was working out his political views, which as Byron Hulsey has written, "reflected the provincialism of the small-town Midwest," where in the 1920s the Ku Klux Klan had a strong presence. Writing to Louella while on a trip to Mississippi in 1924, Dirksen used harsh language, including racial slurs, to denigrate the African Americans he encountered, along with southern Jews who, he said, seemed to dominate the business district of Vicksburg, a place "never intended for white men." Dirksen struggled for years, Hulsey wrote, "to overcome the narrow intolerance of his upbringing."[8]

Dirksen biographer Neil MacNeil, the longtime congressional correspondent for *Time*, said Dirksen grew up surrounded by Republicanism. His commitment to the party was almost spiritual, certainly instinctual—"emotional, sentimental, irrational, like his sense of the meaningfulness of Lincoln: it was not predicated on intellectual postures or reasoned logic." A stint on the nonpartisan Pekin City Council deepened Dirksen's interest in politics as a career, and he made what must have seemed a mildly reckless decision to challenge the local incumbent US Representative William Edgar Hull in the Republican primary. "The ambition to sit in Congress is probably similar to the 'flu,'" Dirksen said years later, "everybody gets it at some time or other; while it had been lurking in my system like some deadly virus, it did not become virulent until 1930."[9]

The *Peoria Star* disparaged Dirksen's youth and inexperience—"the suggestion that he should be sent to Congress was on a par with sending a schoolboy"—local Republican business interests withheld support; and since the Klan disparaged Catholics as well as ethnic minorities, supporters of incumbent congressman

EVERETT M. DIRKSEN

Republican
Candidate for

CONGRESS

16th District

"The best evidence of his service is that he has been endorsed and recommended for re-election by labor, farm and business organizations."

A campaign card from one of Everett Dirksen's earliest Illinois congressional campaigns, circa 1934. (*Collection of the US House of Representatives*)

William Hull distributed a flyer in heavily Catholic areas smearing Dirksen as a Klansman. The conservative and Republican *Chicago Tribune* reduced the race to a contest between a "dry" incumbent and his "wet opponent." In fact, Dirksen tried to have it both ways on the controversial issue of prohibition, neither embracing nor rejecting either position, perhaps an early indication of the political agility that became central to his career and eventual success as a Senate leader. Dirksen narrowly lost the primary, but impressed voters with his energy and enthusiasm. This was the only election Dirksen ever lost. Even the local newspaper came around, saying Dirksen had "waged one of the most astonishing campaigns this district has ever witnessed. That he came so close to victory is a tribute to his ability as an orator, his good nature, and his unbounding energy." The newspaper concluded that Dirksen "has arrived"—and indeed he had.[10]

Dirksen plotted how to win a rematch with Hull (who positioned himself as a regular Republican and committed Herbert Hoover man) by skillfully distancing himself from the toxically unpopular Hoover and the worsening depression—the city of Chicago alone spent $2.5 million on unemployment relief in May 1932, nearly $50 million in 2022 dollars. "The desperate conditions of the Great Depression inspired Dirksen to buck party doctrine," historian Byron Hulsey has written, "and advocate lower taxes and federal relief for the unemployed." Dirksen won the primary and, remarkably, carried his central Illinois district by almost exactly the same margin as Democratic presidential candidate Franklin D. Roosevelt, an outcome

Dirksen termed an "exhibition of impartiality." It was more like a political miracle. The *Bureau County Tribune* noted that Dirksen was one of the few Republicans in Illinois to survive the broad Democratic landslide in 1932.[11]

Dirksen, now thirty-six years old, was among the youngest members of the House of Representatives and one of only 117 Republicans when he arrived in Washington early in 1933. He immediately took to the place, marveling at the monuments, the statues, and the perks. "When I got my first taste of Congress in 1933," he later said, "and was called Honorable, and invited to dinners without having to pay for them, and people saluting me in my office, I thought, 'This is for me.'" Dirksen's political apprenticeship took place during the heady, frantic early days of Roosevelt's New Deal, when a torrent of transformative legislation flooded through Congress. The rookie congressman's political flexibility was evident early on, when he bucked Republican leaders to support much of Roosevelt's program. Dirksen voted for the National Industrial Recovery Act, the Agricultural Adjustment Act, and the Federal Emergency Relief Act, all passed in the first hundred days of FDR's presidency. He later voted for the Social Security Act and the National Labor Relations Act, which established a minimum wage and limited workers' hours. Dirksen justified his vote, which again strained against party bonds, by saying, "Too long has our party been identified as the champion of the big, the rich, the powerful, and the entrenched."[12]

While many Republicans supported Roosevelt's Economy Act of 1933, an effort to reduce federal spending by cutting federal salaries, including some benefits for veterans, Dirksen again displayed his penchant for political flexibility. "Are we going to sacrifice our veterans and civil employees on the altar of balancing the budget?" Dirksen asked home-state voters. Almost immediately, the young congressman began getting attention in the House and in the press for his quick wit and seemingly inexhaustible supply of one-liners and humorous stories. In March 1933, a United Press dispatch termed Dirksen "the best yarn spinner" in the new congressional class. But there was substance behind the pithy speeches and laugh-inducing yarns. Dirksen worked hard to master the rules and traditions of Congress, and he went deep into the details of legislation. Republican leaders rewarded his work ethic by appointing him to the Appropriations Committee in 1937, where he concentrated on agricultural issues important to his constituents. And he kept winning elections, even as Republican numbers in the House shrank in 1934 and 1936. In nine consecutive successful House elections, only twice did Dirksen fail to win in commanding style, and he won five elections with at least 60 percent of the vote.[13]

In one important area, at least until US entry into World War II seemed nearly inevitable in late 1941, Dirksen hewed to midwestern Republican foreign policy orthodoxy. He was very much an isolationist in the spirit of the influential *Chicago Tribune* and its imperious publisher, Robert McCormick. Dirksen voted in favor of every Neutrality Act measure in the 1930s and opposed Roosevelt's 1941 Lend-Lease Act, designed to provide vital military and other supplies to the beleaguered United Kingdom. But six weeks after voting against extending the first peacetime draft in American history, Dirksen turned on a dime—"somersaulted" the *Tribune* said—and embraced Roosevelt's foreign policy objectives. Roosevelt's opposition to Nazi Germany, Dirksen said, was "known to all the world. To disavow or oppose that policy now could only weaken the President's position, impair our prestige, and imperil the nation." This was the first evidence of what became Dirksen's bipartisan deference, fully evident during the Kennedy and Johnson administrations, to presidential primacy in matters of foreign policy. Dirksen's somersault stunned many fellow Republicans, some of whom suggested the move had been orchestrated by Republican presidential candidate Wendell Willkie or had occurred because Dirksen was plotting a 1942 primary challenge to Illinois Senator C. Wayland "Curly" Brooks, a passionate isolationist. But Dirksen, now an internationalist, would postpone his Senate aspirations, stay in the House, and be joined there in 1942 by an ambitious young Democrat from Montana.[14]

One-time Butte and Silver Bow County resident Myron Brinig wrote in his auto-biographical novel *Singermann*, "The copper mine ruled Silver Bow, and the state of Montana as well. Nowhere else in the world was there such a rich treasure of copper as that which ran in ruddy veins under the turbulent, unexpected streets. Thousands of miners were employed, and very few were American born." Among this multiethnic melting pot were thousands of Irish Catholics. Butte was, in fact, "one of the most overwhelmingly Irish cities in the United States." It was a community Mike Mansfield identified with throughout his life. Mansfield grew up in Great Falls, and lived and worked in Missoula, but Butte, where he worked in the mines from 1922 to 1931, was his Montana touchstone. In his winning campaign for the House of Representatives in 1942—Mansfield had lost a Democratic primary for Congress two years earlier—Silver Bow County gave him nearly 69 percent of its vote, and Butte always came through for Mansfield. In eight elections between 1944 and 1970 he never received less than 68 percent of the vote in Silver Bow County.[15]

Butte was, however, more than a dependable source of Democratic votes. It was the beating heart of the Montana Democratic Party, wielding influence vastly out of proportion with its population. At the time of Mansfield's 1942 victory, both of the state's US senators, Burton K. Wheeler and James E. Murray, hailed from Butte. Frank

A young Mike Mansfield at the time he was
transitioning from copper miner to university
professor. (*Archives and Special Collections,
Mansfield Library, University of Montana*)

Walker, who practiced in Butte as a young lawyer, was Roosevelt's postmaster general
and chairman of the Democratic National Committee in the early 1940s. Another Butte
lawyer, James Rowe Jr., was a top Roosevelt aide, a friend of Mansfield's, and a close
associate of an ambitious young congressman from Texas, Lyndon B. Johnson. Rowe
touted his friend, the new Montana congressman, to Roosevelt and to House Speaker
Sam Rayburn of Texas. Noting that Wheeler and Murray were locked in a perpetual
fight for supremacy among Montana Democrats, and that Mansfield deftly avoided
their feud, Rowe advised Rayburn, "Mansfield has a lot of common sense, and in fact
has many of the qualities of Lyndon in his ability to get around." Rowe told FDR that
Mansfield was "an intelligent New Dealer with an international point of view [who]
combines the excellent background of a hard-rock miner and history professor."[16]

Rowe was almost certainly the instigator of Mansfield becoming a presidential
envoy to China in 1944, an unlikely appointment for an untested backbencher. He

undertook the high-profile mission with eagerness and immediately after winning a second term in the House. It was, as Don Oberdorfer has noted, "the single most important event of Mike Mansfield's career in the House, elevating him from obscurity to national prominence." Rowe, no doubt with enthusiastic concurrence from Mansfield, envisioned the trip and its official sanction as a means not only to bolster the Montanan's standing as an Asia expert, but also to position him for a primary challenge in 1946 to Democratic Senator Burton Wheeler, a controversial Roosevelt foe whose noninterventionist foreign policy views had eroded his standing with Montana voters. The Asia trip took Mansfield to New Delhi and along the Ledo Road, a logistical lifeline snaking into China. He met three times with the Chinese Nationalist leader Chiang Kai-shek and was photographed with Montana GIs he encountered along the way. After the mission, Mansfield produced an extensive report presented to Roosevelt, which created opportunities for him to speak to both Congress and the Montana legislature about his findings. Butte's *Montana Standard* reported the trip brought "great credit to Montana as well as high honor to the ability of Congressman Mike Mansfield." While the trip had the desired effect of enhancing Mansfield's foreign policy credentials, it was not enough to persuade him to challenge Wheeler for the Senate seat. After detailed reconnaissance of his chances of winning a Senate race, Mansfield decided, as he said years later, "that I couldn't win." His political radar was well calibrated. Wheeler lost the Montana Democratic primary in 1946, but the Democrat who defeated him was subsequently crushed in what turned out to be a huge Republican sweep—the GOP won control of Congress for the first time since 1930—a political tsunami that Mansfield survived by staying in the House.[17]

Mansfield's reputation for foreign policy expertise continued to grow in the House, but he also paid careful and detailed attention to the bread and butter of Montana politics. "There are many opportunities for development in Montana and I want to see them developed," Mansfield said at the 1948 dedication of Hungry Horse Dam, a massive Bureau of Reclamation hydropower and flood-control project in the northwestern corner of the state. Mansfield, the populist, emphasized that development should not benefit "the few, the big corporations . . . but benefit all the people of Montana so this commonwealth may become in fact as well as in name a real Treasure state for all who live within its borders." Later that year, during the run-up to Harry Truman's surprising come-from-behind presidential election victory and his own reelection campaign, Mansfield echoed Truman in blasting the "do nothing" Eightieth Congress for its failure to address a chronic postwar housing shortage, an issue of particular concern to Montana veterans.[18]

Early in 1949, Mansfield criticized the Truman administration's decision to locate the nation's "new atomic power reactor plant" in the eastern Idaho desert rather than in Montana. Montana was not, he said, "given the consideration she deserves and is entitled to." Mansfield's involvement with Montana issues would remain broad and deep. For example, he supported improving a flood-control levee near Billings, increased appropriations for Montana tribal governments, and raised compensation for the relatives of thirteen firefighters who died in the tragic Mann Gulch fire near Helena. In late October 1949, there was press speculation that Mansfield would resign his House seat to become the State Department's assistant secretary for public affairs. A week later, after a meeting with Truman, Mansfield publicly declined the position, saying he thought he could be of greater service by staying in Congress. The *Great Falls Tribune* hailed Mansfield's decision as good news for Montana.[19]

Mansfield turned down a second invitation to join the Truman administration in 1950, when he was offered the position of undersecretary at the Interior Department, and after he was easily reelected to a fifth House term that year, speculation increased about a Senate run in 1952 when the lackluster incumbent, Republican Zales Ecton, next faced voters. Again, Mansfield's political timing was immaculate.[20]

—

Dirksen's activity in the House before and during World War II, as well as in the postwar period, had a distinctly national orientation. Increasingly, Dirksen became a GOP spokesman, defending liberal Republican Wendell Willkie during his 1940 presidential campaign and assailing what he considered the too-liberal policies of the Roosevelt administration. Dirksen's legislative activities ranged from reforming the budget process to advocating that unemployment offices be run at the state rather than the federal level. *Fortune* magazine described him in a flattering 1943 profile as "a big, tough, shrewd, and hearty fellow who loves his job and is very good at it." Part of Dirksen's appeal, as the political scientist Burdett Loomis has noted, "derives from his memorable physical appearance" with one observer describing him as a "massive, silo-shaped man with an unruly shock of silvery hair."[21]

Dirksen's work ethic contributed to his growing reputation. He worked often eighteen-hour days, traveled extensively, and spoke constantly. Dirksen's curated rhetorical style—he was said to be one of the few members of Congress who could influence votes with a speech—was the product of hard work, study, and practice by a skilled actor who loved to perform. Mansfield would later say that Dirksen's voice was "rich and colorful," backed "by a rich and rounded personality."[22]

Frankie Bozeman Faver analyzed Dirksen's speaking style and use of humor in a master's thesis, concluding that Dirksen's nonverbal communication, the little things he did to supplement his voice and language, were important to his effectiveness as a speaker. "His wrinkled suits which were bought when he was fifty pounds heavier, the horn-rimmed glasses and the diamond ring which he wore on his little finger were evocative props, artistically chosen," Faver wrote. "It was not any single aspect of his non-verbal communication that was outstanding. It was the combination that made people listen even when they had heard the joke before; laugh when they were well ahead of the punch line; and, in many instances, vote for something they did not believe before the speech began. Such was speech-making, Dirksen style."[23]

By 1943, there was considerable speculation that Dirksen had ambitions beyond the House, including rumors that he might chair the Republican National Committee, perhaps run for governor of Illinois, mount a challenge to Senator Scott Lucas, or even seek the presidency. Dirksen stoked the White House speculation with his own petition, circulated among House Republicans, extolling his ability and availability. Eventually thirty-six House Republicans, all but four from Midwest states, signed the petition, and on December 2, 1943, Dirksen announced his candidacy for the GOP presidential nomination in 1944. The maneuvering and announcement raised Dirksen's profile both in the House and nationally, even though few considered him a serious presidential candidate. The *Chicago Tribune* dismissed Dirksen's ambitions as amounting to nothing more than being "a stooge for Willkie," who was planning to run again. While Dirksen did make campaign-style appearances in twenty-seven states, even his supporters eventually admitted that his real objective was the number-two spot on the Republican ticket. Not until some years later would Dirksen acknowledge—according to his son-in-law Howard Baker—that after 1944, his presidential boat "had pulled away from the dock."[24]

Dirksen's ambition was again on display when Republicans gained control of the House in 1946. He immediately sought the job of majority leader but lost out to Indiana Congressman Charles Halleck, who would later garner his own share of fame when, after Dirksen moved to the Senate, the two starred in weekly "Ev and Charlie" appearances before the Washington press corps. Dirksen became a leading House advocate of what became the Legislative Reorganization Act of 1946, sweeping legislation that reduced the number of congressional committees, professionalized many operations of Congress, increased staff, established a coherent budget process, and required registration of lobbyists. Mansfield also supported the legislation, and Dirksen stated its budget provision was "the first real ray of hope that taxpayers have had in eighteen years for a balanced budget."[25]

Dirksen was also a forceful voice in the continuing reorientation of GOP foreign policy away from isolationism and toward internationalism. At the same time, he fully endorsed Republican anti-communism, a position he articulated in a well-publicized speech in 1947 even as he walked back a position he had taken in 1933. During the speech, which he labeled "Red Fascism," Dirksen recalled Roosevelt's ambitious agenda for the first one hundred days, including the passage of the National Industrial Recovery Act, the centerpiece of FDR's economic recovery efforts and legislation Dirksen supported. Fourteen years later he termed the measure, albeit significantly dismantled by a Supreme Court ruling in 1935, a step in the direction of greater collectivization. The ubiquitous symbol of implementation of the National Recovery Act was a blue eagle, displayed on billboards and businesses from coast to coast, and Dirksen went into a rhetorical, and not entirely understandable frenzy in recalling the law and the times: "You need only review the whole picture of this very fantastic situation which was a mixture of the blue eagle, and Sally Rand, and of Hitler and Mussolini, and Pearl Harbor, and penicillin, and the Maginot line, and Senator Claghorn, and dipsy doodle, and flat-foot-floogie, and all the rest, to get a kind of fantastic picture of what happened in the generation that is now slipping away when we put our feet in the path way of a departure from the very fundamentals of freedom." The great menacing force in the world today, Dirksen continued, was "red fascism. That is just another term for communism, but I think it is a little more impressive and accurate when you call it 'red fascism.'"[26]

In the same "red fascism" speech, Dirksen enthusiastically backed the work of the House Un-American Activities Committee, the controversial committee on the hunt for communists and subversives, which especially during the 1940s and 1950s, engaged in what historian Walter Goodman termed "endless harassment of individuals for disagreeable opinions and activities." Dirksen supported many of the committee's initiatives, including investigations of Hollywood figures and "some of the labor unions that are dominated by red-fascism." Dirksen was confident the committee would protect civil liberties—in fact, it often did not—by ensuring "that everybody gets a fair shake, gets the right of appeal, does not become the recipient of the tarred stick until we make sure that there is an appeal and that it is unemotional and fair." The point of the investigations, Dirksen said, was vital: to "get at the very heart of disloyalty in Government." Dirksen's anti-communism never flagged. He supported Wisconsin Senator Joseph McCarthy and his red-baiting campaign to the very end, and later based his support for US policy in Southeast Asia on a belief that the United States had to contain and stop the expansion of world communism.[27]

Mansfield's postwar House career was, in many ways, the flip side of Dirksen's anti-communism. He became a target of Montana Republicans, who steadily advanced the fiction that Mansfield's foreign policy views were dangerously left-wing. Montana Senator Zales Ecton, an ultraconservative elected in the 1946 Republican sweep, was the most aggressive adherent of this theme. Ecton, whom Mansfield would challenge in 1952, essentially had one message: Democrats were dangerous, and many were closet communists. Ecton, who became a close ally of McCarthy's, worried constantly about "Communistic infiltration into the government" and the risk that Americans would become "slaves of the state." In 1948, Mansfield's Republican opponent linked him to congressional big spenders who would "work for laws that will lead to socialism and eventually communism," and in Mansfield's last House campaign in 1950, his conservative opponent accused the Asian expert of "appeasement" and of not understanding the threat of Chinese communism. Mansfield won each election with ease, but the smears continued.[28]

Early in 1948, Dirksen shocked his central Illinois constituents and all of Washington with the announcement that he would not be a candidate for reelection. He cited "compelling personal reasons" for the decision, but friends soon confirmed he was suffering from an eye ailment, explained by one doctor as an inflammation that often led to blindness and by physicians at the Mayo Clinic and Johns Hopkins as retinal cancer. The final diagnosis was chorioretinitis, an inflammation of the lining of the retina deep in the eye. Dirksen refused surgery and opted for total rest, vitamin therapy, and prayer, and he reveled in the bipartisan accolades that accompanied his retirement. A newspaper in Dirksen's district called the announcement "bad news," since he was popular, dedicated, and destined one day to be Speaker of the House. The *Washington Evening Star* said Dirksen was a great Republican asset, but "never a narrow partisan and always constructive." House Democratic leader Sam Rayburn commented, "As far as I'm concerned I don't want too many Republicans around, but if they are going to send Republicans to Congress I want more Republicans like Everett Dirksen." Dirksen resisted efforts to reconsider his retirement decision and, while he served out the rest of his term, he also drastically scaled back his work. By spring his eyesight was improving and would eventually recover. By the fall of 1948 he was already plotting his political future.[29]

Dirksen returned to elected political life in 1950 with an upset victory in a Senate race. Mansfield accomplished the same feat two years later.

3   APPRENTICE TO LEADERSHIP

The first rule of Senate behavior, and the one most widely recognized
off the Hill, is that new members are expected to serve a proper
apprenticeship.

—DONALD R. MATTHEWS, 1960

Anti-communism is deeply embedded in the political DNA of American politics.
The post–World War I "red scare" featured widespread and usually warrantless raids
by federal agents on socialists, anarchists, and labor organizers, and while these
actions frequently involved gross violations of civil liberties, many Americans also
deemed them necessary to defend democracy. Suspicion about the global reach of
communism made the United States one of the last major counties to recognize
diplomatically the Soviet Union, an action that did not occur until 1933. Soviet
hegemony over eastern Europe immediately after World War II—a war won in no
small part as a result of blood spilled by the Red Army—only deepened American
hostility toward communism, and "containment" of Soviet expansionism became
the cornerstone of American foreign policy. In 1947, President Harry Truman,
largely disregarding the civil liberties implications, used an executive order to create a "loyalty program" for federal employees designed to screen out communist
sympathizers. Thousands of workers were dismissed or resigned as a result. Having won a global war against totalitarianism only to have to confront a new and
seeming even more dangerous global threat was profoundly unsettling. Where
Americans—and particularly American politicians—stood on "the Communist
issue" became a defining postwar political stance, as well as a ready explanation for
a host of uncomfortable changes remaking the county and the world. "The nation,"
as David Halberstam wrote, "was ready for witch-hunts," and the Republican Party,
locked out of power for nearly two decades, sought to capitalize on what proved to

be a powerful cause. This political issue under cover of democracy-saving crusade found its champion in one of the most controversial figures in modern American politics, a brash, bullying, but also beguilingly charming Republican senator from Wisconsin.[1]

Joseph R. McCarthy, the Irish Catholic pride of Appleton, Wisconsin, whose reckless and relentless anti-communist demagoguery came to define an era of American politics, figured prominently in the first Senate elections of both Everett Dirksen and Mike Mansfield. McCarthy sought to help elect Dirksen and defeat Mansfield, and each campaign—Dirksen's in 1950 and Mansfield's two years later—did much to shape their subsequent Senate careers.

—

Dirksen's retirement from politics in 1948 was a short one. His eye ailment resolved quickly, and almost immediately after announcing he was ending his sixteen-year House career, Dirksen began plotting a challenge to the sitting Senate majority leader, two-term Illinois Democrat Scott Lucas. In every respect it was a bold, even audacious decision. Dirksen and Lucas were longtime acquaintances, both grew up in central Illinois in less-than-prosperous farm families, were World War I veterans, and were active in the American Legion. Elected to the Senate in 1938, Lucas became majority whip and then leader when his predecessor, Alben W. Barkley, became Harry Truman's vice president. "Lucas was handsomely suave, always impeccably dressed in expensive suits, his hair gracefully combed," Neil MacNeil wrote. "He was articulate, if not eloquent, and he adopted to his purposes a manner somewhat stand-offish, the bearing of a statesman burdened with the cares and responsibilities of great office. There was a gentle irony in his voice and the suggestion of the sardonic in his words. Dirksen cultivated a totally different manner, a rumpled 'just folks' approach to the voters."[2]

Lucas struggled as majority leader, burdened with Truman's unpopularity and the increasingly difficult task of keeping a diverse Democratic Party unified. Conservative southern Democrats, who controlled most important Senate committees, chafed at the party's northern liberals with their emphasis on civil rights and Truman's Fair Deal agenda. Lucas was the man in the middle, often on the outs with both factions. Most observers of the Senate in this period acknowledge that the real institutional power was held by Robert A. Taft of Ohio, leader of the Republican conservatives, and Richard Russell of Georgia, who led the conservative southern Democrats, "The job of the Senate Majority Leader in that era was a misery without splendor," Rowland Evans and Robert Novak wrote. "While Russell and Taft

pulled the strings from the cloakroom, the 'leader' was out there on the floor trying
to keep the Senate's creaky machinery in operation." Lucas would later admit he
hated being majority leader and that his years in the job were the unhappiest of his
life. He suffered the worst of two worlds: the visibility of the position made him a
target, and his identification with the administration, including his advocacy for
the unpopular Truman's programs, left Lucas, as he told a constituent, flexing "my
conscience a bit on some things." McCarthy's anti-communist crusade and the
Illinois penchant for political corruption added to Lucas's burdens.[3]

Early in 1950, McCarthy, a barely known senatorial backbencher, agreed to deliver
a series of Republican Lincoln Day speeches, fulfilling a tedious, if necessary, stint
on the political rubber chicken circuit. Since McCarthy's notoriety was still to
come, as biographer Thomas Reeves noted, he was assigned a rather drab schedule.
McCarthy's "tour [began] in Wheeling, West Virginia, and ended in Huron, South
Dakota. The only bright spots were stopovers in Reno and Las Vegas, where Joe
could exercise his passion for gambling." McCarthy gave little thought to what
he might say to these Republican crowds. He was, in the words of David Halberstam, "the accidental demagogue" without a real plan beyond publicity but with
genuine skill as a conspiracy-minded storyteller. McCarthy's speech in Wheeling,
delivered to the Ohio County Republican Women's Club—"pompous campaign
oratory designed for an unsophisticated audience," by one account—launched his
spectacular national rise. McCarthy's accusation that the State Department was
lousy with communists—"I have here in my hand a list of 205"—who were suppos-
edly shaping US policy proved explosive, and by the standards of 1950, the story
went viral. The day after the West Virginia speech, the *Chicago Tribune* published,
deep inside the paper, a short wire service account of McCarthy's accusations. The
headline read: "205 Reds on Job in State Department McCarthy Says." Two days
later McCarthy's allegations, repeated during a speech in Reno, were prominently
displayed on the *Tribune*'s front page. The Wisconsin senator demanded that Truman seek from his own secretary of state the names of communists employed at
the State Department. The sensational headlines, often reporting McCarthy's latest
numbers, which shifted almost daily, now came in waves.[4]

   In the wake of his increasing prominence, McCarthy made five speeches in
Illinois in 1950 promoting Dirksen's candidacy, boosting the Republican ticket,
and blasting Lucas, who became, along with Democratic senators Millard Tydings
of Maryland and Brien McMahon of Connecticut, McCarthy's principal targets.

Each senator had objected to McCarthy's sweeping, unsubstantiated allegations, and Tydings even investigated and discredited the claims. McCarthy was unbowed. "Lucas provided the whitewash when I charged there were communists in high places in government," McCarthy said in one speech. "McMahon brought the bucket; Tydings the brush. This trio . . . in my opinion have done more than any others in this nation to shield the traitors, protect the disloyal, and confuse Americans in their desperate fight to clean out the communists." McCarthy, in a Chicago speech, contended that a vote for Dirksen equaled a "prayer for America," a "vote against [Truman's secretary of state] Dean Acheson," and a vote against the "commicrat party." Dirksen, campaigning frantically, reinforced the anti-communist message in his own speeches. Voting for Republicans, he said, would tell Joseph Stalin "that there will be a housecleaning of his sympathizers and party liners such as this country has never seen before." At the Illinois state Republican convention Dirksen suggested Democrats were involved in a "long and steady sit-down strike against action on Reds and Pinks on the home front," and in a flight of rhetorical excess that violated his own habit of using colorful but not nasty language, Dirksen lashed out at Lucas, calling him "a faker and a moral fraud," as well as a "puppet" of Truman.[5]

Lucas's campaign, hampered by the demands of the candidate's more than full-time job as majority leader, which kept him tied to Washington, seemed far removed from Dirksen's frenetic travel schedule. Dirksen claimed to have traveled a quarter-million miles during the campaign, and the Republican's relentless attacks on Truman, hidden communists, and socialized medicine landed telling blows on the Democrat. Lucas's major campaign theme—that Dirksen was inconsistent—was tame by comparison. His staff produced a four-hundred-page paper entitled *The Diary of a Chameleon*, which detailed Dirksen's voting record during eight terms in the House of Representatives and charged that he "has literally stood for nothing." The *Chicago Sun-Times*, considerably more liberal than the *Tribune*, also harped on Dirksen's inconsistencies, "reminding readers of Dirksen's frequent changes of position on foreign and agricultural policies." Dirksen responded, as he later did whenever his political "flexibility" was criticized, by saying, "In a society such as ours you can't plow just that one furrow. You have to re-examine your premises in the light of changing conditions." Lucas also attempted to make an issue of Dirksen's support from the *Chicago Tribune*, since the newspaper had often been ambivalent about Dirksen in the past. Dirksen flatly dismissed the issue, saying, "I wear no man's halter."[6]

The Lucas-Dirksen campaign was "a knock-down and drag-out battle with no holds or punches barred," wrote Joseph Driscoll, national correspondent for the

St. Louis Post-Dispatch. The Illinois donnybrook was one of the premier contests in the nation, Driscoll wrote, and would turn on how Illinois voters viewed three issues. First, hostilities in Korea—Dirksen was critical of Truman's policy following the outbreak of war in June 1950. Second on whether the Democrats' health care plans amounted to "socialized medicine"—both candidates opposed government involvement in health care. And, third, on whether Dirksen's flexible record on issues was a liability or an asset. The newspaper suggested in its editorial endorsement of Lucas that Dirksen had flip-flopped in support for the Marshall Plan to aid war-ravaged Europe in exchange for support from McCormick's *Tribune.* Whether Dirksen made an accommodation with McCormick or simply benefited from the *Tribune* editors' dislike of Scott Lucas, there is no doubt that Dirksen received better treatment from the influential newspaper in his first Senate election than he had to that point in his political career.[7]

But historian Brian Deason, Lucas's biographer, contends that the attacks from Dirksen and McCarthy, as blistering and as widely repeated as they were, were not as fatal to Lucas as was a Democratic-led investigation of organized crime that swept into Chicago in the middle of the Senate campaign. Days before the election, the *Sun-Times* published an explosive story from this high-profile probe of organized crime chaired by Tennessee senator Estes Kefauver, an ambitious Democrat with presidential aspirations. A Chicago police captain, Daniel A. "Tubbo" Gilbert, who was also the Democratic candidate for Cook County sheriff, had testified about his gambling habits before Kefauver's committee in closed session. Gilbert admitted during his testimony to amassing a $360,000 fortune by betting on sporting events, elections, horse races, and even the stock market. Gilbert was widely described in Chicago as the "richest cop in the world." The unspoken assumption that organized crime figures controlled the gaming that had enriched Gilbert implicated a top Democrat in the nationwide investigation. The cop's testimony was supposed to have been kept confidential until the committee completed its investigation, but details leaked and the resulting headlines landed, from top to bottom, like an anvil on the entire Democratic ticket. The election impact was amplified because the *Sun-Times* was generally regarded as a Democratic newspaper and had endorsed Lucas but not the candidate for sheriff. Illinois's other senator, Democrat Paul Douglas, called the Democratic campaign in 1950 a "debacle" and admitted, in something of an understatement, that Gilbert's testimony "showed that he did have an enormous income for which he could not satisfactorily account."[8]

The allegations of Democratic corruption clearly contributed to Lucas's loss even though he was not personally implicated. The *Tribune* noted that Lucas ran poorly in Chicago, at least by historic Democratic standards, while Dirksen piled up impressive downstate totals. Dirksen's winning margin was more than 290,000 votes. "The downstate area apparently agreed with Republican campaigners that the people are tired of war, high prices, and high taxes," the *Tribune* said, crowing in a headline: "Lucas and His Entire State Ticket Beaten." And Tubbo Gilbert lost the Cook County sheriff's race by a landslide. Dirksen's victory, or perhaps more correctly Lucas's loss, was seen as a direct repudiation of Harry Truman. Dirksen waited only hours before demanding further investigations of communist influence in the federal government and a reexamination of the Marshall Plan, and he basked in the victory, putting a sign on the front door of his modest Pekin home that read simply "Come In." Mail sacks filled with messages of congratulation piled up on the front porch. An East Peoria man seemed to echo the general sentiment of Republican voters when he wrote Dirksen: "It's time among other things to get rid of the Communists in all departments of the government."[9]

McCarthy, of course, claimed credit for the election outcome. The Wisconsin senator appeared to be wielding "awesome—and to some frightening—power." Newspaper coverage confirmed the image of McCarthy's influence. "In every contest where it was a major factor, McCarthyism won," columnist Marquis Childs wrote. Yet, Dirksen ran such an energetic campaign, and Lucas such an ineffective one, that he might have won in a strong Republican year without McCarthy's communist hectoring. Robert Taft, thought to be in some trouble in Ohio, coasted to reelection, for example. Meanwhile, Dirksen, along with the victorious Republican challenger to Millard Tydings in Maryland and Senate candidates Richard Nixon in California and Herman Welker in Idaho, made the most of drafting in McCarthy's wake. The Republican ticket was also bolstered by other issues, including fears about inflation and a general postwar worry about the state of the world. Dirksen and fellow Republicans, as Taft's biographer wrote, "benefited from a tide that was sweeping many Democrats out of office and that was to leave the Truman administration defending itself against partisan onslaughts for the next two years." Dirksen arrived in the Senate an experienced, respected politician. He had observed firsthand the power of the anti-communist political message, and he would stick with McCarthy even when it became awkward to do so. But the campaign against Scott Lucas also highlighted the benefits of political flexibility, a characteristic Dirksen eventually wore as a political medal. He would face competitive challengers throughout his Senate career, but Dirksen always won by comfortable margins, and he retains the distinction of being one of only three candidates to defeat a sitting Senate majority leader.[10]

The historian William E. Leuchtenburg noted of the 1946 election, "Conservative Republicans viewed the midterm outcome as a massive national revulsion
against liberalism." Convinced that 1946 was not his year to attempt a move to
the Senate, Mansfield was content to stay in the House of Representatives, where
his foreign policy expertise continued to grow. For example, Truman designated
Mansfield a delegate to the United Nations, and his reputation grew in Montana
thanks to diligent constituent service. Despite Truman's slumping popularity and
the Democratic Party's general fall from favor, Mansfield firmly embraced the New
Deal legacy of the Democratic Party. As representatives of a working-class party,
Democrats focused on support for organized labor, attention to the needs of both
farmers and small businesses, and belief in the power of the federal government
to improve the lot of the middle class. Historian Jeffrey Bloodworth has written
about "quantitative liberalism's hydroelectric dams and other internal improvements," precisely the type of issues Mansfield paid close attention to. A cursory
glance at Mansfield's output of news releases—on grain exports; timber harvest;
and rail, air, and highway improvements—underscores that the scholar of Asia
also kept track of the price of a bushel of Montana wheat. By 1952, Mansfield was
ready to try for the Senate.[11]

Zales M. Ecton, the wealthy Gallatin County farmer-lawyer who became the
first popularly elected Republican senator in Montana history in 1946, developed
only one significant theme in his campaigns and during his short Senate career:
he was a fighter against communism and socialist Democrats. It was a given that
Ecton would become one of Joe McCarthy's biggest supporters, and McCarthy
came to Montana in 1952 to help Ecton beat back the challenge from the former
college professor and congressman. It was a brutal campaign, by far the toughest
of Mansfield's political career. Ecton railed against the "socialist tendencies" of all
Democrats, including Mansfield, bashed Truman's handling of the war in Korea,
asserted that high taxes and inflation, products of socialism, were destroying the
economy, and claimed the administration was coercing Montana Native Americans
into voting for Democratic candidates. "I have consistently and persistently fought
any compromise by our government with Communism," Ecton claimed. Deeming
Mansfield's China mission during World War II an "issue which he cannot ignore by
trying to avoid it," Ecton made a barely veiled insinuation that the trip was somehow
evidence of Mansfield's communist sympathies. Not surprisingly, the Associated
Press compared the candidates' voting records and deemed them nearly opposite.[12]

Mansfield was well known and well regarded in his western Montana congressional district but largely an unknown quantity in generally more conservative
eastern Montana, a fact Republicans were determined to capitalize on. The GOP
strategy was to use the McCarthy playbook or, as one Mansfield friend recorded, to
"try to connect [Mansfield] with Red China and Communism . . . the Republicans
have plenty of money & you know the things they say or print don't have to be true."
Ecton lambasted Mansfield for his description of Chinese communists as "agrarian
reformers" and mailers began appearing across Montana charging that Mansfield
"aided the Communist line" that directly brought about the Korean War. Taft and
another of McCarthy's close Senate collaborators, Idaho Republican Herman
Welker, came to Montana to boost Ecton and savage Mansfield, while Dwight
Eisenhower, the party's presidential candidate, and Richard Nixon, his running
mate, both campaigned in the state. McCarthy himself joined the fray late in the
campaign. Before a large crowd in Missoula, McCarthy cited a favorable mention
of Mansfield in a 1947 edition of the *Daily Worker*, the newspaper of the Communist
Party USA. Though he did not precisely say Mansfield was a communist, McCarthy
did say he was "either stupid or a dupe" for not recognizing the threat posed by
communist China and the Soviet Union. In response to criticism of his methods,
McCarthy said, "you don't hunt skunks with a top hat and a lace handkerchief."[13]

McCarthy's attacks on Mansfield went well beyond the passionate excesses of
the campaign trail. A paid FBI informant, a shifty, unreliable ex-communist named
Harvey Matusow, parachuted into Montana at McCarthy's request to further the
Mansfield smears. "McCarthy had a violent hatred for Mansfield," Matusow wrote
years later, even telling him that "you might as well have an admitted Communist in
the Senate," since having Mansfield there was "the same difference." It is impossible
to know whether the Wisconsin senator really despised the Montana congressman,
and Matusow later served a jail sentence for perjury. He admitted to lying repeatedly to congressional committees, and one columnist suggested Matusow might
have been lying about his lying.[14]

For most of the campaign, the mild-mannered Mansfield tried to keep the political debate focused on his record versus Ecton's on Montana issues. Mansfield contended that Ecton had opposed important Rural Electrification Administration
projects in Montana, had voted against funding to expediate the Hungry Horse Dam
project, and had voted to cut soil conservation funding. But, uncharacteristically
and perhaps believing that the Senate seat was slipping away from him, Mansfield
went on the offensive in a radio speech broadcast statewide on the eve of the election. "The people of Montana are now being bombarded by *These Desperate Men*

who will do anything, tell any lie, for a vote," Mansfield said. "*These Desperate Men* are the frustrated politicians. They are so hungry for power—so eager to take over the destiny of this country—so anxious to regain the seat from which the American people drove them twenty years ago that they will do anything. In their slick and ugly way they are trying to blacken the record of every honest man who dares to oppose them." Without mentioning Matusow by name, Mansfield called out "the carpetbagger, a Communist brought into Montana to attack me, my record, and my integrity."[15]

The speech, broadcast from Billings over at least twenty stations, likely saved the election for Mansfield. Montana went heavily for Eisenhower and elected a Republican governor, while Mansfield won the Senate race by fewer than six thousand votes. He later admitted that had he known how nasty the campaign would become, he would have declined to run, and it is clear that the 1952 campaign left an indelible mark on his psyche. "What in heaven's name has happened to us as Americans?" Mansfield asked Montana voters during his final appeal. "Is it not intolerable that a man seeking high office with its agonizing burdens would have to suffer the indignity of having to defend, not his political beliefs, but the very honor of his soul?"[16]

Mansfield's campaign style in the future would mirror his leadership style— little or no harsh, partisan language but instead appeals to reason, a focus on issues, patience, trust in the democratic process, and respect for voters. Rarely did Mansfield engage in the fairly standard arts of partisanship, especially not after reaching Senate leadership and developing his close working relationship with Everett Dirksen. One notable exception came two years after his own narrow brush with defeat, when he took to the Senate floor immediately after the 1954 midterm elections where Democrats regained control of the Senate and Lyndon Johnson became majority leader. In a lengthy speech he entitled "Gutter Politics" Mansfield dissected Vice President Richard Nixon's role in the recent campaign. "Nixon campaigned throughout the nation labeling the Democratic Party as socialistic, left-wing, soft on Communism," Mansfield said, accusing the vice president of willful distortion and "driving a wedge" between the parties. "Nixon and his associates have dragged politics to its lowest ebb," Mansfield said. Twenty years later, as majority leader, Mansfield would organize the Senate investigation into then-President Nixon's lawlessness during another campaign. In 1954, he had formed a view of what Nixon was capable of and offered a prescient preview of where American politics was headed: "The sort of campaign we witnessed is unworthy of the high offices in our Government. At least they should be above 'gutter politics.' Unless the deterioration of our political system is not averted, it will not be the Communists and foreign agents that we have to worry about, it will be those within who will deprive the Americans of their liberties."[17]

The Senate class Mansfield joined in January 1953 included some of the most significant figures in modern political history: John Kennedy of Massachusetts, Henry Jackson of Washington, Stuart Symington of Missouri, Albert Gore Sr. of Tennessee, and Barry Goldwater of Arizona. Among the Senate old guard were Democrats John Sparkman and Lister Hill of Alabama, J. William Fulbright of Arkansas, Richard Russell and Walter George of Georgia, John Stennis and James Eastland of Mississippi, Harry Byrd of Virginia, Robert Kerr of Oklahoma, and Russell Long and Allen Ellender of Louisiana. Influential Republicans included the majority leader Robert Taft, William Langer of North Dakota, Karl Mundt of South Dakota, John Sherman Cooper of Kentucky, and the Senate's only woman, Margaret Chase Smith of Maine. Mansfield immediately aligned himself with the Senate Democratic leader, Lyndon Johnson of Texas.

When Mike Mansfield entered the Senate in 1953, the institution was dominated by a group of clubby insiders and powerful committee chairmen. Mansfield (second from right) is pictured here with (from left to right) Senators James Eastland of Mississippi, Spessard Holland of Florida, and Arthur Watkins of Utah. (*James O. Eastland Collection, Archives and Special Collections, University of Mississippi Libraries*)

Johnson and Mansfield had served in the House together but were hardly friends. So Johnson, seeking support to become the Senate's Democratic leader, reached out to Jim Rowe, the Montana native, skilled political operative, and mutual friend of both, asking him to find out whether Mansfield would support Johnson. Even though Montanan Jim Murray, backed by several Democratic liberals, was also a candidate for the leadership position, Mansfield had already decided to support Johnson, appreciating the Texan's energy and political skill. While Mansfield always spoke well of his Montana colleague, an unabashed New Deal liberal, he almost certainly knew Murray would struggle in such a high-profile role. Murray was a less-than-polished speaker who at seventy-six was showing his age. Mansfield's decision paid off handsomely. The minority leader immediately saw to it that the Montana freshman senator vaulted over several more senior members to take a seat on the Foreign Relations Committee, an extraordinarily rare appointment for a newly elected senator. Eager to add depth to the Democratic ranks on the committee, Johnson also appointed Minnesota's Hubert Humphrey. Knowing that a new Republican administration and congressional Republicans would continue to critique—savage where possible—Franklin Roosevelt's legacy and Truman's foreign policy, and that GOP leader Taft was joining the committee, Johnson sought to add intellectual heft to the Democratic contingent. After his service on the House Foreign Affairs Committee and with his knowledge of Asia, Mansfield was a natural for the committee where he would serve throughout his Senate career. "Mansfield out-knows Taft and Humphrey can out-talk him," Johnson told fellow senators. Mansfield—and Rowe—were grateful that Mansfield received his dream assignment. "I don't know how you did it," Rowe wrote to Johnson, "but I know who did it . . . And so does Mike."[18]

The first mention Mansfield received in Montana newspapers after he took his seat in the Senate in 1953 related to his appointment to the Foreign Relations Committee, but press statements coming from Mansfield's office made little of the assignment, highlighting instead his work on legislation to improve US Highway 2, a vital transportation corridor across the northern "Hi-Line" of Montana. And Mansfield was surely pleased that less than three weeks after he took his Senate oath, both the *Billings Gazette* and *Great Falls Tribune* prominently featured a photo of the freshman senator with four other new members of Congress, all Marine Corps veterans. Mansfield was the only Democrat in the group.[19]

—

Everett Dirksen began the Eisenhower era on the outs with the first Republican president in twenty years. Dirksen struggled, not always successfully, to find positions that permitted him to reconcile his instinctive support for the GOP old guard without completely alienating the forces of Republican moderation, represented by the former general, which were frequently at war over the future of the party. Dirksen broke dramatically with the eastern, more liberal wing of the party at the Republican Convention in 1952, denouncing two-time presidential candidate Thomas Dewey who, Dirksen said, had taken "us down the path to defeat." Dirksen threw his full backing behind the much more conservative Taft, amid speculation that the Illinois senator might end up as the vice presidential candidate on a Taft ticket, something Dirksen clearly desired. But Taft and his slogan "Taft for me. Taft for you. Taft will win in Fifty-Two" was no match for the popular Eisenhower and the simple "I Like Ike." Dirksen's blistering convention attack on Dewey did nothing to deny Eisenhower the presidential nomination but did reveal "the depth of the geographical and ideological divisions plaguing the Republican Party" and, at least temporarily, left Dirksen outside Eisenhower's circle. Dirksen revered the cerebral, introverted Taft and doubted whether Eisenhower was a genuine conservative. In reality, Taft—Mr. Republican to many in the party during the 1940s—was already seriously ill with the cancer that would claim his life in less than a year. Dirksen's reputation for political and partisan flexibility was still developing, and at least during the early going of the Eisenhower administration, Dirksen was committed to a philosophy of government closer to Taft's midwestern conservatism than Ike's modern Republicanism. As a result, the historian Byron Hulsey has written, Dirksen and Eisenhower "treated one another with a standoffish acceptance reflective of the conflict and consensus that defined the Republican party in the early 1950s."[20]

As chairman of the Republican Senate campaign committee, Dirksen traveled the country boosting GOP candidates in 1952 and deserves some of the credit for the narrow Republican Senate majority that resulted from that election. He also did not flinch in his support of Joe McCarthy, declaring a need to rally behind the Wisconsin senator against "eastern money and propaganda." After the Republican victory, Dirksen dedicated himself to keeping moderate easterners—the Dewey wing of the party—out of Eisenhower's government. To that end he joined with ten other very conservative Republicans, including McCarthy and the newly elected Goldwater, to oppose Eisenhower's appointment of Charles E. Bohlen, a top FDR advisor at the 1945 Yalta Conference, as the US ambassador to Moscow. Yalta by this time had become a flash point for conservative Republicans, who had convinced themselves that Roosevelt, influenced by left-leaning or even communist advisors, had sold out eastern Europe to communism. The Republican platform in 1952 repudiated Yalta, and the very word and anyone associated with the conference became a conservative rallying cry. "I have studied the Yalta agreements at great length," Dirksen told the *Chicago Tribune*—the newspaper also opposed Bohlen's appointment—and "come to the conclusion that if you are going to repudiate Yalta, you have to reject the Yalta men." Eisenhower pushed hard for Bohlen's confirmation, and despite hyperbolic pleas from McCarthy and a handful of other Republicans, most of them loyal McCarthyites, the Senate did approve the appointment. Mansfield supported the president's selection. One Eisenhower biographer called it "a remarkable fight, and Ike stood his ground," but the president was also, as he confided to his diary, surprised by the vehemence of the conservative opposition. Eisenhower also drew the wrong lesson about McCarthy from the mostly intraparty fight. "I really believe," Eisenhower said, "that nothing will be so effective in combating his particular kind of trouble-making as to ignore him." It was not to be, and Dirksen would continue to be in the eye of the storm surrounding McCarthy.[21]

Everett Dirksen with then–senate minority leader Lyndon Johnson. The two became close friends in the Senate, and the relationship grew even closer after Johnson became president. (*US Senate Historical Office*)

Dirksen also joined, again in opposition to Eisenhower's wishes, the sustained fight over the Bricker Amendment, named for its sponsor, conservative Ohio Republican senator John Bricker, and cosponsored by Dirksen. This proposed constitutional amendment amounted to a sweeping effort to constrain presidential power in the field of foreign affairs, and Eisenhower saw it for what it was: an affront to a Republican president and his ability to implement foreign policy. Dirksen claimed his opposition to the president and co-sponsorship of the amendment was motivated by his "feeling of responsibility" for his oath to support and defend the Constitution. Dirksen's position was squarely at odds with the internationalism he had embraced during World War II, a contradiction that can only be explained by Dirksen's Senate leadership aspirations. He was struggling to harmonize a last-gasp effort by the old isolationist wing of the Republican Party with Eisenhower's determination to build on the foreign policy consensus that had developed in the immediate postwar period. When he had to choose which way to tilt, Dirksen in this period usually stuck with Republican conservatives, but his political flexibility was growing. The historian Jean Torcom Cronin, who analyzed Dirksen's leadership style, contends that Dirksen's full-throated embrace of anti-communism, as manifest in his support for McCarthy and his return to his earlier isolationism arose from "base political opportunism," a fierce ambition that led Dirksen to abandon principle. This reputation for rank opportunism would, Cronin wrote, "stay with him and color his image for the rest of his life." Her assessment is true, but only to a point. The opportunism Dirksen exhibited in the early 1950s, while clearly a manifestation of his political ambition, was also evidence of his independent instincts, as well as his willingness to change his position in the interests of reasonable progress.[22]

In the 1950s Mansfield often sided with the Republican president on foreign policy issues, saying, for example, that "the Bricker Amendment would make our treaty-implementing procedure the most cumbersome in the world. In this atomic age it would appear that such a policy would be a perilous handicap in our relations with other countries." It became a defining Mansfield characteristic, first evidenced during Eisenhower's presidency, to try and support any president on foreign policy, even as he often candidly offered different advice or advocated specific approaches to issues in private. This attitude—respect for and deference to presidential leadership—would bring Mansfield criticism as well as praise, but would also foster great respect for his integrity and thoughtfulness. Restraint and respect were simply how Mansfield approached politics. His vision of leadership involved careful listening and informed counsel, but never partisan point scoring.[23]

In the early years of his Senate career, Dirksen was attempting to find a way to straddle the ideological divide in his party. He would be neither a throwback to prewar Republican conservatism nor an adherent to the moderate liberalism of Republicans like New Yorker Jacob Javits or Californian Thomas Kuchel. Dirksen would find a way to be accepted by both Republican factions in the Senate, while maintaining working relationships with both conservative southern Democrats and a new generation of Democratic liberals like Mansfield and Humphrey. Over time Dirksen came to exemplify a practical bipartisanship that afforded him a nearly two-decade-long title role—what more could an actor wish for—in the nation's most important political debates.

Meanwhile, Mike Mansfield was creating his own Senate path, in part by deepening his foreign policy portfolio. Mansfield's foreign travel—he was easily the most traveled member of Congress—and the detailed, scholarly writing informed by those trips are, by today's congressional standards, astounding. Don Oberdorfer calculated that by 1957 Mansfield had made five trips to East Asia, seven to western Europe, two to North Africa, and four to Latin America during his fourteen years in the House and Senate. A current member of Congress who set such a travel pace would likely be pilloried in attack ads for excessive foreign junketing. And few members today would have the ability or inclination to detail their views about foreign policy and world events in the very public manner Mansfield did. "In 1956," Oberdorfer wrote, "Mansfield made ten lengthy speeches on the Senate floor reviewing, one by one, U.S. policies in every part of the world and virtually every important country." These speeches were hardly boilerplate, but rather the work of a scholar well read and deeply interested in history whose aim was to enlighten and inform policy rather than merely score partisan debating points. Mansfield could certainly be critical of Eisenhower administration policy, but, as Oberdorfer points out, his speeches and other writings "were restrained in rhetoric and tone and often suggested alternatives. In their depth and breadth, they were scholarly speeches of a sort rarely heard in the Senate in that day and almost never since."[24]

As early as 1954, the *Washington Post* was describing Mansfield as "probably the Senate's leading authority on the complex situation in the Far East." With an uneasy armistice in place in Korea, Mansfield increasingly focused his attention on the growing crisis in Vietnam, which he visited both before and after the bloody French defeat at Dien Bien Phu in 1954 and the subsequent French departure from

Indochina. His first trip, in mid-1953, took Mansfield to Laos, Cambodia, and Vietnam in the company of a researcher from the Library of Congress, Francis Valeo, who would become Mansfield's top foreign policy aide and, later, secretary of the Senate. Mansfield returned from the 1953 trip committed to the idea that international communism must be stopped in Southeast Asia, and in broad terms he supported the Eisenhower administration's policy in the region. A year later, after another visit to Vietnam as the French were preparing to abandon Hanoi, Mansfield's views had grown more nuanced and more realistic. Against the backdrop of the Cold War and the continuing power of anti-communism as a political issue, Mansfield was charting his own approach to foreign policy and American security interests, one grounded in firsthand observation and a detailed understanding of history.[25]

As Oberdorfer notes, "He had begun to see the situation in Vietnam as fundamentally an internal problem with political roots that could not be solved by military means alone." Mansfield was a trusted, thoughtful, measured, and bipartisan source of advice and counsel for the Republican administration, and he also developed close working relationships with officials at the State Department. After yet another visit in 1955, Mansfield authored an article for *Harper's* in which he endorsed Ngo Dinh Diem, the South Vietnamese president, with great enthusiasm as the last—and perhaps only—hope to create a unified, non-communist Vietnam. Mansfield, who had first met Diem in 1953 in the United States, praised Diem, whose political corruption and authoritarianism was not yet entirely obvious, as a man of courage, integrity, and conviction, a person who could best North Vietnamese leader Ho Chi Minh in a contest over the future of the country. "In short," Mansfield wrote, "Diem's star is likely to remain in the ascendancy and that of Ho Chi Minh to fade, because Diem is following a course which more closely meets the needs and aspirations of the Vietnamese people." Mansfield's vision, vastly more realistic than that of many Americans about the stakes and likely outcomes in Vietnam, was still wildly optimistic. His confidence in Diem, which caused many others to have faith in Diem as well, would soon enough be shown to have been misplaced.[26]

In this period Mansfield also expressed some of the earliest and most prescient concerns about the Central Intelligence Agency (CIA). In 1954, during a Senate speech, Mansfield acknowledged the value of a central government agency devoted to foreign intelligence gathering and analysis, as well as the need to keep certain secrets, but he rejected the broad secrecy that surrounded the agency. "Secrecy now beclouds everything about the CIA—its cost, its efficiency, its successes, and its failures," Mansfield said. Secrecy "has been mustered against questions or proposals regarding CIA by members of Congress. It is difficult to legislate intelligently about this agency because we have no information which we can be positive is correct." Mansfield proposed a joint congressional committee to provide intelligence agency oversight, modeled on the successful Joint Committee on Atomic Energy. Mansfield got his legislation to the Senate floor in 1956, where the proposal was defeated fifty-nine to twenty-seven—John F. Kennedy for, Lyndon B. Johnson against. Mansfield's proposal never again made it to a Senate vote. Still, during the Kennedy administration, Mansfield continued pressing for genuine oversight of the CIA. "Many members of Congress have long been concerned with the intelligence structure within the Executive Branch. I am among them," he wrote to Kennedy in 1961. Mansfield's prophetic concerns included the scope of CIA clandestine activity, the lack of budget oversight, and the potential for unchecked influence by the agency inside the government and foreign policy communities. Mansfield recommended Kennedy appoint a presidential commission to review such issues, including "defining intelligence functions," creating a budget process to provide oversight of clandestine activities, and delineating presidential and legislative responsibilities. While Mansfield's call for congressional oversight in the 1950s and early 1960s was little noted at the time, and Congress took no significant action, he identified many of the concerns that would culminate with his creation, as majority leader in the 1970s, of a Senate select committee—the Church Committee—that conducted a wide-ranging and historic investigation of the nation's intelligence community.[27]

Early in 1953, shortly after being sworn in as the new senator from Montana, Mike Mansfield had a chance encounter with Joe McCarthy as the two rode the underground trolley that connected the Senate Office Building to the Capitol. McCarthy, now the hail-fellow senator rather than the attack artist who had assaulted Mansfield in Missoula just weeks earlier, asked, "How are things in Montana, Mike?" Mansfield, rarely testy with anyone, responded, "Much better since you left."[28]

It is impossible to overstate how much McCarthy and McCarthyism dominated the Senate and all of American politics in the 1950s. Most Republicans "could not and would not disavow" the issues and methods the Wisconsin senator employed, the Eisenhower administration had no strategy to deal with McCarthy, and the Senate, at least until McCarthy unraveled on national television during the Army-McCarthy hearings in 1954, had little stomach for disciplining a demagogue. Like the actor he had once aspired to be, Everett Dirksen played a curious, tragicomic role in the Senate's McCarthy saga. As we have seen, in his first Senate election in 1950, Dirksen benefited from McCarthy and his tactics. He then supported McCarthy, defended him, attempted to derail efforts to sanction him, and ultimately suffered reputational damage for sticking with McCarthy to the bitter end. One Dirksen biographer, Jean Torcom Cronin, writes correctly, "his behavior in the McCarthy episode was the nadir of Dirksen's political career." And Neil MacNeil, generally an admirer of Dirksen's, offered some of his harshest criticism in discussing Dirksen's role in the McCarthy censure. Dirksen's defense of McCarthy, MacNeil wrote, shredded "any remnant of the extraordinary prestige he had commanded as a member of the House of Representatives. He was bitterly hated by men who had once admired him. He was now almost as constant a target of the press as was Senator McCarthy." Where colleagues had once laughed with Dirksen, they now laughed at him. Powerful Oklahoma Democrat Robert Kerr took to calling Dirksen "Irksome Dirksen." *Time* coined the "Wizard of Ooze" moniker, which stuck and was repeated constantly. Some who had praised Dirksen's political flexibility now wondered why he had not found a way to distance himself from the cratering McCarthy. One overly simplistic explanation held that Dirksen had become nothing more than an "errand boy" for the *Chicago Tribune*.[29]

Less than a month before McCarthy was formally censured by the Senate, Dirksen was a guest on the NBC program *Meet the Press*. He was asked, "Are you the leader of the forces who oppose the censure of Senator McCarthy?" Dirksen responded: "I'm afraid that word 'leader' is not very well applied. I can only say that as a member of the United States Senate, I have spoken my piece, I sought to defend him. I think this censure is a mistake, and I am prepared to say so on the Senate floor with what feeble talent and energy and vigor I possess." The McCarthy censure vote came on December 2, 1954, and at 67–22, it was overwhelmingly against the Wisconsin senator. As MacNeil wrote, "the names of those voting against censuring read like a roster of the Taft wing of the Republican Party in the Senate . . . the Republican senators voting for censure were the Eisenhower bloc." Dirksen was isolated, or so it seemed, in the shrinking, McCarthy-defined reactionary wing of the GOP. As MacNeil noted, "The Senate vote did more than censure Senator McCarthy: it repudiated as well the men who had stood with him, none more than Dirksen." Dirksen's dramatic arrival in the Senate and his thumping of Scott Lucas just four years earlier—powered in part by a welcome boost from Joe McCarthy—seemed like ancient history. But reports of Dirksen's demise in Republican politics and in the Senate were decidedly premature. The old actor still had a second and even a third act to play.[30]

For his part, Mansfield quietly went along with Lyndon Johnson's strategy of letting Senate Republicans fight it out over McCarthy, although one Senate insider noted that the Montanan was worried about McCarthy's broad support among Irish Catholic voters and "was glad that he and at least two other Catholics in the Senate will vote for censure. But he is very conscious of those nuns scattered throughout the gallery"—and scattered throughout Montana as well.[31]

In 1966, sixteen years after Dirksen defeated the sitting majority leader and went to the Senate, Scott Lucas, then a lobbyist, was hospitalized in Washington, DC. A blood clot caused problems with circulation in Lucas's left leg, and doctors were forced to amputate. Dirksen heard about the operation from Lucas's physician and arranged to visit the hospital before the surgery. Lucas was in good spirits, and the two of them, old friends reacquainted after a bruising, long-ago political battle, had a wide-ranging discussion that covered, as Dirksen recounted, "our days together in the American Legion, in Congress, and in politics; and it was then that I confessed to him a sense of shame that I had used a harsh epithet ["faker"] in the campaign of 1950." This telling anecdote is illustrative of Dirksen's decency, his humanity, and his capacity for self-reflection. He was able, as many in public life are not, to grow and develop, to be flexible, to get better at his job. Dirksen included the story of his visit with Lucas in his autobiography; he made no mention of Joe McCarthy.[32]

ELEMENTS OF LEADERSHIP
Eloquence, Cornpone, Substance, and Humor

...a voice that was like honey dripping over metal tiles.

—JACK VALENTI ON
EVERETT DIRKSEN, 1991

A premise of this book is that few members of the US Senate today, given the Senate's deep and often paralyzing partisanship, are willing, or able, to function within the institution in the manner Mike Mansfield and Everett Dirksen did. Beyond a commitment to comity and bipartisanship, characteristics in short supply in today's Senate, Dirksen and Mansfield displayed other political behaviors that now seem obsolete, old-fashioned, or simply unthinkable. Both senators were, of course, partisans, but their party responsibilities rarely, if ever, superseded the genuine respect, even affection they felt for each other, for colleagues—even the difficult ones—and for the Senate itself. Perhaps if more current senators were to model such behavior, the American public would again come to value Mansfield's egalitarian approach to leadership and Dirksen's willingness to make a deal. Yet, so long as voters view their senators as purely partisan warriors, there is no reason to believe the Senate can transcend what one scholar has called the current political preference for propaganda over persuasion.[1]

Senate leaders of the 1960s clearly lived in an era vastly different than our own, when politics often depended more on memorable oratory than on ten-second sound bites; when appearance, style, and humor could define a political brand, and when the ability to turn a phrase, elicit a laugh, or skewer an opponent with a well-chosen sentence set a politician apart. In personal style the senators from Montana and Illinois could not have been more different: Mansfield, lanky, ramrod straight, laconic, had a scholar's precision with words. Dirksen, a perpetually rumpled bear of a man whose wavy silver hair seemed perpetually in need of a comb, was dedicated, as one reporter said, "to the proposition that a man should never use one word if he can dredge up twenty." Yet each man's approach to rhetoric, humor, language, and political substance related directly to both men's success and longevity as political leaders. It was not a matter of style over substance in either senator's case, but rather an example of how style can enhance substance and provide strength and effectiveness in leadership.[2]

"By a variety of devices peculiarly his own, Dirksen contrived to look and act differently than other men," his biographer Neil MacNeil wrote. "Part of this, plainly, was his inner yearning to be distinguishable from his fellows; part also was the calculated decision of a politician to make himself readily remembered by those who met him, saw him, or heard him." The strategy was a spectacular success. Indeed, as the political scientist Burdett Loomis wrote, "as Dirksen moved from House to Senate, and then to Senate leadership, his hair became progressively wayward, apparently taking on a life of its own." The comedian Bob Hope quipped that Dirksen's curly mop made him look "like a man who had been electrocuted, but lived." In a profile, *Esquire* magazine said, "Everett Dirksen's secret is that he, alone among major American politicians, has mastered the technique of translating style into power."[3]

Everett Dirksen, "the Wizard of Ooze," in mid-sentence. (*US Senate Historical Office*)

When Dirksen first came to Congress, in the days before an amplification system made a speech on the floor of the House of Representatives a shouting contest, he employed a "booming style" that he modeled on William Jennings Bryan, the rousing Midwest orator Dirksen had encountered as a youngster. Gradually, he refined his approach, and with refinement came both greater substance and wider influence. "He speaks, and the words emerge in a soft, sepulchral baritone," *Time* wrote in 1962. "They undulate in measured phrases, expire in breathless wisps. He fills his lungs and blows word rings like smoke. The sentences curl upward." Dirksen knew that at least half of political persuasion involved knowing his audience and entertaining it.[4]

Roger Mudd, the CBS News congressional correspondent, filmed a half-hour documentary profile of Dirksen in the summer of 1965 and asked the minority leader about his rhetorical style.

> *Mudd:* Are you aware, senator, that many people who hear this style you have, and hear you on television, think that you are a buffoon and a gasbag, if I may use an inelegant phrase?
>
> *Dirksen:* Oh, you can be candid with me. I don't know what they think. I judge from the mails that they give approval of the way I undertake to express myself on the issues of our time.

The interviewer was smiling his way through the conversation, with both men clearly enjoying the opportunity for Dirksen to explain himself.

> *Mudd:* Your vocabulary and your general oratorical style causes, I'm sure you're aware, a great deal of comment. Why, for instance, do you say, instead of, "I think there's going to be quite a fight tomorrow," you say, "I apprehend there will be a substantial fulmination." Why do you put it that way?
>
> *Dirksen:* Well, it invests it of a certain finality, knowing that it might not turn out quite that way, so you adopt slightly flexible ground. Suppose I stated to you I'm as positive as we're sitting here now, that it's going to rain tomorrow? Well, how do I know it's going to rain tomorrow? I haven't seen a forecast. I may very well put that another way around and say, in your language, 'I apprehend from a certain feeling in my bones, that there is a possibility of precipitation tomorrow.' You see, you can't come back at me later and say that just shows what a bum forecaster you are.

The exchange was worthy of a P. G. Wodehouse story.[5]

The most famous and widely quoted of Dirksen's lines—"a billion here, a billion there and pretty soon you're talking real money"—may not have been said by him at all. The Dirksen Congressional Center has searched extensively and unsuccessfully for evidence that Dirksen uttered the line. The quotation does have the benefit of sounding like something Dirksen would have said, and he did speak often about deficit spending and the debt ceiling, once saying: "We cannot spend the country rich. It has been tried before under the philosophy of John Maynard Keynes. I believe that greatest thing he ever said was, 'In the long run, we will all be dead.' He ought to know, because he is dead."[6]

In the "Senior Diseases" section of his high school yearbook, Dirksen's "illness"— "bigworditis"—was accompanied with a prognosis of "absolutely hopeless." "To the eye he looks like a Chautauqua Hamlet in the process of melting," journalist Ben Bagdikian wrote. "To the ear he sounds like a machine for reproduction of Victorian speech: call nothing by its simple name, use no plain words, smother each inconsequential thought in cubic yards of rhetorical excelsior." Bagdikian recounted one occasion when members of the Senate were "trying to agree among themselves not to conduct business on July 10 so that they could attend the All-Star baseball game in Washington." This otherwise routine moment of business on the floor of the Senate became a vintage example of Dirksenian style. "I presume there is some quandary," Dirksen rumbled, "regarding the possibility of taking votes during the session tomorrow, in view of a certain well-known athletic contest which is to transpire in the Capitol City. I assume that, other things being equal, there will be no recorded votes to disturb the poise and enjoyment of those who may attend that event."[7]

During a November 1954 appearance on NBC's *Meet the Press* Dirksen, then the chairman of the Senate Republican Campaign Committee, was pressed on why the GOP had lost its Senate majority. The explanation for the loss, Dirksen said, "would require a recital I suppose of all the reasons why a candidate fails in a given state. That would involve the personality of the candidate. It would involve the gripes that people have. It would involve the stay at home vote of which there were a great many. It would involve local conditions. And probably a great many other reasons. And then of course, the inevitable tendency to change even after an administration has been in office for only two years." Dirksen's response combined deflection, obfuscation, insider speculation, and eventually a substantive answer. A *Newsweek* profile correctly assessed how Dirksen's style reinforced his electoral

A photo that speaks a thousand words: Dirksen admires a portrait of himself while Mansfield looks on. Mansfield as usual wears his Marine Corps lapel pin. (*US Senate Historical Office*)

success and contributed directly to his political leadership in the Senate. "Because of his frequent television appearances and his recorded recitations, his scrambled hairdo and his basso profundo voice, he may be regarded by some merely as a camp entertainer who happens to hold public office. Politicians never make this mistake. They recognize him as a politician who happens to be entertaining and who uses entertainment to serve political ends."[8]

The journalist Annette Culler Penney assembled a collection of the mostly affectionate descriptions of Dirksen, including "Honey Tonsils," "Buttered Larynx," and "The Rumpled Magician of the Metaphor." Dirksen's voice became one of the most identifiable political voices of the 1960s, perhaps superseded only by John Kennedy's Boston accent and Lyndon Johnson's Hill County twang. He was compared favorably with the greatest orators of the Senate, including Daniel Webster. "In an age that practically has forgotten what rhetoric is, Senator Dirksen was the closest thing we had to a Ciceronian rhetorician," wrote fifteen-year-old Doug Frazer, a Rock Island, Illinois, high school student whose eloquent tribute was printed in the formal record of Dirksen's memorial service.

Perhaps when all else about him is forgotten, he will be remembered for that. Words fell from his mouth mellifluously. Listening to him in comparison with most other contemporary Senators was like listening to a 33-rpm recording of the New York Philharmonic played on the best stereo set, in contrast to a 78-rpm of the local fifth-grade band played on grandpa's old Victrola. He knew what well-chosen words, well-spoken and properly laced with humor, could do. For him, and for the United States, they did a great deal.[9]

Dirksen and his wife were injured slightly in an automobile accident in 1963. Dirksen's glasses were broken and he had a gash on his hand, while Louella suffered a broken bone in her foot. In describing the accident, Dirksen implored reporters: "Don't magnify it. You'll make me a candidate for a headstone."[10]

One running Dirksen gag played out over several years. Dirksen wanted to have his beloved marigold designated as the national flower. He was a serious gardener who loved his flowers, so the legislation Dirksen proposed was at least semi-serious, although he played it for laughs and the Senate enthusiastically went along, never seriously considering Dirksen's proposal. In 1963 he told his Senate colleagues:

> Two or three years ago, I introduced a joint resolution to make the marigold the national flower. That stirred quite a controversy; and, as a result, the corn tassel and the rose and other flowers were advanced as candidates for our national floral emblem.
>
> But I still find myself wedded to the marigold—robust, rugged, bright, stately, single-colored and multicolored, somehow able to resist the onslaught of insects; it takes in its stride extreme changes in temperature, and fights back the scorching sun in summer and the chill of early spring evenings. What a flower the marigold is! I am looking forward to the time when these gay flowers will salute and intrigue our sense of beauty.
>
> So, once more I find myself impelled to introduce a joint resolution to make the American marigold—its botanical name is *Tagetes erecta*—the national flower of our country.

The debate—or more accurately monologue—went on long enough that Majority Leader Mansfield asked for unanimous consent to extend Dirksen's time "in view of the extraordinarily exhilarating speech the distinguished Minority Leader is making."

Dirksen's response was classic:

O, I shall not take fifteen minutes, because it takes only a moment for one to express the sense that is in his heart about the beauty of flowers. I remember what Wordsworth wrote in his poem on the daffodils: Ten thousand saw I at a glance, Tossing their heads in a sprightly dance.

In those two lines Wordsworth captured a sentiment which probably I could not capture if I took not only the fifteen minutes allowed me, but even much more time, in order to extol the grace, the beauty, and the loveliness of that flower. . . . So, in order to make sure that our discriminating public will have a chance to evaluate the importance of the matter . . . I humbly submit the marigold." [11]

During his marigold speech, journalist Milton Viorst wrote, "Dirksen is at his carefree best." But Viorst also wondered about an obvious question, especially given that the speaker was the Senate's Republican leader: "What other grown man in America would have the courage" to speak as Dirksen did on such a subject? On one occasion as Dirksen waxed on about his marigold resolution, Louisiana Democrat Allen Ellender wondered why he had never "tried to get action on this

Dirksen tends to some of his beloved marigolds outside the Senate Office Building. (*US Senate Historical Office*)

bill and dispose of it?" After all, Ellender said, it cost $44 to introduce one bill. "The Judiciary Committee, where my bill goes," Dirksen replied, poking fun at one of the South's most committed segregationists, "has been busy in recent years with such non-controversial legislation as civil rights and is unable to give attention to my humble bill." Dirksen's purpose was not really to pass a marigold resolution, but to talk about flowers and illustrate through entertainment how a Senate debate should be conducted. It may have been frivolous but it was also fun, and it garnered him vast attention.[12]

Dirksen's humor was old-fashioned and often self-deprecating. *Time* captured the essence of Dirksen's approach: "His manner, leavened by an exquisite sense of self-parody, conjured up Americana, suggestions of snake-oil peddlers, backwoods Shakespeareans, the gentle rapscallionary of Penrod Schofield's or Pudd'nhead Wilson's world."[13]

It is a rare politician who speaks openly of having a taste for liquor, but Dirksen did, once telling a reporter, "We have a standing rule in our family. My wife sticks to champagne and I prefer a fellow by the name of Jonathan Daniels." By all accounts Dirksen held his liquor well, rarely drinking to excess but drinking almost continuously, Winston Churchill-like, and he certainly understood the political value of lubrication. The minority leader cordoned off a section of his office and dubbed it the Twilight Lodge. In Dirksen's Twilight Lodge it was always cocktail hour. The clock face featured only the numeral 5.[14]

Like many capable speakers, Dirksen was strategic with his use of a good story, as he wrote in an essay about how to make an effective speech. "After a time an audience becomes a little restive and weary," Dirksen said, "and that is the time for a good anecdote that helps to rush blood to the head and rekindle the attentiveness." MacNeil recounted a typical story of Dirksen making a point about the need for citizens to be vocal about their government. As Dirksen related the story, an Irishman named Pat sent a talking bird home as a gift to his wife.

"Mary, did the bird arrive?" Pat asked when he arrived home.

"Yes, it did," Mary responded.

"Where is it?"

"Why, I've got him in the oven," Mary replied.

"But that's a valuable bird. He speaks eight languages!"

"Why didn't he speak up?"

"In a wave of laughter," MacNeil wrote, "Dirksen made his point."[15]

In 1967, during some of the most trying days of the Vietnam War, Dirksen's golden voice and celebrity status earned him a Grammy award for a spoken-word recording entitled "Gallant Men," an ultra-patriotic prose poem backed by stirring music. "Tyrants must know," Dirksen intoned as the music swelled, "now, just as then, they cannot stand, not as long as there are Gallant Men." Some critics poked fun at Dirksen, but the record (on the Capitol label) ran up the pop charts. "In achieving hit status, the *New York Daily News* commented, "the Senator now finds himself in the strange company of the Monkees, the Mamas & the Papas and the Kinks—all top record sellers. One record company executive has admirably tagged Dirksen 'the senior citizens' answer to Elvis Presley.'" The success of the recording landed Dirksen guest spots on Johnny Carson's *Tonight Show* and ABC's *Hollywood Palace*, and he served as grand marshal of the Tournament of Roses Parade. When Dirksen accepted his Grammy during a televised ceremony, he reveled in the moment: "I have been the target of a certain amount of levity concerning my voice," he said. "I believe it was Mr. [Bob] Hope who said I sounded like a duet between Tallulah Bankhead and Wallace Beery. He also challenged the right of a Senator to invade the sanctum sanctorum of show business. Well, Mr. Hope, I make my position clear. I have been speaking for the record for thirty years. I have merely moved from one Capitol to another." One recording industry survey reported Dirksen's record sold more copies in 1967 than any recording by Elvis Presley, Dean Martin, or Bob Dylan. A Twentieth Century Fox executive observed Dirksen at the time of his Grammy award acceptance and declared him a new media star. "What a ham! What a winning way that guy has with people! We should sign him. We could turn him into another Will Rogers." It was an accurate assessment.[16]

As flamboyant as Dirksen could be with both his rhetoric and body language, he was also capable of holding his own in terms of substance. He applied himself fully to his Senate duties, and in debate was typically more comfortable with a thrust and parry that drew a laugh rather than blood. Where a lesser talent might have used a Senate speech to scald a Democratic president Dirksen used humor to greater effect in critiquing Lyndon Johnson:

I like that one phrase that the President uses, He says, "I shall advance." I can just see him, making that forward motion. You see, Mr. President, when you act, as Shakespeare said, you "suit the action to the words."

I shall advance. Yes, I was going to say, I hope not on borrowed money and high interest rates, but I had better not say it.

The *Congressional Record* noted that the comment drew laughter. "I can only say that my own language both in and out of the Senate is on the restrained and temperate side," he once explained in an interview. "I hold no brief for unrestrained language. I don't always throw the book at somebody where there is provocation like someone who lets his temper slip." Dirksen was describing his own methods, but he might as well have been talking about Mike Mansfield.[17]

Mansfield also had a sense of humor, but his was as dry as the eastern Montana prairie. In August 1964, with senators eager to adjourn to attend to party political conventions and campaigns back home, the Senate became tied in knots over Dirksen's proposal to somehow override the Supreme Court's decision about apportionment of state legislative seats. Mansfield, eager to get back to Montana to campaign for his own reelection, broke the news to the Democratic Conference that adjournment was just not possible. He deadpanned, "Our hopes for a sine die adjournment before the convention, I am afraid, have been reapportioned." Mansfield rarely found room in his scholarly, erudite speeches for the kind of illustrative stories Dirksen so skillfully employed. His quiet, reserved, almost shy personality did not translate into slapping backs or telling jokes. Senators, Mansfield once explained, are "a bunch of independent people. I appeal to their reason and I try to appeal to their logic. If they have doubts, I advise them to give me the benefit of the doubt. Sometimes it works and sometimes it doesn't." The vast volume of Mansfield's speeches and other writings, including magazine articles, pieces for scholarly and popular journals, and confidential memos to presidents, reveal a spare, taut style of expression, the writing of a historian applying logic, facts, and perspective, not the approach of a tub-thumping politician. The historian Gregory Olson subtitled his study of Mansfield and Vietnam "A Study in Rhetorical Adaptation." Mansfield's actions, Olson wrote, "epitomized Aristotle's definition of rhetoric as 'the faculty of discovering all the possible means of persuasion.' Mansfield was able to adapt to changing world conditions, changes in administrations, and changes in his own party positions. All the while, he was attempting to influence the sitting administration."[18]

One example illustrates Mansfield's method. Before John Kennedy's historic and not altogether successful summit with Soviet leader Nikita Khrushchev in Vienna in 1961, Mansfield sent one of his trademark memos to the president. The document was definitive, insightful, discerning, and full of recommendations. Mansfield had a particular talent—his scholarly training perhaps—for synthesizing an issue. In this case, Mansfield hoped that the summit would be a meeting of "an older man and a

There was nothing flamboyant about the
scholarly Mansfield, who was often content to
spend time alone, thinking, reading, writing,
and smoking his ever-present pipe. (*US Senate
Historical Office*)

younger man, each with great power and responsibility, ready to explore together
soberly and without bombast new ways of achieving a more durable peace." But
Mansfield also predicted, more in keeping with how the summit eventually unfolded,
that the meeting could become "a slug-fest of words" where Khrushchev would
attempt to intimidate the new American president. After a series of often-bitter
exchanges with Khrushchev, Kennedy departed Vienna disappointed and feeling
defeated. He predicted, "It will be a cold winter" as tensions between the Soviet
Union and the United States increased over a central issue of the meeting—the
future of Berlin. Mansfield's follow-up to this major foreign policy development
was an example of his melding of policy and language. By suggesting "a third way
on Berlin" he created a minor foreign policy controversy. In one sense, Mansfield
said in a Senate speech following the summit, "the Vienna talks were useful. They

swept away the chaff. They revealed to both Mr. Khrushchev and Mr. Kennedy the hard kernel of the problem." He essentially suggested that Berlin become an open, international city, with both the Americans and the Soviets stepping back from the sharp edge of confrontation. "Sooner or later," Mansfield said, "the Western nations and the Soviet Union must seek a new way, a third way to solution of the Berlin problem along the lines which I have suggested or some other. Unless this search is pursued with energy and dispatch and to fruition, sooner or later, Berlin is likely to become the pivot of a new disaster for mankind." Proving his ability to turn a phrase and paint a dramatic picture, Mansfield continued, "Berlin is the lever which may ease Europe towards a more durable security or push the Western nations and the Soviet Union into a new vortex of irrationality at whose center lies the graveyard of humanity."[19]

Some commentators suggested that Mansfield was merely launching a trial balloon at the instigation of the Kennedy White House. But casually floating major foreign policy ideas was simply not a part of Mansfield's makeup. He used rhetoric strategically in an effort to shape policy and was driven to present what he saw as logical solutions to complex problems, often demonstrating a remarkable ability to recast an issue in a new and productive way. Mansfield's "third way" speech was a means to expand the foreign policy discussion on Berlin, and few who knew him would disagree with syndicated columnist Holmes Alexander's assessment of the controversy that ensued: "Mike Mansfield's word is as good as his oath and nobody should doubt that these ideas are his own and not piped from the White House."[20]

Mansfield was a speech crafter. Dirksen was a speechmaker. The Illinois Republican often seemed to speak extemporaneously, but he typically committed his thoughts to memory, ideally, as he said, while staring at a wall. "If there is a crack in the wall, so much the better; there is no greater stimulus to the imagination. How did that crack get there? Does it go completely through the plaster? The mind seeks the answers and out of this reflection you make a start, you lay out a text, you develop it, and you prepare the final clout." Frequently, Dirksen would hold up a scrap of paper or the back of an envelope and tell his audience, "I scribbled a few notes on this and out of it will come thousands of words. I wonder what they'll be."

Dirksen insisted, "I always extemporize. I love the diversions, the detours. Without notes you may digress. You may dart. And after you've taken on an interrupter, you don't have to flounder around the piece of paper, trying to find out where the hell you were." Mansfield's approach was decidedly different. His speeches were written carefully, often crafted from his own memos and supplemented by research from his staff. "He put the final touch on everything," his long-time administrative assistant Peggy DiMichele said. "He was very good about writing a lot of that stuff. He used to write out notes from time to time on a sheet and it would be on his desk. Eventually you'd see those paragraphs appear into a speech."[21]

In the late 1950s, Mansfield delivered a series of Senate speeches on various foreign policy issues. These talks, dealing with issues in Asia, Europe, and the Middle East, rarely received great attention from fellow senators, but the content was consumed eagerly by foreign embassies, journalists and columnists, academics, and officials at the State Department and elsewhere in government. Mansfield also used his speeches—almost lectures—on international relations and history to educate and inform his Montana constituents on the great issues of the day. No doubt the authoritative nature of Mansfield's foreign policy work, coupled with his unrelenting attention to home-state issues, helped insulate him from the common refrain that politicians who serve on the Foreign Relations Committee and become specialists in international issues necessarily lose touch with folks back home. Francis Valeo, who became Mansfield's most consistent collaborator on reports, memos, and speeches, often traveled with Mansfield on extensive foreign trips, the two men spending hours in near-total silence as Mansfield read or just thought. Valeo confessed that in many ways, even after years of close contact with the senator, Mansfield remained something of a mystery. "He was his own man. He certainly . . . was a deep thinker in his own right," Valeo said, "he thought like a historian."[22]

During the summer of 1967, Everett Dirksen appeared as the mystery guest on the popular CBS television game show *What's My Line*. The four panelists on the show, including actress Phyllis Newman and Random House publisher Bennett Cerf, were blindfolded when Dirksen walked on stage to immediate recognition and wild applause from the studio audience. As was the show's practice, Dirksen signed in, using his looping cursive to scrawl his full name in chalk on a blackboard. He then took a seat next to the show's host, John Charles Daly. Each panelist in turn asked Dirksen a question, in hopes of getting a clue as to the identity of the mystery guest.

Newman went first, asking, "That was an extraordinary reception. Are you somewhat of an institution?" The audience again erupted in applause and laughter, while Dirksen used every muscle in his ever-expressive face to indicate that indeed he was an institution. There was no way Dirksen could respond with anything other than a monosyllabic answer because his voice was too recognizable, so Daly answered, "Certainly, yes."

To subsequent questions about whether he was making a film or involved in the sports world, Dirksen responded with different versions of no, *nyet*, or *nein*. When Newman asked, "Are you tall and wildly attractive," Dirksen timed the audience's laughter perfectly and responded *oui*. Cerf followed up on a question about whether the mystery personality was in government by asking, "Do you sometimes on the side make a record or two?" and the mystery of the guest's identity was solved.

As Dirksen ambled off the stage, he stopped to place a gallant kiss on Phyllis Newman's hand. The audience applause continued for several more seconds before Daly remarked that it was "as bright a moment" as any in the show's seventeen-year run.[23]

It hardly bears noting that Mike Mansfield never appeared on a game show.

4 HIGHEST ASPIRATIONS—MOVING TO SENATE LEADERSHIP

There are a lot of Senators who are worse than they look. Dirksen is better than he looks.

—*LIFE* MAGAZINE, 1965

There were no "nonpersons" in Mike Mansfield's Senate unless they wanted that status for themselves.

—ROSS K. BAKER, 1991

As the Eighty-Fifth Congress convened in January 1957, the *New York Times* published side-by-side profiles of the two men who had been chosen as Senate whips, the number-two leadership position in their respective parties. Democrats, who held a slim majority of two votes in the Senate, selected Mike Mansfield to be Lyndon Johnson's deputy. The cutline under Mansfield's photo simply said "Devoid of theatrics." The words below Everett Dirksen's picture—he had been selected as Republican whip—read "A good political showman." Both Mansfield and Dirksen came to Senate leadership, and set the stage for eventually assuming the top leadership positions, through a combination of being in the right place at the right time and cultivating their party's leader. Mansfield's relationship with majority leader Johnson paid dividends, as did Dirksen's relationship with minority leader William Knowland of California. At the same time, both for the most part rejected the approach of the leader they now worked under.[1]

Johnson's chief lieutenant in the previous Congress, Kentucky senator Earle Clements, lost his reelection bid in 1956, opening up the whip job. There are many conflicting stories about Johnson's thought process in selecting a replacement for

Clements before he finally decided to offer the position to Mansfield. On the one hand, Johnson being Johnson, the majority leader wanted an understudy whom he could be absolutely confident would be loyal, but also one he could dominate. Johnson, as is well documented, was demanding and occasionally abusive of subordinates. At the same time, Johnson had to navigate the realities of Democratic politics in the Senate and find, as he had found in Clements, a senator able to straddle the party's divides, acceptable to both Dick Russell's southern conservative camp and the party's liberal faction occupied by Northerners like Minnesota's Humphrey and Westerners like Oregon's Wayne Morse. By most accounts, Johnson's first choice for the whip position was the moderately conservative George Smathers, a suave, handsome Floridian whom critics dismissed as "Gorgeous George" but whom Johnson liked and trusted. Smathers held the Democrat's number-three leadership position in the Senate and had often filled in for Clements during 1956, while the latter was campaigning for reelection in Kentucky, and also while Johnson was recuperating from a serious heart attack. Smathers seemed a natural to become Democratic whip except that, at least by his telling, he did not want the job. The long hours and constant pressure of working under Lyndon Johnson's heavy hand had left a mark. When he was summoned to Washington to meet with Johnson about the leadership position, Smathers' wife asked him bluntly, "Why do you keep putting up with Lyndon Johnson? He's just destroyed your life?" Johnson—who brought his top staffer, Bobby Baker, "the bouncy, ingratiating and immensely able" secretary of the Senate with him to the meeting—was not happy when Smathers declined the whip job. "His nostrils flared, his eyes sort of looked funny," Smathers remembered. Johnson, angry and unaccustomed to being turned down, turned to leave, but then asked Smathers who should have the post. "Lyndon," Smathers said, "the only guy that could probably put up with you is that angel, Mansfield. Mansfield's nature is such that he could probably stand it."[2]

Other accounts of this game of insider Senate politics contend that Smathers may have been blackballed by House Speaker Sam Rayburn, who disliked Smathers' campaign tactics against a fellow Democrat. Mansfield biographer Don Oberdorfer claims Montana native Jim Rowe lobbied LBJ to select Mansfield. Johnson may also have considered Humphrey for the whip position but rejected him as too liberal for southern Democrats. Mansfield, too, initially rejected Johnson's offer of the leadership position, telling the majority leader that he preferred to focus on his work on the Foreign Relations Committee, but Johnson eventually won out with an assessment that Mansfield was the least objectionable candidate for the post.

"It was not a flattering argument," Mansfield admitted, "but after several meetings I finally lost my resolve against becoming whip."[3]

Democratic Policy Committee aide Harry McPherson was another who championed Mansfield. "I wrote a memorandum urging Mansfield for the job," McPherson wrote in his memoir. "He was Western, liberal enough to satisfy the North but not so compulsive as to alienate the South." Mansfield would not be as aggressive in the job as Earle Clements had been, McPherson admitted, "but Johnson, with Baker working for him, did not need a drover. He needed a reliable man who could manage the flow of legislation in his absence." Smathers ended up formally nominating Mansfield for the position, even after being implored by several Democratic colleagues to assume the position. "We all love Mansfield," Louisiana Senator Russell Long told Smathers, "but Mansfield is too sweet and too nice." Smathers responded, "Christ, we need someone to offset Johnson." Mansfield was unanimously elected by the Democratic Conference.[4]

Mansfield was universally respected in the Senate for his fairness and integrity. Little wonder that colleagues trusted him to call balls and strikes. Massachusetts senator John Kennedy is catching, while Washington senator Henry Jackson is at bat. (*Archives and Special Collections, Mansfield Library, University of Montana*)

The *Times* profile of Mansfield made the point that the Montanan's Senate standing had been enhanced by the retirement of Georgia senator Walter George, a Mansfield mentor and the respected chairman of the Foreign Relations Committee. Mansfield was now not only in Senate leadership, a genuine insider, but also one of the Senate's preeminent experts on foreign policy. He had, the newspaper said, "become a great power almost overnight." Mansfield's reputation was expanding in another way as well. "Senator Mansfield is a man about whom humorous anecdotes do not gather; quiet, competent, restrained, he has been conspicuous mainly for a total lack of personal theatrical quality in a forum where prima donnas may be found at every second or third desk."[5]

Mansfield's elevation to Senate leadership was greeted with a certain amount of pride in Montana. "Montanans, regardless of party affiliations, will congratulate the junior senator," the *Billings Gazette* wrote, "the honor bestowed upon Senator Mike is made especially significant by reason of the fact that the Montanan is serving only his first term in the Senate." James A. Nelson, a Shelby, Montana, constituent and lawyer, wrote Mansfield, "it pleaseth us in the hinterland to know that our Montana Senator is 'well across the threshold of the Inner Club of the United States Senate.'" Nelson said he had just read William S. White's widely quoted *Harper's* article— "Who Really Runs the Senate," and was celebrating Mansfield's elevation to "the club." No Montanan, with the possible exception of Senator Burton K. Wheeler in the 1920s, had arrived at Senate prominence so quickly or risen so rapidly to a position of real influence.[6]

Like Mansfield, Everett Dirksen rose to Senate leadership at a time when his party was fractured; divided between the remnants of the old Taft partisans— Dirksen had been a charter member of this group—and "modern Republicans" who embraced the moderate conservatism of Dwight Eisenhower. Dirksen rose in this Republican environment for much the same reason Mansfield rose in the Democratic Party: "he was acceptable to all shades of Republicans because of his pleasant personality, tolerance of all viewpoints, and his reputation for hard work." But Dirksen's path to the number-two Senate Republican job was circuitous route through a thicket of intraparty intrigue supplemented by some political sleight of hand. Taft's death in the summer of 1953 elevated William Knowland, a burly, mostly conservative Californian known "more for his determination than his finesse" to the top Republican leadership position. Dirksen was undoubtedly disappointed that Taft had effectively picked Knowland as his successor, thereby sidelining his own leadership aspirations, at least temporarily. But Dirksen was not part of a conspicuous group of some of the Senate's most conservative members who, while not openly opposing Knowland—the Californian was, after all, a kindred spirit with the dissenters on many issues—nevertheless made known their disapproval of him as the Republican leader. Dirksen is recorded in the minutes of the Republican Conference as joining in the unanimous vote for Knowland.[7]

Knowland, a dozen years younger than Dirksen and lacking his humor and winning personality, proved to be a less-than-inspiring leader, overshadowed by Lyndon Johnson and often at odds with the Eisenhower administration while nursing his own presidential ambitions. It was an open secret in the Senate that Knowland was looking to position himself for a future White House bid, and he eventually gave up his Senate seat in 1958 to run for governor of California in an effort to advance his candidacy. The strategy was a flop, but it did serve to advance Dirksen's leadership prospects. By 1957, Dirksen was widely seen as a logical replacement for Knowland, particularly since, unlike Knowland, Dirksen had largely made his peace with Eisenhower. Given Knowland's expected departure from the Senate, the old guard, pro-Taft Senate conservatives were determined not to see party leadership devolve on a Republican like Whip Leverett Saltonstall, the Boston brahmin who was the very definition of a card-carrying member of the "eastern-liberal-internationalist" wing of the GOP. To accommodate these intraparty ideological realities, a leadership switch was engineered. Saltonstall would officially step down from the number-two GOP position and become chairman of the Republican Conference, a face-saving demotion at best. Then Knowland and Styles Bridges, the senior Senate Republican, acting "with equal deftness," as Neil MacNeil noted, sponsored Dirksen for the whip job. With such support, Dirksen easily turned back a challenge from Minnesota senator Edward Thye, another Republican with liberal leanings, and the Republican Conference elected him as whip by a ten-vote margin. "It was paradoxical," Dirksen's biographers Edward and Frederick Schapsmeier have commented, "that the legatees of the Taft wing engineered Ev's election at a time when Dirksen was so closely identified with Eisenhower's policies." Like Mansfield, Dirksen was in the right place at the right time to capitalize on the sponsorship of his party's Senate leader.[8]

The Dirksen profile in the *Times* published at the time of his rise to Senate leadership recounted Dirksen's record: his blistering denunciation of Dewey at the Republican National Convention in 1952; his support for Joe McCarthy; and his distance from and then his embrace of Eisenhower. "The Senator's florid tongue has led to controversy over his place among the great orators of history," the newspaper said. "Some regard him in the long, and perhaps passing, succession that began with Demosthenes. Others think of him as 'an artist in rock-and-roll without music.'"[9]

Dirksen's agile political "flexibility," previously derided as inconsistency in the service of opportunism, was now viewed more as asset than liability. Where he was once openly skeptical of Eisenhower's moderation, now he was more and more the administration's wheelhorse in the Senate. Pressed to take even minor exception to an Eisenhower State of the Union speech, Dirksen employed the full range of his rhetorical skills. "There may have been some things to which I have exception," he responded, "but I thought all in all it was an excellent document, and crammed with detail, and it will make an excellent reference work." Responding to pointed criticism of Eisenhower from iconoclastic Oregon senator Wayne Morse, a Republican turned Independent turned Democrat, Dirksen said:

> I hope we can be a little more circumspect in the way in which we talk about one another. We can speak and still maintain the intensity of our political disagreements. But to do so does not call for personal castigation or reflection upon character. I can only hope, out of a sense of pain and distress, rather than anger, that we can watch our tongues and make certain that false impressions are not created abroad, impressions which can do no good to the esteem of this country, its people or its noble and beloved leader.[10]

Little wonder then that ideologically diverse Senate Republicans, spanning the political spectrum from a southwestern conservative like Barry Goldwater to a northeastern liberal like Jacob Javits, warmed to Dirksen's leadership style. "Knowland was more a personal advocate, more a persuader of the country in the Senate than a tactical mover," Javits recalled. "Dirksen had more of the inside-the-club feeling. . . . And he was a big man, in a genuine sense. He had size in his outlook. . . . I liked Bill Knowland . . . his word was absolutely good. . . . He never would give you answers that might go both ways. Dirksen did, but that doesn't mean—his word was perfectly good, but he didn't give it." Carl Curtis, a Republican Senate conservative from Nebraska and a politician as far removed ideologically from Javits as the Platte River is geographically from the Hudson, also praised Dirksen's leadership, particularly his willingness to seek compromise "and bring people along." Curtis said "to Dirksen compromise was a strategy to do the greatest amount of good. I believe that to Knowland, compromise was distasteful—to him it meant evading of principle."[11]

The experience Dirksen and Mansfield accumulated through serving as understudies to powerful, even dogmatic leaders shaped their own individual approaches to how they would eventually manage the top Senate positions. Considering his regard for Robert Taft, Dirksen might have been expected to follow Taft's approach to Senate leadership, which William S. White explained as "the view that the business of the opposition was 'to oppose,' partisanship was not only desirable but in a public man a public duty." Taft was, White wrote, "prepared to suspect, if not say, the very worst of almost any Democrat in power." Yet, Dirksen did nearly the opposite. And, likewise, Dirksen would not emulate Knowland's leadership style, which could be bellicose and peremptory. Political scientist Burdett Loomis argues in his assessment of Dirksen's leadership that he observed closely Lyndon Johnson's approach but rejected the Texan's aggressiveness. One senator said Dirksen "was never pushing anyone around. He'd try to reach agreement. I never heard him threaten or talk tough, like LBJ. He was a gentleman." It was also clear from the beginning of Mansfield's tenure as whip that he would spend not a minute attempting to mimic Johnson's ironfisted approach to leadership, a posture that almost immediately caused observers to wonder whether the "shy, sharp featured" Montanan had what it took to be effective. *Time* speculated Mansfield's "soft, low-pressure approach may work against him; the job sometimes requires a wheeler-dealer with a big stick."[12]

Perhaps realizing that his domineering, personalized style of leadership, an approach that kept the majority leader from Texas at the center of absolutely everything happening in the Senate, was growing old with his Democratic colleagues, Johnson made a minor pivot as Mansfield became his whip. "Assistant Democratic leader Mansfield" the Associated Press reported in March 1957, "soon will take over some of the work done by majority leader Johnson . . . who has been told by doctors to take it easy." The story was good spin, but in reality Johnson maintained tight control. Nevertheless, the AP story received great press attention in Montana and, Mansfield being Mansfield, he made sure the story was more about Johnson than himself. "Lyndon Johnson is in my opinion one of the great leaders in the history of the Senate," Mansfield said. "He is a tolerant, decent, understanding man and a great leader to work with."[13]

Johnson responded in kind, writing to Mansfield, "As far as I am concerned, there is only one thing wrong with that Associated Press article . . . there was too much in it about what Mansfield thinks about Johnson, and not nearly enough about what Johnson thinks about Mansfield." Johnson suggested that the next time a reporter wanted to do such a story, Mansfield should send the reporter his way. "I am a Mike Mansfield man first, last, and always, and I want the world to know about it." The mutual admiration notwithstanding, few bought the idea that Mansfield was much more than a well-titled errand boy for Johnson, an assessment Mansfield confirmed years later.

Lyndon attempted to be the whole show. Instead of letting committee and subcommittee chairmen handle their bills on the floor when he called legislation off the Calendar, he demanded that they fill him in quickly on the subject and then he would serve as floor manager. He gave me no duties, and about the only thing I did as whip was to pull on his coattails when he was talking too long and beginning to lose votes because of this. Sometimes he sat down before it was too late.

Johnson's approach to leadership certainly brought efficiency to the Senate, but at substantial cost. As Mansfield told historian Richard A. Baker, "There was a feeling that the new senators were not being given the opportunity to act as much on their own responsibility as they would like. Lyndon Johnson was an extraordinary Majority Leader and had a system which was productive but, while he served in that capacity, the feeling of unrest was quite apparent among the younger and newer members and even among some of the older ones, as well." Mansfield was watching and learning. "What I learned was through observation, and not through training," he admitted. As the Senate was changing and tentatively but surely moving on from Johnson's controlling methods, Mansfield was shaping his own approach to leadership.[14]

Everett Dirksen's place in American political history was secured in 1964 when he played a central role in ending a historic filibuster and passing the landmark Civil Rights Act, but Dirksen's apprenticeships in civil rights legislation and how to navigate the slippery footing of southern opposition to such bills had occurred seven years earlier. In the wake of the US Supreme Court's 1954 *Brown v. Board of Education* decision, which required the desegregation of public schools, and with increasing demands from Black Americans for voting rights and vast resistance to these basic rights from White Citizens' Councils across the South, Dwight Eisenhower proposed a civil rights bill in 1956. As with every previous effort to bring about greater equality for Black Americans—legislative efforts dated back to 1875—the Senate, led by segregationist southern Democrats, balked. Mindful of the need to appeal to minority voters in metropolitan Chicago to further his own reelection bid, Dirksen endorsed the administration's proposal in 1956, and he did so again when Eisenhower, prodded by his attorney general Herbert Brownell, made another civil rights push in 1957. Dirksen's views on race relations had matured and political realities demanded his engagement, but it is also clear that he genuinely abhorred racial discrimination. Thanks to his leadership position and a seat on the Senate Judiciary Committee, Dirksen became a major spokesman for the administration's civil rights efforts. Lyndon Johnson, meanwhile, was having his own moment of political maturity, a political epiphany that required the Southerner to separate himself from his party's segregationist wing if there was any chance he might be a future contender for the presidency. To that end Johnson seized the moment to push a civil rights bill acceptable to the North but not so sweeping as to trigger a southern filibuster.[15]

"What neither the press nor most of his fellow legislators (with the exception of Sam Rayburn) realized," Roland Evans and Robert Novak wrote, "was how indispensable to Johnson's national political aspirations it was to get credit for passage of [a civil rights bill], and how fatal it would be for him to oppose it." Johnson was unfolding a careful and calculated political and personal strategy, holding close his own position—editorials speculated that he would ultimately oppose a civil rights bill—while knowing that if he could transform an Eisenhower civil rights bill into a Johnson civil rights bill he would, once and for all, as Evans and Novak put it, "emancipate himself from the Confederate yoke that had destroyed Richard Russell's presidential ambitions [in 1952]." Johnson's maneuvering in 1957—and on another piece of civil rights legislation in 1960—would go some distance in informing how Dirksen and Mansfield met their own civil rights challenges later in the 1960s. In the meantime, the 1957 Senate debate would pit Johnson against fellow southern Democrats, create an unlikely coalition of liberal Democrats and conservative Republicans, and unite southern Democrats opposed to a civil rights bill with western Democrats who supported civil rights but who also wanted a massive public power project at the bottom of the deepest canyon in North America.[16]

—

Before debate on a civil rights bill commenced in July 1957, a vote took place on a seemingly totally unrelated piece of legislation. "By an odd twist of Senate cloakroom politics," *Time* reported, "two far-apart issues—Negroes' civil rights in the South and federal power policies in the Northwest—got linked together on Capitol Hill last week, with surprising results." Just a year earlier, the Senate had easily defeated legislation authorizing a federally developed hydroelectric dam in Hells Canyon, the mile-deep gorge through which the Snake River flows, forming the border between Idaho and Oregon. Congress opted instead to allow Idaho Power Company, an investor-owned utility, to develop a series of three smaller dams in the canyon. Now, suddenly, the entire outlook for a federally developed dam changed in the Senate, and dramatically so. Johnson's biographer Robert Caro has made much of this switch that saw five southern Democrats who had long opposed a federal dam flip to support one. Caro, and others at the time, alleged a quid pro quo: southern Democrats like Mississippi's James Eastland, North Carolina's Sam Ervin, Louisiana's Russell Long, Florida's George Smathers, and even the leader of the segregationist forces, Richard Russell of Georgia, voted for the dam, a project broadly supported by western Democrats. Allegedly, in the other side of the deal, these western Democrats, including Mansfield, signaled by their votes on Senate procedure related to the civil rights proposal a willingness to water down Eisenhower's bill, including specifically to support an amendment providing for jury trials in civil rights cases. The jury trial issue was important for at least two reasons: southern segregationists insisted on the provision, confident that all-white southern juries would refuse to convict under the new law and, at the same time, without such an amendment it was unlikely any bill could pass the Senate.[17]

Amid all this backroom intrigue, Michigan Republican senator Charles Potter was certain he sniffed a rat. The Eisenhower civil rights bill, Potter claimed, was "sold down the river" in exchange for a dam. Mansfield bristled at the suggestion that he had traded his vote, particularly after newspapers in Montana highlighted the alleged deal. A headline in the *Anaconda Standard*, for example, read "Sellout Charged as Senate Approves Hells Canyon Bill." There "was no deal of any kind, sort or nature," Mansfield insisted, "and there were no trades on the part of any Democrat with any other Democrat for votes." As proof that no deal prompted the Southerners' vote switch, Mansfield pointed to three Republicans, including his close friend George Aiken of Vermont, who switched their previous no votes on the Hells Canyon dam to yes. Mansfield asked Potter to withdraw his charge, an invitation the senator declined. Evans and Novak concurred with Potter's assessment: "Far from experiencing a miraculous conversion to the cause of public power, these southerners were merely storing up IOUs for Lyndon Johnson—and themselves—for the days of reckoning on the civil rights bill." Dirksen, meanwhile, joined most Senate Republicans in opposing the federal dam.[18]

Frank Church, the freshman Democratic senator from Idaho who had campaigned in support of a federal dam in Hells Canyon and who stood to gain the most politically from the Senate vote, was equally adamant that there was no deal either nefarious or pragmatic. "There was never any understanding between Lyndon Johnson and me that I would take a role in the Civil Rights bill or I would join in the sponsorship of the Jury Trial Amendment in exchange for his help on Hells Canyon," Church said. "That's pure fiction utterly without any basis in fact." In a

1969 oral history interview, Church perhaps got to the heart of what Johnson pulled off in 1957, not strictly a quid pro quo but simple old-fashioned persuasion married to a pledge of cooperation. "[A quid pro quo] really wasn't the way that Lyndon Johnson worked at least as far as my experience goes," Church said in explaining Johnson's approach to a deal. "He may have [made deals] with other senators. He never did that with me. I think his method, at least as I saw it, was a very different one." It seems entirely plausible that Johnson, who it is well documented could be extremely persuasive, did not need to engineer an explicit deal, but rather could simply tell Mansfield, Church, and other liberal Democrats who supported both a civil rights bill and a federal dam in Hells Canyon that if they truly wanted both, they must compromise. A long-shot chance to authorize the dam was better than nothing. It was a long shot since the House would likely never pass the legislation (in fact, the House killed the proposal again in 1958) and Eisenhower, after all, continued to hold ultimate veto power. Meanwhile, a civil rights bill, even in watered-down form, was better than no bill at all. Another of Johnson's biographers, Robert Dallek, summarized what he believed happened when a link was created between a hydropower dam in the Northwest and a political strategy to pass a civil rights bill. "Although the westerners did not make specific commitments to back changes in the civil rights bill Lyndon and Russell deemed essential, they had an unspoken, gentleman's agreement to do just that." Johnson worked some of his magic because he "was absolutely determined that there would be a bill," his aide George Reedy said. "Virtually singlehanded, he kept a large body of very strong-minded and willful men concentrating on a purpose which most of them thought could not be achieved."[19]

Both Mansfield and Dirksen supported the version of the civil rights bill that passed the Senate by a wide margin—seventy-two to eighteen—on August 8, 1957. Church offered what became the critical jury trial amendment, and Mansfield immediately joined as a cosponsor. Prior to approval, an entire section of the bill was removed that Southerners contended would force federal action to desegregate schools. Mansfield and his more liberal Montana colleague, Jim Murray, supported the elimination. For his part, Dirksen resisted the compromises but ultimately advised Eisenhower to take what the Senate was able to give him. After reconciling with the House-passed version, the Senate completed action on the first civil rights bill since 1875, but only after South Carolina Democrat Strom Thurmond held up a final vote by engaging in the longest speech in Senate history, a slightly more than twenty-four-hour-long marathon. Two hours into Thurmond's monologue—among other things, he read the election statutes of all forty-eight states, the Declaration of

Independence, and Washington's Farewell Address—Dirksen passed word to his colleagues, "Boys, it looks like an all-nighter." It was. Thurmond did not quit talking until after nine o'clock the following morning. Thurmond's record-breaking stunt was widely described as a filibuster, but Mansfield was quick to point out that it was in fact merely a one-man demonstration, and not an effective one, since the goal of a genuine filibuster is to block action. There had been no real filibuster. But there was a bill, a piece of legislation that created a federal Commission on Civil Rights, established a Civil Rights Division of the Justice Department, and authorized federal prosecution, albeit with the promise of a jury trial, for anyone accused of violating another person's right to vote. Still, as most of its supporters knew, the 1957 Civil Rights Act was inadequate for its time and the nation's needs, since it did almost nothing to advance voting rights or eliminate the worst excesses of Jim Crow. But the legislation was a start. The southern bloc veto on civil rights legislation had been broken, and a handful of Southerners even voted for the bill. At long last the Senate had ceased to be, as William S. White truculently put it, "the only place where the South did not lose the Civil War." As historian Robert Mann observed, the 1957 bill was "*the* important first step in the evolution of modern civil rights legislation and the starting point for the civil rights policies of Presidents John F. Kennedy and Lyndon Johnson."[20]

The long civil rights debate held important lessons for both the Democratic and Republican whips. Each observed the value of legislative patience, the importance of having a plan, and the power of bipartisan compromise. Mansfield embraced some of Dirksen's flexibility, and Dirksen found that a dose of Mansfield's reticence could sometimes be of real value. "Dirksen hamstrung himself by speaking out so clearly in the early stages of the debate," Byron Hulsey wrote, "in the future, he kept his thoughts to himself and thus retained more flexibility as legislation snaked its way through Congress." These lessons learned would be manifestly applied during another grueling Senate debate over civil rights seven years hence.[21]

When minority leader William Knowland announced that he would not seek reelection to the Senate in 1958, but would instead run for governor of California, Dirksen, whom many observers considered Knowland's certain replacement as the leader of Senate Republicans, was pressed to address his own political ambitions. During an appearance on *Meet the Press* in 1957—Dirksen appeared nearly a dozen times on the show between 1951 and 1969—he was asked by Associated Press reporter Jack Bell whether he had ambitions beyond leading the Senate minority.

Bell: Do you expect to be a candidate for the Republican nomination for President in 1960?

Dirksen: I do not.

Bell: Would you turn it down?

Dirksen: It has never been offered, and I wouldn't know what I might do.

Bell: Would you not even try for it, as Republican leader of the Senate? All Republican leaders always try to become President, don't they?

Dirksen: No, indeed not, and you are looking at one who would certainly not seek it.

Bell: You wouldn't want to be President?

Dirksen: That is quite a different matter, if on a silver platter, as they offered the head of John the Baptist, they might. . . .

Bell: Senator, you know nobody ever offers you that on a silver platter. Wouldn't it be worthwhile going after?

Dirksen: I am confident it would never be offered, and I am no seeker.

Bell: You don't even want to try for it?

Dirksen: I am definitely, Mr. Bell, not a candidate and would make no effort to seek the nomination.

Bell: I think we have set a record, here, Senator. We have found a man who is absolutely not running for the Presidency under any conditions.

Dirksen: That is as honest and honorable a statement as I can possibly make, and it represents my deepest conviction, believe me.[22]

A substantial portion of the television interview was consumed with Dirksen's explanation of why, even as the number-two Senate Republican, he had rejected many of Eisenhower's budget priorities. Reminded that he had once been an "isolationist" who changed his mind about foreign policy, Dirksen was asked whether he had changed as a Republican. Was he still the Taft Republican who had chastised Dewey's leadership in 1952, or was he a "modern Republican" as Eisenhower described himself? "I have seen no good definition of a 'modern Republican,'" Dirksen responded. He then turned the question back on reporter Richard L. Wilson, the Washington bureau chief for Cowles newspapers, asking him for a definition of "modern Republican." Wilson responded, "I would much rather have you give me one," to which Dirksen said, "I will still revert to the fact that I am a Republican." It is difficult not to conclude that Dirksen was in the process of refining his political identity and enlarging his appeal to all Republican factions in the Senate.[23]

While Dirksen was the clear favorite to lead Senate Republicans into the 1959 session of Congress, he had to withstand a challenge from the party's more liberal wing. Ultimately, the leadership contest came down to Dirksen and moderate Kentucky Republican John Sherman Cooper, a bookish, dapper Harvard Law graduate whose pedigree aligned him more closely than Dirksen with the Eisenhower wing of the party. Employing his gift for flexibility, Dirksen sought to conciliate and console his Republican colleagues, combining, as Byron Hulsey said, "the cajolery and compromise that would mark his Senate leadership for the rest of his career." Barry Goldwater, the Arizona conservative, blessed Dirksen's candidacy—Dirksen would be "a happy compromise" and not "as hide bound as some of us might be." So did New England moderate Margaret Chase Smith, who described Dirksen as "a polished speaker and excellent parliamentarian and clever tactician." Moderate Senate Republicans recognized that Dirksen was equipped to hold his own against Lyndon Johnson, the powerful presence across the Senate's center aisle. Working the phone, Dirksen called in chits and doubled down on his promise of support for Eisenhower's agenda. The lobbying was more than enough to win the leadership position. Senate Republicans balanced their leadership team, selecting liberal California senator Thomas Kuchel as Dirksen's whip. House Republicans shuffled their leadership as well, selecting Indiana congressman Charles Halleck as their leader, a conservative "roughly comparable in political leanings" to Dirksen. The Republican duo became known simply as Ev and Charlie.[24]

Dirksen biographer Neil MacNeil, who reported on Congress for years and became a well-regarded expert on the Senate, contended that the responsibilities of leadership changed Dirksen. "When he first came to the Senate, he was an arrogant and vain politician, full of himself," MacNeil wrote, "a rightwing kind of guy." The militancy of Dirksen's conservatism, best illustrated by his vitriolic support for Taft over Eisenhower in 1952 and his last-stand defense of Joe McCarthy, gave way to pragmatic bipartisanship. After Dirksen became Republican leader in 1959, MacNeil claimed, "he was a changed man," and he never reverted to his old ways. "The Senate now was the achievement of a lifetime, and he loved the job, he loved the whole business of it," MacNeil said. "You have to hear them out," Dirksen would later say of his approach toward Senate colleagues. "You have to be careful not to be too precipitous or capricious in pointing out what the weakness of the other fellow's case may be, especially

Like his Democratic counterpart, Dirksen led an ideologically
diverse party in the Senate. Dirksen, generally identified with
Republican conservatives, is pictured here with the party whip,
California Senator Thomas Kuchel, a GOP liberal. (*US Senate
Historical Office*)

if he is on your side of the aisle, politically speaking. So that requires, I think, gentle
discussion and a gentle 'oilcan' art, as I call it, so that the bearings never get hot."[25]

Meanwhile, the Democratic whip won one of the most impressive reelection
campaigns in the country in 1958, carrying every Montana county and winning
by 120,000 votes over Lou W. Welch, an unknown thirty-one-year-old Republican
challenger. Welch, a millworker, said he ran to give voters a chance to vote for
"some common man instead of fancy politicians," a not very effective line of attack
against Mansfield, who claimed to have logged 31,000 miles campaigning and was
"not taking anything for granted." In only one Montana county did Mansfield get
less than 60 percent of the vote.[26]

During the last two years of Eisenhower's presidency, Mansfield remained ideally positioned to observe how the relationship between the Senate's majority and

minority leaders was evolving. Party unity for Republicans and Democrats was vastly complicated by the ideological range that existed in each party in the Senate in this period. By 1960, Dirksen had largely mastered the complexities of satisfying both conservatives and liberals in his caucus, and Johnson had tamed similar splits in the Democratic ranks, a job that entailed, as Harry McPherson quipped, preventing "Dick Russell from walking across the aisle and embracing Everett Dirksen." The bipartisan cooperation was never, and could never be, perfect, but a level of civility and mutual regard tended to polish down the rough spots. "We have fought—gently—I hope, but always with understanding," Dirksen wrote Johnson at the end of the 1959 session. "We have asserted our various party causes, but always with good grace. We have shared a high mutual pride in the Senate." Johnson responded in kind, saying no Republican leader had been better at wielding "the partisan stiletto" but that Dirksen's jab "never stings."[27]

Johnson, capable of bluster and crassness, especially with his staff, could also inspire great respect and in return deliver remarkable affection. "Sorry I failed you on the Fulbright bill yesterday," Mansfield wired Johnson after failing to get Senate action on legislation to create a federal economic development loan program in 1958. "My defeat only goes to show the acting boss is the straw boss and there is only one majority leader." Johnson, who was in Texas, wired back the next day: "You have failed no one . . . it is not very important whether the Fulbright bill is passed this week or at all but it is very essential to our country and to me that we have men like you on our side." On another occasion Johnson playfully chided Mansfield in a telegram about one of the majority leader's frequent critics: "I understand you let [Senator] Paul Douglas cough the other day without asking my permission." Mansfield's loyalty to the man who had secured his seat on the Foreign Relations Committee then elevated him to Democratic leadership was never in doubt. Despite Mansfield's regard and deep affection for John Kennedy, he would support Johnson for president in 1960, even as most Montana Democrats embraced Kennedy.[28]

Not surprisingly, the last year of Dwight Eisenhower's presidency amounted to a slow winding down rather than a sprint through the tape. Political attention turned from the still-popular seventy-year-old president to the question of who would replace him, with Vice President Nixon being the front-runner. While meeting with Eisenhower in 1959, Dirksen and House Republican leader Charles Halleck wondered if Republicans had blundered in backing the Twenty-Second Amendment to the Constitution, which limited presidents to two terms, a decision more about slapping

Franklin Roosevelt than improving the presidency, Eisenhower dismissed their talk about a third term for him, but he seemed wistful. "You won't hurt my feelings if you speak to repeal," Eisenhower told the Republican congressional leaders, "and maybe if I read some of your eloquent speeches I'd be convinced!" But Eisenhower was worn out by the job and not at all enthused about his likely replacements. He had no particular regard for Nixon and was convinced Democratic contenders John Kennedy and Lyndon Johnson would be disasters. Eisenhower was also dealing with difficult issues, including the downing of a US spy plane over the Soviet Union and a complicated revolution in Cuba. When Dirksen came to the White House to tell Eisenhower the Senate would not sustain his veto of a bill raising the pay of civil service employees, Ike muttered that it was hard to maintain the image of the GOP as "the party of responsibility when the majority of Republicans vote exactly the opposite." Eisenhower privately said he was "disgusted" with Republican leaders and wondered "why anyone should be a member of the Republican Party"—Dirksen, now a loyal supporter, would have been wounded by the critique.[29]

As Nixon moved to secure the Republican nomination in 1960, the Illinois delegation to the GOP Convention—the gathering was in Chicago—unanimously touted Dirksen as the vice-presidential nominee. As columnist Marquis Childs wrote, Dirksen "answered the desires of a segment of the party that cannot be lightly dismissed. It is the Republicanism of the Midwestern small town—the solid, respectable, work-hard-six-days-of-the-week and go-to-church-on-Sunday Republicans. Everett McKinley Dirksen is their man." Privately, most of the delegates, as the Associated Press reported, "expect the Dirksen boom . . . will soon fizzle." The boom did fizzle quickly, but Dirksen, perhaps realizing it would be his last go-round, his last chance even to be mentioned as a national candidate, said he would be grateful to be considered. "I'll do as I always have done," Dirksen said of the speculation that he might become Nixon's running mate, "accept the chores and responsibilities for our party." There is scant evidence Nixon seriously considered Dirksen for the number-two spot, and he also ignored conventional political wisdom about utilizing a vice presidential pick to broaden the ticket's appeal. Selecting former Massachusetts senator and United Nations ambassador Henry Cabot Lodge, a candidate unable to swing his own state let alone other states Nixon had to win, may have been a historic mistake. "Illinois is absolutely necessary to the election of a Republican President," said Illinois governor William Stratton, one of Dirksen's most enthusiastic boosters. Stratton's analysis was later borne out by the closeness of the presidential election in Illinois. Dirksen's only role at the convention was to introduce Eisenhower.[30]

As Democrats gathered in Los Angeles to select their ticket, Mansfield was forced to deny that he was, as a *Billings Gazette* headline put it, trying "to stall Kennedy's bandwagon." Reports that Mansfield was holding himself out as a Montana favorite-son candidate in order to deny Kennedy a first-ballot convention victory were "absolutely untrue" Mansfield said. Undoubtedly, Mansfield's heart was with his one-time Senate seatmate, yet he never wavered in backing Johnson for the nomination while championing his friend, Washington Senator Henry Jackson, as the party's vice-presidential candidate. Jackson would bring depth to the ticket, Mansfield said, and was "acceptable to all parts of the country," a comment that did not precisely describe the senator who eventually filled the second spot on the Democratic ticket. After Kennedy won the nomination on the first ballot, he, unlike Nixon, approached the selection of his vice-presidential running mate with Electoral College math in mind, which is not to say that he did not agonize over the decision amid conflicting advice from numerous advisors. Kennedy's selection of Lyndon Johnson as his running mate virtually assured Texas would be in the Democratic column in 1960, but the selection shocked many of Kennedy's closest aides and supporters. Labor and civil rights leaders, for example, had been assured that Kennedy would never pick Johnson, and Kennedy's close aide Kenneth O'Donnell warned the nominee that "this is the worst mistake you ever made," since it meant turning "against all the people who supported you." Kennedy was stunned and angered by the blowback—"livid with anger," O'Donnell remembered—but Kennedy had also made his decision by calculating the impact of his choice should he win the White House. "I never forgot what he said next," O'Donnell wrote in a memoir, quoting Kennedy. "I'm forty-three years old, and I'm the healthiest candidate for president of the United States. You've traveled with me enough to know that. I'm not going to die in office, so the Vice-Presidency doesn't mean anything. I'm thinking of something else, the leadership of the Senate. If we win, it will be by a small margin and I won't be able to live with Lyndon Johnson as the leader of a small majority in the Senate. Did it occur to you that if Lyndon Johnson becomes Vice-President, I'll have Mike Mansfield as the leader of the Senate, somebody I can trust and depend on?"[31]

Shortly after Kennedy made the surprising, to some astounding, decision to make Johnson his running mate, a Johnson staff member encountered Mansfield on the crowded floor of the Democratic National Convention and cheerfully opined, "Well, Senator, I guess you're going to be majority leader." Mansfield, looking glum according to witnesses, remarked, "I don't want to be majority leader." The historian Ross K. Baker noted, "From most politicians, such an expression of unwillingness to serve in an exalted post might be viewed with suspicion as false modesty, but with

Mansfield the account rings true." Indeed, once Johnson joined the Democratic ticket, press accounts noted that Mansfield, by virtue of his assistant majority leader position, was the obvious favorite to become majority leader should the Kennedy-Johnson ticket prevail. Yet an Associated Press report from the convention noted that Mansfield was "not anxious to step up to the post."[32]

As the 1960 presidential campaign escalated into the fall, both Mansfield and Dirksen did their partisan duty. If Dirksen was nursing a hurt from being passed over for the second spot on the ticket, or harbored reservations about Nixon—which he did—it was not obvious in his political performance. During the mostly-for-show Senate sessions in the period immediately after the party conventions, and with Kennedy and Johnson often absent from the Senate while on the campaign trail, Dirksen poked fun at the empty seats on the Democratic side of the aisle. "And what about the empty saddles in this new frontier?" he joked, playing off Kennedy's branding of his campaign manifesto. On another occasion Dirksen described Kennedy's New Frontier as "out where the waste begins."[33]

For his part, Mansfield seamlessly shifted from Lyndon Johnson backer to John Kennedy booster as the Democratic ticket now included both of his Senate colleagues. But before taking to the stump, Mansfield tried out a suggestion that he would continually champion for the rest of his political career. He decried the "hoopla and sign-waving shenanigans" of the party convention ritual—this was well before the conventions became entirely packaged, extended television commercials for the parties—and proposed federally financed primaries as the best way to select presidential candidates. Such a move, he said, would help neutralize "the factor of money in the nominating and electing process." One newspaper editorial opined it was clear "that Sen. Mansfield didn't like the live television show which the Democrats staged in Los Angeles, nor was he favorably impressed with the well-heeled campaigns carried on by the rich men of both parties." Time and again over the next decade and a half Mansfield called for election reforms, including a single six-year presidential term, public financing of elections, direct election of the president (eliminating the Electoral College), and lowering the voting age, which at the time was twenty-one in most states.[34]

Mansfield primarily confined his pre-election comments to a critique of Republican "vagueness" on foreign policy while touting Kennedy as a man of substance and good judgment. Eisenhower's partial economic embargo against Castro's Cuba, Mansfield said, was "worthless, valueless and most ineffective," since the embargo would not prevent Canada or other nations from continuing to trade with Cuba. Additionally, the embargo reinforced the image of the United States as a "Yankee colossus" imposing "imperialism from the north." Mansfield sat next to Jacqueline Kennedy at a watch party for the second Kennedy-Nixon debate and afterward declared Kennedy the winner "by decision." When Johnson brought the campaign to Montana for a late-October campaign speech at the Civic Center in Great Falls, the vice-presidential candidate took time to call on Mansfield's family—as Kennedy would three years later. The cozy gathering was depicted in a front-page photo in the local newspaper, with Johnson, Stetson in hand, in the middle of a group that included Mansfield's father, stepmother, and half-brother. At an earlier rally, carried on local radio and heard by Mansfield's father, Johnson called the Senate whip "one of the best loved men in the free world." "I cried when you said those things about my son," eighty-four-year-old Patrick Mansfield said.[35]

Knowing the importance of Illinois to the election outcome, Dirksen campaigned with Nixon in Peoria and Rockford in September and stumped for the Republican ticket in October in Mount Carmel, Illinois, where he contended, not very convincingly, that the election result equated to the "continuity of the Republic." With Nixon during a campaign stop in Springfield, Dirksen provoked what the *Chicago Tribune* described as "a storm of laughter" when he chided former president Harry Truman for saying that any Democrat who was thinking of voting for Nixon ought to go to hell. "He is the last man," Dirksen said of the former president, "of the 2½ billion people on earth who, I think, would be consulted by the Lord about their spiritual destination." It was a typically Dirksenian performance—jabbing with laughter rather than wounding with harshness. Nixon made a final Illinois appearance in Chicago on election eve and proclaimed that the "tide has turned to me," but Dirksen, perhaps reading the mood of his voters better than the vice president had, was across the state in Rock Island, making a last-minute appeal for the rest of the Republican ticket. It is impossible to know whether having Dirksen on the ticket would have helped Nixon in the Midwest, a critical region in what turned out to be one of the closest presidential elections in history. Nixon and most statewide Republicans, including Governor Stratton, lost in Illinois in 1960. Kennedy's statewide margin was 8,858 votes and his margin in Chicago was more than 456,000 votes, while Democratic Senator Paul Douglas cruised to reelection. Nixon also narrowly lost Michigan. Had he won both Midwest states, the election might have been decided in the House of Representatives. In 1960, with vastly more credible reasons to do so than in more recent elections, Republicans demanded recounts in as many as thirteen states, even as Nixon's campaign manager said the odds of reversing the outcome were one thousand to one. The very conservative editorial page of the *Chicago Tribune* said Kennedy had won "a highly qualified" election "clouded" by "allegations of wholesale fraud." Dirksen's administrative assistant chaired a committee seeking a broad recount in Illinois, an effort that ultimately fizzled, thanks in part to Democratic maneuvering around the recount procedures.[36]

—

The election of 1960 barely changed the partisan makeup of the US Senate: sixty-five Democrats to thirty-five Republicans, a net gain of a single seat for Dirksen and the GOP. Syndicated columnist Robert S. Allen confidently reported two days after the election that Mansfield was "assured" of replacing Lyndon Johnson as majority leader, but Mansfield remained genuinely conflicted about whether to take the job, which he characterized as involving "a number of difficulties and problems." He would, he said, rather simply be a senator from Montana doing "the job which the people sent me here to do." Few others, including the president-elect, were in doubt about whether he should be majority leader.[37]

Two days after the election Kennedy called and, as was his habit, Mansfield kept detailed notes of the conversation. "At about 11:45, Sen. Kennedy called me and told me that he wanted me to take the majority leadership," the notes read. "I told him I didn't want to take it. He insisted that I take it—said he had talked it over with Johnson and others, and he wanted me to do it. I said that because of his recently acquired position as president-elect, he has put me in a very delicate situation—that I didn't want the job but I would consider it and let him know." The two then discussed who might be whip. Mansfield said that both George Smathers and Hubert Humphrey wanted the job. Later that day Mansfield got a second call. This time Johnson was on the line, likely at the suggestion of the president-elect, to give Mansfield "the Johnson treatment."

Johnson: Why did you stay out all night? I tried to reach you last night. Did you go to bed with the chickens?

Mansfield: No, I went to a ball with my wife and daughter.

Johnson: You better get yourself a new white tie. You're going to need it.

Mansfield: Congratulations to you. You did a magnificent job and we are all very proud of you.

Johnson: Well, I did the best that I could. Listen, now, I want you to take this Leadership. Everybody wants you to. Have you talked with Jack this morning? Did he tell you the same thing?

Mansfield: I don't want to do it, Lyndon, but I will think it over.

Johnson kept pressing. Assuming that Smathers would be the Democratic whip, Johnson assured Mansfield he would see to it Smathers helped share the workload, and Johnson floated an audacious plan to maintain his influence in the Senate. "I'm going to sit in on the Policy and Steering Committees," Johnson said, a suggestion that would soon cause both men problems. Everybody was for Mansfield, Johnson insisted, the northern liberals, "Russell and everybody," and if the Montanan failed to accept the leadership role, he threatened, "you'll break up this party." Over the course of the conversation, Johnson's promises and flattery only elicited from Mansfield, on three separate occasions, "I'll think it over." He promised to call Johnson before saying anything more publicly. Three days went by as Mansfield thought it over, then Johnson's top Senate aide, Bobby Baker, called. "Lyndon asked me if I had any influence with you at all and if so, to use it," Baker said. "Have you prayed over this?" Mansfield responded, "I am still praying over it because I do not want it." Mansfield admitted years later that he could resist Johnson's pressure, but not that of the man who would soon be president of the United States. "Both asked me," Mansfield told the historian Gregory Olson. "I declined Johnson's request and accepted Kennedy's." In the history of the Senate there has likely never been so reluctant a leader who was at the same time so assiduously advanced for the job.[38]

As Francis Valeo, Mansfield's longtime aide noted, "in winning the leadership, Mansfield had made no promises and entailed no debts," no mean feat for a politician who supported a presidential candidate who lost the nomination but was both needed and wanted in leadership by the candidate who won. Once Mansfield acquiesced, his election as majority leader by Senate Democrats was a formality. George Reedy, a Johnson associate of long standing, said Mansfield's elevation to majority leader became a coronation. "It was almost impossible to pick anybody else . . . if you added up everything, it came to Mansfield." The vote was unanimous, and a relief. One observer commented, "After eight years of Lyndon Johnson a lot of Senators were just worn out."[39]

The diverse, often contentious Democratic caucus had its man: a quiet, studious Westerner, not precisely a liberal like a Hubert Humphrey or a Paul Douglas, more in the tradition of that special breed, the western progressive, a senator in high standing with everyone. As if to cement his leadership, Mansfield quietly rebuffed Johnson, who wanted to install Smathers as whip. Humphrey became his number two and Smathers got the job of secretary of the Democratic Policy Committee. The unofficial journalistic oracle of the Senate, William S. White, saw a grand design in the new leadership team. As Kennedy knew, Mansfield would be a workhorse in a Senate that would help determine the fate of his legislative agenda. Mansfield was committed to getting things done, as were his lieutenants, and it did not hurt that the new administration, which White noted had "fared ill in the West" in the presidential election, now had a true Westerner in a pivotal national position. But it was Mansfield's style that presented the biggest change, White wrote in *Harper's*:

> He simply happens to have the only kind of personality which could reasonably have been brought forward to succeed the dominant, highly colorful Lyndon Johnson. In politics, as in entertainment, you don't wisely try to top certain star acts with more of the same. You alter the whole tempo and tone of the show. Johnson was brilliantly demanding of the rank and file, *forcing* operating unity by guess and by God, and by generous use of both the carrot and the stick. Mansfield will *seek* unity, either through his own efforts or those of his two associates. It will make no difference to him who obtains it, so long as it is obtained.[40]

ELEMENTS OF LEADERSHIP
Care and Feeding of the Press

The first and most fundamental task of the American politician ought
to be that of public education—the enlightenment of the electorate he
represents, a constituency that in the nature of the case and in the process
of its own business will not have the time, opportunity, or inclination
that he had to inform itself about the realities of an ever more complex
and shrinking world.

—TOM WICKER, 1968

On Sunday, January 14, 1968, Mike Mansfield made political television history.
In the course of a thirty-minute appearance on the Sunday-morning ABC News
program *Issues and Answers*, the Senate majority leader was asked and answered
sixty-two questions. By all accounts, that is still a record.

ABC correspondent Bob Clark moderated the record-setting broadcast. "I should
make the point that Mansfield was one of the figures I almost revere looking back
on the last 40 or 50 years in Congress," he said years later. "Mike did not like television, he didn't like to go on television, and he'd only do the panel shows every year
or two, but when he did his conscience told him to give honest answers to anything
they ask you, so you could make a lot of news with Mike Mansfield." So much news,
in fact, that a lengthy story about Mansfield's ABC interview was the top story in
the next day's edition of the *New York Times*. A photo of Mansfield puffing on his
pipe, taken on the set of *Issues and Answers*, was printed in dozens of newspapers.[1]

On that Sunday morning Mansfield answered questions on tax and housing
policy. He said it was time to reevaluate spending on the American space program,
pressed his ideas about reducing the US military presence in Europe, and called
for a halt on bombing in Vietnam as a necessary step toward negotiations to end

the war. Mansfield answered many questions with a single sentence. His longest answer—four sentences—came in response to a question about the likelihood of racial violence in American cities. Mansfield lamented Congress's failure to pass anti-crime legislation but pointed out that the primary responsibility for addressing crime rested with local officials, not with politicians in Washington. To one question Mansfield simply responded, "I haven't the slightest idea," and to another, "It's hard to say." On seven different occasions during the interview, Mansfield answered with "yes," "no," or "I do." Betty Cole Dukert, the longtime producer of the venerable NBC Sunday show *Meet the Press*, told a C-Span interviewer in 1991, "We often advised guests to be as concise as intelligently possible in order to cover as many subjects [as possible], but in his case [Mansfield] was too concise at times. You would get yes or no answers frequently." Dukert remembered one Mansfield appearance on her show where he answered fifty-seven questions in a half hour. "He was the only guest who I remember left some reporters actually speechless without questions."

The universal respect for Mansfield extended to journalists, who appreciated his candor and accessibility. Here, Mansfield and Minnesota senator Hubert Humphrey speak with reporters outside the White House. (*Kennedy Presidential Library*)

Mansfield displayed an unusual trait, unthinkable to virtually all other politicians: he disdained publicity. "Unusual is not the word," Neil MacNeil said of Mansfield's purposeful avoidance of attention. "It was astonishing." At the same time, Mansfield was held in the highest esteem by reporters who covered the Senate. MacNeil said in an oral history interview,

> I remember a housing bill, and Larry O'Brien [the Kennedy White House congressional liaison] had a big struggle with the vote on it. Mike Mansfield had a big role in it, working the thing, lining up votes and so on. They passed the bill, and at the meeting with the leadership afterward, John Sparkman [senator from Alabama] was there, the chairman of the committee that produced the bill. Mike Mansfield grabbed the microphone and announced that this was a tremendous feat by Senator Sparkman. Sparkman was stunned; he hadn't done a damn thing. Mike wanted all the credit to go to Sparkman, not him. He acted as though he hadn't done a thing.

MacNeil recalled another occasion when he told Mansfield that his editors had decided to feature Mansfield on the cover of *Time*, a singular level of political visibility that is still craved by virtually everyone. "I got Mansfield in the President's Room, took him off the Senate floor," MacNeil remembered. "I said, 'Senator, I have really bad news for you.' He said, 'What's that?' I said, 'the editors of *Time* magazine have decided to carve your face on Mount Rushmore.' He said, 'What!?' I said, 'We're going to put you on the cover.' Mansfield was really upset: 'That's terrible, how can we stop that?' He didn't want publicity."[2]

During thirty-four years in Congress, Mansfield never had a field office in Montana, never owned a home in the state, and never produced a newsletter for his constituents. Mansfield's biographer Don Oberdorfer asked him during an interview:

Oberdorfer: I was told that you never had a press secretary.

Mansfield: No. Didn't need one.

Oberdorfer: You were your own press secretary?

Mansfield: Well, yeah. But the way to handle reporters, just tell them the truth. That's it. I've gone down many times before the opening of the session, and the reporters would come in.

Oberdorfer: I've done it, yes.

Mansfield: I would say 90 to 95 percent of the time was spent with Dirksen. That was okay with me. If they asked me a question, I would answer it. Part of the job.[3]

There are dozens of examples of Mansfield avoiding a camera or positioning himself in a way to downplay attention. In the numerous photographs of the White House signing ceremony of the 1964 Civil Rights Act, for example, it is easy to spot Dirksen and Hubert Humphrey crowding around Lyndon Johnson. Naturally, they wanted to be captured on film as part of the historic scene, documentary proof of their role in passing landmark legislation. Mansfield is nowhere to be seen. When John Kennedy signed the Limited Nuclear Test Ban Treaty in 1963, Dirksen stood directly behind the president, who was seated at a table in the White House Treaty Room. Republicans George Aiken and Leverett Saltonstall were near Kennedy, as were Humphrey and J. William Fulbright. Mansfield stands removed from the group to the photographers' far left, distant enough from the center of the action that when the photo was sized for newspaper publication he was cropped out of the scene. One other classic bit of photographic evidence of Mansfield shunning the spotlight occurred just outside the White House in 1962. The Senate Democratic leadership—Vice President Johnson, Mansfield, Hubert Humphrey, and George Smathers—and the House leadership—Speaker John McCormack, Carl Albert, and Hale Boggs—had just left a meeting with Kennedy. The group was arrayed around a microphone to field questions from reporters, but the moment the session ended, and while every other politician lingered or stood about wondering what to do next, Mansfield turned and quickly departed. Kennedy, who knew Mansfield as well as anyone in Washington, obviously saw the humor in the resulting photo: Mansfield with his back to the camera while everyone else faced forward. Kennedy presented Mansfield with a copy of the photo inscribed, "For Mike, who knows when to stay and when to go."[4]

In the days before the endless loop of twenty-four-hour cable news, social media, and YouTube came to dominate Washington political coverage, reporting on the US Senate was a more orderly but still informal process. Everett Dirksen seems to have loved his role as national spokesman for the Republican Party. Mike Mansfield tolerated his job as spokesman for Senate Democrats. Both considered meeting the press a daily responsibility, and each in his own way mastered the craft. The *Washington Post*'s David Broder recalled,

When I came to Washington in the mid-1950s, the seniority system in the Senate press gallery was almost as rigid as the Senate's. A few minutes before each day's session began, the majority leader, Lyndon Johnson, and the minority leader, Everett McKinley Dirksen, held separate press conferences at their desks on the Senate floor. Reporters gathered around them in a semicircle, the senior correspondents in the inner ring, lesser ones to the back. Johnson and Dirksen were two of the great orators of their times, with lungs and throats that could fill an auditorium without a microphone. But at these press conferences, neither raised his voice above the level of the boudoir; it was all whispered intimacies to familiar friends in the front row. The rest of us learned what our elders considered proper to relay to us later.

While not exactly relishing his role as Senate spokesman, Mansfield accommodated reporters, Francis Valeo recalled, with answers that were "matter of fact, laconically pertinent, sometimes humorous, and only rarely newsworthy." Mansfield had another unusual trait in dealing with reporters. "He never said anything off the record, never," Neil MacNeil said. "Everything was on the record."[5]

Dirksen became so skilled and so comfortable in his often-spontaneous dealings with Washington reporters that he would frequently climb on top of a desk in his office and hold forth sitting cross-legged, Buddha-like, with an ever-present cigarette dangling between his fingers. CBS correspondent Roger Mudd, who covered the epic filibuster against the Civil Rights Bill in 1964, watched Dirksen day after day during that momentous period "maneuver, wheedle, dissemble, cajole, bargain, beg, and borrow," and admitted the senator developed "an intimacy that at times came very close to crossing the line that ought to separate the press from a politician." Reporters called the men "Ev" and "Mike" and clearly appreciated their unrestrained access to the Senate leaders. Beginning in his days as Lyndon Johnson's whip, Mansfield held regular Saturday-morning office hours when congressional reporters were invited to drop in for coffee and a visit. Like Mansfield, Dirksen genuinely liked reporters and appreciated the role journalists play in a democratic system. In turn, each received generally favorable, even affectionate coverage. Both "committed news," as journalists say, with substance and style. Dirksen joked with reporters on one occasion:

> I've decided to be a dull, morose bore at these press meetings. It's the only safe course. You give me no choice. I tell a joke and you convert it into an international incident. I coin a whimsical term and you make it appear that I am at odds with the President. I indulge in some polite banter and you interpret

it as a split in the party. I engage in a bit of twaddle and it becomes a crisis. I inject a bit of flapdoodle into our pleasant relationship and I get on the front page. You have become an unsafe breed. From now on, I shall become the consummate bore. I shall be insufferably dull and blasé. I shall turn aside questions with a shrug or a grunt or a profound silence with "No comment." You have but yourselves to blame.

Naturally, Dirksen was incapable of keeping that pledge.[6]

By one definition a political "gaffe" occurs when a politician misspeaks and reveals the truth. Candor is not considered a prerequisite for elected office, let alone a successful strategy when politicians speak to journalists. Yet, Dirksen and Mansfield had a remarkable capacity for speaking their mind. When the young, handsome, and openly ambitious Charles Percy was elected to the Senate from Illinois in 1966, defeating Dirksen's old Democratic nemesis Paul Douglas and giving the state two Republican senators for the first time since 1931, Dirksen found himself more than a bit threatened by a home-state GOP rival with obvious presidential

Dirksen assumes his typical pose, talking with reporters while sitting atop a desk. (*Dirksen Congressional Center*)

ambitions. When Percy, while denying White House aspirations, let it be known he wanted to be Illinois's favorite son during the 1968 Republican Convention, Dirksen told a reporter who asked for his opinion: "On that subject, you can say that I'm ambivalent."

The reporter persisted. "When you're ambivalent about a person, you swing back and forth between aversion and liking. Sometimes you're attracted to Percy; sometimes you can't stand the guy?"

"Crudely put," Dirksen said, "but you have grasped the idea."[7]

"Over the years, most correspondents have come to realize a development new to their experience," *Chicago Tribune* reporter Willard Edwards wrote in a profile of Dirksen in 1968, "that the Senate minority leader couldn't care less what they print about him as long as he is quoted accurately." And Walter Mears, the long-time Associated Press Senate correspondent, said that a "quote from Dirksen or Humphrey could carry a story," particularly in a Senate that by the mid-1960s lacked many of the authentically colorful characters of a generation earlier. In such a body it is easy to see why Dirksen stood out. He remained authentically colorful. He loved politics and he reveled in the give-and-take of the political game, including volleys with reporters. Dirksen told one television interviewer that his campaign efforts on behalf of fellow Republican senators in 1960 had required "a little gore" to "make it exciting and interesting, but it is more than that. It is a good way to get your story over. And I have tried it out and I am rather happy to report, and I have never had this opportunity before, that in those states where I campaigned, all of the members of the Senate came back, and I stick a little feather in my hat for that one." The questioner followed up by asking whether Dirksen had "conducted a tough campaign." The senator responded, "I laid it on the line as emphatically as a feeble vocabulary could do so." The novelist and essayist Gore Vidal, himself no stranger to the pursuit of celebrity, described with a certain admiration the "idle pleasures" of observing Dirksen at one Republican National Convention "prowling from camera to camera, playing the part of a Senator with outrageous pleasure."[8]

Mansfield's elevated reputation with many reporters—in Montana as well as Washington—came by a different path. His flat, clear voice and clipped, precise delivery were far from colorful, but his command of detailed information and his blunt candor made him both effective and respected. In an early television appearance during his first term in the Senate—the program was the *Longines Chronoscope* on CBS—Mansfield was introduced as the Senate's leading expert on US foreign policy related to Asia. Every question during the fifteen-minute broadcast was on that subject. Ranging from Japan to Vietnam, Mansfield displayed a sophisticated knowledge of issues and personalities. He never seemed at a loss for words, never stumbled to craft a concise, authoritative answer. When asked whether the United States had adequate allies in the region, Mansfield briefly recounted the military manpower capabilities of every US ally from South Korea to New Zealand. Dirksen appeared on the same program in 1952, during the time he was passionately supporting Robert Taft for president. His approach was different but no less informed. Speaking with deep understanding of national labor law and criticizing Harry Truman's decision to seize the nation's steel mills during a nationwide strike, Dirksen danced skillfully around questions about how the Supreme Court might eventually rule on that controversy. William Bradford Huie, then the editor of the conservative *American Mercury*, served up a softball to Dirksen: a question at the heart of the Truman steel seizure case. "Is the judiciary still an adequate check and balance on executive power in this country?" Huie asked. Dirksen responded, half chuckling and with a big smile on his face, "I don't like particularly to pass on that question except to say that I can find you a lot of people in the country who have their fingers crossed on that one and are beginning to wonder whether a political note has included itself into the judicial findings of the country."[9]

Mansfield's standing with Montana voters was so secure that, outside of his own election years, he was typically in the state for brief visits only three or four times annually. A Montana trip often involved a flight to Billings and an interview with the *Billings Gazette*. The next day often began with a flight to Great Falls and a visit to the newsroom of the *Tribune*. Then Mansfield would go to Missoula by automobile. "After he arrived at the *Missoulian* on a Saturday at noon where no reporters had arrived yet for work, we asked if we could get a little advance notice in the future," remembered *Missoulian* political reporter Charles R. Johnson. Thereafter, "his driver would call from Lincoln, where they were eating lunch or grabbing coffee, and I would be called in on my day off to interview him, something I always looked forward to doing." Mansfield's newsroom tour would then continue to Butte and Helena. During one of the low-key weekend visits in the early 1970s, Johnson, the *Missoulian* reporter, very much at the beginning of his long journalistic career, asked Mansfield for an update on the ongoing Vietnam peace talks in Paris. Mansfield asked to use a newsroom telephone to make a call. He returned having spoken to the authority on the subject: Henry Kissinger, President Richard Nixon's national security advisor. Johnson admitted to being stunned.[10]

Mansfield rarely spent time in the Senate cloakroom, the epicenter of whispered stories and exchanged rumors, and according to his top aides, he simply would not repeat gossip, but he would soak up information, including from reporters. "The same year Mansfield was elected whip, [Thomas] Dodd came over from the House and so did Bob Byrd," Francis Valeo remembered:

> I never forgot a conversation at a Saturday meeting, when Tony Vaccaro (an Associated Press reporter) said to him, "Mike, there's some funny people coming over here from the House this year. Do you know it?" [Mansfield] said, "Who do you have in mind?" [Vaccaro] said, "Well, that fellow Dodd, he's a kind of strange guy." Actually, Dodd was alcoholic, but Vaccaro didn't say it in so many words, but he said, "You know, he likes to make long speeches. Then you got that other fellow Byrd," he said. "He's a wild one!" Mansfield only smiled. He would never let himself be drawn into a conversation which might be in the least disparaging of his colleagues.[11]

Worried that John Kennedy's polished, self-deprecating performances during his regularly televised news conferences were swamping Republican messaging— Kennedy held sixty-four such conferences in less than three years in the White House—Dirksen and Charles Halleck, the House minority leader, began staging their own press briefings. The sessions were quickly dubbed the "Ev and Charlie Show," and while Ev and Charlie could be entertaining and network evening news broadcasts featured film of the sessions, Dirksen and Halleck, a stern, combative conservative, were little match for the telegenic Kennedy. David Halberstam torched the duo's presentations as "not primarily designed for television . . . like watching two burned-out old Shakespearean actors playing the role of the tired if not loyal opposition." The political cartoonist Herblock depicted Ev and Charlie as circus clowns, and in one cartoon had Halleck asking Dirksen, "In 10,000 words or less Ev . . . is it true you are verbose?" Dirksen and Halleck received as much pushback about their staging and presentation from fellow Republicans as from Democrats and TV pundits, and Halleck resented the mockery. Dirksen, on the other hand, saw the weekly sessions as a necessary, if incomplete, antidote to Kennedy's mastery of television, and the platform did allow him to score points with his humor, often by riffing off something Halleck said. When the House minority leader mentioned that Kennedy was playing golf as much or even more than Dwight Eisenhower had, Dirksen said he thoroughly approved of the president spending time on the golf course. "I want him to be fit at all times . . . I want him to be able to tee off on Khrushchev at all times." When some mostly younger congressional Republicans suggested in 1963 that Dirksen's cornball humor and "rotund and rumpled" appearance were hurting more than helping the party's image and were choking off opportunities for other Republicans to develop a national profile, Dirksen disagreed. "I think I can say to you that the Ev and Charlie Show as such will continue," he said. "I wish they would call it the joint leadership show, which it properly is, but we don't mind the appellation."[12]

One benefit of the Dirksen-Halleck production was that it generated money, and Dirksen wanted to do his part to refill the party's bank accounts in anticipation of the 1964 presidential election. "Many approving letters to which are attached checks of $5, $10, $25 are coming," the Washington columnist Mary McGrory quoted Dirksen as saying. "If you could arrange to get it in your copy you might say the joint leadership needs money," Dirksen deadpanned. Eventually, Ev and Charlie invited other Republicans to join the conferences, and to avoid the appearance that they were merely "a show," as in a game show or situation comedy, the sessions

House minority leader Charles Halleck of Indiana teamed with Dirksen—reporters dubbed it the Ev and Charlie Show—to provide a counterpoint to President Kennedy's televised news conferences. The effort was not always successful. (*US Senate Historical Office*)

were only scheduled when events demanded that the Republican leadership speak out. Columnist Gwen Gibson may have had the most astute reading of why "the two-man vaudevillian-like performance" finally grew old. Dirksen, she wrote, "with his limitless repertoire of Biblical, Shakespearean and Dickensian quotations" just did not need a second fiddle. "To team Dirksen with Halleck is like teaming the town deacon with the local free-wheeling ward politician—or, perhaps, Liberace with Sonny Liston."[13]

On December 3, 1962, the New York Times tucked a short article datelined Saigon on page twelve. In hindsight the story was underplayed. The headline read, "Mansfield Is Cool on Vietnam War." During this 1962 trip, one of his frequent visits to Vietnam, Mansfield rejected the canned, optimistic, and often superficial briefings that were offered up to visitors by US embassy personnel in Saigon. Instead, he met alone with four American reporters. Mansfield initiated what became a four-hour lunch with David Halberstam of the Times, Neil Sheehan of United Press International, and Peter Arnett and Malcolm Browne of the Associated Press, all of whom had become pessimistic in their assessments of the progress of the war. The lunchtime conversation—Mansfield mostly listened—deepened the majority leader's own pessimism about the deteriorating situation in Vietnam. "What was clear," Halberstam later recalled, "was that Mansfield was really listening. He wanted to know." Halberstam subsequently reported that Mansfield had refused to issue the upbeat statement prepared for him by US ambassador Fredrick Nolting, and instead issued his own statement that "did not go out of [its] way to assert that considerable progress was being made against the guerillas, or Vietcong." Mansfield told his biographer that he valued the views of the skeptical journalists because "they weren't following the line, they were trying to report the truth, and they did, and it finally sunk in. It finally had its effect."[14]

Mansfield's outreach to Saigon reporters, as he surely knew, came at the very time many journalists were under fire from Washington politicians and military leaders for their reporting on the war and on Ngo Dinh Diem's increasingly problematic regime. A marine general had characterized the journalists as weak liberals, and Kennedy had complained personally to Times publisher Arthur Ochs Sulzberger about Halberstam's reporting, pointedly telling the publisher that Halberstam should be replaced. He was not replaced and Halberstam later won a Pulitzer Prize for his reporting from Vietnam. William C. Trueheart, the deputy chief of the US mission in Saigon in the early 1960s, said, "What happened with Mansfield was that he had talked to a lot of people in the lower ranks of the mission probably, and above all I think he'd talked to a lot of the press. Of course, he was a very astute man and he had been following the situation for a long time." Seeking out the opinions and insights of reporters became a Mansfield trademark. He consumed on a daily basis the international reporting of major national newspapers and came to trust journalists more than the often-secret briefings served up to the Foreign Relations Committee. He rarely missed a public session of the committee but routinely ignored the secret sessions. "You don't learn anything from these secret briefings that isn't in the *New York Times* usually sooner rather than later," Mansfield said. "If you attend an executive session or listen in private you're stopped from talking in public about what you already knew before the briefing."[15]

—

Political scientist and one-time White House aide Stephen Hess published *The Ultimate Insiders* (1986), a book exploring why some senators receive more attention from the press and television than others. Hess's analysis, using data assembled by cataloguing newspaper, wire service, and television appearances, found that Everett Dirksen was always in the news more often than Mike Mansfield during the decade they led the Senate, although Mansfield was never far behind in press mentions or appearances.[16]

Journalists are not unlike voters when it comes to political figures: they value politicians who level with them by answering questions directly, they appreciate not having to maneuver for access in order to ask a question or seek clarification, they place a premium on talking to politicians who are knowledgeable, and they enjoy being entertained. Jack Germond, a gruff, hardworking, and well-regarded reporter and columnist of the old school, likely spoke for many of his colleagues when he underscored the relationship between those who report on politics and those who make the news. Germond said a group of reporters tossing questions at Dirksen amounted to "casting imitation pearls before the real swine." Politics is, after all, often about successful communication, and communication can be enhanced by candor, competence, and comity. Working the press, and working with the press, was a fundamental tool in Dirksen's and Mansfield's leadership arsenals. Each understood that a fundamental task of leadership was to educate and inform, not merely for partisan advantage, but rather in the interests of making politics—even partisan politics—work in a democracy.[17]

5   ONE BRIEF SHINING MOMENT

Reaching across the aisle used to get you plaudits in a campaign;
now it just gets you a primary.

—FORMER ARIZONA SENATOR
JEFF FLAKE, 2020

A defining characteristic of Mike Mansfield's approach to political leadership was his overarching sense of propriety. There were certain ways to do things, Mansfield believed, and definite standards to be maintained. This Mansfield principle is illustrated by one incident immediately after the 1960 presidential election, a bitterly contested campaign that ended eight years of Republican control of the Executive Branch, with the seventy-year-old Dwight Eisenhower succeeded by the forty-three-year-old John Kennedy, the oldest president to that point in American history replaced by the youngest. On November 15, exactly a week after the election and while doubt remained about Mansfield's own elevation to majority leader, Mansfield sent Vice-President-Elect Lyndon Johnson a confidential memo. Johnson was scheduled to attend the NATO Parliamentary Conference in Paris, where in his role as Senate leader he would serve as head of the US delegation. Johnson no doubt wanted to make the visit to France for both personal and political reasons, and he intended to call on several European and NATO leaders while there. But in his memo Mansfield warned Johnson to be careful. Unless the trip was sanctioned by Eisenhower, who as Mansfield noted, would continue to have full control of American foreign policy until Kennedy was officially sworn in in January, the foreign travel and high-level meetings could give offense to the outgoing president and might confuse American allies.

"To forestall this danger of looking foolish, therefore, it seems to me that the following course should be pursued," Mansfield wrote. Kennedy should tell Eisenhower of the meeting, while pointing out the advantages of Johnson using the trip to renew relationships and give "a sense of continuity to American policy." Mansfield was adamant about the protocol of the situation. The authorization to visit foreign leaders should come from Eisenhower, "not from Kennedy." Mansfield's memo even included a suggested telegram to be sent to the president, and he ended the communication with a pointed postscript: "Move with great caution and do not do anything without Kennedy's approval. If in doubt, don't."[1]

Mansfield's communication seemed perfectly timed to influence Johnson's European trip, with press accounts noting that "the NATO conference was an important item of discussion when President-elect John F. Kennedy visited at Johnson's ranch" just two days after the Mansfield memo reached Johnson. Whether Johnson followed Mansfield's advice completely is difficult to ascertain, but once in Paris Johnson opened his remarks to the NATO conference with an explanation that he was speaking "only as a parliamentarian" and that "until January, the full and sole Executive authority remains with the Administration of President Eisenhower." Johnson did meet with French President Charles de Gaulle and other French leaders but was at pains to keep the conversations low-key and he made no substantive public comments afterward.[2]

A month later, Mansfield was in Palm Beach, Florida, for a session with Kennedy, Johnson, and House Speaker Sam Rayburn. At Kennedy's request the Democratic congressional leaders had gathered to strategize around the new president's legislative agenda. At the press conference following the meeting, Mansfield was asked only two questions, both about whether the Senate would attempt to change Rule XXII, governing the filibuster. Mansfield said an effort to change the rule was inevitable, but he suggested that he hoped to avoid a fight over the filibuster that might interfere with Kennedy's legislative program. As he typically did, Mansfield prepared a summary of the meeting for his files, where he noted that the discussions involved, among other issues, legislation to address medical care for the elderly. Mansfield also suggested to Kennedy at least two candidates for State Department positions, both of whom Kennedy subsequently appointed. Mansfield also discussed a variety of foreign policy matters and left the president-elect with another of his scholarly memos, a virtual world tour of his views about international concerns. Detailed to a fault, Mansfield noted in his summary that "the luncheon was good—lamb chops, spaghetti, green peas, clam chowder soup, red wine, dessert, coffee and cigars. I left with a full stomach."[3]

President-Elect Kennedy's first post-election meeting with (right to left) Mike Mansfield, House Speaker Sam Rayburn, and Vice President–Elect Lyndon Johnson in Palm Beach, Florida, December 20, 1960. (*Archives and Special Collections, Mansfield Library, University of Montana*)

There may never have been as close a personal and political relationship between a president and a Senate majority leader as that between John Kennedy and Mike Mansfield. Kennedy and Mansfield first became acquainted when both served in the House of Representatives, and their relationship ripened when the two occupied adjoining desks in the back row of the Senate in 1953. Both where Catholics of Irish descent, though Don Oberdorfer noted their different upbringings:

> Kennedy had been brought up amid glamour and opulence as the son of one of the richest and most prominent men in America, and Mansfield, a virtual orphan, had had to make his own way. Kennedy exuded social ease, charm, and self-confidence: Mansfield, to the despair of Washington hostesses, was untroubled sitting at a table for hours without exchanging more than a few compulsory words with his dinner partners. Although both were progressive Democrats with a similar political outlook, they were from opposite ends of the country . . . and Mansfield was fourteen years older.

The relationship blossomed into one of deep affection as well as mutual regard. Robert Kennedy would say his brother "loved" Mansfield.[4]

The depth of connection between the onetime copper miner and the Harvard graduate is illustrated by an exchange of letters immediately after Kennedy fell just short of winning the Democratic vice-presidential nomination in 1956. In a furious few hours of old-style convention politics, Kennedy came close to winning the nomination before a sudden shift among several delegations handed the nomination to Senator Estes Kefauver of Tennessee. But in losing Kennedy had shown both grace and strength. "I tried to call you the Monday after the Convention," Mansfield wrote Kennedy. "I wanted to tell you that if any man came out of the convention with enhanced prestige, it was you." Being nominated would have been satisfying, Mansfield said, but the timing was wrong for Kennedy. "I think in all honesty, that in the long run, it was a break you were not." Mansfield was clearly anticipating that the Democratic ticket of Adlai Stevenson and Kefauver would lose in November, in part because Democratic divisions over agricultural legislation had strengthened Eisenhower's already firm grasp on the Farm Belt. Mansfield gently encouraged Kennedy to begin broadening his national appeal: "It would be my hope, Jack, that during the next several years, you would have the opportunity to visit the Midwest and far west to learn at first hand some of our problems in those parts of the country." Mansfield pledged his assistance, and reassured Kennedy— still only thirty-nine years old—"that your star is just beginning to shine and that in the future the Democratic Party will be tied to it more securely. You have lost nothing because, in reality, you have gained much." Kennedy, who had left immediately after the convention for a vacation in France, responded with a handwritten note when he returned in early September. "I can't thank you enough for your very generous and typically thoughtful note," Kennedy wrote. "Your letter explains why you are the most respected member of the Senate. I agree with your analysis of the situation there and I think that probably the farm vote along with the 'canonical' impediments might have been too much to carry this year. However I did appreciate greatly the help of those who stood up and were counted—and you were one of the best of these." The note was signed "Jack."[5]

After the 1960 election, Kennedy and Mansfield seem to have been in near-constant communication—one-on-one meetings, leadership breakfasts, social occasions, and frequent telephone calls. "At his request I would sometimes furnish memoranda to him on foreign policy questions," Mansfield told an interviewer of these confidential assessments, particularly those related to Indochina, which would become increasingly important to both men. Kennedy "particularly liked and valued

Mike Mansfield," Arthur Schlesinger remembered. Kennedy "approved of Mansfield's announced principles of 'courtesy, self-restraint and accommodation' and
considered him underrated because he did his job with so little self-advertisement
and fanfare." Mansfield described his relationship with Kennedy as deeply personal,
based on his "faith and confidence" in Kennedy, and their interactions as both "very
informal and businesslike." When asked if he could recall an occasion of serious
disagreement with Kennedy, Mansfield responded: "not one."[6]

Everett Dirksen certainly harbored reservations about Kennedy's lack of experience
and was keenly aware that Kennedy's election left him leading a frequently frac-
tious Senate minority. At the same time, with a Democrat in the White House and
Democratic majorities in Congress, Dirksen immediately became the most important Republican in Washington, and arguably in the country. As Robert Kennedy
remembered, "Everett Dirksen liked President Kennedy a great deal," and the feeling
was reciprocated, meaning Dirksen had the chance to become a Senate power broker
leading a coalition of fellow Republicans and conservative southern Democrats, over-
shadowing the quiet, reserved, and untested majority leader. Among other things,
John Kennedy admired Dirksen's speaking ability and sought the older man's advice
when Kennedy began to worry about losing his voice due to the constant speaking
required during the 1960 campaign. "You keep talking off your vocal cords," Dirksen
told Kennedy. "I've been watching you. You need some exercises. You need to throw
your voice down to your diaphragm." He advised Kennedy to retain a voice coach,
then marveled when Kennedy followed his advice. "By golly," Dirksen said, "that's
what Jack did and he never had any trouble after that."[7]

Dirksen was now the Senate's proven commodity. Mansfield represented a question mark. In a December 1960 column, William S. White predicted it would take
all three members of the Senate's Democratic leadership team to replace Lyndon
Johnson and suggested that, while Mansfield was "definitely more relaxed" and
"incomparably less driven" than Johnson, he would also be less effective. Syndicated
columnist Fletcher Knebel—coauthor of the best-selling novel *Seven Days in May*,
about an attempted American military coup—joked that "Mansfield is slated for
Senate leader. Tough job. He has to button-hole 99 senators—and drag them into
Lyndon Johnson's office." Johnson had a similar thought, concocting a scheme to
effectively retain his Senate influence by participating in the Democratic Policy
and Steering Committee meetings while serving as vice president and, in effect,
keeping Mansfield as his deputy.[8]

Johnson floated his audacious idea while trying to persuade Mansfield to step up to the majority leader's job. Johnson cast the idea as a way to support Mansfield, but he really intended to continue to direct the party in the Senate. In effect, as Johnson told Bobby Baker, the Senate was "gonna be just the way it was" when he was majority leader. Mansfield, initially at least, seemed to accept the arrangement, even discussing it with Kennedy then pressing ahead to implement the plan during the organizational Democratic caucus on January 3, 1961. Yet, when Mansfield, immediately after his own election by acclamation as majority leader, made the motion to install Johnson as permanent chair of the conference, the not even remotely veiled power grab by Johnson crashed with a resounding thud.

"There was a moment of stunned silence," Evans and Novak wrote, "followed by a wave of opposition." Francis Valeo said it "was as though [Mansfield] had brought down the east front or the west front" of the Capitol. West Virginia Senator Robert Byrd remarked years later of Mansfield's willingness to accept Johnson's plan, "Can you imagine that? This action by the new Majority Leader reflected the quiet and assuming nature of Mike Mansfield, but it was a mistake." Several senators opposed the scheme immediately over questions about separation of powers. The reactions were blunt. "We might as well ask Jack Kennedy to come back up to the Senate and take *his* turn presiding," Tennessee Senator Albert Gore Sr. fumed. Others thought the sixty-five Senate Democrats would simply appear ridiculous if their conference were overseen by a non-senator. Still others were anxious to be rid of Johnson's influence and could not imagine inviting him back into Senate counsels. Johnson was present for the entire humiliating discussion. Eventually, a strong majority supported Mansfield's motion, but seventeen Democrats objected, meaning Johnson's idea simply did not command anything approaching consensus. A miscalculation had turned into a stiff rebuke. A compromise substitute was eventually approved where Mansfield was authorized to request that Johnson, or any senator, might preside at the conference, yet even this face-saving effort garnered seventeen no votes. Johnson was hurt and angry. He retreated to his majestic suite of offices— the press dubbed it his Taj Mahal—which Mansfield might have commandeered as majority leader but instead allowed Johnson to keep. There, Johnson fumed to Senate secretary Bobby Baker: "Now I know the different between a caucus and cactus," Johnson reportedly said. "In a caucus all the pricks are on the outside." But Johnson got the message. That day he formally resigned his Senate seat. He never attended another caucus.[9]

Johnson nursed a grudge, but not against Mansfield. Mansfield had done precisely what he had told Johnson he would do, even clearing the idea with his own leadership team of Humphrey and Smathers, and reportedly threatening to resign his own leadership position if his support for Johnson was rebuffed. (The compromise made his resignation a moot point.) Furthermore, he accommodated Johnson's desire to continue to occupy the grand, chandeliered Taj Mahal, and Mansfield kept Bobby Baker, Johnson's right-hand man, as his top Senate aide, a move that many of his colleagues considered a mistake. They argued that Mansfield should have his own person as Senate secretary and that dismissing Baker would have signaled a clear break with the past. But Mansfield had other methods of making that break, and he certainly knew that by demonstrating his loyalty yet again to Lyndon Johnson he established his own credibility and cemented his personal integrity more firmly. In short order Mansfield let it be known that the Senate would operate differently under his leadership. There would be fewer late-night sessions and a more predictable schedule. Individual senators would have more influence in floor management of legislation. Critics complained that efficiency suffered under Mansfield's Senate leadership, but efficiency was not his aim. Rather, Mansfield would attempt to mold the Senate in his own image: serious, businesslike, civil, and independent. As Neil MacNeil said, Lyndon Johnson "thought he *was* the Senate." Mansfield intended to make one hundred individual senators the Senate and to create a bipartisan partnership with Everett Dirksen.[10]

Bobby Baker claimed that "working for Mike Mansfield, compared to working for Lyndon Johnson, was like lolling on the beach as opposed to picking cotton," while Harry McPherson, the top Senate Democratic policy aide, said that the change in Senate leadership was so vast, so complete that it was "like going home to mother after a weekend with a chorus girl." Dirksen had to adjust every bit as much as Senate Democrats. Albeit having enjoyed a particularly warm relationship with Johnson, Dirksen was always Johnson's junior partner, never mistaken for having equal or even greater power or influence than the majority leader. With Mansfield across the aisle, things were different. The Senate was in "an extraordinary situation," one Republican observed, "we have a Majority Leader who is generous to the Minority, and a Minority Leader who is the most powerful member of the Senate." Dirksen now stood virtually alone as spokesman for Republican values, and Mansfield's deferential, determinedly bipartisan approach to Senate leadership served to enhance Dirksen's effectiveness. As Burdett Loomis has noted, Dirksen's standing as party leader—and Senate power broker—was "partly the result of Senator Mansfield's unparalleled graciousness as majority leader." Maine Senator Edmund Muskie, who came to the Senate in 1959, said Mansfield's demeanor was intentional. "Mansfield simply did not view the Senate as an instrument of its leadership," Muskie said. "He felt that the way to make the Senate effective was simply to let it work its will. And he believed that the Senate would do just that. And he also believed that senators would rise to that responsibility if it was made clear to them that their responsibility was important."[11]

It is impossible to overstate this aspect of Mansfield's Senate leadership. Mansfield was the ultimate institutionalist, believing the US Senate to be the foundational cornerstone of the Republic, and he advanced this theory in ways that now seem unthinkable. "Mansfield lives in the institution of the Senate," a contemporary observer wrote, "and not in the institution of the Democratic Party. In short, he is a Senate man, not a political man, and in many ways an inscrutable figure."[12]

"Mansfield was very different," Hubert Humphrey wrote in his memoir. "He tried to be effective without being oppressive. He succeeded because he is a man of absolute honor and integrity. He is a quiet, contemplative leader, never forcing his own deeply held convictions on others. Wheeling and dealing are not his style. Mike never seeks to bully, punish, or even reward senators for their votes. If home-state politics or constituent pressure means a senator couldn't follow his lead, he was understanding and forgiving." In contrast to Johnson's top-down management of the Senate, Humphrey said Mansfield gave him wide latitude in his role as whip, "letting me operate pretty much by my own standards."[13]

"Personal fondness can convert intermittent cooperation into a more durable alliance," political scientist Ross K. Baker wrote in his book *Friend and Foe in the U.S. Senate*. Dirksen and Mansfield offer a case study of that idea. Both understood that personal relationships, not merely the stodgy, formal courtesies required by Senate tradition, but genuine personal connections, were—and are—an essential ingredient of political leadership, and legislative progress.[14]

Mansfield's closest Senate relationship, an unlikely one, was with the flinty Vermont Republican George Aiken. Early in Mansfield's Senate career, Aiken had spotted the Montanan eating breakfast alone in the Senate dining room and asked if he could join Mansfield, the beginning of a tradition that continued until Aiken's retirement. Neither man was an avowed partisan, and both were unassuming in a world where outsized personalities thrived. "Mansfield maintained they most often discussed the news of the day rather than politics," Don Oberdorfer wrote, "but there is little doubt he benefited from the sharing of viewpoints and intelligence with his Republican friend." Mansfield said Aiken often helped "when I got into some sort of difficulty." Longtime Mansfield aide Charles Ferris recalled the bipartisan friendship "was very good for Mansfield because Aiken loved to pick up the gossip in the Senate, and Mansfield, in my 14 years up there with him, I can put on the fingers of one hand the number of times Mansfield was actually in the Democratic cloakroom where gossip was the currency. He did not hang around with the guys." The Mansfield-Aiken breakfast, typically coffee and English muffins, "became a Washington institution," with Aiken's wife, Lola, who had been on his staff prior to their marriage, often joining them at the special table reserved for the daily ritual. Mansfield would soon develop a similar level of intimacy with Dirksen.[15]

Mansfield was "the most disarming man in the world," Dirksen said in paying a birthday tribute to Mansfield in 1959. Then, according to a reporter, "in a burst of emotion," Dirksen cried out: "We love you, Mike." Mansfield would later say of Dirksen, "I think for a year or so he didn't know how to size me up." Then in his typically clipped fashion, Mansfield captured the essence of why their political and personal relationship came to work so well. "Never did anything behind his back," Mansfield said. "Neither did he with me."[16]

Mansfield breakfasted nearly every day with Vermont Republican George Aiken, his closest Senate friend, pictured here with Maine Republican senator Margaret Chase Smith. (*US Senate Historical Office*)

Mansfield's deference—including especially to Republicans—his commitment to consensus, and his total unwillingness to twist arms or bargain for deals was, initially at least, seen as evidence of his weakness as a leader, and indeed over time there would be criticism from fellow Democrats that he simply was not strong enough in the leader's role. But Mansfield had a different vision of Senate leadership. He sought to elevate the Senate—and individual senators—by downplaying his own role and operating on the basis of absolute candor. A former senator told Ross K. Baker, "People say he wasn't much of a leader. He was a good leader in this sense—he was believed. Lyndon was a strong leader in this sense—that he could get bills passed; but you just didn't have the trust."[17]

Mansfield would unfailingly consult Dirksen—and vice versa—on issues small and large. There are numerous examples of the majority leader telling a president or a colleague, "You had better check with Dirksen." As a result, says Humphrey aide John G. Stewart, "Republicans seldom took any action which might have embarrassed Mansfield personally in the course of achieving some short-term partisan advantage. Moreover, blind obstructionism and partisan sniping were largely forsaken." One Republican senator described to Stewart how, during the Johnson era, he would often go to the Senate floor late in the afternoon for the sole purpose of engaging in a purely partisan back-and-forth with Johnson. "Lyndon would always get mad and irritated," the Republican said, but he told Stewart he would never treat Mansfield in such a fashion.[18]

"Sometimes it was painful as a partisan to see him be so kind to people who wanted to cut the pensions of widows and orphans," Mansfield aide Teddy Roe remembered, "but that is who he was." Neil MacNeil claimed that Mansfield's deference to Dirksen was so obvious "that even Senate correspondents began to confuse Dirksen's functional role in the Senate as that of the majority leader, not the minority leader. Dirksen was not unappreciative of Mansfield's generosity to him, and he was prepared to requite Mansfield's friendship to the full." Historian Baker contends that "pure friendship" in the Senate is rare "because politicians are wary people; they are constantly on display and surround themselves by an elaborate array of defenses." Mansfield and Dirksen defied these constraints because, while each was a skilled political actor, each was also a genuinely decent person, given to embrace comity, compromise, and candor.[19]

The friendship extended to random acts of kindness, something Mansfield seemed particularly good at. On one occasion, for no obvious reason, Mansfield sent Dirksen a box of cigars, perhaps not the best gift for a determined three-pack-a-day smoker who suffered from both a heart condition and chronic emphysema.

"That box of cigars is really out of this world. A million thanks," Dirksen wrote in reply. Another Mansfield gift was a large box of candy from the Sheppard Candy Company in Butte. "It has been our evening dessert ever since the box arrived," Dirksen wrote in his thank-you note.[20]

He was not "a pusher," one colleague said of Mansfield. "There was something very docile about Mike Mansfield; he was the lay priest of the Senate. As a matter of fact, if he could have gotten into the clergy, I think he would have turned out to be a cardinal. There is something ecclesiastical about the man." Another commented, "Mike Mansfield just wouldn't interfere with anybody under any circumstances. That's the kind of person he was, and they loved him for it. Sometimes it paid off. If Mike Mansfield got up you might have disagreed with him, but you knew he was honest and he had that respect." A "pusher" in leadership "can get under your skin. Mike just never did that."[21]

Dirksen's leadership style was similar, although, unlike Mansfield, the minority leader loved the dealmaker role, and he was not unwilling to cajole and plead for a vote from a fellow Republican. While Republicans occasionally grumbled about Dirksen's style, he commanded universal respect. Republican Len B. Jordan, a conservative from Idaho, said of Dirksen: "He could make the tent big enough to take us all in and, at the same time, he supported enough of the opposition party when he agreed with them. When he didn't, he put up a valiant and courageous fight. So, he operated altogether in a different climate than anyone who would succeed him because he had the confidence of all of us." Mansfield said simply of Dirksen, "He's an old pro. He's got what it takes. It's a pleasure to be associated with a man like that."[22]

To understand the Mansfield-Dirksen era is to appreciate how markedly different the Senate of the 1960s was compared to the hyper-partisan, deeply polarized, party-focused Senate of the twenty-first century. It is not an overstatement to say that in the 1960s members of each political party were frequently united by little more than a shared label and a sense of loyalty to the partisan brand. Democrats, for example, divided along regional and ideological lines into southern conservatives and northern and western liberals. Since southern Democrats dominated powerful committee leadership positions, senators like Russell of Georgia, Eastland of Mississippi, Long of Louisiana, Kerr of Oklahoma, and Fulbright of Arkansas wielded great influence, and members of this bloc—on civil rights particularly—often made common cause with the Senate's conservative Republican faction. Republicans also had at least two factions; conservatives in the Taft mold were generally more isolationist in matters of foreign policy, sought to limit the size and scope of government, and were loath to raise taxes and spend money. Another faction, many of them from northeastern states and represented by moderates or even liberals like Aiken of Vermont, Saltonstall of Massachusetts, and Javits of New York often found ideological common ground with Democrats like Humphrey of Minnesota, Hart of Michigan, or Magnuson of Washington. The lines separating these factions were constantly shifting to be sure, and were often quite flexible. Consequentially, communication and compromise became all the more critical. That Dirksen and Mansfield, as party leaders, successfully navigated these divides speaks to each man's political skill and no doubt contributed to their belief that for the Senate to work, it had at least to try to deal with issues responsibly and with great deference to the importance of the Senate as an institution.

Mansfield aide Charles Ferris, when asked during an oral history interview, could not remember a single significant issue in the fourteen years he worked in the Senate that was decided on a strictly party-line basis. "There were very progressive Republicans and there were very reactionary Democrats," Ferris said. "The reactionaries of each party could join and prevail as could the progressives. . . . Sometimes the conservatives would prevail and sometimes the progressives would prevail." The bipartisan working relationship that Mansfield and Dirksen embraced in the 1960s obviously existed in the context of strong Democratic majorities, but as Burdett Loomis has observed, "most observers concluded had the majority been Dirksen's to lead with Mansfield in the minority, the relationship would have still existed. Even when pushing a Democratic proposal past his political opponents Mansfield never failed to consult with Dirksen. Neither man tried to gain an advantage by surprise or misdirection."[23]

"The leader's job," political scientist Donald R. Matthews wrote in his study of the Senate, published in 1960, "requires vast energy, tolerance, patience, a willingness to pay infinite attention to details, manipulative ability, a sense of 'news,' and a talent for compromise, but the exact mixture of these skills needed for effective leadership varies from one situation to another." Mansfield's laconic nature—one aide said he "would sit on the floor for hours and hours, [and] never show any movement toward ambition or wanting to go forward"—conveyed to some a lack of energy or determination. They were wrong. And Dirksen's florid oratory—"oratorical prowess alone does not make for a master legislator," his biographer observed—served to mask for many the seriousness with which he approached his responsibilities.[24]

"Thank you for your kind words concerning my election as Majority Leader by my Democratic colleagues in the Senate," Mansfield wrote in a form letter he used to respond to hundreds of congratulatory messages he received in his first month as majority leader. "I am not fooling myself about the difficulties in the task ahead, but you may be certain that I will give the job all I have, and I would hope that in those efforts I will continue to merit the trust and confidence which have been placed in me." Mansfield had made no effort to get the job, but once it was his, he was determined to succeed, not for himself, but for the Senate.[25]

Mansfield's work ethic—and Dirksen's as well—was absolutely Herculean. "Dirksen rose every day by five-thirty," Neal MacNeil reported, and was in the office never later than eight in the morning, often earlier. There are numerous stories of Dirksen, a semi-insomniac, perhaps because of his emphysema, working at his home desk by four thirty in the morning. He always transported an armful of work home at night and constantly read reports, bills, and speeches while being driven to and from the Senate. Mansfield, also an early riser, was often in his Senate office in what is now the Russell Senate Office Building, by five thirty in the morning. He would review, often in detail, the previous day's mail from Montana and dictate and sign correspondence. Mansfield's staff devised an ingenious but simple card filing system for correspondence, particularly from Montana, that kept track of every correspondent and the subjects of their letters or telegrams. The card file takes up substantial space in the collection of Mansfield's papers. Both senators maintained extensive Christmas card lists. Breakfast with Aiken would follow Mansfield's Montana office work, and after that, hours in the majority leader's office in the Capitol, on the floor, and in committee meetings, although Mansfield often missed committee meetings, including closed Foreign Relations Committee hearings, that he considered a waste of time. Francis Valeo recalled that Mansfield had a comfortable couch removed from his outer office "so that the uninvited could not lounge but would have to sit in rather uncomfortable upright chairs if they insisted on seeing him." Unlike many public people, Mansfield was content to be alone. He often retreated to his inner office for hours on end to read, write, and think.[26]

Mansfield's egalitarianism, like Dirksen's political flexibility, was genuine but also reflected practical reality in the Senate of the 1960s. Mansfield needed Dirksen's cooperation, and often his vote and those of other Republicans he could persuade, to get anything significant done. They worked, as Mansfield said, "Very closely, and deliberately so and delightfully so. We had the majority, the Democrats, but on various kinds of legislation we did not have a majority, civil rights and the like.

With Dirksen it was a case of putting my cards, I would say, our cards on the table, face up. We knew each other very well."[27]

"Mansfield handled Dirksen beautifully." Francis Valeo recalled:

He deferred to Dirksen a great deal. Dirksen responded. Dirksen was a bit of a ham, and he loved the spotlight. He was not a fool; you couldn't win him over by blatant flattery, and Mansfield never tried that, but he did defer to him, and Dirksen responded extremely well to that kind of treatment. As far as I know, he never crossed Mansfield, never took delight in a defeat that Mansfield may have suffered. He still remained very partisan, and there were a couple of points you could press the button and Dirksen would become extremely partisan. But it was never directed at Mansfield, it would always be directed at other people on the Democratic side whom he thought were trying to maneuver him or manipulate him. He was a charming man.[28]

Dirksen was typically the first to defend Mansfield from any criticism, particularly on the rare occasion when Mansfield's word was questioned. When Wayne Morse, the typically argumentative Oregon liberal, "in effect called Mansfield a liar" during a heated debate in 1962, Dirksen jumped to his feet and silenced Morse for violating the Senate rule against "indecorous language." How dare a senator question "the veracity of the majority leader," Dirksen demanded. Mansfield, showing rare anger, said he could take care of himself, but the episode demonstrated to every senator, as Neil MacNeil wrote, that Dirksen was always ready to defend the leader across the aisle.[29]

"Our working arrangements are excellent," Dirksen told MacNeil:

Mike Mansfield is by all odds one of the most agreeable, amiable people to work with, that it has been my pleasure to be associated with in the Senate chamber. He has a flexibility that is not a lack of firmness. He readily sees all sides of the picture and he can easily decide, as a result what to do. There has never been a time with a divisive spirit in the Senate that Mike could not come in that door and put all his cards on the table. "All right," he'll say, "leadership is a two-way street—what do you think we should do?" Mansfield has humility in the deepest sense of the word. There's no reaching for grandeur, no reaching for headlines. He is a patriot to the core. His whole public life is devoted to that which he thinks is for the benefit of the United States. He is accessible at all times to everybody, to the humblest and the highest. Mike is like that. And those are the great Christian attributes of this fellow.[30]

～

During John Kennedy's abbreviated presidency Dirksen was often at odds with the White House, as well as with Mansfield, on Kennedy's domestic agenda. As Valeo correctly noted, Dirksen could resort to tough partisanship with ease. Yet, the Senate leaders often forged a bipartisan consensus on issues as diverse as funding the United Nations, responding to the Cuban Missile Crisis, and even shielding the libidinous president from sex scandal. The depth of the bipartisanship extended to Dirksen's own reelection campaign in 1962, when Mansfield, much to the consternation of fellow Democrats, went wildly beyond senatorial courtesy to praise his Republican counterpart. It was the beginning of a remarkable decade in Senate history.

In the judgment of most historians, the record of domestic legislative achievements by the Kennedy administration was, at best, underwhelming. Kennedy had campaigned as a transformative liberal—"the most liberal, activist platform in history" by one estimate—and he had promised action on a host of issues that would "get this country moving again." But the rhetoric and promise failed to match reality and disillusionment, or at least disappointment, fairly quickly began to define Kennedy's relations with Congress, particularly the House of Representatives. Kennedy, still very popular with voters and much more focused on foreign policy, expended little political capital to move Congress.[31]

Dirksen exhibited real political skill in resisting elements of the Kennedy program that broadly offended his Republican colleagues—"socialized medicine" and deficit spending, for example—while at the same time offering the young president support when he could or when he read the political popularity of a Kennedy initiative better than many of his fellow conservatives did. "Now the Kennedy program is just what everyone expected," Dirksen said three months into Kennedy's tenure, "deficit spending, increased government controls, increases in the government payroll, more welfare statism—that inevitable price which we must pay the piper—eventually more taxes. It may be called the New Frontier but the Kennedy program is the Old New Deal taken out of an old warming oven. It was hot stuff 25 years ago but time has passed it by."[32]

On March 1, 1961, the US Embassy in Saigon received a cable stressing the overarching importance of South Vietnam to American national security. On the same day, Kennedy issued an executive order creating the Peace Corps, and many Republicans were eager to pounce on what they saw as a fuzzy-headed effort to exert foreign

White House aide Dave Powers with President Kennedy and Senators Dirksen and
Mansfield at a Washington Senators baseball game. (*Kennedy Presidential Library*)

policy soft power, but Dirksen backed off the naysayers. Republicans "should not
take a negative approach to this program," Dirksen said, pointing out that it was a
widely popular idea with "appeal to young people as well as the churches." Mansfield admitted years later that he "had some doubts about the Peace Corps in the
beginning," concerned that the experiment might fail "with adverse repercussions
for the Administration." But after talking it through with Kennedy and Sargent
Shriver, the president's brother-in-law who became the first director of the Peace
Corps, Mansfield embraced the program, later acknowledging "Kennedy was quite
right about the Peace Corps." Dirksen also supported Kennedy's space program,
despite the steep cost, including the promise to put a man on the moon and return
him safely by the end of the decade.[33]

How to structure and regulate the burgeoning satellite communications industry
became a major issue in the second year of Kennedy's presidency. Kennedy had
called for congressional action in 1961 and had made the issue an administration
priority. It was not readily apparent at the time, but resolution of the complicated
Communications Satellite Act (COMSAT) provided a template of sorts for how

Mansfield and Dirksen would later secure approval of civil rights legislation, including ending a filibuster. The satellite fight came down to a not unusual division of
Senate views between progressive Democrats, who feared monopolistic control
over the industry, and conservatives, who worried about too much government
regulation stifling innovation. "When this bill first started out I thought it was as
crooked as a dog's hind leg," Louisiana Democrat Russell Long remarked. "I am
now convinced that that would be a compliment. This bill is as crooked as a barrel of
snakes." Long was in a group with Oregon's Wayne Morse, Albert Gore Sr. of Tennessee, and Paul Douglas of Illinois who were convinced the telecommunications
behemoth AT&T would gain monopoly control of developing satellite technology.
This coalition faced off against Robert Kerr, the powerful Senate Commerce Committee chairman from Oklahoma and, among others, Dirksen.[34]

The voluble Morse, an outspoken liberal on most issues who normally disdained
the Senate tradition of unlimited debate and often opposed the legislative delaying
tactics of southern Democrats, found himself in the uncomfortable position of leading a liberal filibuster in an effort to stop the satellite bill. For days the slowdown
worked, reducing Senate action to a crawl. A substantial Senate majority supported
the legislation, but failure to end the filibuster left the majority powerless. With
growing frustration, Kerr approached Dirksen, increasingly seen as the broker of
bipartisan Senate deals, to seek a path to end the impasse. Dirksen was sympathetic
and the two went to see Mansfield, who not uncharacteristically had kept himself
out of the controversy. Would Mansfield try to convince Morse, a Republican turned
Democrat, to relent? Nope, he would not do that. Mansfield would not interfere with
any individual senator operating under the Senate's rules. How about extending
Senate hours to wear down the bill's opponents? Mansfield reluctantly agreed but
refused to hold an all-night session, which he considered an affront to the Senate's
decorum and prestige. The only clear path, Mansfield pointed out, was cloture—to
secure enough votes to cut off debate. Mansfield effectively ceded control over the
issue to Dirksen, who went to work and ultimately secured the cloture votes of
all but two Senate Republicans—Goldwater of Arizona and Tower of Texas. The
satellite bill passed two days later by a margin of seventy-three to twenty-seven.
"There was jeering and cheering over the outcome," Valeo wrote, "but not from the
majority leader," who had simply disappeared from the Senate floor before the vote
was announced, his quiet role in ceding leadership to Dirksen hardly noticed.[35]

As Valeo has noted, Mansfield's "unrelenting efforts to build a bridge to the
Republicans and particularly to the Republican leader by equal and even differ-
ential treatment had paid off in producing the necessary two-thirds vote required

for cloture on the COMSAT bill." As described in chapter 1, Mansfield employed essentially the same approach to secure ratification of the Limited Nuclear Test Ban Treaty. These accomplishments of subtle leadership unburdened by the issue of who would receive the political credit went mostly unnoticed. What comments were made, inside the Senate and out, tended to describe Mansfield's "restrained style" as "weak, reticent, meek, or even nonexistent."[36]

Dirksen knew better, and he complimented the majority leader for his leadership in general and on the commercial satellite bill in particular. "He has made an effort to harmonize 100 diverse personalities in the U.S. Senate," Dirksen said bursting into full rhetorical bloom. "O great God, what an amazing and dissonant 100 personalities there are—from the orchards of Oregon and Washington, from the cotton fields of Mississippi, from the cranberry bogs of Massachusetts, from the rockbound coasts of Maine, and from the cornfields of Illinois. What an amazing thing it is somehow to harmonize them. What a job it is."[37]

One incident during the legislative struggle over the COMSAT bill illustrates Mansfield's sense of fairness and attention to detail. Due to an oversight, Idaho Democrat Frank Church was recorded as opposing the legislation. Church had informed Mansfield of his position on the legislation and was absent when votes were recorded. Mansfield took to the floor to correct the mistake. "I wish to state for the record," Mansfield said, "so that there will be no doubt as to what actually happened at that time." He went on to explain that Church had informed him of his absence and his support for the COMSAT legislation. "The fact that his position was reported incorrectly is the fault of the senator from Montana, and I want that to be shown," Mansfield said.[38]

Dirksen, the satellite bill notwithstanding, was still skeptical of Kennedy's domestic policy agenda but at the same time broadly helpful in advancing the president's foreign policy objectives. He also displayed remarkable restraint, at least by more contemporary standards, in not criticizing or only mildly sanctioning a series of foreign policy stumbles by the administration. "He had changed his attitude toward Kennedy," Neil MacNeil said. "When Kennedy had international problems, it was 'He's my President,' which was astonishing." Later with Lyndon Johnson in the White House, as MacNeil related, "he would not say, this is Johnson's war the way [Robert] Taft and the others in the '50s denounced Truman for Truman's war in Korea. He held off on all of that partisan stuff all the way through."[39]

"It is a rather interesting thing," Dirksen said later while discussing a president's foreign policy power. "I have run down many legal cases before the Supreme Court— that I have found as yet no delimitation on the power of the Commander in Chief under the Constitution." As a constitutional scholar, Dirksen had a point, but he may also have suffered from what Arthur Schlesinger Jr. called a kind of "intellectual and moral intimidation" that had become a feature of the increasingly imperial nature of the modern presidency. As a result, Schlesinger wrote, Congress forgot "even the claim for foreign policy consultation," and overburdened presidents, including Kennedy, "gratefully accepted the royal prerogative."[40]

When Kennedy returned from Vienna in June 1961 after what was generally regarded as a disastrous summit with Soviet premier Khrushchev, Dirksen was part of a bipartisan delegation that met the president at Andrews Air Force Base. Khrushchev had gone to the summit determined to test and even bully the inexperienced American president, and the plan worked. "He just beat the hell out of me," Kennedy confessed. The wire service photo of Kennedy's return captured Dirksen flashing a big smile as he shook hands with the president before returning to the White House with Kennedy in the presidential helicopter. Frank Holeman, writing in the *New York Daily News*, said Kennedy seemed particularly happy to see Dirksen at the airport, with the two men "chatting for several minutes." Asked for an assessment of Kennedy's meeting with the Soviet leader, Dirksen deflected. "I will have to wait until I have a chance to ask the president what I can say about this," Dirksen said. "I always did that with President Eisenhower and President Kennedy is due the same consideration." This was not an unprecedented show of foreign policy bipartisanship, but today even such a simple gesture from a Senate leader of one party to the president of another would indeed be considered remarkable. Dirksen continued to profess his support for Kennedy—"to uphold the hands of the president and commander in chief"—while occasionally giving in to partisan demands that he bash the administration's handling of specific issues. The badly botched US-backed invasion of Cuba at the Bay of Pigs, occurring just before the Vienna summit, was an example, as Dirksen said, of "blundering incompetence." However, the minority leader opposed any wide-ranging congressional investigation of the debacle, which almost certainly would have embarrassed Kennedy as well as former President Eisenhower. "A few men of knowledge and discernment," might look into the matter, Dirksen said, and quietly report their findings to the president, but a public exposé with partisan overtones was unnecessary.[41]

Such bipartisan restraint kept Dirksen both in the know at the White House and regularly in the news, and presented the image of the leader of the loyal opposition being willing to cooperate with the administration to advance the national interest. The role played to Dirksen's transactional nature. In exchange for muted critiques of Kennedy's foreign policy, Dirksen enjoyed patronage influence in Illinois as well as a certain level of intimacy with the attractive and popular young president. Dirksen recalled of his relationship with Kennedy, "there was one nice thing about it: every time you carried the torch for him, he would call you up almost immediately to thank you without any intervening operator." Louella Dirksen on more than one occasion admonished her husband for his informality in greeting the president simply as "Jack."[42]

Dirksen rarely criticized the Senate's Democratic leadership, even obliquely. A rare, albeit mild Dirksen criticism of Mansfield involved Berlin, where in early August 1961, Khrushchev ordered the construction of a concrete and barbed-wire wall dividing the city into eastern and western sectors. Earlier in the summer, Mansfield had made a controversial suggestion during a Senate speech. Berlin, he said, should be a unified, free city, reasoning that "the way to start to bring about the unification of Germany was first to try to bring about the unification of East and West Berlin. Out of the microcosm of a unified Berlin, I thought, might come the reunification of the two Germanies." Mansfield conceded later that his "proposal met with a great deal of criticism," and he insisted he did not coordinate his remarks with Kennedy.

For his part Dirksen quietly and privately stoked criticism of Kennedy's mishandling of the Berlin crisis while stressing publicly the need "for this nation's officials to speak with one voice of strength and determination." And while initially praising Mansfield for performing "distinguished service" by attempting to reframe issues around Berlin, Dirksen speculated on whether the majority leader's proposal was a "trial balloon" on behalf of the White House, "in the nature of a feeler as to whether the American people felt the solution lies in a free city of Berlin." Adoption of Mansfield's idea—which was certainly counter to long-established US policy—would, Dirksen said, flush "the whole question of unification of Germany . . . down the drain." While Dirksen accepted Mansfield's explanation that the new Berlin policy idea was the majority leader's alone, this was a rare example of the two sparring publicly, even though Dirksen delivered his jab ever so gently.[43]

Early in 1962, Mansfield and Dirksen teamed again to support a United Nations and Kennedy administration plan to pay for expenses related to UN peacekeeping efforts in the Congo and the Middle East. The UN General Assembly authorized a $200-million bond issue, and Kennedy advocated that the United States purchase as much as half the total, but the proposal encountered significant Republican resistance in the Senate. "Dirksen did more than try to persuade his Senate Republicans to go along with the President," Neil MacNeil wrote. "He joined with Mansfield in working out compromise language" to shore up GOP support. The compromise was mostly face saving for Kennedy, removing language that committed the administration to a specific dollar amount of bond purchases while leaving the details to the president. Still, Dirksen got pushback from his side of the Senate aisle. The compromise was "a surrender," Barry Goldwater said, while Indiana Senator Homer Capehart said Dirksen was handing Kennedy a blank check, a charge the minority leader countered by saying, "I haven't forfeited my faith in John Fitzgerald Kennedy. I'm willing, as always, to trust my president because he is my president." By most accounts Dirksen's eloquent Senate speech on the UN issue moved both Republican and Democratic votes to his position. "This is not a financial question," Dirksen said. "This is a moral question. We must stand up and be counted in our generation. It does not make any difference what the mail from back home says to us." The proposal was approved by the Senate on a vote of seventy to twenty-two. "It is agreed on all sides that Dirksen . . . played an indispensable role in rolling up the big Senate vote," the *New York Times* news service reported. "He was a key man in the offstage negotiations that shaped the legislation in such a way that it commanded wide support on the floor." Mansfield credited Kennedy for making "a special effort" to reach out to Dirksen, and Dirksen for responding. "If it hadn't been for Everett Dirksen, I think that we would have failed," Mansfield said. Here was yet another occasion where, as Mansfield often said, "All I wanted were the votes. That's why I say that in many respects at times [Dirksen] was the majority leader. That didn't bother me."[44]

The autumn of 1962 produced a deluge of issues and controversies. In September, Kennedy was forced to send five hundred US marshals and, eventually, federalized National Guard troops to the campus of the University of Mississippi to protect James Meredith, the first Black student ever to be admitted to the school. Mississippi's segregationist governor Ross Barnett, a Democrat, fought Meredith's admission, court orders, and Kennedy's actions at every turn. As thousands of white Mississippians descended on the campus, a riot ensued. Two in the crowd were killed; dozens more were injured, many seriously; and scores were arrested. Meredith was finally admitted, but the scab had been ripped off of racial violence and blatant segregationist racism. "This reminds me a little of the Bay of Pigs," Kennedy aide Kenneth O'Donnell said while the campus violence was underway. "Yeah," Kennedy said, "I haven't had such a good time since the Bay of Pigs." The Ole Miss riot and subsequent civil rights protests and demands both in the South and across the country underscored the increasing sentiment that Kennedy had blundered badly by failing to push an aggressive civil rights agenda in Congress.[45]

The events in Mississippi were "an embarrassment to all concerned," Mansfield stated after a meeting at the White House, "but this is a nation ruled by law and not by men." Dirksen agreed, saying he supported Kennedy's determination to enforce the court orders admitting Meredith to Ole Miss, and he brushed aside an effort by Mississippi's segregationist senator James Eastland, the chairman of the Judiciary Committee, to launch an investigation into the federal actions. Dirksen certainly would not have sanctioned an investigation by a Mississippi senator that many in Congress and the country would rightly suspect of being less than credible, and as the senior Republican on Eastland's committee, he was in a position to stop any investigative effort in its tracks, which he did. Yet Dirksen was also critical of Kennedy for moving too slowly on civil rights. "Had the President kept his campaign pledge and sent his program to Congress in 1961," Dirksen said, "new civil rights statutes would have been on the books before demonstrations and violence were ever precipitated."[46]

Dirksen certainly knew, as historian Alan Brinkley has documented, that there is little evidence to support the view that Kennedy would have been successful had he pushed harder on civil rights in 1961. In truth, there is much evidence to the contrary, including the fact that the civil rights legislation that Mansfield and Dirksen jointly introduced in 1963, amid increasing racial violence and ever wider demonstrations, stalled in the Senate, victim again of southern Democratic opposition. It would take Kennedy's death, the political skills of Lyndon Johnson, and the Senate leadership of Dirksen and Mansfield to finally overcome the inevitable southern filibuster of yet another civil rights bill, but for the time being legislative progress on civil rights was high-centered again in Congress.[47]

From the beginning of 1962, in Washington and Illinois, political speculation churned around one question: who would contest Ev Dirksen's reelection? There was no doubt the Senate minority leader, now sixty-six years old, would seek a third term. He had announced his intentions in September 1961. There was considerable doubt about whether he could be defeated and whether any credible Democrat would even try. Chicago mayor Richard J. Daley encouraged twice defeated presidential candidate Adlai Stevenson, a former Illinois governor and UN ambassador, to run, and Stevenson floated then deflated his own trial balloon. Finally, Chicago-area congressman Sidney Yates emerged as Dirksen's Democratic opponent.

"Yates thought he had a right to expect the president's support," Yates's biographers have written, since he had been "a loyal and consistent vote in Congress for JFK." But Kennedy had a political and personal dilemma, and stories about the president's political calculations began to appear regularly in Illinois and national newspapers. In April 1962, a southern Illinois newspaper headline read "Will JFK Back Yates or Let Dirksen Win?" The *Southern Illinoisan*, recounting Dirksen's pivotal role in gaining recent Senate approval of the UN bond issue, stated the obvious: "the Illinois senator is more willing than any Republican leader to rise above party loyalty when the situation demands it . . . to have another, more hostile, Republican replace Dirksen as his party's floor leader by virtue of his defeat in Illinois could hurt the Administration more than adding just another Democrat to the party's already huge majority in the Senate would help it." With Kennedy's help, the newspaper concluded, Yates had "a chance in November; without it Senator Dirksen is practically home free."[48]

Speculation about just how much Kennedy would support Dirksen's Democratic challenger continued through the summer of 1962, with the *Chicago Tribune*, often critical of Dirksen's political flexibility but now fully in his camp, reporting in August: "Despite White House assertions that President Kennedy will stump Illinois against Sen. Dirksen in October, the word is that the President will voice no criticism of Dirksen and will make only a general appeal for the election of the whole Democratic congressional slate." Kennedy's indifferent support was bad enough news for Yates, Mike Mansfield made matters worse.[49]

Ten days after the *Tribune* offered its informed speculation about Kennedy's posture in the Illinois Senate race, Mansfield took to the Senate floor—the occasion was to commemorate Dirksen's thirty years of congressional service—and offered the kind of effusive praise that any candidate would kill to have from across the political aisle. "There is only one Demosthenes in the Senate," Mansfield said, as he praised Dirksen's "wit and wisdom" and his "scholarly erudition and homespun simplicity." Mansfield literally gushed over how he had received Dirksen's help on many occasions. The minority leader had served the Republican Party brilliantly, Mansfield said, and "our country even more." Dirksen's Illinois colleague, Democrat Paul Douglas, a strong supporter of Yates's candidacy, was livid. Douglas complained to the White House that Mansfield's speech had "done immeasurable damage" to the Democratic candidate in Illinois. Douglas would later write that Mansfield "had gone overboard in praise" of Dirksen and complained that even Hubert Humphrey "joined in this paean of tributes." All the Dirksen tributes were, of course, reported widely in the Illinois press, and flattering profiles of Dirksen in the *Saturday Evening Post* and *Time* were reproduced en masse by his campaign.[50]

One of Dirksen's Illinois constituents objected to Mansfield's Senate floor tribute in a pithy telegram to the majority leader. "Deeply resent flowery encomiums to Ev. Dirksen they are entirely undeserved," the wire read. The sender signed the telegram "a very ex-Republican." Such criticism seems not to have registered at all with Mansfield. His commitment to bipartisanship and his personal relationship with Dirksen only grew stronger. With Congress on the eve of adjournment in early October 1962, Mansfield sent Dirksen a bouquet of begonias—a perfect gesture for the Senate's number-one gardener and lover of flowers. "With that gift you not only enriched my day," Dirksen wrote in his thank-you note, "but you enriched my weeks for as was once remarked, I am in the that category of human being who is always prepared to sell bread to buy hyacinths. Thanks a million."[51]

Mansfield's slow, steady efforts to shape a Senate based on his vision of "decency, courtesy, and restraint" was simply too slow and too unproductive for many of his Democratic colleagues, who complained that Mansfield's methods had contributed to Kennedy's New Frontier stalling out in Congress. Political power had been decentralized under Mansfield who, some complained, lacked "an iron fist." Dictatorial committee chairmen called the shots, it was said, not the leader. Old and unflattering contrasts between Mansfield and Lyndon Johnson resurfaced. One unnamed senator told journalist Robert Albright, "I never thought I would ever say it, but I wish Johnson were back." Rumors even surfaced suggesting that Mansfield would give up his leadership position and might not seek reelection in 1964, speculation that circulated in Montana as well as Washington despite Mansfield's denial. Yet, there was an odd flip side to the complaints that the Senate was bogged down due to the majority leader's soft touch: Mansfield was more popular than ever with his colleagues. "If a secret ballot of senators were taken today," Albright wrote shortly after the Senate passed the COMSAT bill in the summer of 1962, "Mansfield doubtless would emerge the best-liked senator in decades. But in this tough-minded world of Senate prima donnas, popularity doesn't always buy votes." There is zero evidence Mansfield ever considered changing his approach to Senate leadership. He would maintain it was the only way he knew how to operate: treat every senator as an equal, create bipartisan coalitions to "get the votes," and insist that the Senate accept its responsibility to contribute solutions to national problems. Still, the low rumble of criticism about Mansfield's leadership would continue.[52]

⁓

In a way that rarely happens in American politics, domestic political concerns virtually stopped on the evening of October 22, 1962. Pearl Harbor in December 1941 and the terrorist attacks on the World Trade Center and Pentagon on September 11, 2001, would be comparable examples. That night in October Cuba became once again the focus of a worried world. "Within the past week," John Kennedy told a national television and radio audience, "unmistakable evidence has established the fact that a series of offensive missile sites is now in preparation on that imprisoned island. The purpose of these bases can be none other than to provide a nuclear strike capability against the Western Hemisphere." Kennedy had been aware for some days that the Soviet Union had supplied Cuban leader Fidel Castro with the expertise and hardware to create missile sites on the island, leaving much of North America within range of nuclear warheads that could be delivered within minutes of launch.[53]

As Kennedy and his advisors struggled to understand Nikita Khrushchev's motives for precipitating what the Soviet leader must have known would amount to a historic level of brinksmanship, and to devise a response, Kennedy maintained the fiction of normalcy. He kept to his regular public schedule even while in constant private discussions over US options. So as not to tip off the Soviets to the US discovery of the missile sites, Kennedy flew to Illinois on October 19 to deliver speeches in both Springfield and Chicago, where he finally gave a less-than-fulsome endorsement of Sid Yates while declining to say anything that might antagonize Dirksen. Following these speeches, Press Secretary Pierre Salinger told reporters the president would scrap the remainder of his trip, the sole purpose of which was to help Democratic candidates, and return immediately to Washington. Salinger concocted a story that Kennedy had developed a cold and slight fever, and on doctor's orders, would take to his bed in the White House.[54]

"We had to think up some way of confronting America with more than words," Khrushchev would later write. "We had to establish a tangible and effective deterrent to American interference in the Caribbean, but what exactly?" Deploying missiles to Cuba was Khrushchev's answer and, as it turned out, a stunning misreading of Kennedy, since, as historian Michael Beschloss has written, "he almost certainly did not guess that the President would risk nuclear war to get the missiles out of Cuba." Back in Washington on October 21, Kennedy decided on a blockade of Cuba. The president then summoned congressional leaders to a White House meeting and prepared a speech to the nation about the so-called Cuban Missile Crisis.[55]

Mansfield was vacationing with his wife in Florida when he received the summons to return to Washington immediately. A military helicopter took Mansfield to MacDill Air Force Base in Tampa, where George Smathers joined him, and an Air Force jet delivered them to Washington. Dirksen was with his wife on the Illinois campaign trail when the call came to his hotel insisting that he also return immediately to Washington. "Well, Mrs. D.," Dirksen told Louella, "You're taking over the campaign. That was the president. He wants me back in Washington. He's sending a plane for me. It's urgent." Congressional leaders were similarly gathered from locations across the country—House minority leader Charles Halleck of Indiana was pheasant hunting in South Dakota and House Democratic whip Hale Boggs of Louisiana was fetched by helicopter from a fishing trip in the Gulf of Mexico. As they trooped into the White House Cabinet Room at 5:00 P.M., Dirksen attempted to poke a bit of fun at the somber president. "That was a nice little speech you gave for Sid Yates in Chicago," Dirksen told Kennedy. "Too bad you caught that cold making it."[56]

Ignoring Dirksen's attempt at humor, Kennedy was all business. Following a series of briefings from the Central Intelligence Agency and the State and Defense Departments, the president outlined his blockade plan, stressing he was not seeking congressional advice but simply informing Mansfield, Dirksen, and the others of his intentions. Senate Armed Services Committee chairman Richard Russell protested that the blockade was too timid and would invite a nuclear exchange. Surprisingly, William Fulbright, the Foreign Relations Committee chairman, agreed. Dirksen and Mansfield immediately signaled their support for Kennedy's plan, and Mansfield stayed at the White House after the leadership meeting broke up to watch Kennedy's speech from the office of aide Lawrence O'Brien. Later that evening Mansfield issued his own statement. Kennedy's "hand has been forced," Mansfield stated, and the president "alone had to make the decision in the light of all the facts available." Mansfield later told historian Gregory Olson that Kennedy was "contained" and "cool" during the crisis, and during the tense standoff with Khrushchev, Kennedy "attained maturity." In essence, both Dirksen and Mansfield were holding to their established approach to presidents and foreign policy: they would offer advice, even disagree privately with presidents on foreign policy issues, but would rarely if ever voice outright opposition in public statements or actions.[57]

After more hours of tension and worry, Khrushchev finally agreed to a face-saving retreat. The Cuban crisis was resolved with the removal of the Soviet missiles while the world held its breath on the brink of nuclear war. Mansfield told biographer Don Oberdorfer that when he and Maureen returned to Montana shortly after the conference at the White House and Kennedy's historic speech, he noticed that the military aircraft at Malmstrom Air Force Base near Great Falls had been dispersed to civilian airports in fear of a Soviet attack. The historian Serhii Plokhy argues in his 2021 history of the Cuban Missile Crisis that Kennedy and Khrushchev both made multiple, potentially fatal mistakes in October 1962, but in the end, each concluded that a nuclear war could not be won and therefore must not be fought. A clear lesson of the crisis was the need to control nuclear weapons. "With the signing in August 1963 of the partial test ban treaty," Plokhy wrote, "Kennedy and Khrushchev saved the world a second time by drastically limiting radioactive fallout, which threatened life on this planet as we know it. If humanity is lucky enough to survive the new nuclear age and live for another thirty or forty million years, geologists of the future studying ice cores, corals, and rocks will still be able to pinpoint the time when the Kennedy-Khrushchev treaty was signed."[58]

Dirksen, anxious to get back to Illinois to resume campaigning, told Kennedy that with the Cuban crisis cooling down, he planned to leave Washington. It was now Kennedy's turn to joke. "What are you talking about?" he kidded Dirksen. "You're just as good as in." Either Dirksen related the story to a reporter or a reporter overheard the story, and Kennedy's assessment of the minority leader's reelection chances circulated widely in the days leading up to the election. Sid Yates, stunned by his treatment at the hands of fellow Democrats, called the remark an "outright contemptible lie." Dirksen passed off Kennedy's comment as a little private conversation with his wife that "somebody overheard." Then, the day before the election, seemingly adding injury to insult, Mansfield confirmed to the New York Times that he and Dirksen would soon depart together for a round-the-world tour of "trouble spots." The newspaper reported that the White House declined to confirm the trip "from a desire not to influence tomorrow's Senate race in Illinois," but Mansfield clearly had no such reservations. As it turned out, Dirksen did not make the trip, but the mere suggestion that he would was a final blow to Yates's campaign. "With the sharpest of political instincts," Byron Hulsey wrote, Dirksen "drifted between his roles as an indispensable leader of the loyal opposition to partisan critic of the administration's liberal machinations and back again to defender of the White House in times of trouble before the closing of the polls on election day." It was a masterful example of his flexibility and his bipartisanship, and Dirksen won reelection by 200,000 votes.[59]

On November 7, 1962, Mansfield and a small Senate delegation left Washington on the round-the-world tour he had announced just before Election Day. Dirksen begged off on making the six-week trip—"they asked us to go," Louella Dirksen told a reporter, "but we had too much pressure, too many loose ends after the campaign"—so Mansfield, who selected the delegation, was joined by Democratic senators Claiborne Pell of Rhode Island and Benjamin Smith of Massachusetts and

Republican Caleb Boggs of Delaware. Kennedy supplied a presidential aircraft and officially sanctioned the trip in order to get "a senator's view" of international issues. Mansfield set the itinerary—Berlin, Greece, Egypt, Turkey, Iran, India, Hong Kong, the Philippines, Cambodia, and a final stop in Saigon. This would be Mansfield's fourth trip to Vietnam, having last visited the country in 1955. This time he was decidedly unimpressed with what he saw and heard.[60]

That Mansfield would undertake extensive travel at the behest of Kennedy, particularly to Vietnam, was an outgrowth of each man's long interest—and growing worry—about the American role in Southeast Asia. In 1954, for instance, during the second year of Kennedy's and Mansfield's Senate tenures, the two first-termers engaged in friendly debate on the Senate floor. "To pour money, material, and men into the jungles of Indochina without at least a remote prospect of victory," Kennedy said, "would be dangerously futile and self-destructive." Mansfield asked Kennedy about a recent speech by John Foster Dulles, Eisenhower's secretary of state, where Dulles had called for "united action" against Communist guerrillas in Vietnam. What did Dulles mean? Mansfield asked. "There is every indication that what he meant was that the United States will take the ultimate step," Kennedy said. "And that is what?" Mansfield responded. "It is war," Kennedy replied.[61]

Kennedy, Mansfield, and Dirksen were political products of the Cold War. To varying degrees, each subscribed to the so-called domino theory. This foreign policy thesis, which became conventional wisdom during Eisenhower's presidency, held that should South Vietnam go communist, Laos, Cambodia, Thailand, and eventually all of Southeast Asia would inevitably follow. By 1961, Mansfield was rethinking both the domino theory and his longtime support of Ngo Dinh Diem, the increasingly autocratic South Vietnamese president. Mansfield previewed his growing misgivings about American policy in the region during a commencement speech at Michigan State University in June 1962. The majority leader chose the venue for a major speech on Vietnam because faculty at the school had long advised Diem, and Mansfield knew and respected their work. US policy, Mansfield said, was on "a mark time course" that was already entailing huge costs. He recommended a reevaluation of a policy that seemed to hold only the possibility of a "conflict of indefinite depth and duration, depending largely on our forces for its prosecution." Mansfield's speech, Gregory Olson wrote, "received limited attention in the United States, but it caused alarm in South Vietnam." The most informed and influential Senate expert on Southeast Asia, a friend of Diem's, had delivered a sharply critical assessment of American foreign policy.[62]

Back from his globe-circling trip, Mansfield produced two lengthy and remarkable reports, one for public release—Mansfield received hundreds of requests for copies—and a second that he supplied privately to Kennedy. Since the Mansfields were on holiday in Florida, the president and the majority leader met the day after Christmas in Palm Beach and spent the afternoon sailing aboard the presidential yacht, the *Honey Fitz*. Kennedy read Mansfield's report while enjoying the sun on the aft deck. "Kennedy was one of these Evelyn Wood speed readers," Mansfield aide Charles Ferris recalled. "He had this report, and he was going through it and would read down the page. I don't know how many pages it was, but [Mansfield] said it took him about 20 minutes, 25 minutes to go through the whole thing." Mansfield sat and watched the president's neck getting redder and redder, and not from the sun. When Kennedy finished, he said, "Mike, this is not what my people are telling me." Mansfield replied, not trimming his negative assessment in the face of Kennedy's pushback, "you asked me to go to Vietnam." Mansfield admitted later that "it wasn't a pleasant picture that I had depicted for him."[63]

Mansfield's confidential report on the US role in South Vietnam, including his assessment of the continued viability of Diem as a leader and the prospects of even wider American participation, in the words of historian Thurston Clark, "ranks among the most prescient and depressing documents ever written about that conflict." Success in Vietnam might be possible, but Mansfield considered it unlikely. The only alternative to seeing the situation slowly deteriorate was "a truly massive commitment of American military personnel and other resources—in short going to war fully ourselves against the guerillas—and the establishment of some sort of neo-colonial rule in South Vietnam," a course of action Mansfield entirely rejected. The responsibility for prosecuting the war rested solely with the South Vietnamese, Mansfield argued in the report, and should the South Vietnamese fail and the United States attempt to engage militarily in a significant way, it would "not only be immensely costly in terms of American lives and resources but it may also draw us into some variation of the unenviable position in Vietnam which was formerly occupied by the French." In his punchy writing style, Mansfield put a fine point on Kennedy's and the country's dilemma: "Seven years and billions of dollars later . . . it would be well to face the fact that we are at the beginning of the beginning."[64]

Mansfield told biographer Don Oberdorfer that he verbally conveyed to Kennedy his strong belief that the United States should not send more troops to Vietnam and should instead begin a withdrawal. Mansfield worried that momentum would soon be on the side of introducing more American combat forces "which would be

counterproductive to this country's interest as well as Vietnam's." Kennedy questioned Mansfield closely, even sharply and later, according to Kenneth O'Donnell,
arguably Kennedy's closest aide, Kennedy said, "I got angry at Mike for disagreeing
with our policy so completely, and I got angry with myself because I found myself
agreeing with him."[65]

O'Donnell would later write of a Kennedy-Mansfield White House meeting
in the spring of 1963 where, he claimed, after thinking more about the situation
in Vietnam, Kennedy told Mansfield that he had come around to the Montanan's
view that a complete military withdrawal was the correct course. "But I can't do
it until 1965—after I'm re-elected," Kennedy allegedly said. Mansfield, who had a
prized ability to recall names and conversations, recalled the incident in slightly
different ways when several historians and researchers questioned him about it over
a period of many years, and he equivocated when Don Oberdorfer pressed him in
1999 about whether Kennedy, had he lived, would have disengaged from Vietnam.
"Barring unforeseen circumstances he might have," Mansfield said, "I can't say he
would have." The question of what John Kennedy might have done after his likely
reelection in 1964 remains a fascinating and unknowable detail of the long American
experience in Indochina.[66]

~

Dirksen began 1963 as an outspoken opponent of Kennedy's domestic legislative
agenda, but once again his political flexibility prevented him from knee-jerk opposition merely for the sake of opposing. "Both Congress and the Executive will be
confronted with a world still fevered and confused," he wrote just before the new
Congress convened. "Set a finger on any part of the world map and there you will
find unrest or turmoil." Dirksen would support the president where he could but
said "it is the function of the opposition party to oppose unsound proposals," by
which he meant Kennedy's farm bill, a transportation initiative, a tax cut, and
federal aid for education, among other initiatives. At various times Dirksen suggested he could support filibuster reform, but he ultimately sided with conservative
Democrats to shelve a reform proposal. There is scant record of Dirksen expressing much opinion at all about the increasing US role in Southeast Asia, beyond
expressing unqualified support for Kennedy's position. By the summer of 1963,
Kennedy's legislative program had slowed to a crawl in the House and the Senate.
While Republican obstruction certainly contributed to the president's legislative
headaches, the support of southern Democrats hampered Kennedy as well. As

politicians are wont to do, blame was apportioned, with Mansfield getting his share. Kennedy, too, had to shoulder substantial responsibility for his short list of legislative accomplishments. "He spent more of his time than people realized working with Congress," Arthur Schlesinger wrote. "But it cannot be said that this was the part of the Presidency which gave him the greatest pleasure or satisfaction." Kennedy's interest lay in foreign policy.[67]

One important area where Dirksen did attempt to help Kennedy with a festering domestic issue was civil rights. Tuesday, June 11, 1963, would be a historic day: for the first time Black students were admitted to the University of Alabama despite the showy protests of Governor George Wallace. Later that night Kennedy delivered a televised Oval Office speech finally launching his civil rights initiative. Then, just before midnight, NAACP organizer Medgar Evers was murdered by a sniper with a high-powered rifle as he entered his home in Jackson, Mississippi. All the progress, politics, and poison around race was on clear display on this one memorable day.

Kennedy's speech acknowledged the anguish over racial inequality increasingly gripping the nation, what the president called "the fires of frustration and discord." Dirksen immediately responded, "I recognize that Congress has a responsibility in this field, and there should be some action this session on effective civil rights legislation. To this end I will devote my best efforts." Mansfield said Kennedy had "laid it on the line" with his televised speech, not an easy message to deliver, he said, but one "that had to be made to the American public." Mansfield then introduced Kennedy's civil rights bill in its entirety, including the most controversial section dealing with public accommodations. Then, to assuage Dirksen's concerns, he cosponsored a separate bill stripped of the public accommodations section but otherwise identical to Kennedy's proposal. Mansfield next worked with Washington Senator Warren Magnuson to introduce separate legislation addressing public accommodations. He predicted that Congress would pass a civil rights bill, but it was not to be, at least not for another year.[68]

In late September—on the day the Senate ratified the Limited Nuclear Test Ban Treaty—John Kennedy left Washington for a multiday, eleven-state western "conservation tour tinged with politics." Ten of the states on Kennedy's itinerary were holding Senate elections in 1964, and the White House was keenly aware of growing western support for Arizona Senator Barry Goldwater, who was emerging as a favorite for the Republican presidential nomination. The trip included two Montana stops: Billings and Great Falls. When Kennedy spoke to a crowd of seventeen thousand at the fairgrounds in Billings, he tired of the conservation theme, a subject of much less interest to him than foreign policy, and instead lavished praise on Mansfield for helping secure approval of the test ban treaty. "Mr. Kennedy drew a tremendous ovation from the crowd when he praised Senate Majority Leader Mike Mansfield," the *Billings Gazette* reported. "It was difficult to tell whether the crowd was cheering for Mansfield or the treaty." Kennedy spoke to an even larger crowd in Great Falls, but before the speech at Memorial Stadium the president made an unscheduled stop to pay his respects to Mansfield's father and stepmother. "If he'd asked me about it, I would have urged against it, for security and other reasons," Mansfield said later. "We live in a very poor section of town. It's on the wrong side of the tracks, but it was on the way to the airport, and he wanted to do it so we went in and he said to my father, 'well, how do you think Mike is doing?' My father said, 'I think you are both doing well, Mr. President.' Then he talked some about Irish history and that was it."

Mansfield's relatives were amazed by the ten-minute visit, which included the hurried installation of a red emergency phone in the parlor. Kennedy was amazed as well. "I wonder how many majority leaders of the U.S. Senate have had a brother

Two months before his assassination, Kennedy made two campaign-style stops in Montana. Here he is pictured in Billings with Mike Mansfield. Later, the president visited with Mansfield's family in Great Falls. (*Courtesy of* Billings Gazette)

working in the hometown fire department," Kennedy said. "And that fellow wouldn't take a job in Washington for any amount of money."[69]

———

Only once in his long political career did scandal even remotely attach to Mike Mansfield, and that scandal was a legacy of Lyndon Johnson's tenure as majority leader.

Early on, Mansfield's colleagues had warned him about Bobby Baker, the smooth South Carolinian and one-time Senate page who rose, through ambition, scheming, and guile, to become Johnson's indispensable aide as secretary of the Senate. The secretary is technically an elected position, but in fact, the job goes to a confidante of the majority leader who handles an array of legislative, financial, and administrative duties ranging from hiring to payroll to records management. Baker, wielding political power in the same way Johnson did, took the mostly behind-the-scenes role to a new level. Often referred to as the 101st senator, Baker was Johnson's errand boy, his head counter, his "Little Lyndon." Baker knew every senatorial peccadillo, where every secret was stashed away, what every senator needed or wanted, and how to count votes. Johnson loved him. "I have two daughters," Johnson once said of his affection for Baker. "If I had a son, this would be the boy." Despite Baker's closeness to Johnson, despite his flashy style—a huge contrast to Mansfield's quiet rectitude—despite his always seeming to have more money and more favors at his command than common sense explained, and despite his offer to resign when Mansfield became majority leader, Baker was kept on. Perhaps the new majority leader felt he needed the young man who made the Senate schedule function, or perhaps his tendency to expect and think the best of virtually everyone blinkered him when it came to Baker. Or perhaps Lawrence O'Brien, John Kennedy's congressional liaison, explained it best. "I think Mansfield inherited Baker passively," O'Brien said. "Baker had the job, and he wouldn't throw him out." Mansfield clearly liked Baker and spoke warmly of him in 1961, calling the top Senate staffer "one of the country's most distinguished sons and public servants." Dirksen, too, shared the regard for Baker, calling him a "very distinguished" public official. Virtually every senator liked and depended on Bobby Baker, but by the summer of 1963, Baker's days were numbered and Mansfield's handling of the financial and sex scandal that engulfed Baker was brutally criticized.[70]

At least one senator did not hold Bobby Baker in high regard. John J. Williams, a starchy, irascible Republican from Delaware, considered Baker at best a shyster, at worst a crook. Williams, described not altogether favorably as "relentless in pursuit of his perpetrators as a blue tick hound after a raccoon," caught the scent of scandal around Baker and pounced. Taking to the Senate floor to repeat charges first leveled in Drew Pearson's muckraking "Washington Merry-Go-Round" column, Williams demanded an investigation of Baker's finances. How had Baker financed a side business—The Quorum Club—a hangout for lobbyists, congressional staffers, young women, and old senators, located across the street from what is now the Russell Senate Office Building? How had Baker managed to acquire a resort hotel on the Maryland shore? How was a Senate staffer like Baker making all these side investments? Interest in Baker's questionable finances grew when he was sued by a business associate who threatened to expose potentially tawdry details.[71]

At first, as Francis Valeo wrote, Mansfield remained "passive as the scandal swirled around the Senate. He did not make light of the matter, but at the same time he refused to accept Baker's proffered resignation, insisting that the matter needed to be clarified." As the Baker scandal worsened, Mansfield finally invited Baker to attend a meeting in his office with Dirksen and Williams in order to explain himself. Baker failed to show for the meeting and instead submitted his resignation. By this point, the Federal Bureau of Investigation was on the Baker case, and with William's agreement, Mansfield referred the sordid mess to the Senate Rules Committee for further investigation.[72]

Mansfield appears to have been trying to ensure something like political due process for Baker, presuming the thirty-six-year-old hustler innocent until proven guilty, and he diligently kept Dirksen informed and involved regarding the scandal and investigation. Dirksen clearly had little stomach for a probe that might reveal too many Senate secrets, and he warned fellow Republicans not to attempt to politicize any investigation of Baker. "The danger is that this could take on a partisan slant," Dirksen said, "to a degree this involves the Senate as an institution." Still, the Baker case amplified criticism of Mansfield's hands-off management style and caused rumbles in Montana. Pearson's columns, carried in several Montana newspapers, were filled with titillating tidbits—"One lady of the evening has given investigators a statement about pandering and partying with Capitol Hill playboys." A Republican state legislator, Tom Haines of Missoula, wrote Mansfield that he had never supported him politically but had also never questioned his "honesty and integrity" until the Baker affair. Now, Haines said, "I feel ashamed for you." Most Montana editorial pages touched lightly on Mansfield's connections to Baker, but one editorial gently chided the majority leader for being too inclined "to brush off the charges as being nothing but politics."[73]

Within a month of Baker's resignation, and while the Senate investigation was proceeding, Mansfield tapped Francis Valeo as the new secretary of the Senate. The contrast between the quiet, scholarly, mostly apolitical Valeo, a one-time employee of the Library of Congress who, as a foreign policy expert, had been Mansfield's traveling companion to Vietnam and elsewhere, versus the bubbly, backslapping, hyper-political Baker was lost on no one. "If senators were looking for an opposite type to succeed Baker they found him in Valeo," United Press International reported. With perfect hindsight, Mansfield clearly made a mistake in keeping Baker on when he became majority leader. Now, after a scandal, he had a staffer in keeping with his own style. The Baker affair eventually faded from headlines, but Baker's troubles persisted. He was indicted in 1967 for tax evasion, fraud, and theft and ultimately served sixteen months in prison. Baker died in 2017, more than half a century after his name became synonymous with political scandal.[74]

Bobby Baker was also connected, at least tangentially, with sexual allegations involving President Kennedy that emerged in late October 1963. Investigative reporter Clark Mollenhoff broke the story in the *Des Moines Register*, and suddenly what had been a financial scandal became a sex scandal with a money angle. An "exotic 27-year-old German girl," Ellen Rometsch, a "party girl" well known in Washington political circles, had been quietly deported in August 1963. The inference was that Rometsch had been shuttled out of the country to prevent her from talking to Senate investigators looking into the Baker allegations. Ellen was married to a German soldier stationed in the United States and moved, as Mollenhoff reported, "in a crowd that included some well-known New Frontier figures." The FBI suspected Rometsch was an East German spy and identified her as one of "Baker's party girls." FBI director J. Edgar Hoover had pieced together details connecting the young woman to a number of political figures, and Baker himself would later allege that Rometsch frequented the White House for sexual liaisons with the president. By some accounts, Kennedy laughed off the Mollenhoff story, although records exist confirming that the president summoned Mansfield to the White House to discuss "the playing down of this news report." Kennedy's brother, Attorney General Robert Kennedy, took more direct action.[75]

Mansfield would later tell biographer Don Oberdorfer that he had only faint recollection of a meeting with Dirksen and Hoover at his Washington home on the afternoon of October 28, 1963. At the meeting the FBI director provided details about several senators who had been sexually involved with Baker's "party girls." The meeting is noteworthy for many reasons, not least because Mansfield hardly ever conducted Senate business at his home, but apparently the conference was held

at his residence to avoid the curious eyes of reporters wandering the halls of the
Capitol. The Senate leaders, Kennedy biographer Richard Reeves has written, "were
stunned by Hoover's performance" as the FBI director detailed "dates, times, and
the names of senators from both parties, stopping occasionally to make the point
that some of the girls were foreigners or Negros." Robert Kennedy had prevailed
upon Hoover to brief the Senate leaders and assure them that the FBI had no evidence to implicate Kennedy in a sexual relationship with a potential communist spy.
(Nevertheless, the allegations bore a striking similarity to the so-called Profumo
affair in the United Kingdom, in which a senior British politician's sexual relationship with a Soviet spy caused a huge scandal and contributed to the resignation
of Prime Minister Harold Macmillan just days before Hoover's meeting with the
Senate leaders.) Robert Kennedy obviously hoped that Hoover's credibility would
persuade Mansfield and Dirksen to quash any further Senate investigation of sexual
high jinks in high places. After all, if the president was not involved, anything an
investigation might uncover would potentially reflect poorly, as Dirksen said, "on
the Senate as an institution."[76]

Mansfield called Kennedy as soon as Hoover left his residence, presumably to
reassure the president that his name had not come up but also likely to say that
any investigation of sexcapades on Capitol Hill had been stopped cold. When a
senator subsequently tried to inject the sexual aspects of the Baker scandal into
the ongoing Senate investigation of Baker's finances, Rules Committee Chairman
B. Everett Jordan of North Carolina ruled the line of inquiry out of order. It is possible that Mansfield and Dirksen saved the Kennedy presidency, a claim Bobby Baker,
perhaps not the most credible source, made explicitly to Don Oberdorfer. "Mike
Mansfield by that meeting in his house in Wesley Heights saved the presidency of
John Kennedy," Baker told Oberdorfer during an interview in 2001, "and probably
the political future of Bobby Kennedy." Had the meeting with Hoover not taken
place, and had Mansfield and Dirksen acted differently, Baker asserted, political
figures known to the FBI could well have unspooled the sordid details of a world-
class sex scandal. "I'm telling you," Baker said to the reporter Oberdorfer, "you guys
in the press would have had the greatest field day in your history."[77]

Mansfield and Dirksen were among the most perceptive public officials of their
generation. They understood politics, the Senate, and the presidency, as well as
human nature. They were both clearly fond of John and Robert Kennedy and had
an instinctive reverence for the institution of the American presidency. Both were
also extremely sensitive to anything that might bring the Senate into disrepute.
Dirksen apparently left no reaction to the whole "party girl" affair in his papers,

and there is no record he said anything about it to anyone. For his part Mansfield confessed he was not particularly shocked by Hoover's information but also said he mentioned the matter only to Maureen and to no one else. Hoover apparently told Bobby Kennedy nearly the opposite, that Mansfield was "particularly amazed and surprised" by the explicit details.[78]

By the fall of 1963, Jack Kennedy's appetite for sex and indiscretion was becoming more widely known and was threatening, as political scientist Larry Sabato has written, "his personal and political safety." There is ample evidence the president had more than one liaison with the statuesque young German woman who, Kennedy is reputed to have said, provided the best oral sex he ever had. Biographers and historians have since catalogued a dozen other cases of the president's reckless pursuit of call girls, strippers, White House secretaries, and interns, even the actresses Marilyn Monroe and Marlene Dietrich. It stretches credulity to assume that Mansfield and Dirksen were unaware of the rumors. It seems more likely that they concluded preventing the damage to the presidency, the government, and America's standing around the world was simply more important than getting at the truth. As historian Michael Beschloss has observed, had Bobby Kennedy and J. Edgar Hoover, with the help of Everett Dirksen and Mike Mansfield, not effectively contained the Rometsch scandal, Kennedy might well have been subjected to months of investigation and even forced from office in a Profumo-style sex and security scandal that could have roiled American politics for years. "The American Right and others might have explained Kennedy's failure to exploit the American nuclear advantage at the Bay of Pigs, in Laos and Berlin, and during the Missile Crisis as the result of the President's compromise by Soviet bloc intelligence," Beschloss wrote. As a result, Kennedy's efforts to bring about a more stable relationship with the Soviet Union, not to mention his presidency, might have been crippled. None of that happened. Three weeks later, John Kennedy visited Dallas.[79]

6 CAMELOT'S END

Men walked the tight rope between brittle confidence and sudden fear,
never knowing when reality would suddenly intrude and laughter fade
and the dark abyss yawn open and remind them it was waiting there for
a still unhumbled land.

—ALLEN DRURY, 1959

The senior senator from Connecticut, Democrat Thomas J. Dodd, carried himself,
his biographer wrote, "like an actor from the cast of Julius Caesar." With a mane
of white hair and perfect, chiseled features, "nobody looked more like The Senator
than Tom Dodd." If Dodd looked like he could have been at home in the Roman
Forum, he was also a walking, talking collection of contradictions: a northeastern
liberal who supported Southerner Lyndon Johnson for president in 1960, a brilliant
prosecutor at the Nuremberg war crimes trials who delivered lofty speeches on
the importance of propriety while benefiting financially from a host of conflicts
of interest. Perhaps most importantly, Tom Dodd was a politician who regularly
"succumbed to his lifelong predisposition to say whatever he goddamn pleased."
On the Senate floor on the evening of November 7, 1963, almost surely lubricated
with liquid courage, Dodd laid into the Senate leadership of Mike Mansfield and
Everett Dirksen. Concerns about Mansfield's soft approach to leadership—worries
that had simmered among some of his colleagues since January 1961 but that were
still generally confined to cloakroom gossip or the speculation of columnists—and
about Dirksen's cozy willingness to be a full partner with his opposite number finally
boiled over in public on the Senate floor.[1]

"I wish our leader would behave more like a leader and lead the Senate as it should
be led," Dodd intoned in what one reporter described as a "boozy voice." Dodd was
merely channeling common complaints from other senators, he said, including the
lament that Mansfield refused to keep the Senate in session long into the night to

advance critical legislation. The leadership was "being frivolous with the people's business" and taking "a Wall Street attitude of 9 or 12 or 4 or 5 or 6" (apparently an alcohol-influenced reference to a less-than-demanding workday). In fact, Dodd was speaking during an evening session as he complained about the Senate not working late enough. He invoked the memory of the Senate leadership of Lyndon Johnson, "an orchestra leader" who magically "blended into a wonderful production all the discordant notes of the Senate." And Dirksen was no better, Dodd claimed. "The opposition is so weak, so decadent, so fallen, so anxious to curry public opinion, that it does not say what it should be saying."[2]

As muddled, incoherent, and booze fueled as Dodd's critique was—apparently much of what was said was omitted from the *Congressional Record*, leaving newspapers to report the details—the harangue was not delivered in a vacuum. In offering such pointed criticism of his own majority leader, Dodd may have been channeling personal disappointment. Due to the press of Senate business, Mansfield had recently cancelled a Senate junket to Paris that Dodd and his wife were planning to join, but it was also true that the Senate had bogged down. Kennedy's civil rights legislation was floundering, appropriations bills were stalled, and a contentious and prolonged debate involving a foreign aid proposal was barely making headway. At the same time, it was also true that some senators were capitalizing on Mansfield's light hand of leadership to frequently skip floor and committee sessions. There was generally less discipline and more freelancing. Some senators even resented Mansfield sending telegrams reminding them of a key vote. Columnists such as Joseph Alsop continued to lionize Lyndon Johnson and his time as leader, while complaining "that the always-creaky Congressional machinery has degenerated to a really dangerous degree." Columnist Mary McGrory opined that "if the Senate were a horse, it would be turned out to pasture; if it were a business, it would be put on the block and sold, mostly for the fixtures." Mansfield had left for the day when Dodd gained the floor, and that fact, at least for some who were present, was an unforgiveable breach of the type of decorum and civility the majority leader had tried to instill since taking the leadership. "I wish the majority leader were present, because I know this will be construed as a criticism of him," Dodd said. "It is meant to be. It is a criticism of him. I do not think he is leading the Senate as he should, and I believe we should have leadership."[3]

Almost immediately Dodd realized that he had overplayed his hand, overstated the seriousness of the turmoil in the Senate, and insulted Dirksen and Mansfield. Returning to his office after issuing his broadside Dodd told an aide, "I may have gotten myself in trouble." He had. When the Senate convened the next day, Mansfield, not surprisingly and entirely in character, thanked Dodd for his constructive criticism, and said he would resist making "a mountain out of a mole hill." Dodd rather sheepishly admitted that Mansfield had called him and offered to come to Dodd's office to talk. They eventually met in the majority leader's office where Mansfield, Dodd said, "made me feel the size of a peanut." Dirksen was not so forgiving. When the minority leader rose to respond he noted pointedly that Dodd was absent. "The brave crusader from the Nutmeg State on his white charger has great zeal for being here and getting on with business, and he is not here now," Dirksen thundered. He demanded a quorum call in order to allow Dodd to "see if he can find his way to the Senate chamber where the business is done." At an earlier news conference, Dirksen suggested Dodd might need a seeing eye dog to find his way to the Senate floor. When Dodd did show up, Dirksen unloaded on him. The Connecticut senator's allegations about the Senate not doing its work were ironic, Dirksen said, because "the senator is not around enough. I can prove it with the Senate Committee record and with his attendance on the floor." Dodd was guilty of "cerebral incoherence" and "emotional inconsistency," a clear reference to the senator's blood alcohol level. Dodd was using the Senate as "a glorified wailing wall to air his own ineptitude," Dirksen said. Before the dustup subsided, Dodd had a further blistering exchange with Dirksen. "I'm not impressed by menacing words and gestures," Dodd said when Dirksen shook a finger in his direction, then as if his earlier angry words had not been spoken, Dodd apologized and praised both leaders as "great men." Dodd's turnaround, from criticism to flattery, in the space of less than twenty-four hours was so complete the Hartford Courant's headline read simply: "Dodd Reverses Stand, Praises Senate Leaders."[4]

When Mansfield finally addressed criticism of his leadership in a brief statement on the Senate floor, he emphasized that individual responsibility and seriousness of purpose, rather than a heavy whip hand were the keys to the Senate operating successfully. "I'm not going to turn this chamber into a sideshow or a Roman holiday," Mansfield declared, and he defended his leadership and the Senate's accomplishments, which in fact had been substantial. Mansfield promised to address the issues raised by Dodd and others in more detail, and he prepared that speech, a manifesto of sorts defining his leadership approach as well as what he believed the US Senate could be and should be. He planned to deliver that speech on Friday afternoon, November 22, 1963, but all Senate business that afternoon was overtaken by the tragedy in Dealey Plaza in Dallas. Mansfield's speech was inserted instead in the Congressional Record, then largely forgotten until a new generation of Senate leaders invited him to revisit the defense of his unique brand of leadership thirty-five years later.[5]

"When Tom Dodd gave that speech in 1963," Mansfield aide Charles Ferris recalled, "he was really pining for Lyndon Johnson. Some people thought the legislative process should be worked out behind the scenes rather than in an open forum." But working in the shadows, cutting deals in the Senate cloakroom, or trading favors over a glass of bourbon was simply antithetical to Mansfield's notion of leadership. Mansfield's attempt to create a different kind of Senate, as Francis Valeo described it, "could only work if senators were prepared to accept a full share of personal responsibility for what went on and for the image that the Senate projected to the nation. Above all, it required that the Senate's easily abused rules and indulgent practices be used with a maximum of self-imposed individual restraint and mutual consideration. Otherwise, rules intended to facilitate wise decisions became deadly impediments to rational legislative action and covers for inaction and inequity." Even as Mansfield publicly discounted Dodd's criticism, it still stung. He seriously contemplated quitting as majority leader. Ironically, the criticism did serve to underscore Mansfield's insistence that every senator shared the responsibility to make the Senate work. As important as his bipartisan relationship with Dirksen had become, it was not enough. If individual senators did not step up and accept Mansfield's "appeal to the senatorial interests of institutional pride and personal participation," the majority leader from Montana would be completely content to return to the job he truly loved—being a senator from Montana.[6]

Tom Dodd's criticism of Dirksen was less specific and certainly less politically serious than the dissatisfied rumbles that occasionally surfaced from fellow Republicans who charged the minority leader with being too accommodating to Democrats. Dirksen was often forced to straddle the growing tensions between the moderate and conservative factions in his party, a reality that surfaced loudly and decisively when Barry Goldwater captured the Republican Party's presidential nomination in 1964. A New York Republican group, the Republican Committee of One Hundred, publicly demanded that Dirksen stand down as the party's leader in the Senate. The committee accused Dirksen of "continual support for administration policies harmful to the United States." Dirksen, the former Cold War warrior and Joe McCarthy defender, was now allegedly "giving aid to communist countries." The extremely conservative *Indianapolis Star*—the newspaper's publisher was the grandfather of future senator and vice president Dan Quayle—endorsed the idea that Dirksen's leadership was inept. "It sounds very high-minded to declare that the national interest is above party," the *Star* said in an editorial. "But on almost every conceivable political question there

is room for conflicting ideas as to what constitutes the national interest." Dirksen
had failed his party, the editorial contended, and did not deserve to stay in party
leadership. "The role of a majority leader in Congress is to support the policies and
principles of the party in power. The role of the minority leader is to oppose the party
in power. Neither one can fulfill his obligation to the nation in any other way." But
that was simply not Dirksen's way, nor Mansfield's either.[7]

A week before Tom Dodd upset the Senate's delicate decorum, Washington was
stunned by news that South Vietnamese president Diem and his conniving, corrupt
brother, Ngo Dinh Nhu, who headed the regime's security forces, had been killed
during a successful military coup in Saigon. Immediately, it was reported that the
United States was "not unhappy over the move that toppled Diem." In fact, the Kennedy administration had encouraged the coup. Nevertheless, the majority leader
was shocked by the news, even though he had advised Kennedy in August 1963
that a future US role in South Vietnam must not be tied to Diem continuing in
office. Diem and his increasingly isolated and corrupt administration, Mansfield
told Kennedy, was beside the point. "Therefore, we may well ask ourselves, once
more," Mansfield wrote in a memo, "not the tactical question, but the fundamental
question: Is South Vietnam as important to us as the premise on which we are now
apparently operating indicates?" It was *the* important question. The way out of "the
bind" of continued and accelerated US involvement, Mansfield said, "is certainly
not by the route of ever-deeper involvement. To be sure it is desirable that we do
not spend countless American lives and billions of dollars to maintain an illusion of
freedom in a devastated South Viet Nam." South Vietnam was simply not critical to
American interests, but rather "peripheral to those interests." Mansfield would say
years later that he never stopped believing in Diem, but "once he was assassinated,
things went from bad—admittedly—to worse, and worse, and worse."[8]

On the day of Diem's murder—November 1 in Washington—Dirksen and Mansfield jointly sponsored an amendment to reduce the price tag on a contentious
foreign aid bill that had paralyzed the Senate for several days. Dirksen joked that
because action on the legislation was taking so long, he envisioned senators "in their
red flannel pajamas" sitting with their grandchildren in front of the Christmas tree
mumbling to themselves "we didn't finish foreign aid." Instead, the leaders practiced
political realism in cutting the budget Kennedy wanted, which some key senators
thought was too expensive and others thought too spare. Mansfield said he and
Dirksen were acting to head off "random, disjointed, and haphazard reductions of

unknown depth, carrying unknown and uncertain dangers to the nation." As was typical with many Mansfield-Dirksen compromises, no one was completely happy, but an important budget was approved with bipartisan support. The legislation was the last substantive Senate act of Kennedy's presidency.[9]

—

United Press International posted the first bulletin at 1:34 P.M. eastern time: "Three shots fired at President Kennedy's motorcade today in downtown Dallas." The Senate chamber was nearly empty at that hour, but as word spread, senators came to the floor and clustered around Mansfield and Dirksen. Minutes earlier, after a whispered conversation with a reporter, Mansfield had muttered, "This is horrible. I can't find words." Dirksen's initial reaction was "Oh, God. This is the most distressing thing that could ever happen. I am shocked." As the minutes ticked by, the uncertainty grew. At 2:16 P.M. eastern time, Mansfield, surely knowing that the president and Texas governor John Connally had both been shot, took the floor and spoke of "a tragic situation" now confronting "the Nation and the free world." Referring to Kennedy, Mansfield said that extreme danger "confronts a good, a decent, and a kindly man." He and Dirksen agreed, Mansfield said, that it would be appropriate for the Senate chaplain to offer a prayer "in the devout hope that he, the Governor of Texas and others will recover." Reverend Frederick Brown Harris prayed that Kennedy's life might be spared in the face of "this sudden, almost unbelievable news." The prayer completed, Mansfield "unable to find words, motioned to Dirksen. The minority leader quietly moved an adjournment until noon Monday." The US Senate had prayed for the life of John Kennedy, unaware that he had died moments earlier in the emergency room of Parkland Memorial Hospital, the young and vigorous president, friend to both Senate leaders, felled at the hand of an assassin.[10]

After learning from wire service bulletins that Kennedy had died, for the only time anyone could remember, Mansfield asked an aide, "Get me a drink." He then retreated, alone, to his office, where he remained for thirty minutes. "Mansfield was very stoic," Charles Ferris remembered. "He kept his emotions very contained." But the majority leader who had come to the Senate with Kennedy and developed a deep affection for a fellow Irish Catholic, was shaken profoundly. "Jack Kennedy, I think, was like a son to him," Ferris said. Dirksen, for once, struggled to find words. "I'm a little bewildered as I know the nation and the whole world will be," he said. Of the assassin, Dirksen said, "the gates of hell must have congealed inside him." Kennedy was a victim of "a violent and indescribable hate." Mansfield, his wife, and his daughter met Air Force One at Andrews Air Force base when it returned from

Dallas carrying Kennedy's body and the strapping Texan who was now president. Sometime during the next chaotic hours, Jacqueline Kennedy personally phoned Mansfield requesting that he alone deliver a eulogy during the memorial service planned for the rotunda of the Capitol on Sunday, November 24. Mansfield agreed, but it was later determined that protocol required that someone from the House of Representatives also speak. Ultimately, Speaker John McCormack and Chief Justice Earl Warren also delivered remarks in the echoing space below the Capitol dome. Only Mansfield's words are remembered.[11]

Mansfield remembered working on his Kennedy eulogy in the post-midnight despair of Saturday, November 23. Francis Valeo, who wrote so many of Mansfield's speeches, also claimed a hand in the drafting, and apparently Rhode Island Senator John Pastore reviewed a draft. The drafting may have been a collective effort, and it likely was, but the inspiration for Mansfield's remarks, delivered next to the president's casket, was his alone. "The words uttered by Senate Democratic Majority Leader Mike Mansfield Sunday in his eulogy for President Kennedy are echoing through the country," the *Boston Globe* reported. "They were inspired by a poignant gesture by Mrs. Kennedy Friday." On the day of the murder, Mansfield apparently heard a broadcast news account of Jacqueline Kennedy placing a kiss on the lips of her dead husband and slipping her own wedding ring into his hand. That gesture became the connective theme of Mansfield's eulogy. Not everyone who heard the short speech, and hearing was difficult in the awful acoustics of the rotunda, was impressed with Mansfield's words or his use of repetition. David Ormsby-Gore, the British ambassador to Washington and a Kennedy friend, thought the four-hundred-word speech "absolutely appalling," and Treasury Secretary Douglas Dillon was said to have cringed inwardly. But Mansfield had written the eulogy for Jackie Kennedy and for history.[12]

There was a sound of laughter and in a moment, it was no more. And so she took a ring from her finger and placed it in his hands.

There was a wit in a man neither young nor old, but a wit full of an old man's wisdom and a child's wisdom, and then, in a moment it was no more. And so she took a ring from her finger and placed it in his hands.

There was a man marked with the scars of his love of country, a body active with the surge of a life far from spent and, in a moment, it was no more. And so she took a ring from her finger and placed it in his hands.

There was a father with a little boy and a little girl, and a joy of each in the other, and in a moment it was no more. And so she took a ring from her finger and placed it in his hands.

There was a husband who asked much and gave much, and out of the giving and the asking wove with a woman what could not be broken in life, and in a moment it was no more. And so she took a ring from her finger and placed it in his hands, and kissed him, and closed the lid of the coffin.

A piece of each of us died at that moment. Yet, in death he gave of himself to us. He gave us of a good heart from which the laughter came. He gave us of a profound wit, from which a great leadership emerged. He gave us of a kindness and a strength fused into the human courage to seek peace without fear.

He gave us of his love that we, too, in turn, might give. He gave that we might give of ourselves, that we might give to one another until there would be no room, no room at all, for the bigotry, the hatred, the prejudice, and the arrogance which converged in that moment of horror to strike him down.

In leaving us these gifts, John Fitzgerald Kennedy, President of the United States, leaves with us. Will we take them, Mr. President? Will we have, now, the sense and the responsibility and the courage to take them?

I pray to God that we shall and under God we will.

"I shall never forget Mike Mansfield's speech," Lady Bird Johnson wrote, "he, the most precise and restrained of men—repeated over and over the phrase 'and she took a ring from her finger and placed it on his hand.'" Albert Steinberg, a Lyndon Johnson biographer, believed that "Mansfield, in his loud, crisp voice with the Irish lilt" had "delivered a magnificent eulogy." And William Manchester, who interviewed the former first lady for his book *The Death of a President*, wrote: "Only Jacqueline Kennedy could judge Mike Mansfield, and she couldn't believe what she was hearing; she didn't know a eulogy could be this magnificent; looking up into his suffering eyes and his gaunt mountain man's face, she thought his profile was like a sixteenth-century El Greco. To her the speech itself was as eloquent as a Pericles oration, or Lincoln's letter to the mother who had lost five sons in battle. It didn't turn aside from the ghastly reality—'It was,' she thought, 'the one thing that said what had happened.'"[13]

With his final words still echoing beneath the dome, Mansfield walked the short distance to where Mrs. Kennedy was standing and gave her his copy of the eulogy. "You anticipate me," she said. "How did you know I wanted it?" Mansfield ducked his head slightly—bowed some said—and responded, "I just wanted you to have it."[14]

Dirksen offered his own tribute in the Senate on November 25, shortly after Kennedy's funeral. "The memory of John Fitzgerald Kennedy lingers in this forum of the people," Dirksen said. "Here we knew his vigorous tread, his flashing smile,

Senators Smathers, Humphrey, Mansfield, Kuchel, and Dirksen walk from the White House to the Cathedral of St. Matthew the Apostle for John Kennedy's funeral, November 25, 1963. (*Kennedy Presidential Library*)

his ready wit, his keen mind, his zest for adventure. Here with quiet grief we mourn his departure." Dirksen spoke for millions of Americans struggling to understand such a tragedy. "And why, in a free land, untouched by the heel of dictatorship and oppression, where the humblest citizen may freely utter his grievances, must that life be cut short by an evil instrument, moved by malice, frustration and hate? This is the incredible thing which leaves us bewildered and perplexed."[15]

A week after Kennedy's murder, President Johnson placed a telephone call to Mansfield during which he outlined his plans to create what became the Warren Commission, the blue-ribbon panel headed by Chief Justice Warren that investigated the Dallas crime. Before asking Mansfield's opinion of the idea, Johnson handed the phone to Secretary of State Dean Rusk, whose voice betrayed his concerns about the international and diplomatic ramifications of an investigation that leaked or failed to substantiate its findings. Rusk warned of the possibility of a "tremendous storm" before handing the phone back to Johnson. "Mr. President," Mansfield replied, "I think the idea is a solid one. I would suggest that you contact Dirksen. As far as I'm concerned you have my full support all the way, as always." Johnson then told Mansfield of a request from the Kennedy family—Robert Kennedy was the messenger—for temporary financial support from Congress to handle the deluge of condolence mail in the wake of the president's assassination. "I think we ought to do it," Johnson said, to which Mansfield replied, "I think Dirksen and I should co-sponsor it."[16]

Kennedy "was just on the verge of greatness," Mansfield would later say. "He had to feel his way. He had to inaugurate new policies; he had to tread new paths. And I think that if he had continued to be with us, in his second term he would have been one of the great Presidents of the United States and would have accomplished things which would have really paved the way to a better world, a more peaceful world, and a more understanding world."[17]

Now the majority leader Mike Mansfield had replaced had become the president of the United States. Dirksen's political world changed as well. He had enjoyed a warm and candid relationship with Kennedy, if not as close a friendship as Kennedy shared with Mansfield. Now Dirksen would have a true friend in the Oval Office, a fellow political dealmaker, someone who knew the Senate and Washington, and Lyndon Johnson wasted no time cementing his old relationship with Dirksen. "Every chance you get to say, like you did this morning," Johnson told Dirksen on November 23, "and let them know you're part of this partnership and your country comes first would be good."[18]

—

In the vast Mansfield archive, no correspondence is more poignant or more personal than the letters Jackie Kennedy wrote the majority leader after the death of her husband. Maureen and Mike Mansfield called on Mrs. Kennedy a few days after the president's funeral and before Jackie had moved from the White House. She responded to their thoughtfulness with a handwritten note: "I do thank you and Maureen for coming to see me. The only time things are better is when I talk about Jack—and you and he were so close and built so much together. I will always care terribly about your happiness. Love, Jackie." Ten years after the Kennedy assassination, the nation paused to remember the awful day in Dallas. Jackie Kennedy was watching an evening news program with her son when Mansfield's eulogy was rebroadcast. She commemorated the occasion with another handwritten note to Mansfield: "Other people will remember Jack all this weekend—but yours was different—because you are different. There is no one on this earth like you. Thank you dear Mike, with all my heart. Please forgive the incoherence of this letter. It is written with much emotion—and all my love—Jackie."[19]

7 AN IDEA WHOSE TIME HAS COME

Good God, Lyndon's president. He's gonna pass a lot of this
damn fool stuff.

—MISSISSIPPI DEMOCRAT
JAMES EASTLAND

Lyndon Johnson dreamed of the presidency, lusted for it, and seeing his goal slipping
away, settled in 1960 for what he expected to be the dead end of the vice presidency.
Now tragedy had placed him where he was certain destiny intended him to be. Two
days after Kennedy's funeral Johnson stood before the packed chamber of the House
of Representatives, the room "bright in the glare of television lights," and made
John Kennedy's legislative agenda his own. Many of the hardened, even cynical
politicians listening to the accidental president were moved to tears by Johnson's
call to translate Kennedy's "ideas and ideals" into action, Tom Wicker wrote in
the *Times*. Johnson endorsed nearly the entirety of Kennedy's agenda but made
his most dramatic appeal for the passage of a civil rights bill that had been limping
along for months. "No memorial oration or eulogy could more eloquently honor
President Kennedy's memory than the earliest possible passage of the civil rights
bill for which he fought." It was time, Johnson said, to stop talking of equal rights—
"we have talked for one hundred years or more"—now "is the time to write the next
chapter—and write it in the books of law." Wicker noted the chamber "broke into a
storm of applause—though some southern members significantly withheld theirs."[1]

Everett Dirksen called the speech "a very reassuring message to the country.
It is in the great American tradition for us to cooperate in order to see that there
can be an effective organization of the government." Johnson knew he had Mike
Mansfield's support to advance Kennedy's agenda, but he also knew he must secure
Dirksen's support, especially if a civil rights bill were to have a chance. His wooing

of the minority leader was nonstop, with many newspapers the next day printing photos of the new president and the Illinois senator literally holding hands as
Johnson paused to talk with Dirksen as he departed the House after his speech.[2]

~

Having realized his dream, Lyndon Johnson could apply his vision, as biographer Robert Dallek has said, to "picking up where FDR's New Deal had left off—
expanding prosperity, opening doors of opportunity for poor folks, and honoring the
country's rhetoric about equal treatment under the law." Johnson had an expansive,
even wildly ambitious agenda, pushing forward but also expanding on John Kennedy's aspirations and attempting to construct his own Great Society. And, like
any politician, Johnson could not stop thinking about an election in less than a
year when he expected to confront a rising tide of conservatism in the Republican
Party in the person of Barry Goldwater. Goldwater detested Johnson, "thinking
him corrupt and unfit," and for his part, Johnson was stunned that the Republican
Party would hand its nomination to a reactionary ideologue. The two men would
largely define the political direction of their parties for the next generation, but as
1964 unfolded Johnson was more focused on working the political levers on Capitol
Hill, pushing his and Kennedy's agenda, and passing a civil rights bill that would
require the Senate's leaders, Mansfield and Dirksen, to confront and overcome the
longest filibuster in Senate history.[3]

As much as Johnson believed that he had long ago mastered the politics of Congress, as a new president he was "overwhelmed with doubt and a sense of inad-
equacy," as biographer Randall Woods has noted. In early December 1963, Johnson
complained to *Washington Post* publisher Katharine Graham that Congress was
loafing, off on holiday. "Russell was in Winder [Georgia], Dirksen was in Illinois,
Humphrey was on the beach, Mansfield was on the beach in Miami . . . Charlie
Halleck was out hunting turkey." No one was helping him, Johnson complained.
"And they're not passing anything! And they're not going to!" As for his civil rights
bill, Johnson was worrying about how slowly it would move in the House and then
in the Senate, and he was sure his old friend and mentor Dick Russell was ready to
gum up the works. "He will screw them to death," Johnson said of the congressional
leadership, "because he's so much smarter than they are."[4]

Consequential and enduring legislation is frequently described as "sweeping,"
and the Civil Rights Act of 1964, containing eleven major titles, certainly deserved
that description. The legislation addressed uniform standards for registering voters
and eliminated many state-level provisions used in the South, and occasionally

elsewhere, that required voters to pass literacy tests. Discrimination based on race, color, religion, or national origin in public accommodations was outlawed. New powers were granted to the Justice Department and the attorney general to investigate, enforce, and intercede in cases where discrimination was alleged. The life of the US Civil Rights Commission was extended, and the Equal Employment Opportunity Commission established and authorized to investigate unlawful employment practices. The historic legislation, as is all too clear in the twenty-first century, did not eliminate racism in America, but it did, as Clay Risen has written, "reorient the country—both the government and the people—onto a path toward true racial equality."[5]

The path to the 1964 Civil Rights Act was a long, often violent one that involved a massive grassroots effort by Black Americans, civil rights and labor organizations, religious leaders, students, and vast numbers of citizens who longed to see advances toward racial equality. "But paradoxically," as Todd Purdum wrote in his history of the act, "the bill was proposed and passed mostly by men whose personal acquaintance with black Americans was limited to their own domestic servants and the leaders of a movement who had provided more impetus and historical argument for its fierce necessity. Its passage was, in that sense, all the more remarkable."[6]

—

As Lyndon Johnson surely knew, even as he complained about congressional inaction, Everett Dirksen and Mike Mansfield were no loafers. They were legislators.

Early in 1964, Dirksen was beginning the long and complicated political maneuvering that would take him from skepticism about Johnson's civil rights bill, particularly provisions dealing with discrimination in public accommodations, to hero for his role in securing passage of the legislation. The road Dirksen maneuvered was perilous and drew criticism from left, right, and center. Time and again Dirksen's motives and commitment would be questioned and his political strategy misunderstood. He came under intense pressure.

"There will be extensive demonstrations in Illinois," James Farmer, one of the major Black civil rights leaders said in February 1964. "People will march en masse to the post offices there to mail handwritten letters to Dirksen." Farmer promised, "We'll take whatever action is needed" to convince Dirksen and other senators to defeat a southern filibuster of the civil rights bill, end debate, and secure passage. The threats—or promises—of direct political action drew pushback. After reading Farmer's comments, a Billings constituent said in a telegram to Mansfield: "I was shocked and sickened at the stomach after reading the morning paper to find that a man had threatened the entire Senate of the United States if they did not silence their fellow members." Mansfield responded that he "had talked to Senator Dirksen earlier on this matter and expressed to him my extreme disapproval that such pressure had been applied. I want to assure you that to the best of my knowledge no Senator of the United States will be pressured on that basis." Dirksen bristled at both the criticism and the pressure. "In Dirksen's judgment," Neil MacNeil wrote, "he had been shabbily and unfairly treated" by Black leaders in Chicago during his 1962 reelection campaign. "I carried the flag in the Eisenhower administration for all civil rights legislation," Dirksen told the NAACP's Clarence Mitchell, and for his trouble he was now being portrayed as an opponent of civil rights. Mitchell was alarmed at Dirksen's anger toward Black leaders because, like Lyndon Johnson and Mike Mansfield, he knew that without Dirksen there would be no civil rights bill.[7]

When the Civil Rights Act arrived in the Senate on February 17, 1964, having passed the House a week before, Mansfield was ready. Despite his frequent claim that he was no expert in the Senate's complicated, often arcane rules, Mansfield had meticulously worked out his strategy to advance the civil rights legislation, knowing full well that Dick Russell, the wily leader of the segregationist bloc of southern Democrats was also ready. From his earliest days in the Senate in the 1930s, Russell had been an expert parliamentarian. As his biographer wrote, Russell "believed that knowledge was power and set out to learn the minutest details about the Senate's rules, procedures, and traditions." Additionally, Russell's principal southern allies, including James Eastland and John Stennis of Mississippi, Lister Hill of Alabama, and Allen Ellender of Louisiana, were skilled in the ways of the Senate, and particularly in the use of the filibuster. As Clay Risen has noted, "like the Confederacy during the Civil War" Russell and his troops "did not have to defeat their opponents outright, they just needed to draw out the fight long enough that the other side gave up." Mansfield and his allies, eventually including Dirksen, had to meet and overcome this powerful combination of Senate experience and intransigence, and because of Mansfield's commitment to openness and candor, do so without tricks, subterfuge, or misdirection. Success would require the skills of a juggler, the patience of a saint, and the stamina of a long-distance runner.[8]

Mansfield's first move was to stop the House version of the civil rights bill "at the door," in the parlance of the Senate, heading off automatic referral to the Senate Judiciary Committee, the bailiwick of Eastland and the burial ground of civil rights bills. Ordinarily, a bill from the House would be read twice by the clerk and referred to the germane Senate committee for hearings and action before coming back to the full Senate for a vote, but in this case referral of another civil rights bill to Eastland's committee would guarantee delay of the legislation and more than likely its ultimate defeat. As is typical of Senate procedure, Mansfield asked that the bill be read for the first time, then immediately objected to the second reading that would have led to a committee referral. Mansfield would hold the bill on the Senate calendar subject to action when he determined action was warranted. While unusual, Mansfield's action was not unprecedented and, in fact, he had informed Eastland of his plans well in advance. In explaining his approach and the need for the Senate to act on civil rights, Mansfield made one of the most important and eloquence speeches of his career.[9]

"The procedures which the leadership will follow are not usual," Mansfield told the Senate, "but neither are they unprecedented. And the reasons for unusual procedures are too well known to require elaboration." Ever senator knew the majority leader was referring to the ultimate deadly fate of a civil rights bill that went to Eastland's committee, and besides, Mansfield said, the issues addressed by the legislation had been "discussed and debated, not for a week or a month, but for years." It was time for action.

Demonstrating the transparency that Mansfield thought critical to Senate action, he spelled out his approach. "It is my intention to have the majority whip, the able Senator from Minnesota [Hubert Humphrey], together with the distinguished Senator from Washington [Warren Magnuson], the Senator from Pennsylvania [Joseph Clark], and the distinguished Senator from Michigan [Philip Hart] assume direct responsibility for the handling of this legislation on the floor. They will be ready to state the case for this bill and to answer the questions to which it may give rise."

Mansfield's choice of Humphrey as manager of the legislation was welcomed warmly by civil rights advocates who appreciated the Minnesota liberal's long commitment to the cause. The move was also critical to keep Mansfield in the position of an honest broker who could remain above the hourly wrangling over legislative details while keeping communication open with all Senate factions, particularly the southern opponents of civil rights legislation and Dirksen and those Republicans the minority leader might influence. Here again was an example of Mansfield, a politician with seemingly no ego and zero lust for the limelight, doing what was necessary to get the votes. Mansfield's speech on the Senate's duty to deal responsibly with the civil rights bill distilled all his beliefs about how the institution and its members should behave. It is worthy of quoting at length:

Speaking for myself, may I say at the outset that I should have preferred [that] the issue had been resolved before my time as a Senator, or it had not come to the fore until after. The Senator from Montana has no lust for conflict on this matter. Yet this question is one which invites conflict. For it divides deeply.

But, Mr. President, great public issues are not subject to our personal timetables. They do not accommodate themselves to our individual preference or convenience. They emerge in their own way and in their own time. We do not compel them. They compel us.

We look in vain if we look backward to past achievements which might spare this Senate the necessity of a difficult decision on the civil rights question. We hope in vain if we hope that this issue can be put over safely to another tomorrow, to be dealt with by another generation of Senators.

The time is now. The crossroads is here in the Senate.

To be sure, the issue will not be fully resolved by what we do today. Its resolution depends also on what is done tomorrow and on many tomorrows. Nor will the issue be fully resolved by the Senate or the Congress. Indeed, it will involve all Americans and all the institutions, public and private, which hold us as a society of diversity in one nation, and it will involve all for a long time to come. In truth, it is a universal issue which, for this nation, having begun with the Declaration of Independence and persisted through the decades, will hardly dissolve in the Senate of the 88th Congress.

Nevertheless, at this moment in the nation's history, it is the Senate's time and turn.

But, insofar as the majority leader is concerned, he must state to the Senate that it would be a tragic error if this body, as a whole, were to elect the closed-eyes course of inaction. That course, Mr. President, would disclose a cavalier disinterest or a legislative impotence on this issue, and either would be completely inconsonant with the serious domestic situation which now confronts us.

It is bad enough to evade decision on any major proposal of any President. It is inexcusable in this issue, which has drawn a curtain of uncertainty and insecurity over the entire nation, and over which blood has already run in the streets.

In these circumstances, I cannot believe that this Senate will abdicate its constitutional responsibilities.

At this critical moment, the majority leader, for one, is not prepared to say to the President and to the courts: Resolve this present manifestation of the divisive issue of civil rights as best you can. We wish you well or we wish you ill. But most of all, in the Senate, we wish no part in the process.

If the Senate were to choose such a course at this time, Mr. President, the course of evasion and denial, we would leave this body a less significant and less respected factor in the Government of the United States than it was when we entered it.

I implore the Senate, therefore, to consider deeply the consequences of such a course, not only to the nation, but also to the reputation of the Senate, as one of the great institutions upon which the nation rests. And may I say, Mr. President, that when we have considered deeply, I do not believe that this Senate will choose the course of evasion and denial.

If we are to reach a point of decision in this matter, in the last analysis it will be not because of what the majority leader alone does or the majority leader and the minority leader jointly do or fail to do. It will be because the whole membership is prepared to look at the world and at the nation as it is, not the way we may wish for it to be. It will be because the members of this body are ready to face this decisive moment in the nation's history and the Senate's history. It will be because the members of this Senate, all the members, on both sides of the aisle, are prepared to assume full responsibility, along with their rights in the Senate—full responsibility for writing an honorable chapter in both histories, irrespective of what their views may be on this particular issue.

We will not write that chapter, Mr. President, if we dawdle, if we evade. And we cannot write that chapter on the basis of the Senate rules. We can write it only by facing the substance of the issue itself, by debating it and voting on it.[10]

Mansfield counseled senators not to search in Senate rules for a roadmap to consider civil rights legislation, but rather to search "in the Golden Rule," and he encouraged examination of "the dark chasm of ignorance and arrogance which divide, and . . . the slender bridges of understanding and humility which unite." Then, as if forecasting the long, often bitter accounting of race in America that still haunts the nation, Mansfield reminded the Senate: "An issue of this magnitude carries the accumulated action and neglect, the accumulated achievements and failures, the accumulated commissions and omissions of generations of Americans. And it will take, for many years, the combined contribution of all the sources of reason and unity within the Nation to bring the issue to adequate resolution."

Finally, Mansfield became specific with several of his Senate colleagues, calling on Republicans and Democrats—and particularly Dirksen—to bring their best to the coming debate.

> And, so, Mr. President, as we approach this issue, I appeal to the Senate to put aside the passions, the sectionalisms, and the inertia which may plague us. I appeal to the distinguished minority leader, whose patriotism has always taken precedence over his partisanship, to join with me—and I know he will—in finding the Senate's best possible contribution at this time, to the resolution of this grave national issue.

> I appeal to the Senator from Vermont [Mansfield's close Republican friend George Aiken] and the Senator from Iowa [conservative Republican Bourke Hickenlooper], whose many years of outstanding and exceptional service have given them a deep perception, not only of the needs of their States but of the needs of the Nation's progress. I appeal especially to the Senators from those States where this issue is not necessarily acute at the moment, to the Senators of many of the Western and Central States. I appeal to them to provide an active and objective participation, if not in terms of the future problems of their States, then on behalf of the Senate itself and on behalf of the Nation of which their States are an inseparable part.

> I appeal to the Senator from Illinois [liberal Democrat Paul Douglas], to the distinguished Senator from the State of Lincoln, to lend us not only of his profound convictions on human freedom but of his warm and compassionate nature to help close the wounds of division.

> And I appeal to the Senator from Georgia [Richard Russell], not as the leader of any bloc, not as an outstanding legislative tactician, but as the great American and the great Senator which he is, and I beseech him to give us not only of his immense parliamentary capacity but even more of his legal wisdom and of his heart in order that this Senate will be remembered, not for what it did not do, but because of what it did for the Nation.

> And, finally, Mr. President, I appeal to every Member of this body to bring to this issue, when it is before the Senate, all the resources of wisdom, courage, perseverance, and understanding, so that we may, with mutual restraint and in all humility, fashion a contribution to the freedom, order, and well-being of American life which is worthy of ourselves, of the Senate, and of the Nation.[11]

At that time, Dirksen, still coy about how far he was willing to go to help Mansfield and still expressing concern about how the legislation would address public accommodations, offered encouragement. He would, Dirksen said, "cooperate in every possible way, consonant with my duty to render an independent judgment, not for one group but for all the people." He was "keeping an open mind."[12]

Compounding his role as legislative strategist, Mansfield also had to control nearly constant rumors, including a report that a deal had already been struck between the White House and southern Democrats to water down the legislation to forestall a filibuster. "There is absolutely no deal of any kind. That's all poppycock," Mansfield said. Dirksen agreed. "I have no reason to believe there has been any deal," he said. The civil rights bill now hung in a kind of procedural limbo, awaiting action, certain to be filibustered, as Mansfield and his lieutenants plotted the moment to make the bill the pending business of the US Senate.[13]

Mansfield also moved immediately to reassure Dick Russell that during the pressure-filled weeks to come he would not blindside the influential Georgia senator. "On Wednesday, February 19, 1964, I met with Senator Russell relative to the Civil Rights Bill," Mansfield wrote in an after-action memo for his files. Mansfield made five points during the meeting that took place in his office: (1) he would keep Russell "informed fully"; (2) he was trying to do "what is best for the President, the Senate and the party"; (3) he wanted Russell's "advice and help"; (4) failure to pass "some reasonable legislation" would be a major political setback for Lyndon Johnson; and (5) pressure tactics directed at senators supporting or opposing a filibuster were "threats to the integrity of the Senate." Mansfield twice asked Russell whether he would attempt to delay action on pending tax cut legislation in order to delay action on civil rights. Russell twice said "no." Mansfield then told Russell precisely what his next move would be—placing the bill on the Senate calendar. "I informed him that I would give him plenty of notice of any move I would make; that the cards would always be on the table," Mansfield recorded. "[Russell] said he appreciated that and since I have been Leader, he has had no 'guard' on the Floor, indicating that he had full confidence that I would do nothing untoward nor questionable and on that note the meeting broke up." Mansfield told his biographer that he "kept Russell informed of every move we made on the civil rights bill. I don't think he took me too seriously at first, but he did with the passage of time. [There were] no back strokes, no hidden areas." The candor and straightforwardness were quintessential Mansfield.[14]

Meanwhile, intense pressure continued to squeeze Dirksen from both left and right. Civil rights leaders pressured the minority leader and protesters picketed his home, a tactic Mansfield characterized as "not beneficial." Russell hoped the protests would backfire and push Dirksen in the direction of the southern Democrats,

Georgia's powerful, segregationist Democrat Richard B.
Russell led the Senate's anti–civil rights Southerners.
(*US Senate Historical Office*)

yet Dirksen was offended but unmoved in his determination to conduct his own deliberate consideration of the civil rights bill. Dirksen also received pressure from the press. The *Chicago Tribune*, the influential newspaper voice of the heartland that was often lukewarm at best about Dirksen's political flexibility, constantly found ways to object to the House-passed legislation. One *Tribune* editorial headlined "The Commissars" trashed Title V of the bill, the section dealing with the federal Commission on Civil Rights, as little more than American communism. The editorial quoted segregationist Virginia Congressman William Tuck as saying the commission would "turn loose on the people of the nation a swarm of investigators, detectives, hawkshaws, and inspectors with unlimited authority to inaugurate inquires, to harass the people, to issue subpoenas, to bring miscreants before federal judges and have them enjoined, fined, and imprisoned."[15]

Republican liberals in the Senate were also pushing Dirksen for a firm commitment of support. In partial response, Dirksen borrowed a page from Mansfield's strategy and appointed his whip, liberal California Senator Tom Kuchel, to manage the Republican side of the civil rights bill. Every move, even minor ones, involved complications. Kuchel's role was viewed with skepticism by many Senate conservatives, while Republican liberals, eager for movement, complained of a lack of coordinated strategy in a barely veiled criticism of the majority leader. By one account, Republican liberals, "yet to be convinced that Mansfield will fight to the bitter end for a strong bill," were close to fracturing the pro–civil rights forces. Dirksen had also to be mindful of the House-Senate dynamic. The senior Republican on the House Judiciary Committee, William McCulloch of Ohio, had played a pivotal role in House approval of the civil rights bill and had extracted commitments that his handiwork would not be compromised to end a Senate filibuster. This wicked mix of competing and overlapping interests stood in sharp contrast to Russell's unified southern bloc, leading columnists Roland Evans and Robert Novak to suggest, "Thus all the ingredients for a nasty brand of personal competition are present among the leaders of the Senate's bi-partisan civil rights bloc. This is precisely the recipe that, if allowed to cook on a hot political stove, could possibly lead to a Russell victory."[16]

Mansfield was also hearing from his voters. A Eureka, Montana, constituent wrote, "It is my firm conviction that the Civil Rights Bill is a radical, unconstitutional and thoroughly unacceptable proposal, in that it will destroy the basic rights of all individuals through federal intervention." A couple from Billings told Mansfield, "Individual freedoms cannot be removed, either collectively or one at a time, without leading us along the road to socialism which will enslave us all, black and white alike." In what was clearly a coordinated lobbying effort, several letters to Mansfield in early 1964 used the same language: "The Civil Rights Bill before the Senate now, is 10% civil rights and 90% take-over of all activities of life." Always attuned to home-state sensibilities, Mansfield prepared a summary of the bill, "The Civil Rights Bill and Montana." Not altogether correctly, this summary dismissed the legislation's impact on Montana "because in the first instance there is no problem of discrimination in Montana."[17]

Seemingly immune to criticism of his strategy and undeterred by the widespread skepticism about the likelihood of success, Mansfield pressed on, systematically clearing the Senate calendar of pending business. Ignoring advice from President Johnson that he immediately take up the civil rights bill, he kept everyone talking about the path forward, encouraging and facilitating working groups that included Attorney General Robert Kennedy and his staff, Republicans, and Humphrey and his team. He maintained a laser-like focus on Dirksen and those Republicans the minority leader could influence, knowing that without Dirksen's eventual active engagement he could not create a sufficiently large bipartisan coalition to defeat a filibuster; and he refused Johnson's advice to keep the Senate in round-the-clock session as a tactic to wear down Russell and his troops.

"I am not going to turn the Senate into a circus," Mansfield said when challenged about his rejection of all-night or even late-night sessions. The dignity and respectability of the Senate would be tarnished by news accounts of elderly, unshaven senators padding about in bedroom slippers, napping on cots in the cloakroom, or answering quorum calls in their pajamas. "He just thought it was senseless to do it," Charles Ferris remembered of the demand for around-the-clock sessions, "and ineffective in passing the legislation. There is a natural rhythm to an event of this magnitude and the all-night sessions would have worked against the passage of the strongest bill possible. It also demeaned the dignity of the Senate." President Johnson, of course, disagreed, bitterly criticizing Mansfield in a telephone call with his chief congressional lobbyist Lawrence O'Brien. "I just want to be sure the attorney general approves of this," Johnson said of Mansfield's strategy. "Because I sure don't. And if they agree with him, all right. But my judgment is they ought to start right out going around the clock until they get it." Robert Kennedy and other civil rights strategists did agree with Mansfield's approach, but it hardly mattered since the decision was nonnegotiable. "He could hardly abide Mansfield and Humphrey's refusal to follow in his footsteps," Clay Risen wrote of Johnson's reaction to the Senate strategy. "They were charting their own path, and only time would make clear whether it was the right one."[18]

Lyndon Johnson receives, and is due, great credit for his determination to pass a meaningful civil rights bill in 1964, but Johnson was also extraordinarily concerned that should a bill fail or be compromised to insignificance, he would receive the blame, a failure that would certainly reflect poorly on his presidential election plans. Therefore, Johnson could not help himself. He wanted to determine Senate strategy but also have plausible deniability for doing so. "Be *awful* careful," he admonished Humphrey about implying that the White House was calling the shots for the Senate. At the same time, he encouraged Humphrey, saying you have to "get" Dirksen, a reality Humphrey certainly understood. After Humphrey praised Dirksen's patriotism on a Sunday-morning interview program, Johnson called him. "Boy, that was right. You're doing just right now. You just keep doing that. Don't let those bomb throwers . . . talk you out of seeing Dirksen," Johnson said. "Ev is a proud man. So don't pull any damn protocol. *You* go see *him*. And don't forget that Dirksen loves to bend at the elbow. I want you to drink with him until he agrees to cloture and deliver me two Republicans from the mountain states." Then, in another breath, Johnson taunted Humphrey, "You have got this opportunity, Hubert, but you liberals will never deliver."[19]

On another occasion Johnson's desire to stage-manage literally everything found him insisting that Mansfield call *Washington Star* columnist Mary McGrory who, Johnson said, was complaining that the majority leader lacked a coordinated strategy to get a bill passed. Certain that Robert Kennedy was trying to embarrass him, Johnson speculated that McGrory was getting her information from Kennedy's Justice Department. Call McGrory, Johnson insisted to Mansfield, and tell her that the majority leader's strategy was "satisfactory to the White House, but that you make those decisions yourself." Mansfield responded, "Well, she hasn't been around to see me. She hasn't been around to see Hubert." Mansfield did talk to the columnist, who subsequently wrote a piece emphasizing how frustrated Johnson was about the Senate's pace and strategy on civil rights. An unnamed White House aide— almost certainly aide Bill Moyers—was quoted as saying Johnson "can suggest, but he cannot command. He is frustrated." Neither Johnson nor McGrory understood fully the wisdom of Mansfield and his strategy. He was determined to elevate civil rights by elevating the Senate. Mansfield wanted to pass a bill but not create a confrontation so bitter that it would poison relationships and permanently tarnish the Senate. As events played out. it became increasingly clear that Johnson's steadfast public support for the House-passed bill was his most important contribution to the civil rights battle. The blocking and tackling of Senate battlefield strategy was set by Mansfield and implemented by Humphrey. They now had to demonstrate patience while Dirksen's political flexibility allowed him to work his way to yes.[20]

⸻

If Johnson was trying to manage public and political expectations around the looming civil rights fight, Dirksen, laid up in early February when he was hospitalized with a bleeding ulcer, was doing the same. "How ya feeling?" Johnson asked when he reached a clearly groggy Dirksen in the hospital. "Well, I'm doing pretty good," Dirksen replied. "That ulcer hit me about midnight." Johnson, at his folksy best, told the minority leader, "Well, if you'd quit drinking that damn Sanka and get on a good Scotch whiskey once in a while." Dirksen chuckled, "Well, I think you got a point there." "What you need to do," Johnson continued, "is go out and get you about three good half glasses of bourbon whiskey, and then go down to the Occidental [the Washington, DC, steakhouse] and buy a red beefsteak and then get you a woman." Dirksen, completely devoted to his wife, only chuckled. Johnson then pivoted to ask about a nominee to the Federal Deposit Insurance Commission. The civil rights bill was not mentioned, perhaps a strategic decision by Johnson not to get ahead of Dirksen and his own process. "Go back to sleep and don't let anybody else call you," Johnson said as he signed off. "I just wanted to wish you well and tell you I was thinking of you and hoping you hurry up and get back." Dirksen spent his short hospitalization plotting his own way forward, still raising concerns about portions of the House bill, trying to keep GOP liberals on the nest, and working to convince Republican conservatives in the Senate that he was not caving to the Democratic administration.[21]

Dirksen was facing, in the words of columnist William S. White, "the most powerful and open pressure upon a single senator . . . ever applied in the memory of old Washington hands." Dirksen was a politician of conviction, honor, and courage, White wrote, but he needed room to operate politically; too much pressure would clearly be counterproductive. "If pressure groups, however earnestly motivated, can picket a senator in the exercise of his duty and conscience, as though he were some industrial plant refusing a wage increase, were does the picketing stop?" Dirksen biographer Byron Hulsey has written that Dirksen was holding his cards on the civil rights legislation so close that not even his staff was clear about his intentions, but the uncertainty—and the time involved—contributed to a larger strategy. Washington journalists and civil rights activists saw delay as a sign that failure loomed, but Dirksen needed time to persuade twenty to twenty-five of his Republican colleagues that a civil rights bill was more than a priority of a Democratic administration, but indeed was a national imperative. Dirksen was invoking the political equivalent of "all good things come to those who wait," an approach Mansfield clearly understood. As James Marlow reported for the Associated Press on February 21, Mansfield was asked how long a southern-led filibuster might last before an attempt was made to end it. His one-word answer: "Months."[22]

For nine days after its arrival in the Senate the House-passed civil rights bill resided in procedural purgatory. Mansfield moved to change that on February 26, when he asked to have the legislation read for a second time then placed on the Senate calendar, ensuring the bill would remain out of the clutches of Jim Eastland, the Judiciary Committee chairman. Russell, who knew Mansfield's request was coming, jumped immediately to his feet objecting with a point of order, and the Georgia senator was joined by a surprising ally, the iconoclastic Oregon liberal Wayne Morse. Russell, considering the subject, used an explosive word to characterize Mansfield's action—"Lynch law rather than a parliamentary law" was being practiced, he said, leading to destruction of Senate tradition. Morse, a fierce supporter of civil rights but a stickler for procedure, said bypassing the Judiciary Committee would preclude developing a detailed legislative record of the bill. Mansfield received a minor shock when another strange bedfellow, Dirksen, joined the naysayers, arguing that hearings were necessary to consider the impact of a fair employment practices commission that had not been included in the original administration bill. Mansfield's Montana colleague, Lee Metcalf, was presiding in the Senate and, as the *New York Times* reported, "reading from a typed sheet prepared in advance, ruled against the point of order, thus sustaining Mr. Mansfield." Russell challenged Metcalf's ruling and heated debate commenced.[23]

The Senate eventually upheld Metcalf's ruling by a comfortable fifty-four to thirty-seven margin, including twenty Republicans, handing Mansfield a win on "the first skirmish in the civil rights bill." It was evidence of strong, if not overwhelming bipartisan support for the legislation. After prevailing, Mansfield did a very Mansfield thing: he requested unanimous consent to have the civil rights bill referred to Eastland's committee on condition that it be returned the Senate in two weeks without changes. Mansfield may have been hoping the gesture would win over Alaska Democrat Ernest Gruening, who had supported sending the bill to committee and was an unsure vote to end a filibuster. Or just as likely, Mansfield may have been looking for a fair middle ground. In seeking unanimous consent, Mansfield said a legitimate argument had been made for hearings, albeit limited ones. All sides objected: Eastland argued against any time constraints on his committee, while liberal New York Republican Jacob Javits contended a vast committee record had already been developed during consideration of previous legislation. The session ended amid some confusion, but a strong civil rights bill was on the Senate calendar. News accounts noted the obvious: "Senate Southerners led by Russell are expected to mount an all-out filibuster once the bill comes up for debate."[24]

Lyndon Johnson, meanwhile, worried constantly about "Old Dick Russell" working against him. "He's the one I worry about," Johnson said, warning Humphrey in a phone call that if "you damned liberals don't get off your asses and do something, Russell is gonna wind up with your peckers in his pocket." Mansfield stuck to his plan: win over Dirksen and with bipartisan support defeat a filibuster and pass a bill. On March 9, shortly after noon, Mansfield requested unanimous consent to dispense with the reading of the Senate *Journal*. Russell objected and the clerk read it. When Mansfield formally moved to make the civil rights bill the Senate's pending business, the first of ultimately two filibusters against the civil rights bill officially began, since even the question of taking up the legislation was subject to "extended debate." Mansfield appealed simply for responsible behavior:

Now it is the time and turn of the Senate. Racial inequities are among the oldest and most dangerous faults in the structure of this Nation. What we do here in the 88th Congress will not, of itself, correct these faults, but we can and must join the wisdom—the collective wisdom of this body—to the efforts of others in this Nation to face up to them for what they are, a serious erosion of the fundamental rock upon which the unity of the Nation stands.

There is an ebb and flow in human affairs which at rare moments brings the complex of human events into a delicate balance. At those moments, the acts of governments may indeed influence, for better or for worse, the course of history. This is such a moment in the life of the Nation. This is that moment for the Senate. If ever the Members of this body have needed to strive to put aside personal advantage and partisan political considerations, and to seek the national good in its noblest terms, now is that time. I now move that the Senate proceed to the consideration of H.R. 7152, the civil rights bill.[25]

A month later, what some have termed a "phony" filibuster—a debate about debating—was still droning on, Mansfield and his staff estimated which senators would support a cloture vote. The calculation was not encouraging: 48 sure votes to end debate, 38 almost certainly opposed, and 14 uncertain, with 67 votes required to end the filibuster. Dirksen was listed on Mansfield's Senate vote tally sheet as "no." Yet, through the often-tedious debate that alternated between southern complaints that the Judiciary Committee had been bypassed improperly and substantive debate on the specifics of the legislation, Mansfield's grand strategy held. His decision to deputize Humphrey as the floor leader of the civil rights effort was affirmed time and again. The peripatetic Minnesotan confirmed his organizational genius, and even opponents of the bill were impressed by Humphrey's work ethic. Humphrey's commitment to the civil rights cause was beyond question, and in the Senate of comity and character Mansfield was trying to create, as historian Robert Mann has written, "even the most racist of southern conservatives found it impossible to dislike [Humphrey]." And Humphrey steeled himself to the task. "I truly did think through what I wanted to do and how I wanted to act . . . I made up my mind I would not lose my temper and that if I could do nothing else, I would try to preserve a reasonable degree of good nature and fair play in the Senate."[26]

On March 26, more than a month after the civil rights legislation landed in the Senate, Russell kept his commitment to Mansfield that he would not indefinitely debate the question of whether the Senate could even consider the bill. A motion to proceed to consideration passed with precisely the number of votes needed—sixty-seven—a victory for Mansfield but also a warning. "Voting to take up the bill was not an endorsement of it," Clay Risen wrote, "or even a vote on for cloture on the main filibuster yet to come." Mansfield also won victory when he defeated another effort by Morse to send the bill to the Judiciary Committee. The Senate deck was clear, but as the cagey Russell knew, the real fight was just beginning. "A battle has been lost," Russell said. "We shall now begin to fight the war."[27]

At the precise moment the Senate finally agreed to move to consideration of the civil rights bill, the nation's two most prominent Black leaders were watching from separate parts of the gallery. Martin Luther King Jr. and Malcolm X, the activist and Muslim minister, later held separate news conferences. As the *Detroit Free Press* reported, "The two Negroes differed both on their goals and on the means to achieve them. About the only thing they had in common was a desire to see the civil rights bill passed." King had words of praise for President Johnson and "courageous" senators in both parties who supported the legislation, while "Malcolm issued a thinly veiled threat to Mr. Johnson by warning that Negroes may abstain from voting in the presidential election this November" if there was no action on civil rights. The two men were captured in a photo awkwardly shaking hands, with Malcolm wisecracking to King, "now you're going to get investigated."[28]

One tactic of the pro–civil rights forces was to explain the legislation systematically and thoroughly, and at the same time actively engage opponents in real debate, an approach not always taken with previous civil rights bills. "This exercise seemed worthwhile for several reasons," Humphrey aide John G. Stewart wrote, "it put the proponents' case on the public record; it replied to many of the charges leveled by the Southern Democrats; it continued to generate news favorable to the civil rights cause and thereby encourage the people working in behalf of the legislation outside of Congress," particularly the diverse faith communities that rallied around the legislation. Nevertheless, this approach would not speed Senate consideration, which as April days slipped by on the calendar continued at a glacial pace, and still Dirksen remained noncommittal. A *Louisville Courier-Journal* headline summed up much of the attitude of official Washington: "Dirksen's Rights Strategy Baffles."[29]

By contrast, Humphrey's charm offensive directed at the minority leader was moving like a political blitzkrieg. "I was his Jiminy Cricket," Humphrey would later

It was clear from the beginning of the long debate over civil rights that Dirksen wanted to support a bill, but he had to persuade fellow Republicans to join him. Dirksen is pictured here in 1963 meeting with leaders of the March on Washington, including (left to right) Whitney Young, National Urban League; Dr. Martin Luther King Jr., Southern Christian Leadership Conference; Roy Wilkins, NAACP; Walter Reuther, United Auto Workers; and John Lewis, Student Non-Violent Coordinating Committee. (*Walter P. Reuther Library, Archives of Labor and Urban Affairs, Wayne State University*)

say of his relationship with Dirksen, "visiting with him on the floor, in the cloakroom, in the corridors and on the elevators. I constantly encouraged him to take a more prominent role, asked him what changes he wanted to propose, urged him to call meetings to discuss his changes." Humphrey's public courting of Dirksen was, some thought, shamelessly close to pandering. "On my first TV appearance I praised Senator Dirksen," Humphrey recalled, "telling the nation that he would help, that he would support a good civil rights bill, that he would put his country above party, that he would look upon this issue as a moral issue and not a partisan issue. I did so not only because I believed what I said, but because we also needed him ... we couldn't possibly get cloture without Dirksen and his help."[30]

It was an open secret that Dirksen, despite his public position of noncommittal, had prepared a raft of possible amendments—seventy in all—knowing that Lyndon Johnson was insisting there be no changes in the House-passed legislation. Historian Frank H. Mackaman has argued that Dirksen's stance was strategic, and his "reserve was calculated." The minority leader's flexibility was showing. He was trying out options and in doing so creating "room to move and, by testing the waters constantly, [Dirksen was able] to gauge the feelings of the key group of Republican senators who would need to end the filibuster." Dirksen stayed aloof from the drama on the Senate floor and worked with a team of lawyers in a small office tucked away on the third floor of the Old Senate Office Building, now the Russell Building. "Dirksen was nothing if not crafty," Mackaman wrote. He mastered the details of the legislation to the point he could recite much of it from memory. While other lawmakers operated at a conceptual level, Dirksen did the hard work of drafting and redrafting language. Thus, gradually things seemed to be moving. A bipartisan staff group met regularly. Dirksen began to talk more often to Robert Kennedy. More meetings were held on Dirksen's turf, a symbolic and practical acknowledgment that he was assuming a leadership role, perhaps the leadership role. "Let's not kid ourselves," one Democratic senator fumed. "This has become the Dirksen bill! I deplore it but that's it." Humphrey—and Mansfield—were unmoved. "I don't care where we meet Dirksen," Humphrey said. "We can meet him in a nightclub, in the bottom of a mine or in a manhole. It doesn't make any difference to me. I just want to meet Dirksen. I just want to get there."[31]

Ironically, a maneuver orchestrated by Russell opened the door to active collaboration between Dirksen and Mansfield. Georgia Democrat Herman Talmadge, at Russell's instigation, offered an amendment to expand the right to a jury trial for individuals accused of criminal contempt in federal courts. The move, designed to weaken the legislation, very much appeared to be a replay of a similar amendment offered during the Senate civil rights debate in 1957. "Given the history of 1957," John G. Stewart wrote, "Mansfield, Humphrey and Kuchel recognized at once that Russell had played one of his strongest cards. The Talmadge amendment appealed to all Southern Democrats as a way of limiting the federal government's role in enforcing the bill, but at the same time the amendment would likely win significant support among Republicans and some Northern Democrats by its attractiveness as a civil liberties issue." The amendment might well be approved, giving Russell a win while signaling weakness among the pro–civil rights forces. Stewart, who staffed the leadership meetings where a response was developed, observed that "the Talmadge amendment . . . represented a substantive issue likely to affect the distribution of forces within the Senate, a distribution which ultimately might decide the entire contest." Mansfield and Humphrey immediately decided to violate the "no amendment" pledge, offer their own jury trial language, and ask Dirksen to cosponsor the amendment with Mansfield. Wording was worked out quickly and

Dirksen presented the alternate version to the Senate. "I trust," Dirksen said, "it will be agreeable to everyone when it is finally called up for a vote."[32]

It would not be agreeable to Russell, of course, who realized a Mansfield-Dirksen united front was hardly in his interest. Russell did what he did best in such circumstances, he stalled, while Dirksen took an important step—a visit to Lyndon Johnson—the motives for which historians still disagree. Dirksen's message for the president, telegraphed in advance in comments to reporters, was simple enough: it was unreasonable to expect the Senate would accept the House version of a civil rights bill without amendments. "Now it's your play," Dirksen told the reporters, previewing what he intended to tell Johnson. "What do you have to say?"[33]

"Mike, what should I tell Dirksen when he starts trying to put me on the spot down here on this civil rights thing," Johnson asked Mansfield in a telephone conversation just before Dirksen arrived at the White House, "just work it out with the leadership?"

"That's right," Mansfield replied, "tell him I gave a report to you yesterday, that I told you that Dirksen and I are in constant contact and are working together agreeably and it would be your suggestion that he and I just keep working together and it's our responsibility now."

Johnson said he would reiterate to Dirksen that he was supportive of "a strong civil rights bill," but then he abruptly veered off to complain about the Republican leader's tough-guy comments to the press. "I don't know what's happening to him lately," Johnson said. "He's acting like a shit ass." Johnson also grumbled that Dirksen had criticized a recent photo of Johnson lifting his dogs by their ears, proof, some dog lovers contended, that Johnson was mistreating his hounds. "Oh, I didn't know he said that," Mansfield responded. "It's none of his damn business how I treat my dog," Johnson went on, "I'm a hell of a lot better to dogs and humans, too, than he is." Mansfield only chuckled. The whole business with his dogs, the president said, was a manufactured controversy and "too little a thing for a big man like Dirksen." The conversation abruptly returned to the civil rights bill and a discussion of the status of cloture and whether the Senate would try to cut off debate on the new jury trial amendment or on the entire bill. Mansfield said he preferred a vote on the bill but that Dirksen had balked, and the majority leader repeated again his mantra: "we've got to get those twenty-three to twenty-five [Republican] votes." Johnson ended the conversation by assuring Mansfield that he would tell Dirksen that he was not going to negotiate details of the civil rights bill from the White House, that he trusted Attorney General Kennedy, Mansfield, and Humphrey to work out the details. "Yes, sir," Mansfield said, "put it back on us and stroke his back."[34]

Johnson did not precisely follow Mansfield's suggestion. He gave not an inch to Dirksen's plea that the bill needed wholesale amendments. Some historians have suggested Dirksen blundered badly by offending Johnson and getting nothing for his visit. But it seems more likely that the wily old negotiator knew precisely what he was doing. By signaling publicly what he intended to tell Johnson, Dirksen sent a message to fellow Republicans: he was going to drive a hard bargain. And by having Johnson restate his commitment to the process Mansfield and Humphrey were following, Dirksen defined the shape of subsequent negotiations. "Such information was crucial to Dirksen's strategy with the recalcitrants in his own party," Mackaman wrote. This view is supported by a contemporary account of Dirksen's thinking. "For ordinary Republican Senators to have heard how strenuously Everett Dirksen has thought an issue through amounts to their having thought it through themselves," Murray Kempton wrote in the *Spectator*. Having pushed on Lyndon Johnson, Dirksen was now in a position to engage fully in the process to pass a bill that would garner widespread Republican support.[35]

Dirksen walked a political high wire as he entered negotiations. On one hand he acted tough, demanded amendments, and demonstrated to fellow Republicans that he was influencing the legislation as much as he possibly could. Yet, Dirksen had clearly concluded that he wanted, and for the sake of the Republican Party needed, to pass a bill. Dirksen brought all of his proposed amendments to the first negotiating session, but it soon became apparent that the parties were not really all that far apart on substance. "It was like labor negotiations," one participant said. "Everyone started out in adversary positions and overstated their cases. It took some time for it to become clear that they really weren't so very far apart." For seven weeks, even as the filibuster against debating the bill continued on the Senate floor, the detailed work continued out of sight, with Dirksen's staff, Mansfield's staff, and lawyers from the Justice Department meeting every morning. In the afternoon the most involved senators would huddle to get updates and make decisions. It was detailed, painstaking work, with almost all of the meetings occurring in Dirksen's office—"it was Dirksen who needed special attention and the limelight," Charles Ferris said. The majority leader thought nothing of making the small concession even when some of his colleagues objected. A genuine spirit of bipartisanship took over. Alfred Steinberg quoted one Republican senator as saying, "We knew Mike Mansfield well enough to know that his integrity was complete, and he would work out a fair bill and a strong bill."[36]

And Mansfield missed no opportunity to grease the bipartisan gears. On the last day of April, he addressed the American Good Government Society in Washington and lavished praise on Dirksen. "The Senate is one of the great institutions in the

Dirksen in his minority leader's office, where, in 1964, many key meetings were held to thrash out details of the landmark Civil Rights Act. (*US Senate Historical Office*)

nation," Mansfield said. "But the Senate functions, on occasion, in bizarre and almost incomprehensible ways, as you have undoubtedly noticed in connection with the current debate on civil rights. I am frank to admit that one of the strangest aberrations in Senate behavior is that the institution can get along without a Majority Leader, but it cannot possibly function without a Minority Leader. Moreover, it must be a Minority Leader of exceptional tact, forbearance and cooperativeness, a Minority Leader willing to put the basic operation of the Senate above all considerations of party." Dirksen was "a tower of national strength," Mansfield said, a "personal friend as well as a legislative colleague." Similarly, Hubert Humphrey later readily admitted his job amounted to "a public massage" of Dirksen's ego and an unabashed appeal to the minority leader's vanity. "The gentle pressure left room for him to be the historically important figure in our struggle," Humphrey wrote in his memoir, "the statesman above partisanship, the thoughtful architect, the master builder of a legislative edifice that would last forever. He liked it."[37]

Whether motivated by political necessity, ego, a genuine desire to place his stamp on a historic piece of legislation, or perhaps by all three, Dirksen's bipartisan political calculation in the spring of 1964 was astounding for one overridingly important reason. As the titular leader of the GOP, Dirksen's embrace and essential leadership on civil rights placed him squarely at odds with the man almost certain to be the Republican presidential candidate in the fall, and at the same time Dirksen was providing an enormous political boost to Barry Goldwater's Democratic opponent—Lyndon Johnson.

From the first moment of Senate consideration of the civil rights bill, Goldwater, armed with the legal analysis of a Yale Law School professor by the name of Robert Bork, had been among the most outspoken critics of the bill. The public accommodation section, Goldwater said in February, "would force you to admit drunks, a known murderer or an insane person into your place of business." And to Goldwater, fair employment opportunities meant hiring "incompetent" workers. Dirksen would eventually plead with Goldwater to reconsider his opposition—"you just can't do it," Dirksen argued, "not only for yourself, but you can't do it for the party"—but to no avail. Dirksen's willingness to oppose the presidential candidate of his own party on the highest-profile issue in the country remains a remarkable statement about the minority leader's conviction that the time had come for the Senate to address civil rights.[38]

Since the end of March, CBS News correspondent Roger Mudd had spent all his time covering the glacially slow pace of filibuster developments. CBS placed a camera outside the Capitol, and since cameras were not allowed in the Senate chamber, hired a sketch artist to create illustrations for Mudd's reports. He often filed a dozen or more radio and television stories each day during the run of the filibuster, and thanks to the "talent fees" broadcast reporters received for each piece aired, Mudd did quite well financially. To dramatize the length of the filibuster, CBS placed a large clock outside the Capitol registering the hours consumed by the debate. The attention from Mudd and other reporters covering the dilatory tactics of the anti–civil rights forces underscored not only what was at stake with the legislation, but also how determined Russell and his troops were to thwart the majority will of the Senate. As the filibuster groaned on and more sightseers descended on Washington, Roger Mudd, reporting from the Capitol steps, became a genuine Washington tourist attraction.[39]

Press attention was worrisome to the anti–civil rights forces, but Russell and his like-minded colleagues worried even more about the impact of a broad-based, grassroots coalition of religious leaders who were pressuring individual senators. The National Council of Churches spent $400,000 on the effort, a demonstration by mainline denominations of a level of political clout never before mobilized on such a scale. Ministers, priests, and rabbis wrote letters, participated in prayer vigils, made phone calls, and showed up in person to buttonhole senators. After conservative South Dakota Republican Karl Mundt, at best an uncertain supporter of the legislation, threw in with civil rights supporters on one key vote, he left the Senate floor muttering, "I hope that satisfies those two goddamned bishops who called me last night."[40]

The bipartisan negotiations over the civil rights bill were nearly unprecedented in Senate history to that time, ironically more like how major issues are handled in the Senate now than how they were typically addressed in the 1960s. "A kind of ad hoc committee [took] the place of a regular legislative committee," a procedure that left Russell livid and worried even some civil rights advocates. Russell complained that an unconstitutional "troika"—Dirksen, Humphrey, and Robert Kennedy—were short-circuiting the Senate's legislative functions, but still the negotiations ground on.[41]

From the beginning of the civil rights debate, dating at least to John Kennedy's push for legislative action after the showdown with George Wallace that forced the president to send National Guard troops to the campus of the University of Alabama, Mike Mansfield knew that the Senate itself was on trial over the question of how and whether it would address civil rights. As Humphrey aide John Stewart observed, "The power of the Southern Democrats, grounded firmly in the Senate's explicitly established right of extended debate, had been able to defeat or largely emasculate all earlier civil rights proposals. There was no compelling reason why their prior successes should not be repeated in 1964." Yet, failure to address the legitimate, historic, and widespread demands of Black Americans, and the millions of other Americans who also supported a strong legislative response to civil rights, might call into question the legitimacy of the Senate as an institution. Stewart, who was a daily participant in the legislative negotiations, has said there was genuine worry that "a massive outpouring of public sentiment against the institution itself might result in widespread civil disobedience in the District of Columbia, the intimidation of Senators, disruption of the public sessions, or even violence." Mansfield missed no opportunity to remind senators of their duty. It was critical, Mansfield said, to maintain the "stature of the Senate in this matter."[42]

With Dirksen now working with urgency and tenacity, the Southern forces pressed their position on the jury trial issue including "four drama-laden roll-calls," and lost. It was a win, albeit it a narrow one, for the bipartisan leadership. The two steps forward, one step back nature of the negotiations caused frayed nerves and at any number of points a belief that the entire civil rights effort would once again fail. One firsthand observer noted "the group started in the morning saying 'the bill is dead.' In the afternoon, the group was saying 'it's a fine bill.'" Ultimately, the extended process of talking, negotiating, and refining that gave Dirksen his maneuvering room—the approach Mansfield had insisted on from the beginning—worked. On May 13, "with the bourbon and the conversation both flowing," and after ten days of intense negotiations, Dirksen stepped out of his office to speak to waiting reporters. "We have a good agreement," he said of the full bill. Humphrey agreed. "We've got a much better bill than anyone dreamed possible," he said, and there was no backsliding on the House legislation. "In some places we've improved it," Humphrey said.[43]

Dirksen's imprint on the final version of the civil rights bill was both politically enormous and substantively minor. Dirksen would insist that his contributions had been substantive, but his own words belied the claim. "Well, there have been some modifications in language," Dirksen told reporters, "paragraphs have been transposed; there have been some shadings that we had to take account of; sometimes you delete a phrase; sometimes you had to add a phrase." Minnesota Republican Clark MacGregor, who helped craft the House bill, would later say Dirksen "felt he had to put his stamp of authority on a lot of little niggling amendments that really didn't amount to much, so that the bill would come into law as a Dirksen bill and more importantly, that he would be perceived as pouring the healing salve on the whole controversy."[44]

The bipartisan Senate civil rights agreement would be embodied in a Mansfield-Dirksen substitute for the House bill—so much for Johnson's determination that the House legislation not be amended—and while Dirksen was now completely on board, the Republican leader still had considerable work to do inside his own conference. Influential conservatives still needed to be satisfied if they were to ultimately provide the Republican votes needed to end the filibuster. Word reached Mansfield that Iowa's Bourke Hickenlooper, a senator with more seniority than Dirksen and always sensitive to slights real and perceived, was angry that his concerns were not being heard. Mansfield immediately phoned Hickenlooper with an invitation to come and discuss whatever was bothering him. Hickenlooper arrived to find several Justice Department attorneys in Mansfield's office, including Robert Kennedy's top deputy, Nicholas Katzenbach. Before Hickenlooper's arrival Mansfield admonished the lawyers simply to listen to the Iowan's concerns, agree where possible, but in no event to engage in a legal debate. "Hickenlooper was somewhat taken aback," Francis Valeo recalled, "by finding himself the center of attention in the Democratic leader's office and, unexpectedly, in the midst of the Justice Department's legal talent." Hickenlooper pointed out his concerns, most of which were minor, and left saying his proposed changes would make for a better bill but that Mansfield should not yet count him as a vote for cloture. The majority leader said he understood and promised that any amendment Hickenlooper or other conservatives wanted to offer to the Mansfield-Dirksen substitute would be given fair consideration. Amendments from conservative Republicans were eventually considered, as Mansfield had promised. None passed, and Hickenlooper voted against the bill on final passage, but critically he voted in favor of cloture.[45]

Lyndon Johnson, now confident that the Senate would pass a strong bill, called Dirksen to congratulate him, laying on the full Johnson treatment. "The attorney general said you were very helpful and did an excellent job," Johnson said, "and that I ought to tell you that I admire you, and I told him I had done that for some time." Dirksen mumbled his appreciation. "I talked to Dick this morning," Dirksen said of his conversation with the leader of the filibustering southern coalition, "and he gave me no comfort . . . we're going to keep the show going," he reported Russell as saying. Dirksen said he told Russell, "Dick, you're going to have to fish or cut bait because I think we have gone far enough, and I think we've been fair." Johnson, impatient for a decisive vote to end the filibuster, now accepted that Dirksen was working his magic. "We don't want this to be a Democratic bill we want this to be an American bill," Johnson said. "You're worthy of the Land of Lincoln," Johnson drawled, "and the man from Illinois is gonna pass the bill and I'll see that you get proper attention and credit." Dirksen, barely audible on the White House recording, said, "ah, thanks, bye."[46]

Richard Russell immediately recognized the bipartisan power of Mansfield and Dirksen and now knew that he was close to losing his war. Russell could hardly contain his anger. "Unless I am badly fooled," Russell groused, "[Dirksen] has killed off a rapidly growing Republican Party in the South, at least so far as his party's prospects in the presidential campaign are concerned." That turned out to be one of Russell's worst political predictions.[47]

There continues to be debate about the role Dirksen played in passing the monumental bill. Was he just out for personal political recognition? Was he motivated by a desire to reposition the Republican Party as broadly supportive of civil rights? Did Lyndon Johnson's persuasive magic bring Dirksen around? Or did Hubert Humphrey, with his flattery, patience, and organizational ability, manufacture an image that Dirksen was in effect writing a bill to which he made only minor adjustments? The simple answer is that Dirksen, like Mansfield, was a legislator. One aide described Dirksen's approach to legislation as that of "an activist in the middle," reminiscent of Mansfield's contention that enduring political change required broad consensus. Dirksen's goal, one observer remarked, "was a bill that would satisfy the vast majority of Americans, most of whom are somewhere in the middle on most political issues." Even the *Chicago Tribune*, often skeptical of Dirksen's willingness to work with the other party, acknowledged the minority leader's approach to the civil rights bill was in keeping with Dirksen's "familiar role—easing the path of a President, regardless of party label." Dirksen had helped John Kennedy and Mansfield with the Limited Nuclear Test Ban Treaty and UN funding, the newspaper recalled, now he was helping Johnson with civil rights. Readily admitting that "he is, without question, an extraordinary man, the newspaper concluded, "Beyond his "picturesque and determinedly flamboyant exterior, under an embroidered curtain of florid phrases, Dirksen is the calm and practical politician."[48]

The Senate drama surrounding the civil rights filibuster continued to the last moment. With nearly every senator in attendance, Mansfield began the debate on the cloture motion on June 10—the Senate was in the third month of consideration of a civil rights bill—by reading a letter from a Montana constituent, identified by Mansfield as a twenty-nine-year-old white woman, the mother of four children:

> At night, when I kiss my children goodnight, I offer a small prayer of thanks to God for making them so perfect, so healthy, so lovely, and I find myself tempted to thank Him for letting them be born white. Then I am not so proud, either of myself, nor of our society, which forces such a temptation upon us. And that is why I don't feel that this is a southern problem. It is a northern problem, a western problem, an eastern problem. It is an American problem, for all Americans.[49]

Richard Russell was unmoved by what he called Mansfield's "emotional appeal," an appeal that might be made, he said, for every "purely socialistic or communistic

system that would divide and distribute among all our people every bit of the property and wealth of the people of these United States." Senate approval of a civil
rights bill, Russell predicted, "will result in vast changes, not only in our social
order but in our very form of government." Humphrey then spoke briefly, recalling
King Henry V's "we band of brothers" speech before the Battle of Agincourt, and
finally it was Dirksen's turn.[50]

Dirksen was clearly not feeling well, having been laid low by a cold as well as a
flare-up of his ulcer, but in this career-defining moment, he was in prime rhetorical
shape. "Incredible allegations have been made. Extreme views have been asserted,"
Dirksen said. "For myself, I have had but one purpose, and that was the enactment
of a good, workable, equitable, practical bill having due regard for the progress
made in the civil rights field at the state and local level." The moment for action had
arrived, Dirksen said, paraphrasing Victor Hugo: "Stronger than all the armies is
an idea whose time has come."[51]

Lee Metcalf, presiding over the Senate, declared that time for debate on the
question of cloture had expired, and he called for the vote. As the clerk began the
roll call the gallery was jammed, but Mansfield said he had never heard the chamber
so quiet, the only sound the names of individual senators being called. The tally
mounted until there was a brief pause when the clerk reached the name of Clair
Engle, a fifty-two-year-old California Democrat. Recovering from brain surgery
and absent for weeks, Engle had insisted on returning to the Senate floor for the
critical vote. Unable to speak, sitting in a wheelchair, Engle struggled to raise a finger to his eye indicating his "aye" vote for cloture. Engle also supported the bill on
final passage. Six weeks later he was dead.[52]

Delaware Republican John Williams—reporters dubbed him "Whispering
Willie" because he rarely raised his voice—mumbled a quiet "aye," giving the
two-thirds majority needed to end the filibuster. Mansfield had at least one vote in
reserve, that of Carl Hayden, the octogenarian Democrat from Arizona. Hayden,
who in thirty-seven years in the Senate had never voted for cloture, waited out the
roll call in the cloakroom after pledging that he would vote to cut off debate, but only
if his vote was essential. It was not, and Mansfield told him, "It's all right, Carl. We're
in." Hayden voted no on cloture. The final count was seventy-one to twenty-nine,
four more votes than necessary. This historic example of Senate bipartisanship
was the first defeat ever of a filibuster against a civil rights bill—eleven times
before the filibuster had killed bills—and only the sixth time to that point that
the Senate had voted on cloture. Dirksen had worked his magic. Twenty-seven of
thirty-three Senate Republicans voted with their leader.[53]

There were now more amendments to consider and dispose of, and North Carolina Democrat Sam Ervin mounted a pointless post-cloture filibuster that irritated nearly everyone, but final passage of the Civil Rights Act of 1964 came on June 20, the eighty-third day of debate. The marathon of speeches and maneuvers consumed 534 hours, 1 minute, and 51 seconds. The final vote was seventy-three in favor, twenty-seven opposed. It was, said Mansfield, Everett Dirksen's "finest hour . . . the Senate and the whole country are in debt to the Senator from Illinois." Mansfield also praised the leadership of Humphrey and Republican whip Thomas Kuchel, but quickly added there was "no room for unwarranted sentiments of victory" and there should be "no sense of triumph, but a profound humility" among those had worked on and supported the legislation.[54]

As Mansfield intended and was totally comfortable with, the laurels attached to Dirksen. He graced the cover of *Time*, and the *Chicago Defender*, the world's largest Black-owned newspaper, went from Dirksen critic to praising him for "his generalship" in passage of the most important civil rights measure "since Reconstruction." A headline in the *Daily Press* of Newport News, Virginia, read, "Dirksen Given Major Share of Credit for Civil Rights Bill Success." A *Kansas City Star* editorial claimed Dirksen's "leadership performance . . . on behalf of the civil rights bill was one of the finest we have ever seen on Capitol Hill." Roy Wilkins, the executive secretary of the NAACP and one of the most respected civil rights leaders, wrote Dirksen, admitting he had been wrong in thinking the minority leader would end up gutting the legislation. The strong vote for cloture, Wilkins told Dirksen, "tended mightily to reinforce your judgment and vindicate your procedure." The NAACP's Washington lobbyist, Clarence Mitchell, also long skeptical of Dirksen's commitment to the legislation, gushed his congratulations: "It's simply fantastic," Mitchell said. "[Dirksen] worked steadily and effectively for the bill. No one deserves more credit from our point of view." The columnists Evans and Novak agreed. "Of all the heroes who made it happen, Dirksen stands the highest."[55]

Mansfield, consistent in his view that the only thing that mattered was getting the votes, told his biographer years later that "Dirksen was in large part responsible for the passage of the Civil Rights Act, and I'm not denigrating Hubert Humphrey who did a superb job, but you had to get the votes. Dirksen was the one who had to get the votes. It took a long time, made many visits to his office, did so deliberately, wanted to." Asked by Don Oberdorfer about criticism he received from fellow Democrats for ceding so much control to Dirksen, Mansfield was at his most succinct: "Yeah, I was after the votes, not the publicity. And we got them."[56]

The House of Representatives concurred rapidly with the Senate's version of the civil rights bill. On July 2, before television cameras in a packed East Room of the White House—Dirksen sat in the front row next to Bobby Kennedy—Lyndon Johnson signed the legislation. "Let us close the springs of racial poisoning," Johnson said before handing out seventy-five pens to Dirksen, Humphrey, Kennedy, Charles Halleck, Dr. Martin Luther King Jr., and a score of others. Among the many photographs of the historic event is one of Dirksen and Humphrey, surrounded by a scrum of other politicians, hovering over Johnson's right shoulder as he signed the act. Mansfield is nowhere to be seen. (Mansfield also managed to evade the cameras during a celebratory gathering in his own office immediately after the civil rights legislation passed the Senate.)[57]

In their account of Johnson's presidency, published in 1966, the columnists Roland Evans and Robert Novak offered what became conventional wisdom: Lyndon Johnson was the ultimate hero of the epic civil rights struggle in the Senate, exerting "control over Congress with no thought of compromise." The historic milestone was achieved, Evans and Novak suggested, because Johnson's "political imperatives as a *Southern* President foreclosed compromise, whereas Kennedy's would not have." The journalists further speculated that Richard Russell's filibuster would likely have ended sooner had Mansfield "ordered around-the-clock sessions as Johnson desired." In defeat, Russell also gave Johnson the credit for steamrolling the southern roadblock to Senate action on civil rights. "You know," Russell said, "we could have beaten John Kennedy on civil rights, but not Lyndon Johnson." The emphasis by journalists at the time and some scholars since on Johnson's role in civil rights legislation reflects, at least in part, a tendency in matters of complicated legislation to overemphasize the presidency and minimize the role of Congress. The president is, after all, a single well-known person and therefore his actions are easier to describe, or perhaps amplify, than are the lengthy, confusing actions of Congress that always involve multiple personalities. Greater historical perspective on the events of 1964 leads to a more nuanced conclusion about the president's role in passing the Civil Rights Act.[58]

Arguably Johnson's greatest contribution to the passage of the legislation was not exercising "control over Congress," which Johnson was unable to accomplish despite his desire to do so, but rather the unstinting public support the president provided to the legislative effort. After Kennedy's death, Johnson made the civil rights issue his own and elevated the national consciousness about racial equality in a way no president had before, or arguably has since. Yet, without the strategy devised by Mansfield and implemented by Humphrey, and without the vigorous efforts of Dirksen to create a political environment where fellow Republicans could support the legislation, the Senate may well have failed, as it had so many times before. Passage of the legislation was, as Humphrey aide John Stewart concluded—and Stewart was a firsthand observer at every significant moment in the long battle—"a striking vindication of the strategy which the Democratic party leaders began devising a year earlier, as well as the tactical decisions which had been made in the course of the debate itself."[59]

Mansfield's understanding of the need to create a political process—one that was fair, candid, and inclusive—was essential to the outcome. The majority leader knew the ultimate goal had to be defeat of a filibuster, but defeating southern obstruction required elevating the Senate rather than fracturing the brittle norms and traditions that define the institution. Mansfield's insistence that the Senate and its individual members had to function responsibly, civilly, and procedurally in order to deal with an enormous issue of overriding national importance remains an enduring example of both principled and effective political leadership. As Stewart has written, "The Senate had not merely survived its most notable institutional challenge of the post-war era, but its supposed outworn and unworkable procedures never looked better [than] when the Southern Democrats were beaten at their own game." At the same time, the Dirksen-Mansfield commitment to bipartisanship, a bipartisanship where the majority frequently deferred to the minority, remains historic.[60]

—

While the praise rained down on Dirksen and columnists assessed the historic importance of the Senate action on a civil rights bill, Mansfield continued to act in a manner that he hoped his colleagues would emulate. He wrote a thank-you letter to every senator.

> We have come through a most trying period in the Senate. In retrospect, the issues were such that they might have opened schisms which would have been years in closing. That did not happen, and I want you to know how grateful I am for the help, the understanding and the cooperation which you gave to me in striving to prevent it.
>
> The character of the Senate's handling of this issue, I believe, will mean a great deal to the nation. I know that it meant a great deal to me personally. Members, regardless of views on the substance of the measure, treated me with the utmost kindness and consideration and I am deeply appreciative.[61]

Democratic leader Mike Mansfield and Republican leader Everett Dirksen developed
what Mansfield termed "a dream relationship." (*Archives and Special Collections,
Mansfield Library, University of Montana*)

Responses to the majority leader's letter came from both supporters and opponents of the Civil Rights Act, with nearly all praising the tone Mansfield had insisted
upon establishing and the leadership he provided the Senate. "Permit me to acknowledge and thank you for your letter," Richard Russell wrote. "The long fight was indeed
trying and I am grateful indeed that it did not leave any more permanent scars than
it did. This is in large measure due to your patience and understanding and the complete confidence which all the members of the Senate have in your sense of fairness."
Georgia's Herman Talmadge, another opponent of the legislation, wrote, "Thanks
to your effective operation of the Senate under such conditions with no more rancor
than we had and with the esteem and affection of every member of the Senate which
you have obtained this was an outstanding accomplishment. I know of no legislator
in this century who has been more beloved by his colleagues than you. I am proud
of your friendship and leadership." Similar letters came from southern Democrats
Russell Long, John Sparkman, and Olin Johnson, while Nebraska's Roman Hruska,

one of the Republican conservatives Dirksen brought around, wrote, "Dear Mike—your restraint and forbearance during those trying weeks were remarkable. In spite of decided differences in our respective views and convictions, my heart often went out to you for the bitter torment you must have suffered so often."[62]

Liberal New York Republican Jacob Javits wrote Mansfield: "In the first place, the Bill was a triumph of bipartisanship; secondly, it was a triumph of Senate personalities, and this is where you shone, for you knew when to speak and when to refrain from speaking. . . . Your hand at the controls was historic in its import, and your relation and confidence with Everett Dirksen were so strong as to bring within their influence Hubert Humphrey."[63]

Frank Lausche, an Ohio Democrat often disdainful of party considerations, wrote Mansfield: "The credit for what has been achieved while it has gone to others, in my opinion mainly belongs to you. If it had not been for your gracious and temperate consideration of the individuals who were deeply involved in the controversy, a split in the Senate might have occurred which would have been most damaging. You acted as a mediator in a most noble fashion; you kept tempers from breaking loose into violence." Humphrey, increasingly mentioned as the favorite to become Johnson's vice-presidential running mate, wrote Mansfield, "You are without a doubt the most unselfish, kind, and considerate man that I have ever known. It is a rare privilege to be associated with you, and I am eternally grateful for the opportunities that you have given me to make some contribution to our country."[64]

It was not in Dirksen's nature to write letters to colleagues, as Mansfield often did, but his heartfelt response to Mansfield's note underscores the level of personal affection and political partnership that had developed across the Senate's center aisle. "I don't know what we would have done about the civil rights struggle if it had not been for your humility, your understanding, your self-effacement and your appreciation of every problem as it arose," Dirksen wrote. "When all is said and done you are the one who should have had the lion's share of the credit because you are the Majority Leader and because you cooperated so superbly at every step of this tortuous road. You will never know how deep my appreciation is and my admiration and respect for you."[65]

Mansfield's closest Senate friend, Vermont Republican George Aiken, may have come closest to capturing the sentiment about Mansfield inside the Senate club: "The fact remains that those of us who were in on the Conferences . . . know full well that without your leadership and the esteem in which you are held, particularly by Republican Senators, this bill would not have been passed. Unfortunately, the public and the press is unaware of the leadership you took in this legislation."[66]

Hundreds of letters came to Mansfield's office from New York, Wyoming, Alabama, California, Kentucky, Georgia, Illinois, Nebraska, even British Columbia. The union leaders of the AFL-CIO wrote to congratulate Mansfield, as did church groups, schoolchildren, the Japanese American Citizens League, and the United Steelworkers of America, among many others. Mansfield responded to many of the letters, always highlighting the work of the Senate, and he sent a thank-you note to every Montanan who wrote, including Reverend Orville E. Lanham, the pastor of the First Presbyterian Church in White Sulphur Springs. Reverend Lanham noted that it was rare for a Presbyterian to take the trouble to thank a Catholic, but he said he wanted to thank Mansfield for his "work in this vital issue . . . I know you will receive many letters criticizing you for your stand. But, I appreciate all you have done to secure passage of the bill."[67]

The Civil Rights Act of 1964, a triumph of bipartisanship that began the still-unfinished work of reorienting American law and attitudes about race and equality, remains the single most significant piece of legislation passed during the twentieth century.[68]

8 A GREAT SOCIETY AND A BITCH OF A WAR

The fires of the 1960s may have burned the liberals' house to the ground, but when the smoke had cleared, its foundation—The Great Society—remained and remains intact.

—RANDALL B. WOODS, 2016

When Everett Dirksen made his closing speech on the Civil Rights Act of 1964, he knew that Barry Goldwater was almost certainly going to be the Republican Party's presidential candidate against Lyndon Johnson. He savaged Goldwater's opposition to the legislation anyway. Anthony Lewis of the *New York Times* called Dirksen's speech "a biting attack on the party's leading Presidential prospect," and it was. Dirksen never mentioned Goldwater by name, but in refuting the Arizona senator's contention that the civil rights legislation was unconstitutional, he looked directly at Goldwater and theatrically thrust his right arm in that direction. "Utter all the extreme opinions that you will," Dirksen said, but the legislation meant human progress, and human progress would always carry on. "You can go and talk about conscience!" Dirksen said in response to Goldwater's claim that his "no" vote was dictated by his conscience. "It is man's conscience that speaks in every generation!" Yet, while Dirksen could slash a fellow Republican—remarkable for a party elder—he was also a loyal Republican, he knew how to count, and he was not about to step in front of a party turning hard right. "Barry earned his spurs as a Republican," Dirksen said, telling Washington reporters, "show me a Republican who has campaigned as hard, then bring me a straw hat, and I'll eat it." Dirksen also certainly knew that Goldwater's candidacy was doomed but, no novice to national campaigns, he would not undertake a fool's errand to try to stop the inevitable. When approached by an emissary of Pennsylvania governor William Scranton, a liberal Republican rival to Goldwater, with the suggestion that Dirksen would be a formidable favorite-son candidate who just might help derail Goldwater's momentum, Dirksen was livid and definitely not interested. "What do they think I am," he huffed to an aide, "a rookie or a patsy?" It was one thing to openly defy Republican conservatives to help a Democratic president pass a civil rights bill, quite another to sabotage the party's presidential candidate.[1]

When Dirksen agreed to give the convention nominating speech for Goldwater in July 1964, the *Times* editorial page could not resist tweaking him for what the newspaper called "a disappointing anticlimax to all who recall how skillfully and with what high principles he riddled Senator Goldwater's arguments against the civil rights bill." Dirksen's decision to pivot from Senate floor denunciation of Goldwater to convention praise in San Francisco was proof, many Republicans thought, that the party could unite behind arguably its most conservative candidate since Calvin Coolidge. Doing all he could to make the case for Goldwater, Dirksen laid it on thick in what journalist Theodore White termed "one of the most tasteless nominating speeches ever made." Admitting that Goldwater's controversial votes "won him no applause" and "did nothing for his political advancement," Dirksen said such actions demonstrated the "blazing courage of the man—in refusing to take the easy course." Repeatedly referring to Goldwater's pioneering ancestors and calling the Arizona's senator "a peddler's son"—Goldwater was heir to a department store fortune—Dirksen worked hard to position the nominee in the political mainstream. The Republican convention delegates, however, wanted no moderate.[2]

Less than a month earlier, Dirksen had been on the cover of *Time*, which extolled his singular role in the passage of the Civil Rights Act. The magazine quoted Dirksen's powerful closing speech on the bill: "America grows. America changes. And on the civil rights issue we must rise with the occasion." Now the ever-flexible Dirksen was touting the presidential candidacy of the most prominent Republican opponent of civil rights. It was a jarring juxtaposition. Neal MacNeil would later write that Goldwater's refusal to follow Dirksen on civil rights "took away part of the savor of his greatest legislative triumph. Dirksen had imposed his will on the Senate, but not on the leader-to-be of his own Republican Party." Furthermore, MacNeil reported to his *Time* editors from the Republican Convention, Dirksen was concerned about Goldwater's tendency to talk himself into embarrassing headlines. Dirksen unrealistically suggested that during the campaign Goldwater only take reporters' questions in writing. "We've got to stop this hip-shooting," Dirksen told MacNeil, not for attribution of course. "It is simply too dangerous in the world as it is, with Latin America and Vietnam." Yet Goldwater, as he did with Dirksen's advice on civil rights, rejected the counsel of moderation. When Goldwater told the stomping, cheering crowd in San Francisco—not a few Republican delegates embraced the John Birch Society or held white supremacist views—that "extremism in defense of liberty is no vice . . . moderation in the pursuit of justice is no virtue" he was not so subtly turning his back on Dirksen's politics of principled bipartisanship, pragmatism, and compromise. One reporter listening to the candidate's acceptance speech remarked, "My God. He's going to run as Barry Goldwater." The very next day, Dirksen tried in vain to explain what Goldwater had been saying to the convention and the nation, suggesting the candidate had edited his remarks about extremism too tightly, but few who heard the speech had any doubt as to Goldwater's meaning, or that the words reflected his genuine beliefs. The modern Republican Party, a party Ev Dirksen would hardly recognize today, was born with Barry Goldwater's nomination in the drafty old Cow Palace on July 16, 1964.[3]

—

In the summer of 1964, Mike Mansfield was less concerned with a presidential campaign than with his own third-term reelection campaign in Montana. Nevertheless, he was drawn deeply into the intrigue Lyndon Johnson manufactured around the question of who the president would select as his vice presidential running mate. (The Twenty-Fifth Amendment to the Constitution had yet to be adopted, so the vice presidency was left vacant after Johnson came to the presidency.)

In early July, Johnson's favorite columnist, William S. White, anointed Mansfield as a serious contender for vice president. Since official Washington often read White's columns and imagined Johnson's lips moving—Kenneth O'Donnell said "White often sailed a kite for Johnson" to allow the president to gauge the political winds—the Mansfield speculation assumed a level of seriousness that transcended both the majority leader's lack of interest and Johnson's desire to manage any political fallout attached to his burning desire to make sure the Democratic Convention did not stampede him into selecting Robert Kennedy for the number-two position. Mansfield was a Catholic, White wrote, and "selection of a Catholic running mate would be fitting" since the first Catholic president's term had been tragically cut short. Moreover, "Mansfield is a Westerner—and no one doubts that Goldwater's strength is most of all in the West. Mansfield is a moderate liberal, much like the President in basic philosophy." *New York Daily News* columnist Ted Lewis was another who pronounced Mansfield a solid choice for vice president. In an August 14 column, Lewis remembered Johnson's praise for Mansfield, including a Senate speech in which he said, "although Mrs. Johnson and I have never had a boy, if we had a boy and if he grew to manhood, we would like to have him become the kind of man Mike Mansfield is." Lewis called Mansfield "a definite dark horse" whose potential candidacy would more seriously be considered "if he had taken the same active interest this summer in seeking [the vice presidency] that Humphrey and [Eugene] McCarthy have. But this would be contrary to his philosophical nature." Neither columnist had checked with Mansfield, or they would have gotten a one-word answer from the senator: no.[4]

Kenneth O'Donnell, the Kennedy loyalist who stayed on to work for Johnson, thought the president was more serious than not about Mansfield, as did Francis Valeo, perhaps as near as anyone could be to a Mansfield confidante. If the idea of Mansfield as a running mate was serious, perhaps Johnson was motivated by the same desire, but in reverse, that drove John Kennedy to want Mansfield as his man in the Senate. If the Montanan were tucked away in the vice presidency, Humphrey might, as majority leader, be a more aggressive advocate for the administration in the Senate. Or perhaps the endlessly manipulative Johnson just wanted to tweak Humphrey in the interest of securing, as he eventually did, an ironclad pledge of loyalty from Humphrey, the kind of pledge it is hard to imagine Mansfield making. Even when O'Donnell reminded Johnson that Humphrey was the consensus choice of Democratic leaders, and besides that Mansfield would refuse the position no matter what, he quoted Johnson as saying: "Let me tell you something. That's what they said about old Lyndon Johnson in 1960. But when they lead you up to the mountain, and show you those green fields down below and that beautiful White House standing there—you know what you do? You take it. They all take it."[5]

Humphrey, undoubtedly at least a little embarrassed to be buffeted by the Mansfield rumors, would later downplay the rumors as just Johnson's way of maintaining suspense leading up to the Democratic Convention while also keeping every would-be contender off-balance. Besides, Humphrey later maintained, the increasing division between Johnson and Mansfield over Vietnam policy ruled out the majority leader as a running mate. "Johnson said to me," Humphrey wrote, "You'll find in every man from Montana a little bit of Burton K. Wheeler," a reference to the once-powerful Montana senator, a leading antiwar noninterventionist prior to World War II. O'Donnell would later claim that Mansfield told him after seeing William White's column, he went to the White House and told Johnson that under no circumstances would he accept the vice-presidential nomination. Even after Mansfield gave Johnson his firm "no," speculation about a Johnson-Mansfield ticket continued until the eve of the Democratic Convention. Mansfield finally issued a formal statement disclaiming any interest. Mansfield dutifully headed the Montana delegation to the 1964 Democratic National Convention, served Johnson loyally as floor leader, and selected Rhode Island Senator John Pastore, a fiery speaker, as the keynoter. But he had long ago grown weary of the carnival atmosphere at national political conventions. He was much more focused on Montana.[6]

There was never much doubt about Mansfield's reelection, even with a respectable Republican opponent, Great Falls attorney Alex Blewitt, trying to paint him as too close to Johnson, "a mascot of the White House." This criticism was tepid stuff, particularly as Mansfield engineered a Johnson stop in Great Falls in September designed to highlight the president's signing of the Columbia River Treaty with Canadian prime minister Lester Pearson. The treaty cleared a path for construction of Libby Dam, a huge hydroelectric project long championed by Mansfield, on the Kootenai River in northwestern Montana. Given such tangible evidence of Mansfield's political effectiveness, it was nearly impossible for any critic to tarnish his popularity. Mansfield's campaigning was decidedly old school retail politics, consisting almost exclusively of speeches and informal meetings over coffee at cafés on Montana's main streets. "It's a wonder he didn't drown in coffee," recalled long-time aide Peggy DeMichele, as he "met a lot of everyday people," heard their concerns, and put his staff to work trying to help.[7]

The president was back in Montana in early October, honoring a commitment John Kennedy had made to campaign in Silver Bow County. Before a crowd the Butte police chief estimated at 46,500, the president lavished praise on Mansfield. "It would be a wonderful thing," Johnson said, "a kind thing, if you would give him the largest majority of any senator elected this year." In his prepared remarks, the president recalled the effort to ratify the test ban treaty a little more than a year earlier. "Senator Mike Mansfield and Senator Lee Metcalf are Democrats from Montana," Johnson said. "Senator Everett Dirksen is a Republican from Illinois, but they worked together for all mankind to approve that treaty. That is responsible government."[8]

Dirksen not only did nothing to help Mansfield's Republican challenger but went out of his way to indicate his preference for Mansfield's reelection. Dirksen was reported to have said "he would go to the moon to help Republicans, 'but, please, don't ask me to go to Montana.'" Two weeks before the election, *Newsweek* ran a small item that was widely repeated in Montana: "GOP Senate Leader Everett Dirksen candidly told Montana Republicans that he wants his good friend, Democrat Mike Mansfield, re-elected." Mansfield was reelected, and easily. Johnson also carried Montana in 1964 with nearly 59 percent of the vote on the way to a crushing landslide victory over Goldwater. Mansfield did even better, defeating Blewitt two to one and losing only five small counties.[9]

The end of the Eighty-Eighth Congress also marked the end of any serious grumbling about Mansfield's leadership of the Senate. Though the Civil Rights Act dominated the headlines, the remainder of the legislative record spoke for itself, and Mansfield allowed himself a modest victory lap during an interview with Kenneth Scheibel, the *Missoulian*'s Washington correspondent. Mansfield noted that Johnson had sent Congress 52 specific legislative proposals, "the Senate passed 52, and 46 became law." The impressive list of legislative accomplishments was a preview of Johnson's wildly ambitious Great Society legislative agenda that would reach full steam in 1965. Congress had already produced on Johnson's agenda: the Urban Mass Transit Act; the first significant Clean Air Act; a variety of education measures; a major tax cut; creation of the Land and Water Conservation Fund; the Food Stamp Act, championed by, among others, Mansfield's close friend George Aiken and passed by the Senate on a voice vote; and the Economic Opportunity Act of 1964, which created, among other programs, Head Start, the Job Corps, and work-study grants for college students. Dirksen and the Senate's most conservative Republicans voted with southern Democrats against the Economic Opportunity Act, but ten Senate Republicans supported Mansfield and the administration. All the legislation was passed with bipartisan support.[10]

After a multiyear effort, Congress also finished work on the Wilderness Act in 1964, another landmark piece of legislation that preserved more than nine million acres of national forest land by sharply limiting development and motorized access. The legislation was controversial in Montana, particularly with livestock and mining interests, but it passed the Senate with a strong bipartisan vote of seventy-three to twelve. Johnson called the collection of environmental legislation "some of the most far-reaching conservation measures that a far-sighted nation has ever coped with." It was, Mansfield said, "a record which will compare with any one year in the history of the republic!"[11]

The majority leader, characteristically, refused to claim credit for himself. "I think it was the cooperation of Senator Dirksen and the Republicans who many times gave us four to ten votes—the difference between defeat and victory," he told Scheibel. "What did you do differently this year?" Scheibel asked. "Nothing," Mansfield replied. The *Missoulian* reporter persisted: Mansfield must have done something differently. "No, I wouldn't if I could. I treat senators as I want to be treated. The Senate went out of its way to be cooperative, and helpful to me." "Any regrets?" Scheibel asked. "None, really," Mansfield said. What about South Carolina Senator

Strom Thurmond abandoning the Democratic Party to become a Republican" "No, I appreciate his honesty," Mansfield said. "I wish him well. He'll be happier with the Republicans."[12]

Dirksen's age, not to mention his heavy cigarette habit and fondness for bourbon, was becoming a constant concern, and the minority leader landed in the hospital again just before the 1964 election. This time it was a fractured vertebra caused, his wife said, by a "twist or misstep." Dirksen was in and out of hospitals for most of November. On the eve of the election, Mansfield wrote him, "I want to express my appreciation for the privilege of sharing membership with you in the Senate of the 88th Congress. It was a deeply gratifying personal experience to have worked with you. Whatever we accomplished in the way of constructive contribution to the nation was achieved by the membership as a whole. Personally, I shall be ever grateful to you for your patience, forebearance [sic] and help and, most of all, for your under-standing friendship." Dirksen responded immediately, noting that never before had he spent an Election Day "immobilized in a hospital," but he would content himself with watching the election outcome on television. "I am grateful indeed," he told Mansfield, "for your generous note and I can say as much for what I deem to be the high privilege of having had such an intimate and friendly relationship with you throughout our legislative careers and particularly in our capacity as Senate leaders."[13]

—

Even accounting for Thurmond's party switch, Mansfield began the new Congress in January 1965 with the largest Democratic majority since Franklin Roosevelt's second term, but the numbers did not tell the complete story of the profound changes underway in American politics. The election outcome had as much to do with the electorate's objections to Goldwater as it did with the president's popularity, and Johnson's prediction that passage of the Civil Rights Act would cost Democrats dearly in the South was proving correct. The party still claimed, in name if not always in policy, old-line Southerners like Dick Russell and Jim Eastland, but Goldwater had broken the once "solid South," romping to huge majorities in Georgia, Louisi-ana, Alabama, and South Carolina; in Mississippi Johnson lost every county and commanded less than 13 percent of the total vote. The only other state Goldwater won was Arizona, but Republicans won five congressional seats in Alabama and one each in Georgia and Mississippi. The total Democratic vote in the South was lower than it had been in 1960. Senate Democrats—and to a lesser degree Senate Republicans—would remain deeply divided on many issues, making the Mansfield-Dirksen bipartisan collaboration more important than ever.[14]

In a long speech to the Democratic conference in January 1965, Mansfield stressed that many issues coming before the Senate were "of such transcendent importance to the nation that the only acceptable answers can never be either Republican or Democratic but only American." The Senate must seek national unity, Mansfield said, and in a clear reference to Goldwater's campaign, "work without the kind of reckless and irresponsible divisiveness which was so decisively rejected in November." As for his approach to leading the Senate: "As Majority Leader for the past four years," Mansfield said, "I have not allowed the partisan wedge to drive so deeply in the Senate as to alienate the minority members, so deeply as to force them out of the house of the nation. And I have every intention of continuing to work, as in the past, with the minority leadership, with the restraint and respect and mutual understanding and with that high degree of comity and civility which are the foundations of the house."[15]

The one great issue that would come to dominate the Senate and divide the country in the second half of the decade of the 1960s was an issue Mansfield and Dirksen could not find a way to confront together. Vietnam had been almost an afterthought during the 1964 presidential campaign, emerging only as an issue that underscored Goldwater's penchant for bellicose pronouncements about American foreign policy, a tendency that Johnson used masterfully to portray the Republican candidate as dangerously irresponsible. Goldwater advocated bombing North Vietnam, for example, and talked colorfully if not rationally of using nuclear weapons against the Soviet Union.[16]

Mansfield's concern about American policy in Vietnam was by now well known, and his doubts had grown along with his determination to provide verbal public support to the president while continuing to offer unvarnished advice privately. Mansfield never attempted to lead the Senate's antiwar faction, a fact that engendered criticism, but he did through his speeches, reports, and position on the Foreign Relations Committee attempt to shape the way policy was made. As early as 1962, for example, when a Republican seat became available on the Foreign Relations Committee, and perhaps anticipating that Vietnam would only become a more pressing issue for the Senate, Mansfield conducted what for him was an unusual public lobbying campaign to get Dirksen to join the committee. One published report said Mansfield—and President Kennedy as well—was pushing the idea with the "feeling . . . that Dirksen's stature as Republican floor leader and one of those called in by the White House on major foreign policy [issues], would strengthen the committee." The *New York Times* noted that Mansfield and Kennedy "are extremely grateful to Senator Dirksen for the general support he has given to the administration's foreign policy." In the end, the Republican seat on the committee went to Karl Mundt of South Dakota, who had more seniority than Dirksen, was a frequent administration critic, and was a conservative hard-liner on Vietnam. Dirksen's decision not to engage more directly on foreign policy issues—he often deferred to Mundt or the equally conservative Bourke Hickenlooper of Iowa—seemed like a minor issue at the time, but over time it would limit his exposure to the kind of detailed discussion of Vietnam policy that came to define the Foreign Relations Committee after 1965. Dirksen remained a Cold War, anti-communist hawk, almost always inclined to defer to the occupant of the Oval Office.[17]

During a January 1965 appearance on *Meet the Press*, Dirksen was asked about US options in Vietnam. He stressed that he would not attempt to dictate policy to Lyndon Johnson and candidly suggested that the best option was to "muddle as we have been muddling" in hopes of creating a "situation responsibly stabilized." Dirksen also offered a full-on endorsement of the Eisenhower-era domino theory, an article of foreign policy faith that Johnson also embraced, which held that once the Vietnam "domino" fell to communism so would the rest of Asia. "Let me remind you," Dirksen said during the interview, "if we pull out of Vietnam—and I am not one of those who counsels that course—it will mean that the southernmost flank of the line that runs from Korea to Vietnam and which is our outside defense perimeter will suddenly have that flank turned and then all the trusted islands in the Pacific as well as the Philippines are in danger, and I will not counsel that kind of a course." Even while Republican congressional leaders were formally saying that a robust debate about foreign policy "should be encouraged," Dirksen was deferring to his old friend Lyndon Johnson. "Is there any alternative except to fight through to a victorious conclusion?" Dirksen asked reporters. "And besides," he said, "don't forget for a moment that the prestige and the face of the country is involved in all of Southeast Asia." Dirksen's position placed him in lockstep with Johnson, who in early 1965 made the decision to dramatically expand the war.[18]

As he had done with Kennedy, the majority leader attempted to influence Johnson's thinking not merely to criticize his policy. For example, on December 7, 1963, in one of his first actions after Kennedy's death, Mansfield sent the new president copies of the Vietnam memos he had provided to Kennedy, along with a copy of his Michigan State speech from 1962 in which he had warned against the growing US involvement. Mansfield offered Johnson three suggestions: shift American strategy from military activity to political and social action; engage in aggressive multinational diplomacy to seek a peaceful solution to the conflict; and encourage a neutral Cambodia. Mansfield told Johnson, and he hardly wavered in his advice in the months ahead, that there was no military solution in Vietnam and that pursuing such a course risked widening the war, perhaps drawing in China. He made no references to American vital interests or domino theories. As Mansfield said, he kept "pounding away" on his strategy suggestions, sending multiple detailed reports to Johnson and often being the only person in meetings to offer a counter to further military escalation. At the same time, Mansfield assiduously avoided direct criticism of Johnson. The apparent contradictions in Mansfield's approach— disagreeing fundamentally with Johnson's policy but offering public support for the president—exasperated opponents of the war who wanted the Senate leader to lead on the biggest issue of the day. But such an approach would have been directly counter to Mansfield's view of the personal responsibility of every senator.[19]

On February 17, 1965, two Democrats—Frank Church of Idaho and George McGovern of South Dakota—launched the first sustained Senate debate on US policy in Vietnam. Both called for a negotiated end to the bloodletting, with Church saying the current policy could only lead to "[sending] American land forces into battle, thus converting the struggle into an American war." McGovern said his mail from constituents overwhelmingly supported negotiations, since "the hard fact was the problem resisted a military situation." Dirksen was livid about the implied criticism, and that evening he called Johnson. "I just listened to your friend and brother in the faith, Mr. Church, tee off on your administration for 45 minutes," Dirksen said, "and Mr. George McGovern of South Dakota is now teeing off on your Vietnamese policy and I thought you needed a little defense on the floor of the Senate from your friend on the other side of the aisle." Johnson chuckled and said, "Good." The worst things happening, Johnson told the minority leader, "are the speeches . . . about negotiations." Knowing that Dirksen would agree, Johnson launched into his interpretation of the domino theory. "If they take South Vietnam, they take Thailand, they take Indonesia, they take Burma, they come right on back to The Philippines." Dirksen occasionally interjected a "yup," but Johnson did the talking. "The Communists take our speeches," he said, "and they quote what Mansfield . . . or McGovern says, and they think that's the government of the United States." Johnson did acknowledge that in public statements Mansfield was supporting the president but admitted "his heart's not in this thing, as you know." The next day Dirksen, in full rhetorical flower, was on front pages all across the country defending Johnson from the criticism of fellow Democrats.[20]

Calling for negotiations, Dirksen said, was the same as proposing to "run up the white flag before the world and start running away from communism." In the minority leader's opinion, negotiations were pointless since no agreement would be honored by communist leaders. It was, Dirksen said, a "strange experience" to listen to such a "chorus of despair" on the Senate floor. Meanwhile, the joint Republican leadership—Michigan's Gerald Ford now led House Republicans, having defeated Charlie Halleck in a leadership contest—issued a statement supporting Johnson and asserting that there "can be no negotiations on the Vietnamese question as long as there is communist-promoted infiltration of South Vietnam."[21]

Dirksen was not alone in bashing McGovern and Church. Democrats Tom Dodd and Gale McGee joined the piling on, as did Russell Long, who had replaced Humphrey as Democratic whip. The debate brought into clear focus the profound divisions among Democrats about Vietnam. Consistent with his belief that every senator should chart his own course, Mansfield defended the dissenters, saying they reflected "great credit upon the Senate." Meanwhile, Dirksen's "white flag" speech still stung years later—"a very excoriating and ridiculous address," Church called it. "I think that it is fair to say," Church added, "that Everett Dirksen was [Johnson's] principal lieutenant in support of the war in the Senate."[22]

In March 1965, the first 3,500 US combat troops—from Mansfield's beloved Marine Corps—arrived in South Vietnam, augmenting the 25,000 American military advisors and security troops in the country at the start of the year. By the end of 1965, more than 185,000 US troops were in Vietnam. In what became known as the Tonkin Gulf resolution, the Senate authorized the Johnson administration to use force in response to a still-murky incident involving US destroyers and North Vietnamese patrol boats that ultimately became Johnson's legal rationale for increased American involvement. Outside of this resolution, the vast expansion of the war took place with minimal debate or even discussion outside the White House. (Mansfield and Dirksen supported the Tonkin Gulf resolution, although during a leadership meeting at the White House, Mansfield was alone in objecting to the retaliatory air raids Johnson ordered. He was also deeply skeptical of official explanations of what had happened off the North Vietnamese coast. Later, he cosponsored the Senate measure to repeal the resolution.)[23]

In the spring of 1965 the leftist journalist I. F. Stone offered a scathing denunciation of the lack of real debate about the escalating war: "It looks as if while the rest of us may be plunged into war, Lyndon Johnson wants to keep as far away from it as possible," Stone wrote, sarcastically suggesting that Johnson blame the escalation on Dirksen, "who was foolish enough to say plainly that he feared [the escalation] would 'transform this into a conventional war.' That is the kind of candor that lost Republicans the last election."[24]

Mike Mansfield, who knew Lyndon Johnson as well as Ev Dirksen did, understood that whatever limited influence he had with Johnson on the Vietnam issue would disappear entirely if he broke openly with his old Senate mentor. The mere perception that Mansfield was offering even mild criticism of the administration's Vietnam policy infuriated Johnson, who took to calling the majority leader "that man from Montana." Moreover, Johnson disdained Mansfield's knowledge of and firsthand expertise in Asia. In one exchange with McGovern, who like Mansfield once taught history, Johnson said, "Goddamn it, George, don't give me another history lesson. . . . I've got a drawer full of history lessons over there from Mansfield, another professor. I don't have time to be sitting around this desk reading history books!" As if to underscore that any Mansfield critique amounted to mere petty politics, the White House leaked a story—a favorite White House tactic to try to intimidate other senators as well—that Mansfield was on the outs with Johnson over an administration decision to close a Veterans Administration hospital in Miles City, Montana. But the pettiness was all Johnson's. Mansfield understood, as the Wisconsin Democrat William Proxmire said years later: "Any such outspoken dissent from Mansfield could have made Johnson harder to handle, not easier. Johnson's position on the Vietnam War could not be influenced by Mansfield or any other member of the Senate or the Congress or the administration." George Reedy, Johnson's aide, said much the same. "Critics reinforced Johnson, locked Johnson into a position. Public criticism wouldn't have worked with Johnson." Nonetheless, Mansfield's strategy of private counsel and public support ultimately failed, while Dirksen, always willing to express unfailing support for Johnson's foreign policy, saw his influence at the White House increase. Historian Byron Hulsey has argued that only late in 1967 and into 1968, when Dirksen's own Senate leadership was under attack from fellow Republicans, in no small part because of his close relationship with Johnson, did the minority leader recalibrate and begin to push back, ever so subtly, on the president.[25]

Still, even accounting for complex and shifting Senate politics, including the chasms existing within both parties on Vietnam, the fact that Mansfield and Dirksen, who were so skillful in advancing bipartisan consensus on critical national priorities in the 1960s, failed to find constructive common ground on Vietnam ranks as their singular leadership failure. "It haunts me still," Mansfield told his biographer of the catastrophe of Vietnam. With tears in his eyes and his voice breaking, Mansfield told Don Oberdorfer, "What a shame—55,000 dead, 305,000 wounded. Costs which we will be paying well into the middle of the next century . . . a tragic mistake."[26]

Lyndon Johnson may not have had time to sit at his desk and read history books, but he did understand the history of a president's window of opportunity to legislate. After his 1964 landslide, Johnson enjoyed a huge partisan numerical advantage in Congress, a majority with new moderate and liberal Democrats who by their numbers reduced substantially the influence of southern conservatives. "I want you to work for my legislative program and get as much passed in the next 90 days and in 1965 as is humanly possible," Johnson told a meeting of legislative liaisons from his Cabinet agencies. Johnson knew the power of his landslide was ephemeral. He had to move quickly, and he had to discourage public and congressional discussion of a faraway war. Johnson, a master at political multitasking, wanted the country and the Congress, as historian Robert Dallek has written, to focus on "the explosion of Great Society legislation—federal aid to elementary, secondary, and higher education, Medicare, Medicaid, Voting Rights, clean air and clean water bills, immigration reform, the creation of a Department of Housing and Urban Development and the National Endowments for the Arts and the Humanities. Johnson believed that conservatives eager to kill off his programs of domestic reform would have been all too happy to seize upon the expanding war as an excuse to stall and ultimately kill the Great Society and war on poverty."[27]

The blizzard of Great Society legislation that cascaded out of Congress in 1965—most of the significant initiatives passed with bipartisan support—marked "the fabulous Eighty-Ninth Congress" as akin to the second coming of Franklin Roosevelt's New Deal. But before Johnson could hope to perfect his vision of the country and Congress, he had again to face the fierce urgency of civil rights.

"Selma Marchers Routed" read the headline in the *Nashville Tennessean* on Monday morning, March 8, 1965. The *Great Falls Tribune* led with "'Bama Troops Bar Negro March," while the *Chicago Tribune*, beneath a bold banner—"Marines Land in Viet Nam"—ran a smaller headline: "Negroes Routed by Tear Gas." The voting rights march from Selma to Montgomery, Alabama, a demonstration of civil rights leaders' determination to register Black Americans to vote, was stopped by nightstick-swinging state troopers at the Edmund Pettis Bridge on the outskirts of Selma.[28]

Alabama Governor George C. Wallace gave the order to stop the marchers. "The troopers rushed forward," the *New York Times* reported, "their blue uniforms and white helmets blurring into a flying wedge as they moved. The wedge moved with such force that it seemed almost to pass over the waiting column instead of through it. The first 10 or 20 Negros were swept to the ground screaming, arms and legs flying, and packs and bags went skittering across the grassy divider strip and on to the pavement on both sides. Those still on their feet retreated." One marcher, beaten to the point of requiring hospitalization, was John Lewis, then the chairman of the Student Non-Violent Coordinating Committee and years later a member of Congress from Georgia. "Next time we march," Lewis said before being taken to the hospital, "maybe we have to keep going when we get to Montgomery. We may have to go on to Washington."[29]

Nothing—not the March on Washington in the summer of 1963, not the ambush murder of Medgar Evers, not the Birmingham police commissioner turning fire hoses on protesters, not even a church bombing that killed four young African American girls—galvanized the country like "bloody Sunday" in Selma. Millions of American saw the shocking images on television, many viewing them that very Sunday night when ABC News broke into the network's airing of the Academy Award–winning film *Judgment at Nuremburg* to broadcast a special report. Lyndon Johnson, who had told Dr. Martin Luther King Jr. early in 1965 that he could not get a voting rights bill through Congress that year but was "going to do it eventually" now had no choice but to act. Mansfield and Dirksen were incensed by the violence in Alabama, and the usually calm and circumspect majority leader was upset by the president's reticence and perhaps also, at least in Johnson's opinion, by the White House rushing to consult only Dirksen. After Selma, Mansfield told Larry O'Brien, White House congressional liaison, that he would introduce his own voting rights bill if Johnson failed to act quickly.[30]

Events did now move quickly. On March 9, Johnson publicly said for the first time that work was underway on a voting rights bill, and the president instructed Justice Department officials quietly to begin work with Dirksen on shaping the legislation. Civil rights demonstrators marched outside the White House on March 11, and a handful staged a sit-in. The same day, a group of sixteen clergy members met with Johnson for two hours and came away incensed by "Johnson's failure to act on the racial crisis in Selma." On March 13, Johnson met at the White House with Governor Wallace—"the most amazing conversation I've ever been present at" recalled Attorney General Nicholas Katzenbach—resulting in an agreement that Wallace would ask the president to send federal troops to Alabama to protect the next voting rights march. On March 14, a Sunday, congressional leaders met with Johnson, and it was agreed that he would address Congress the next day. The *New York Times* noted in its story previewing Johnson's speech that a voting rights proposal had been worked out between Katzenbach and Dirksen, while legal aides to Dirksen, Mansfield, and Republican whip Tom Kuchel "put the draft in near-final form."[31]

Johnson's March 15 speech to Congress, televised in prime time, would be one of the greatest of his presidency, perhaps the greatest. "At times history and fate meet at a single time in a single place to shape a turning point in man's unending search for freedom," Johnson pronounced to a hushed House chamber. "So it was at Lexington and Concord. So it was a century ago at Appomattox. So it was last week in Selma, Alabama." Anticipating objections from southern conservatives that a federal voting rights act was unconstitutional or a violation of states' rights, Johnson dismissed the charges out of hand. "There is no constitutional issue here. The command of the Constitution is plain. There is no moral issue. It is wrong—deadly wrong—to deny any of your fellow Americans the right to vote in this country. There is no issue of States rights or national rights. There is only the struggle for human rights."

As Richard Goodwin, who wrote the speech, remembered, Johnson spoke that night "in loud deliberate tones," creating one of the most dramatic rhetorical moments of the 1960s. "What happened in Selma is part of a far larger movement which reaches into every section and State of America. It is the effort of American Negroes to secure for themselves the full blessings of American life. Their cause must be our cause too. Because it is not just Negroes, but really it is all of us, who must overcome the crippling legacy of bigotry and injustice. And we shall overcome." The proposed voting rights legislation was affront enough to Johnson's one-time southern Senate colleagues, but the president actually invoking the language of civil rights activists was just too much. Richard Russell pronounced his protégé "a turncoat if ever there was one."[32]

John Lewis was in Selma watching the speech with Dr. King and a handful of others. "I looked at Dr. King and tears came down his face," Lewis said, "and we all cried a little." As the House erupted in cheers and applause, Goodwin noticed that "tears rolled down the checks of Senator Mansfield of Montana."[33]

Compared to the Civil Rights Act a year earlier, the Voting Rights Act moved on a fast track in the Senate. Bills were introduced in both the House and Senate shortly after Johnson's speech. The Senate legislation, sporting sixty-six cosponsors, was referred to Eastland's Judiciary Committee with a strict deadline that it be returned to the full Senate by April 9. Mansfield forecast passage within two weeks, before the scheduled Easter recess, a prediction that turned out to be overly optimistic. Conservative southern Democrats, their influence depleted and with Richard Russell in poor health, still managed a delaying filibuster. Meanwhile, events far from Capitol Hill continued to influence the political action. Dr. King, now leading the march from Selma to Montgomery, completed the fifty-four-mile walk with a triumphant speech at the steps of the Alabama state capitol on March 25.

Yet, that night a thirty-nine-year-old white civil rights activist from Detroit, Viola Liuzzo, a mother of five, was shot and killed. Liuzzo had come to Alabama to aid the voting rights cause. Members of the Alabama Ku Klux Klan murdered her on the same highway the marchers had walked along.[34]

As before, Dirksen was the key to passage of another landmark civil rights bill, but he faced an old problem—how to end a filibuster when many conservative Republicans, who might ultimately support the bill, resisted on principle efforts to limit debate. As before, Dirksen's office became the control center where legislative details were hashed out and resolved. "We had the same process of coming out every day at 4 o'clock and Dirksen would talk to the cameras and the press," Charles Ferris recalled. "Mansfield would stand in the background and smoke his pipe and say nothing, just nod his agreement to Dirksen's daily report." Dirksen also became the principal conduit to Lyndon Johnson, and as was always the case with their relationship, everything involved a transaction.[35]

In a telephone call with Johnson on April 5, Dirksen admitted, "I'm bushed. This Goddamn voting rights bill." Dirksen was clearly conveying a message from Mansfield as well as from himself. "That reminds me," Dirksen told the president. "I just had a talk with Mike. Don't make any statements about driving that damn thing through before Easter. We think now we've got a good bill. We had twenty guys around a table putting the finishing touches on it on late Saturday afternoon." Both Dirksen and Mansfield were worried that presidential pressure to move the voting rights bill more quickly might get in the way of senators' Easter plans. "There is going to be grousing to beat hell up there because they've all made plans," Dirksen told the president before promising him there would be a good bill and soon. Johnson expressed concern about more Selma-like unrest if the debate dragged on much longer. Dirksen said he understood, and like any self-respecting senator, complained that the House was messing around with "all other kind of Goddamn stuff." Yet he assured Johnson that when the process was complete, "it will be the bill we have drawn up because I think it's a good one."[36]

A politician with a bigger ego or one worried about the perception of his political power might have resented the Johnson-Dirksen friendship—one observer suggested it was a relationship of "honor among crooks"—but Mansfield knew that Dirksen now commanded Johnson's ear a good deal more than he did, and he seemed fine with that. "Not that I wasn't friendly," Mansfield said of his relationship with the president, "but they sort of had a pal-ship."[37]

Lady Bird Johnson looked in on her husband and Dirksen hammering out strategy around the voting rights bill, "in earnest conversation . . . two brother artisans

President Lyndon Johnson confers with Everett Dirksen in the Oval Office. Dirksen was recovering from a fall. Note his crutches leaning against the cabinet enclosing Johnson's wire service machines. (*US Senate Historical Office*)

in government, heads close together." Checking back two hours later, the first lady found the two old pols "in practically the same posture." During another telephone call in this period, Dirksen let it slip that he had spoken with a Democratic senator about one of his frequent conversations with the Democratic president. Johnson was taken aback. "You don't know these little boys, my friend," Johnson said. "I catch more hell because they think you're running the government these Democrats . . . but I've got to talk to you, but don't you ever let 'em know I do. Don't you tell 'em."[38]

While Senate respect for Mansfield was universal, not every Republican appreciated Dirksen's close friendship with the majority leader, and some Democrats had difficulty grasping, or perhaps accepting, Mansfield's extremely close relationship with Dirksen. "He and Mansfield were enormously close," Kansas Republican Senator James Pearson said. "It's difficult to find adequate adjectives to describe the closeness." Charles Ferris recalled receiving a call from a top aide to Illinois Democrat Paul Douglas during the deliberations on the voting rights bill. Why did all the meetings have to take place in Dirksen's office? the aide demanded to know. The television camera only showed the Republican leader's lair. What would be wrong with having half the meetings in Mansfield's office?

> I thought that was fairly reasonable, so I went into Mansfield and said, "The natives are getting a little restless here, can we meet in your office half the time and Dirksen's office half the time, so the cameras will capture the Democratic leader's office at least half the time?" Again, the perspective of Mansfield was so incredible. He said, "No, Charlie, we're going to meet in Dirksen's office every day. We've got overwhelming Democratic majorities in the Senate and the House. This is probably the most important piece of social legislation in history for this country." He said, "It's very, very good if the people of this country realize that this legislation is being put together not just by Democrats but by Republicans. If Everett Dirksen can go before the cameras every day and talk about what we're doing on this bill, that's an important message for the country."

Ferris remembered Mansfield adding, "Last year in the presidential election the Republicans left the mainstream. They left the mainstream of American political and social life in that campaign, and this is an opportunity for them to get back on track."[39] Mansfield knew best and Dirksen succeeded again.

The filibuster against the voting rights legislation consumed twenty-four days, roughly one-third the time southern Democrats had talked against the Civil Rights Act. The cloture vote on May 25 was seventy to thirty, with the bill passing the next day by a vote of seventy-seven to nineteen. Several southern Democrats who had opposed the Civil Rights Act the year before now switched and embraced voting rights. The House and Senate versions of the legislation had to be reconciled, and in the end Mansfield and Dirksen brokered an agreement permitting poll taxes to continue but giving the attorney general the power to investigate any potentially discriminatory use of poll taxes at state and local levels. Some liberal Democrats, including the newly elected Senator Robert Kennedy of New York, wanted the legislation to include a prohibition against state-level poll taxes. It was a painful, weakening concession to some, but eventually Dr. King endorsed the compromise. As historian Julian Zelizer has noted, "The final legislation contained almost everything that was in the deal reached by Dirksen and Johnson before the congressional deliberations began," including provisions to end discriminatory tests that prevented many from voting, as well as a critical preclearance provision that required federal approval for any changes in voting law in states that had a record of discrimination. The law also contained a provision for criminal penalties for violations.[40]

For the first time since Herbert Hoover's presidency, a president signed legislation in the President's Room in the Capitol. The date was August 6, 104 years to the day since Abraham Lincoln had sat in the same room and freed slaves who had been forced to serve in the Confederate Army. "Today is a triumph for freedom as huge as any victory that has ever been won on any battlefield," Johnson said. "Today the Negro story and the American story fuse and blend." As Johnson signed the legislation, he gave the first pen to Vice President Humphrey and handed the second to Dirksen. Mansfield received a pen as well but avoided appearing in any photo of the historic event. Almost immediately, federal officials departed for several southern states to begin registering voters.[41]

After the ceremony, Johnson wandered his old haunts, and as the president approached the double doors of the Senate chamber, Mansfield asked if he wanted, as protocol dictated, to be formally invited on to the floor. "I'm sorry, I forgot," Johnson responded, as Mansfield held the doors. Johnson made his way to his old desk, now Mansfield's, where he sat for a moment. Wayne Morse, who was presiding, recognized the uniqueness of the moment. "The chair recognizes the senator from Texas, and the majority leader," Morse proclaimed. There were chuckles as Johnson rose, returned the seat to Mansfield, and said, "this chair is too hot for me." The handful of gallery watchers applauded as the president left the Senate. It was, reporter Ben Cole wrote, "an hour of jubilation."[42]

─

When asked to characterize Lyndon Johnson's Great Society, the usually voluble Everett Dirksen did so in four words: "A blueprint for paradise." That pithy statement was not intended as praise. The minority leader bristled at much of what Johnson proposed as too big, too expensive, and too unworkable, but when he did oppose, he did so in a measured way. On one occasion Dirksen said Johnson was pursuing his massive agenda with "the pop-eyed ardor of Harpo Marx chasing blondes." Yet his outnumbered Republican conference had two basic options: oppose the Johnson program or attempt to shape it. Dirksen chose the latter course. "He seldom makes an open declaration in favor of a Democratic measure that would offend many Republicans," Ben Bagdikian wrote in a New York Times profile of Dirksen in 1965. "He agrees, or seems to, with the initial Republican grumbling, gathering party leaders to his camp and at the same time raising his price for peace talks with the Democrats."[43]

So it was with the torrent of legislation that threatened to swamp Congress in 1965. Dirksen was never a fan, for example, of what became Medicare, worrying, not unreasonably, about the program's eventual cost. "I would be eligible," the often-hospitalized minority leader said. "Why should I be allowed to use dollars the government is taking from some young factory worker in Cleveland in the promise of providing for his old age?" Ironically, Dirksen was in the hospital and unable to vote when the Senate, by a strong bipartisan margin, approved Medicare—technically amendments to the Social Security Act—in July 1965. Despite years of conservative opposition to government-funded health care of any type, Dirksen worked with Mansfield to avoid procedural roadblocks to Senate action on the legislation, and he was recorded as "paired" in favor on final passage.[44]

Dirksen, son of immigrants, supported Johnson's immigration legislation that ended a strict quota formula which dated to the 1920s. Dirksen also supported Johnson's Appalachian Development Act, designed to direct federal aid to one of the nation's most depressed regions. Fifteen Senate Republicans, including the most conservative, voted no. And legislation to create the national endowments for the arts and the humanities, agencies that became the focus of GOP criticism in the 1990s, passed the Senate in 1965 by a voice vote. That the Senate functioned as well as it did in churning through an immense volume of Great Society legislation during what Lyndon Johnson referred to as "the fabulous Eighty-ninth Congress" is surely a testament to the president's ambition and drive, as well as to Mansfield's management of his often-fractured Democratic supermajority. The legislative output also evidenced Dirksen's essential pragmatism, his willingness to influence rather than merely to oppose. Dirksen was "shrewdly conciliatory," *Life* magazine's Paul O'Neil wrote, "exquisitely aware of the country's problems and tirelessly dedicated to both the Senate and the country."[45]

Mike Mansfield's dedication to the Senate was every bit as tireless and complete as Dirksen's. As majority leader, Mansfield rarely called a meeting of the entire Democratic conference, the forum Lyndon Johnson had used to whip his party in a specific direction. When Mansfield did summon all Senate Democrats, his message was rarely about pending legislation or partisan strategy. He always spoke of the responsibilities senators had to the Senate. His speech to his Democratic colleagues in the summer of 1965, amid the glow of Senate accomplishment, was a fitting epitaph for the remarkable 1965 session:

As you know, I am not given to overstatement, but I do want to say that this Senate has contributed much to the nation during this session in a manner very close to that which, in my judgement, the Constitution intends it to contribute. That has been possible only because of the abilities, responsive-ness and dedication of the Senators, individually, and as a body. I want to say, too, in this connection that the Minority side under the leadership of Senator Dirksen has operated in the best tradition of a loyal opposition and its contribution to the record of this session has been exceptional.

Insofar as the Leadership is concerned, it continues to function solely on the basis of cooperation, restraint, and understanding of the individual Members and under the concept that every Senator from the youngest to the oldest, from the most eloquent to the least—a distinction which I claim for myself—from Committee Chairmen to the least senior Members of the committee—all have equal rights and equal responsibilities under the Constitution. I regard it as a major responsibility of leadership to interpret that principle into effective practice. That is how it has been; that is how it will be and no other way, so far as I am concerned.[46]

Lyndon Johnson wrote Mansfield at the end of the 1965 session, praising his leadership and the work of Congress but also pointedly noting that "23 major pieces of legislation" were still awaiting action. Mansfield's response was to recommend a pause in the frantic legislating, shifting emphasis to "the perfection, the elaboration and refinement" of all that had been created. It was sound political advice that Johnson dismissed. He wanted more and more, telling Congress in 1966 "the nation is mighty enough, its society healthy enough, its people are strong enough, to pursue goals in the rest of the world while still building a Great Society here at home." Yet budgetary pressures, exacerbated by the growing cost of an expanding war, congressional fatigue, and divisiveness driven by Vietnam (the subject that consumed half of Johnson's State of the Union speech in 1966) combined to stall the president's legislative ambitions.[47]

Lyndon Johnson told the biographer and presidential historian Doris Kearns Goodwin in 1970:

I knew from the start that I was bound to be crucified either way I moved. If I left the woman I really loved—the Great Society—in order to get involved with that bitch of a war on the other side of the world, then I would lose everything at home. All my programs. All my hopes to feed the hungry and shelter the homeless. All my dreams to provide education and medical care to the browns and the blacks and the lame and the poor. But if I left that war and let the Communists take over South Vietnam, then I would both find it impossible to accomplish anything for anybody anywhere on the entire globe.[48]

To be sure, Johnson did have legislative successes after 1965, creating a Cabinet-level Transportation Department, children's nutrition programs, and environmental protection measures, among others, but his proposals—dozens of them—were, as Robert Dallek has written, "a pale imitation of those of 1965." Even after counseling Johnson that he would be wise to proceed more modestly, Mansfield, as the *New York Times* reported, "was prepared to be a good soldier" in pushing the administration's latest initiatives, even while warning "you don't get everything at once." Dirksen, perhaps with an eye toward midterm elections, balked at another civil rights bill in 1966, and he led the Senate effort, a filibuster, to defeat repeal of Section 14-B of the Taft-Hartley Act, the provision allowing states to enact so-called right-to-work laws that limit the power of labor unions. That constituted an important victory for conservative Republicans and lessened, at least temporarily, conservative grumbling that Dirksen had been too willing to help a Democratic administration. Dirksen's often tepid resistance to the administration's legislative agenda after 1965 centered on the need to pay for the war. "To keep expenditures in balance," Dirksen said in 1966, "[Johnson] is going to have to cut somewhere, and he certainly can't cut the war." The whole tone and tenor "of the second session of the 89th Congress," *Time's* Neil MacNeil wrote, "has been dictated by the ominous and oppressive war in Vietnam."[49]

On the same day Mansfield pledged to do what he could to advance Johnson's legislative agenda, Walter Lippmann, the influential syndicated columnist, wrote on what he called "the Mansfield report," a white paper on Vietnam that the majority leader prepared with Republicans George Aiken and Caleb Boggs and Democrats Edmund Muskie and Daniel Inouye. The report followed yet another Mansfield visit to Saigon, a trip at the end of 1965 that Johnson sanctioned, at least in part to avoid the appearance that an open split over the war had developed with Mansfield. "Here for the first time," Lippmann wrote, "we have a report on the war which is responsible, informed and trustworthy," in contrast to official statements and briefings that had created "a crisis of credibility" for the administration. Scripps-Howard columnist Richard Starnes was even more pointed. "A more sobering document than the Mansfield Report is difficult to imagine," Starnes said. "It strips away the deceit, the foolishness and the wishful thinking, and exposes gathering disaster in Southeast Asia in all its naked horror." Mansfield's report asserted in straightforward terms that Johnson's policy was leading to "a military situation which is, in effect, open ended." Lippmann lamented that the report had not received the attention it deserved, although it was apparently widely read within the Senate. The headline above the column in the *Missoulian* was stark: "Mansfield Report Shows Viet Nam War Could Be Endless."[50]

Hundreds of requests for Mansfield's Vietnam report poured into the majority leader's office. Dozens of Montanans requested copies, but requests came as well from academics at the University of California, Indiana State College, Finch College, the University of Oregon, and Northwestern University. The publication manager of Ford Motor Company and the Harris County, Texas, Republican Party requested copies. Marriner Eccles, the former chairman of the Federal Reserve, wrote Mansfield with his views about the need to withdraw American troops from South Vietnam and received a copy of the report. Two copies of the white paper were sent to every college library in Montana.[51]

"He didn't like it," Mansfield said of Johnson's reaction to his blunt reporting. "Four or five times I was the only one who spoke out [against the course of action] in White House meetings. Everyone else would agree. I felt lonely." At the heart of Mansfield's advice, consistent over the course of Johnson's presidency, was his contention that only a sustained international effort that included all-party negotiations offered a realistic path to end the fighting in Vietnam. Mansfield's gloomy report was part of Johnson's motivation when he did give in to pressure and pause the bombing campaign of North Vietnam late in 1965, hoping the gesture would encourage peace talks. Privately, the majority leader pressed the president to take other actions as well, advice that Johnson ignored. Asked why the president so completely rejected his advice, Mansfield replied succinctly: "He didn't want to lose. He didn't want to withdraw."[52]

When Johnson finally resumed bombing, intensifying the war in the north, only Mansfield and Foreign Relations Committee Chairman Fulbright objected during a leadership meeting at the White House. Johnson grumbled about both men: "Fulbright's awful mean, and awful narrow, and awful little," Johnson said, "he's almost as tough to get along with as Mansfield." Dirksen, meanwhile, encouraged Johnson to do whatever it took to win the war militarily, but while he pointedly criticized antiwar Democrats by name, he never criticized Mansfield. Occasionally Dirksen questioned Johnson's methods in prosecuting the war, but he never criticized Johnson. More than ever, the minority leader's views on Vietnam influenced the president. Dirksen became "the White House's indispensable agent," as biographer Byron Hulsey put it, on all matters pertaining to the war.[53]

—

The Great Society did not translate into a great midterm election for congressional Democrats in 1966. Republicans flipped forty-seven seats in the House of Representatives and three in the Senate, including an election won by Dirksen's son-in-law,

Dirksen talks, Johnson is ready to talk, Mansfield listens. (*US Senate Historical Office*)

Howard Baker of Tennessee, who had campaigned as a critic of the Great Society. Dirksen was very proud and said of Baker, who would himself one day also occupy a Senate leadership post: "He is very able, very capable, and has a sense of public service . . . he is right independent in his thinking."[54]

In the all-but-inevitable political backlash against Lyndon Johnson's ambitious agenda, the Senate's output of significant legislation slowed to a trickle in 1967. Nevertheless, history was made on August 30 when then solicitor general and former civil rights lawyer Thurgood Marshall became the first Black American to be confirmed for a seat on the Supreme Court. "I haven't the slightest doubt that he will be confirmed," Dirksen said when Johnson announced his nominee. "He's a good lawyer, and the fact of his color should make no difference." Mansfield promised Marshall's confirmation would be handled "expeditiously," but, as was his practice, he did nothing to pressure Judiciary Committee Chairman Eastland, who presided over confirmation hearings that stretched out for more than two months. The committee's Southerners eventually grilled Marshall for five straight days, then took a week's recess before advancing the nomination to the full Senate. Dirksen rallied every Republican with the exception of Strom Thurmond in strong bipartisan support of the historic appointment. The opposition came from die-hard conservative southern Democrats, including North Carolina's Sam Ervin, who called Marshall "a constitutional iconoclast" who "would make it virtually certain that for years to come, if not forever, the American people will be ruled by the arbitrary notions of Supreme Court Justices rather than by the precepts of the Constitution."[55]

In spite of the passage of important civil rights legislation, and in the wake of widespread recognition that an accomplished Black lawyer should finally sit on the Supreme Court, racial turmoil exploded across the country in the "long hot summer" of 1967. More than 150 urban riots, including a brutal outbreak of violence in Detroit that left forty-three dead, shook Washington and shocked the nation. Dr. King delineated the causes as "white backlash," unemployment, still-widespread discrimination, the war, and "features peculiar to big cities: crime, family problems, and intensive migration." King said the Johnson administration was "more concerned with winning the war in Vietnam than in winning the war on poverty," and the Southern Christian Leadership Conference formally condemned "the racist pressures of the real estate lobby," which the group blamed for congressional inaction to end housing discrimination.[56]

CBS correspondent Daniel Schorr, who often covered Congress in the 1960s, began to notice a change in the Senate as the decade progressed. Despite Mansfield's constant efforts and personal example, civility was suffering. Schorr had to admit that television coverage was responsible. Senators, Schorr recalled, "frequently raised their voices for no reason at all, just because they knew it would get our attention by doing that." Dr. King complained to Schorr that the now-ubiquitous presence of television, always seeking out conflict, also influenced the civil rights movement by focusing on the most inflammatory, radical language while exhibiting little interest in King's nonviolent approach to protest. "When Negros are incited to violence, will you think of your responsibility in helping produce it?" King asked him. "Did I go on seeking menacing sound bites as my passport to the evening news?" Schorr asked himself in response. "I'm afraid I did."[57]

⁓

After seven years of what Roland Evans and Robert Novak dismissed as Mansfield's "ever docile" Senate leadership, the institution had changed. Gone was the notion that a small group of clubby, secretive insiders led by a domineering majority leader ran the show. For good or bad, and there were strong opinions both ways, Mansfield had brought something like democracy to the Senate, in no small part because of his remarkable political and personal relationship with Dirksen. "We've shifted our way of doing things in a bloodless coup, and outsiders have hardly noticed," Michigan Democrat Phil Hart said. "If [Mansfield] had tried something like this eight years ago—or even five years ago—he would have a full-fledged revolt on his hands. Even at that, I wouldn't make book that it would have happened under other leadership." The deference Mansfield exhibited to every senator, even the most junior ones in the minority, served to defuse power, particularly so when the majority leader purposely ceded power to the minority leader. Senate individualism was enhanced, a change that would only grow over time, along with the ability of a single senator or a determined leader, often acting on purely partisan or personal grounds, to abuse the institution's norms and complicated rules. Mansfield succeeded with Senate democracy, but he could not force senators to be responsible to the institution or to embrace Dirksen's pragmatic bipartisanship. Those who longed for the days when Lyndon Johnson and a few insiders dictated Senate decisions by stroking backs and twisting arms could not quarrel with the legislative accomplishments of Mansfield's and Dirksen's Senate. That record stands as a monument to one of the most productive and significant periods of legislating in the history of Congress.[58]

The relationship Mike Mansfield built with Everett Dirksen has few if any precedents in Senate history. It came to transcend the desire, acknowledged by both leaders, for bipartisan cooperation in running the Senate and reached a level of genuine personal affection, illustrated by occasional and apparently random gifts from Mansfield. Dirksen reciprocated the kindness, co-chairing in 1967 an effort to endow the Mike Mansfield Lectures in International Relations at the University of Montana. Dirksen wrote letters to many of his own financial supporters, soliciting contributions for the effort. The campaign, in which Mansfield refused to participate, raised a modest sum for the lecture program and created partisan backlash for Dirksen. "Sorry Ev," a Cincinnati businessman scrawled on Dirksen's letter, "let [Thomas] Dodd do it," apparently a reference to an ongoing ethics investigation of the Democratic senator. Another recipient of a Dirksen letter, one of the original founders of the John Birch Society, wondered what had happened to the minority leader who, the correspondent suggested, had clearly abandoned his conservative principles to raise money for a liberal Democrat. "Nothing has happened to me," Dirksen responded. He disagreed with Mansfield "fervently on many things," Dirksen wrote, "but is that any reason why we shouldn't pay tribute to his Americanism and his public service?" Mansfield was a "great American who came up the hard way.... I respect him greatly." In closing his response, Dirksen delivered a stinger. "The question in my mind is how reactionary have you gotten. All in good spirit, and with every good wish." Dirksen writing letters to his own supporters soliciting contributions for an effort to celebrate his partisan opposite number was as remarkable then as it is unthinkable today.[59]

As was their habit, Mansfield and Dirksen exchanged letters at the end of the 1967 session of Congress. Dirksen, slowed by his many ailments and worn out by his unrelenting pace of work, wrote more poetically and more personally than ever:

> The Senate of the United States could be a difficult adventure and a tortu-ous road to travel if it were not for your superb tolerance, your devotion to the country, and the humility with which you have accepted the slings and arrows of outrageous fortune as Shakespeare once put it.
>
> Truly it has been a pleasure to be across the aisle from you in the knowl-edge that that aisle does not separate us in our convictions, devotions, and our friendship.
>
> I share your concern about the future and sometimes I wonder whether we haven't seen the best of this country. We can continue to make progress in the most majestic manner and still refrain from the kind of violence and pettiness which marks the attitude of some of the groups in our county who are willing to resort to any measure in order to accomplish their objectives. All the more need, therefore, for us to stand steadfast and be forthright in our devotion to the Republic.
>
> As the door of the New Year beckons, let me wish for you and Maureen every one of life's choicest blessings.[60]

9 END OF AN ERA

> You get a partner like Dirksen and form a dream relationship once
> in a century.
>
> —MIKE MANSFIELD

On the evening of January 31, 1968, Vietcong troops stormed the US embassy in Saigon and held parts of the most secure American outpost in South Vietnam for more than six hours. Communist troops simultaneously attacked eight other cities across the country. It was the beginning of what became the Tet Offensive, a defining moment in the long American war in Vietnam. Shortly after the embassy compound was secured, with the loss of several American and many more Vietnamese lives, General William Westmoreland, the US military commander in Vietnam, walked through rubble. "The enemy exposed himself by virtue of his strategy and he suffered great causalities," Westmoreland told disbelieving reporters, including Don Oberdorfer, then a *Washington Post* correspondent and later Mike Mansfield's biographer. "The reporters could hardly believe their ears," Oberdorfer recounted. "Westmoreland was standing in the ruins and saying everything was great."[1]

Two days later in Washington, amid much speculation that Lyndon Johnson would call up reservists to insert yet more Americans into the war, Mike Mansfield called for the administration to "reassess the whole picture" in Vietnam. "On the basis of the past three days, we must take a new look and a harder look at the situation in Vietnam," Mansfield said. Two weeks earlier, Everett Dirksen had reaffirmed his support for the war. "What are we going to do other than what the president is doing right now?" Dirksen asked. "We can't retreat, we can't pull out and we can't get the other side to negotiate." Dirksen and Mansfield, so often able to find common ground amid great controversy, never got close to common ground on Vietnam.[2]

Tet was just one tumultuous, transformative event in a year of transformative events. From Chicago to Prague, 1968 was a year of global turmoil, "a spontaneous combustion of rebellious spirits around the world," as historian Mark Kurlansky put it. During the year of upheaval, an unwinnable war drove a president to abandon his hopes of reelection; a US senator, brother of a murdered president, and Dr. Martin Luther King Jr., the foremost advocate of peaceful protest in the service of civil rights, both died at the hands of assassins; the Democratic National Convention in Chicago descended into chaos and riots and smoothed the way for the second act of Richard Nixon's political life. A Senate fight over a Supreme Court nominee created a template for virtually every subsequent appointment to the court, and Mansfield risked his political future to support a gun-control measure. It was also the year Mansfield and Dirksen worked together to help pass a third major civil rights bill, a feat accomplished while Dirksen's health was in precipitous decline, his leadership grip on Senate Republicans was weakening, and he successfully sought a fourth Senate term.[3]

Historian Robert Dallek was correct when he wrote, "By 1968 the great mandate of the 1964 election had been lost in the flames of Vietnam. And along with it, the national consensus for Cold War policies abroad and liberal social reforms at home." Yet, Lyndon Johnson's Great Society had one last gasp—the Fair Housing Act, which completed the trifecta of transformative civil rights legislation that arguably remains the hallmark of bipartisanship in the Mansfield-Dirksen era. The minority leader's Senate maneuvering to overcome one more filibuster and pass a bill with broad bipartisan support had all the earmarks of classic Dirksen legislating, including a sharp reversal of position and almost certainly a deal with Lyndon Johnson that virtually assured Dirksen's reelection.[4]

After Johnson's State of the Union speech in January 1968, Mike Mansfield pledged Senate action on a long-stalled housing bill, legislation Dirksen had long opposed in the belief that almost any proposal would infringe on individual property rights. When fair housing legislation had been considered in 1966, Dirksen rose on his crutches to condemn "a package of mischief for the country." Mansfield, always the realist, expressed doubt that Dirksen would rediscover his old flexibility from 1964 and 1965 and join him in getting a bill passed to address housing discrimination.[5]

Dirksen's influence with the Republican Senate caucus was clearly slipping, but he could, if he chose, still kill a civil rights bill. A cloture vote on a housing bill on February 20, 1968, failed with Dirksen voting no. He claimed federal legislation was unnecessary and appeared to indicate he was solidly opposed to any bill. "I will take nothing on the federal level," Dirksen said. But powerful Senate and White House forces were in play. Half the Senate Republicans had voted for cloture and against Dirksen, a much different outcome than in previous votes on similar legislation. A second cloture vote six days later also failed, but one more Republican, conservative Norris Cotton of New Hampshire, voted in favor. The next day—February 27—Dirksen turned on a dime, perhaps a case of what Senator Paul Douglas termed his "weather-vane sensitivity," and announced he would now support a bill and intended to meet with Mansfield to work on the details. "Chain-smoking and gulping cups of cold coffee," Byron Hulsey wrote, Dirksen explained his latest switch to reporters. "Time and reality make you older and wiser," the minority leader said. When Dirksen was asked whether the increasing number of Republicans abandoning him on cloture indicated his influence was slipping, he responded, "Maybe I can find comfort in the fact that you have to be a pretty strong bastard to take the slings and arrows." Another way perhaps of acknowledging yes, a good part of his caucus had left him, and he was now racing to rejoin them. Still, Dirksen maintained, and for Mansfield this was the critical issue, that he had rescued the bill. There would be a chance to legislate.[6]

Another critical calculation seems to have influenced Dirksen's about-face. Illinois Democrats had several attractive candidates ready to challenge Dirksen's reelection, including then state auditor Adlai Stevenson III, but these were still the days when the makeup of the statewide Democratic ticket depended on the preference of just one man, Chicago's autocratic mayor Richard J. Daley, a close ally of Lyndon Johnson's. On February 28, Daley announced his slate and the *Chicago Tribune* noted in a headline, "Democrats Fail to Pick Adlai." Rather than select the strongest Democratic candidate against Dirksen—others widely considered serious contenders included Eunice Kennedy's husband Sargent Shriver and future senator Paul Simon—Daley had chosen the weakest one available, Illinois attorney general William G. Clark, a lackluster party functionary, Daley loyalist, and candidate unlikely to present much of a challenge to Dirksen. A contemporary observer, Tom Wicker of the *New York Times*, saw clearly what was going on. "Dirksen's support for civil rights just might cause President Johnson and his ally, Mayor Richard Daley . . . to lose interest in a strong opponent for Dirksen, just as President Kennedy gave little if any help to Sydney [sic] Yates who ran against him in 1962." Dirksen, the consummate dealmaker, had seemingly engineered a political twofer: his switch on the fair housing bill got him right with a majority of his caucus and he got a weak reelection opponent.[7]

UCLA law professor Jonathan Zasloff details these events in a 2017 article entitled "The Secret History of the Fair Housing Act." Zasloff acknowledges that, short of a séance, it is impossible to know for sure what quid pro quos were actually fashioned among Johnson, Dirksen, and Daley, but he makes a persuasive case that the timeline reveals an intricate political deal. "The Senate was at an impasse [on fair housing legislation] for virtually all of January and February," Zasloff writes. "Dirksen had already loudly rejected fair housing on both policy and constitutional grounds. For dozens of civil rights bills, that was a recipe for a successful filibuster. Then, in late February, Dirksen started negotiating privately with the White House; a few days later a vague compromise was announced; Daley chose Clark; and Dirksen voted for cloture on the new bill." After talking with Dirksen in late February, Johnson reportedly told members of his staff, "We are going to get the Civil Rights bill! Dirksen is going to come out in support . . . and don't ask me what I had to give him." Dirksen maintained he came around because of concerns about more urban unrest. Whatever his motivation, Dirksen had indeed saved the bill.[8]

The Senate passed the Fair Housing Act on March 11, 1968, with the usual southern Democrats voting no. It was a stronger bill than those Dirksen had earlier opposed, and only three Senate Republicans voted in opposition. It was the third time in five years that Dirksen and Mansfield had succeeded with a bipartisan strategy to end a Senate filibuster and pass a major piece of civil rights legislation. But unlike on the previous occasions, there was little celebration. The latest bipartisan accomplishment was overshadowed by press reports of a contentious appearance before the Foreign Relations Committee by Secretary of State Dean Rusk. "Why are we in Vietnam?" Mansfield asked Rusk, who mumbled an answer about preventing an attack from North Vietnam. Rusk refused to commit to further bombing halts or negotiations.[9]

The fair housing legislation immediately stalled in the House of Representatives, where many members, as historian Randall Woods has written, were "besieged by white middle-class constituents determined to keep Blacks out of their neighborhoods." Tragically, it was the murder of Dr. Martin Luther King in Memphis on April 4 that finally forced favorable House action. Johnson signed the legislation on April 11. The *Chicago Tribune* placed the story on page 7 with no mention of Dirksen, but the paper did note that his reelection campaign would get a boost from actress Shirley Temple Black, who would appear at a fundraiser for Dirksen.[10]

Lyndon Johnson's decision to end his political career—announced at the very end of a televised speech on March 31, 1968, where Johnson also announced limits on future bombing of North Vietnam—remains one of the most astonishing surprises in presidential history. Mansfield received a call one hour before the speech. "I was shocked and dismayed," he said. Deep differences over Vietnam had strained their relationship to the breaking point, but Mansfield immediately praised Johnson's decision—"a very strong initiative"—to begin peace talks. Dirksen, issuing a statement from his hospital bed at Walter Reed Army Medical Center, seemed to convey a certain resignation that Richard Nixon, never a favorite of his, would now likely become president. Johnson's fellow Democrats had assailed the president with "personal and sometimes ugly" attacks, Dirksen said, and that vitriol finally took its toll on Johnson.[11]

Johnson was immediately a lame duck, but he hardly behaved like one, and Dirksen and Mansfield continued to work in a bipartisan fashion to help him finish his presidency with a victory. Johnson leaned particularly hard on Dirksen to help elevate Associate Justice Abe Fortas to chief justice of the Supreme Court, replacing retiring chief justice Earl Warren. When Johnson announced the nominations of Fortas, an old friend—some would say crony—of his, and Texas judge Homer Thornberry, another old friend, to replace Fortas, Dirksen pronounced both men qualified and confirmable. Mansfield also predicted confirmation. But once again Dirksen had misread the Senate Republican conference, and particularly his ability to deliver votes for a president in the twilight of his career. Before the ink dried on the Fortas nomination paperwork, nineteen Senate Republicans vowed to oppose Johnson's lame duck appointments. Even Dirksen's son-in-law, Howard Baker, said he would oppose the nominees. Michigan Republican Robert P. Griffin was the opposition ringleader. Griffin, appointed to the Senate in 1966, was representative of a new breed of Republicans, more combative, less willing to defer to a bipartisan dealmaker like Dirksen, and determined to present a different, updated image of the party. As a member of the House, Griffin helped engineer the party coup that replaced minority leader Charlie Halleck with Gerald Ford. Griffin now resented, as historian Byron Hulsey wrote, "Johnson's assumption that a retiring president and a few anointed leaders on Capitol Hill could ram contentious nominations through the Senate."[12]

Griffin and like-minded colleagues, aided by conservative southern Democrats who considered Fortas too liberal, delayed the confirmation hearings long enough for serious questions about the nominee's ethics to come to light. Those questions eventually soured Mansfield on the nomination, as did Johnson's failure to produce votes supporting Fortas from southern Democrats. When Dirksen finally abandoned the Fortas nomination, signaling he would not support a cloture motion while also getting on the right side of his caucus again, the nomination tanked. Ironically,

Johnson had predicted the outcome. "I know him," Johnson told an aide, "I know the Senate. If they get this thing drug out very long, we're going to get beat. Ev Dirksen will leave us if this thing gets strung over very long." Asked if Dirksen's about-face would hurt Fortas's chances, Mansfield said, "It sure as hell will." Predictably, a cloture vote fell far short, and Fortas asked that his nomination be withdrawn. This marked the first time in Senate history that a Supreme Court nominee was defeated by a filibuster, and arguably, the beginning of the now-routine and profoundly partisan Senate battles over Supreme Court appointments.[13]

On September 18, 1968, Mike Mansfield cast the most controversial vote of his political career. He voted for the Gun Control Act of 1968, which restricts interstate sales of rifles, shotguns, and ammunition, and he caught political hell for the vote in Montana. After the assassination of Senator Robert Kennedy in June 1968, Mansfield cosponsored a proposal requiring state-level action on gun registration and licensing, a much stronger proposal than eventually cleared the Senate. Bobby Kennedy's murder profoundly affected the majority leader, who had developed a deep affection for both murdered Kennedy brothers. One aide remembered Mansfield as "maybe the most emotional I ever saw him" after Bobby was shot minutes after winning the Democratic presidential primary in California. "What in the name of God has happened to us?" Mansfield asked in a statement. He worried about the blind hatred of gun violence and wondered whether Americans were "so immersed in ourselves that we cannot live with one another in peace and amity." While Bobby Kennedy's assassination affected Mansfield profoundly, he was also stunned by another murder that occurred at the same time in Washington, DC. Twenty-year-old Thaddeus Lesnick, a Marine second lieutenant from Fishtail, Montana, a tiny unincorporated town just north of Yellowstone National Park, was eating lunch with two other Marines at a hamburger joint in the Georgetown neighborhood when all three and a woman with them were shot. Lesnick and a second victim died. Mansfield wrote Lesnick's mother, saying he had "been deeply shocked by similar tragedies which befell two close personal friends and colleagues, John F. Kennedy and Robert F. Kennedy. Yet, it was the death of your son . . . which was decisive in bringing me to a soul-searching reexamination of the question of gun-control."[14]

Mansfield's mail, overwhelmingly opposed to his gun-control position, was the heaviest on any subject during his thirty-four years in politics. "Who in the world does Mike Mansfield think he is?" asked a letter to the editor in the *Billings Gazette*. "Is his intelligence so superior to his constituents that he can decide what's best in gun legislation when by his own admission his constituents are three to one against his stand?" Mansfield said his position was one of "conscience." In closing Senate debate on the gun bill, Mansfield told his colleagues: "We should remember that we all wear two hats, one is as Senator from our state and the other as a Senator of the United States. Those of us who come from the rural West have an obligation to the rest of the country to help cut down on crime." The *New York Times* noted his appeal fell on deaf ears, as few western senators supported him. Still, the bill passed the Senate seventy to seventeen, a strong bipartisan showing. Dirksen joined Mansfield in voting yes. That thirteen senators did not vote indicated the sensitivity for some of even being recorded on the issue. Mansfield's Montana colleague Lee Metcalf was one of the no votes. "Mike is the only man in the Senate from a western state," Metcalf later said, "who can run against the gun lobby and still get elected."[15]

In November 1968, Mansfield drove to remote Fishtail, Montana, to call upon the Lesnick family. In a follow-up letter to the mother of the murdered Montana Marine, Mansfield said "it was a personal privilege for me to have the opportunity to call on you . . . because of Thad and you, a great impression was made on my thinking, and a position which I had held down through the years was changed completely." His position on gun control would become the dominant issue in Mansfield's last reelection campaign in 1970. Nevertheless, he won easily against the owner of a sporting goods store who criticized the gun-control vote and said Mansfield was "soft on communism."[16]

—

Everett Dirksen won his last campaign in 1968 in a contest that was closer than most had expected. Ironically, with Republican Richard Nixon now in the White House replacing Dirksen's friend Lyndon Johnson, Dirksen's very short fourth term marked the nadir of his political influence. Dirksen had known Nixon for years but had never developed the personal chemistry or lust for dealmaking that made Dirksen so influential during Johnson's presidency. It likely did not help the relationship that Nixon selected the virtually unknown Maryland governor Spiro Agnew as his running mate, against the wishes of Dirksen, who was pushing his son-in-law, Howard Baker. Mansfield as well faced a new political reality after 1968. He no longer had the responsibility of championing an administration's agenda in the Senate, and while Mansfield maintained cordial relations with Nixon—regular breakfast meetings at the White House, for example—he was now cast as the most important Democrat in the nation. In his measured way, Mansfield challenged much of Nixon's domestic agenda, continued his own efforts to end the war while growing increasingly skeptical of Nixon's strategy in Vietnam, and enthusiastically supported Nixon's opening to China.[17]

Two weeks after Nixon took office, Mansfield convened a luncheon meeting of the Democratic Policy Committee, the party's senior leadership in the Senate. His remarks to the eight members, a diverse group that included Southerners like Russell and Fulbright and liberals like Ted Kennedy and John Pastore, were remarkable in 1969, and even more so now in light of the profoundly partisan divides of the Senate of the twenty-first century. "We must put, above all else," Mansfield said, "the interests of the nation and the President's unique role in safeguarding them as well as the demeanor and effective operation of the Senate as the Constitutional institution through which each of us serves those interests. These are the highest priorities." It was a quintessentially Mansfield-like plea for the Senate, with Democrats in the majority, to rise above partisanship now that a Republican occupied the White House.[18]

At the same time, Mansfield certainly knew—as Dirksen did—of Nixon's dark side. A rare Mansfield partisan broadside in 1954 accused then vice president Nixon of dragging "politics to its lowest ebb" with his attacks on Democrats "as socialistic, left-wing, [and] soft on Communism." And Lyndon Johnson took Dirksen into his confidence at the very end of the 1968 presidential campaign when the president found out, by wiretapping the South Vietnamese embassy in Washington, that Nixon's campaign was using a third party to encourage the South Vietnamese government to slow-walk peace talks. "I'm reading their hand, Everett," Johnson told Dirksen in a state of high agitation. "This is treason." Dirksen mumbled, "I know."[19]

Ironically, in 1969, Dirksen often gave Nixon more grief than Mansfield did. The minority leader opposed several Nixon appointees, a decision that baffled some of his closest friends and sparked criticism from Republicans. "Dirksen has confused if not confounded many in Washington by his cavalier and at times defiant attitude toward some of the people his own Republican President has sought to recruit," John Averill wrote in the Los Angeles Times. Criticism of Dirksen grew more pointed as he defied the new president. He was too old, it was said—Dirksen was seventy-three—and had too many scores to settle. He was said to be out of touch with the country, and with Johnson gone, merely to be trying to demonstrate that he still had influence. Dirksen's own explanation for challenging a Republican president, viewed in light of his knowledge of the Nixon campaign's tactics related to Vietnam, seems more plausible. He was, Dirksen said, protecting Nixon "from people I feel do him no good and could do him harm."[20]

Dirksen had clearly slowed down and was now subject to more personal controversy as well. Press reports zeroed in on his finances and ethics. A questionable relationship with a Peoria law firm that paid Dirksen for referring clients generated headlines and calls for a Senate investigation. Dirksen's health problems—an ulcer, emphysema, a bad back, heart issues—accumulated, and when doctors discovered a malignant tumor on his right lung in August 1969, his days were numbered. Dirksen survived the cancer surgery, something his doctors doubted possible, but a few days later suffered severe cardiac and respiratory failure. Everett Dirksen died on September 7, 1969. His death was front-page news across the country.[21]

"To me it is a great personal loss," Mansfield said. "He was a real professional in the real sense of the word. We always laid our cards on the table. It was the kind of relationship I always dreamed of." In remarks in the Senate, Mansfield said "the Senate has lost a Senate man . . . yet, his death does not diminish the Senate. His uniqueness is the stuff of legends, and he leaves here a permanent imprint and an enduring echo." Dirksen's obituary in the *New York Times* led with his role in passing the Limited Nuclear Test Ban Treaty in 1963. "Mr. Dirksen probably assured himself a place in the history books by three great reversals over three years," the *Times's* E. W. Kenworthy wrote, "on the United Nations bond issue of 1962, the nuclear test ban treaty of 1963 and the Civil Rights Act of 1964." It was decided immediately that Dirksen would receive the exceedingly rare honor of lying in state in the Capitol Rotunda, an expression of respect accorded to only three other senators before him.[22]

Columnist David Lawrence wrote of Dirksen's "warm personality" and political astuteness. "Contemporaries in Congress will agree," Lawrence said, "that he showed a knack in leadership which is sometimes called political skill but in reality is a keen understanding of human nature and how to make agreements and compromises in a complex legislative situation."

The widely respected Peter Lisagor, who knew Dirksen well in his role as Washington bureau chief of the *Chicago Daily News*, wrote that many saw the Illinois senator "as an artful dodger and political cardsharp . . . politics to him was a game of compromise and maneuver, and he served so many interests that he was constantly under suspicion." Dirksen was no saint, Lisagor wrote, "nor was he wicked," but he was "an authentic institution, a political original, he will be missed." The *Chicago Tribune*, often conflicted about whether to embrace Dirksen for his bipartisan accomplishments or condemn him for his offenses to conservative orthodoxy, called him "a living legend."[23]

The *Tribune* sampled "man in the street" sentiments about the senator's death, including one from Dr. William Boikan, a Chicago physician who seems to have understood Dirksen as well as any political analyst. "The thing I remember most about Sen. Dirksen was that he was called 'old bear grease' by his detractors," Boikan said. "It is true that the senator often changed his mind on issues, but he judged issues on an individual basis rather than on a partisan one—to my way of thinking his lack of consistency was logical."[24]

At the time of Everett Dirksen's death, Mike Mansfield was only halfway through his record-setting tenure as majority leader, a position he would hold until January 1977. Mansfield immediately formed a close, bipartisan working relationship with Dirksen's successor, Pennsylvania Senator Hugh Scott, a moderate to liberal-leaning Republican, a recognized expert on Chinese art, and like Mansfield, rarely without his pipe. Scott defeated Howard Baker in a leadership contest that was widely seen as a victory for Republican moderates eager to make a pivot from Dirksen's style of personal and personality-driven leadership. Scott did share with Dirksen a reputation for political flexibility, once saying "a wise man changes his mind often and a fool never." Francis Valeo has noted that Scott, like Dirksen, stood squarely with Mansfield "on all matters affecting the status of the Senate and its powers and prerogatives within the government." When in 1974, for example, Mansfield contemplated creation of a select committee to investigate the Watergate affair, he consulted closely with Scott, who agreed with the move. The two leaders also quietly agreed on how the Senate would approach a trial of Richard Nixon should the issue of his impeachment reach the Senate. The two leaders, each with a deep interest in China policy and enjoying a personal friendship, traveled with their wives to China in 1972, a sixteen-day trip that Richard Nixon tried to prevent, fearing that Mansfield intended to use the visit to criticize his foreign policy. On returning to Washington, Mansfield, as he had with Kennedy and Johnson, presented Nixon with his candid, confidential observations and recommendations. He praised without exception Nixon's opening to China.[25]

Mike Mansfield announced that he would not seek reelection to the Senate in 1976, an election almost every observer believed he would have won easily. Consciously or not, in his announcement he invoked the inscription John Kennedy had scribbled fifteen years earlier on the photograph of Mansfield leaving the leadership scrum outside the White House. "There is a time to stay and a time to go," Mansfield said. "Thirty-four years is not a long time but it is time enough." Mansfield had served with seven presidents, a career spanning "one-sixth of the nation's history since independence." Mansfield styled his decision to retire—he would soon have a further career as US ambassador to Japan for a dozen years—as "a final public service; to the nation, to the Senate, and to the people of Montana. A great public trust has been reposed in me in so many ways and for so many years. For whatever time remains to me I shall be grateful to the nation, the Senate and to my state for this confidence. I ask now that this trust be shifted to other shoulders."

"His voice began wavering as he finished reading," the *Times* reported. "He sat down, wiped his nose with a handkerchief and sat with his eyes cast downward and his arms folded across his chest for the next 45 minutes as senator after senator rose to praise his fairness and integrity." One senator who spoke, his voice breaking too, was Minority Leader Hugh Scott. "I have never known a man who is more distinguished by his complete fairness and his total integrity," Scott said. "He has in every instance put the interests of the country above any other consideration." We are taught to believe, Scott said, that there are no indispensable men, but "nevertheless, we believe that there are some people whose services are so great that the very thought of the termination of those services is a recognition of a loss too vast to be smoothly and quickly measured."[26]

EPILOGUE

THE SENATE, MANSFIELD, AND DIRKSEN

Well, he was the greatest American I ever met. I mean, Mansfield was.
I have just absolutely limitless admiration for him in terms of integrity
and foresight and extraordinary modesty. I never knew George Marshall.
People talked about Marshall in those terms, but Mansfield had all
of those qualities.

—DAVID BRODER

As he could persuade, he could be persuaded. His respect for other points
of view lent weight to his own point of view. He was not afraid to change
his position if he were persuaded that he had been wrong. That tolerance
and sympathy were elements of his character and that character gained
him the affection and esteem of millions of his fellow Americans.

—RICHARD NIXON ON
EVERETT DIRKSEN, 1969

Invented as the product of a compromise that created the American Constitution,
the United States Senate was part of a grand bargain struck by the Founders to
"resolve a fundamental power struggle between the most populous states and their
smaller counterparts." Because of how it is structured—two senators elected from
every state without regard to population—the Senate is the most undemocratic,
least representative elective institution of the federal government. It is also one of
the few legislative bodies in the world designed to ensure power for the minority.[1]

The Senate, with the obvious exceptions of the presidency and an increasingly
ideological Supreme Court, may also be the most important institution of the government, "one of the rocks of the Republic," as Mike Mansfield was fond of saying.

The Senate confirms presidential appointees, including federal judges, it passes judgment (as we have seen) on treaties, and its exalted place as the "upper house" of the national legislature gives the Senate special standing on matters of foreign policy and oversight of the executive branch. Yet, the problems of the modern Senate are legion, and seemingly only growing. The most common word used to describe the Senate in the twenty-first century is "dysfunctional."[2]

One of the most obvious examples of Senate dysfunction is the stark fact that "the world's greatest deliberative body" hardly deliberates any more. The great debates that frequently marked the Senate of the past and were certainly features of the Senate in the 1960s, serving to illuminate, educate, and even persuade, have given way to set-piece partisan soundbites typically designed only to abuse the other party while appealing to a polarized electorate. Jeff Merkley, a Democrat from Oregon in his second term, has said during his time in the Senate he remembers witnessing only one actual floor debate between a Republican and a Democrat. "The memory I took with me was: Wow, that's unusual—there's a conversation occurring in which they're making point and counterpoint and challenging each other. And yet nobody else was in the chamber."[3]

Increasing partisan polarization of American politics over the last forty years has only enhanced the power of small states, underscoring the Senate's undemocratic character and further contributing to its dysfunction. Critics frequently observe that sparsely populated states such as Wyoming or Vermont enjoy the same voting clout as highly populated California and Florida. But, as Mike Mansfield, a small-state senator, and Everett Dirksen, a large-state senator, understood in their day, this reality is baked into the Constitution and is unlikely to change soon, or ever. Any remedy for this situation almost certainly requires a political solution; namely, commitment by both parties to compete more credibly for Senate seats in states they now often write off. Given greater population growth in more populous states, failure to address this fundamentally political rather than structural challenge will, as commentators including Jeff Greenfield have noted, "further strengthen minority rule in the Senate." That, in turn, likely further erodes the credibility of the institution for millions of Americans.[4]

Beyond the Senate's constitutional structure lie other fundamental problems that have become chronic since the days of Mansfield and Dirksen. The deference the majority leader once showed to committee chairmen, Mansfield's insistence that individual senators had a right and responsibility to manage legislation, and the equal standing of the most junior and most senior members has largely given way to what congressional scholar Barbara Sinclair has called "unorthodox lawmaking." Continuing resolutions to fund the government, largely dictated by party leaders, have taken the place of annual budgets hashed out in committee, and extending these tenuous agreements inevitably involves a partisan showdown amid threats to shut down the government. Small groups of Senate leaders often craft the most important legislation entirely separate from the committee process. The standard textbook description of how a bill becomes law is an increasingly inoperative relic of the past. The picture of a Senate majority leader standing next to a Senate minority leader to demonstrate legislative bipartisanship, the kind of image that showcased cooperation between Dirksen and Mansfield, is all but nonexistent today.[5]

As we have seen, the filibuster, an occasional feature of the Senate in the 1960s that Mansfield and Dirksen overcame in order to pass civil rights and other legislation, has more recently become the most dominant feature of a dysfunctional Senate. A determined partisan minority now routinely—and vastly more often than in the 1960s—uses the mere threat of a filibuster to thwart the will of the Senate majority. Changes to the filibuster to eliminate its use, for example, for judicial appointments have done little to quell demands for more changes in the Senate's rules, or in the extreme case elimination of the Senate entirely.[6]

Yet, as Mark Schmitt, a former staffer to New Jersey senator Bill Bradley, has asked, "Shouldn't we expect more from the Senate than merely that it not be an obstacle? It's the rare legislative body anywhere in the democratic world that, in theory, gives individual members so much freedom of movement. Reopening its potential would involve far more than just ending the filibuster." Imagine real debates in the Senate again on voting rights, gun control, or the government's response to a pandemic. Or imagine a real filibuster again, when in order to stop consideration of legislation or short-circuit an appointment, individual senators had to actually hold the floor for hours or days on end. A so-called talking filibuster would undoubtedly bring with it Senate chaos, including shutting down committee work, but those consequences once made engaging in obstruction, as Richard Russell could tell us, uncomfortable and often self-defeating for the obstructionists. Long-time Senate watcher Walter Shapiro has observed, given widespread television coverage of the Senate, that "the first few days of a talking filibuster—especially if you add the drama of an all-night session or two—could attract a sizable audience." Imagine watching in real time, for example, partisan political obstruction of a voting rights bill. "It would be instructive," Shapiro notes, "to hear their arguments as fatigue stripped away their masquerade that they are defenders of election integrity."[7]

Nearing the end of his legislative career in 1976, Mike Mansfield, prescient about many things, foresaw clearly where the Senate was headed. The occasion was, of course, a filibuster, the use of Senate rules by a minority to frustrate the clear will of the majority:

> My mind goes back to the days of Dick Russell and others who undertook to make their position substantially known on matters of great import affecting not only their part of the country, the South, but the Nation as a whole, and I refer specifically to the great civil rights debates in this body.
>
> We do not have those kinds of debates anymore. But what has developed in the last two years has been a policy by means of which cloture is almost forced on the Senate on practically every piece of legislation of major significance which comes before this body. Not only that, but the substantial way Dick Russell and his colleagues used to handle the imposition of cloture, once it was invoked, has gone by the board.
>
> Substance has disappeared and form has taken its place. Dilatory tactics are the norm. They are not unusual anymore.

Mansfield never advocated eliminating the filibuster, even noting that he had reservations about changing the cloture rule to require sixty votes, believing that "the minority has its rights . . . they should be protected." But, as Mansfield warned in 1976, "there is a breaking point. I hope that the Senate, both the majority and the minority, and its members singly and in groups, will recognize that the institution means a great deal more than any of us. Because if you do not face up to your responsibility, then you are going to have to pay the penalty in the months and in the years ahead." What the minority was doing to the majority, Mansfield said nearly fifty years ago, is "most demeaning to the Senate."[8]

It is not difficult to imagine what Mike Mansfield would make of the Senate of the twenty-first century. He knew that the Senate, given its essentially undemocratic structure, could only function on the basis of cooperation, civility, and compromise. Any individual or faction or party could stymie a majority and erode public faith in the institution by abusing the rules or putting short-term partisan or ideological interests above the interests of the Senate and the country.

The Senate Mike Mansfield tried to foster in the 1960s, often with remarkable cooperation from Everett Dirksen, was an institution that could be more than an obstacle, a legislative body more important than its individual members or its two parties, a collection of diverse personalities of varied interests that could also consistently function as a decision-making body and that could, at least once in a while, rise above its natural state of partisanship.

The essential ingredient that Mansfield—and often Dirksen, as well—exhibited was the exercise of personal responsibility in service to the Senate:

> The thing that counts is not the individual but it is the individuals collectively. It's the vote. It's the record that will stand the test of time and prove whether or not during your time the Senate was an effective institution, that it operated constitutionally, that it recognized that as an institution it was the equal of the [executive] branch, that there was a line of demarcation that should be strictly adhered to, but that difficulties could be subject to compromises or things of that sort to bring about respectable legislation. Dirksen and I both realized it wasn't us, it was them, the entire Senate, which made the decisions, created the record, that left its mark on posterity.[9]

Perhaps Mansfield's long tenure as majority leader, a record length of time for one leader but a short period in the long history of the Senate, was merely an aberration, an interlude where bipartisan cooperation often triumphed but that quickly reverted to partisan gamesmanship once the quiet man from Montana stepped off the Senate floor for the final time. As Francis Valeo said of Mansfield's time as leader,

> It was almost like a Gandhian attempt to run the Senate by Gandhi's non-violent methods. It was a fascinating experience. It could have only happened under Mansfield. I can't think of another member who would have been capable of trying that trick—or trying that approach. I shouldn't use the word "trick," I don't think he used it as a trick. I think it was his nature. He was that way, and as a result the Senate became another way. It was a brief kind of moment in Camelot, if you will, in the Kennedy words. Not quite the same kind of thing, maybe a moment in New Delhi might be closer to it. But it was a different experience.[10]

John Kennedy's murder in Dallas in 1963 prevented Mansfield from addressing, both bluntly and with genuine eloquence, the criticism surrounding his approach to Senate leadership early in his tenure. "I have no heart to read this report to the Senate," Mansfield said at the time, content to have his thoughts preserved in the *Congressional Record*. It seems certain that every senator read Mansfield's "report," a statement of his leadership philosophy as well as a respectful yet pointed demand for responsibility and civility from every member. It is also clear that Mansfield's leadership was never again seriously questioned. For all but the few who remembered the circumstances surrounding Mansfield's dissertation on leadership, as well as the tragedy that prevented him from addressing his colleagues on November 22, 1963, the speech faded into Senate history, only to be revived in the twilight of Mansfield's long life.[11]

On March 24, 1998, at the invitation of then majority leader Trent Lott, a Republican, Mansfield, at age ninety-five, returned to the Capitol and finally delivered the thirty-five-year-old speech—"The Senate and Its Leadership"—to an audience of senators in the Old Senate Chamber. The occasion was both joyous and solemn, marked by nostalgia mixed with obvious longing for more civil times. Lott remarked in introducing Mansfield that "we have had few like him. But then, with the good Lord's help, it only takes a few." The Senate of the 1990s was dominated by a new generation of political leaders—only four Senators who heard Mansfield's speech in 1998 were serving when he prepared the talk in 1963—and new issues and arguably even sharper partisan divisions now demanded the Senate's attention. Yet the fundamentals necessary for the institution to function, Mansfield insisted, remained the same.[12]

I do my best to be courteous, decent and understanding of others and sometimes I fail at it. But it is for the Senate to decide whether these characteristics are incompatible with the leadership.

I have tried to treat others as I would like to be treated and almost invariably have been. And it is for the Senate to decide, too, whether that characteristic is incompatible with Senate leadership.

And, finally, within this body I believe every member ought to be equal in fact not less than in theory, that they have a primary responsibility to the people whom they represent to face the legislative issues of the nation. And to the extent that the Senate may be inadequate in this connection, the remedy lies not in the seeking of short-cuts, not in the cracking of non-existent whips, nor in wheeling and dealing, but in an honest facing of the situation and a resolution of it by the Senate itself, by accommodation, by respect for one another, by mutual restraint and, as necessary, adjustments in the procedures of this body.[13]

As Mansfield told the *New York Times* in 1998, "I've always felt that the true strength of the Senate lay in the center, not on the right and not on the left, but with those people who could see both sides and were not so convinced of their own assumptions that they wouldn't listen to the other side."[14]

Mike Mansfield never shied away from being described as a liberal. He was always a proud Democrat. Everett Dirksen identified as a conservative, a Republican first, last, and always. Yet, in a way that has become exceedingly difficult, perhaps impossible, a half century on from the Mansfield-Dirksen era, both men were often able to put their own partisan roles to the side in order to address major national issues while also elevating the Senate as an institution.

To be sure the copper miner and history professor from Montana and the Illinois thespian and practitioner of flexibility sat across the aisle from each other in a different Senate in a different era. There is no Twilight Lodge today. A liberal Republican is as rare as a conservative Democrat. Scarce is a genuine bipartisan friendship like that of Mansfield and Aiken, or of Dirksen and a president of the other party. An assault on the policies or legitimacy of a president or a member of the other party—often via Twitter—the type of aggressive partisanship Mansfield avoided always and Dirksen used rarely—has become an accepted tactic to stay in the news while shirking the hard work of real lawmaking. A bipartisan coalition to pass legislation critical to the nation's interest has become as rare an occurrence as when Mansfield and Dirksen effectively endorsed each other for reelection. The Senate of Mansfield and Dirksen was far from perfect. It had its scoundrels and lightweights, its obstructionists and charlatans. The general absence of what some have termed "negative partisanship," the idea that politicians and voters are motivated by sheer hatred of their opponents rather by policies or a legislative agenda, was, of course, never complete in the 1960s. Politicians, even the best of them, frequently revert to tribal instincts. The Senate often fell short of attaining Mansfield's vision, and despite the senatorial behavior the leaders attempted to model, the Senate of comity and compromise they presided over for a decade had limited staying power.[15]

When Mike Mansfield died in 2001, his tenure was broadly remembered as "one of the golden ages" of Senate accomplishment. One suspects, however, Mansfield would have enjoyed more a reference made in one obituary that recounted his willingness to credit Dirksen with much of the Senate's success. "Viewed in contrast to today's Senate," Nick Anderson wrote in the Los Angeles Times, "where Republicans and Democrats are nearly evenly matched and duel for any edge, it is difficult to imagine how a senator could lead a 2-to-1 majority without lording it over the other party. Yet that is what Mr. Mansfield did."[16]

The Mansfield-Dirksen Senate is long gone, yet its example still informs, enlightens, and inspires. Senators today, most far removed from the bipartisan civility, cooperation, and accomplishment of the Mansfield-Dirksen era, cannot for even a day avoid the presence of the senators from Montana and Illinois. The looming Dirksen Senate Office Building—unlike the man a rather bland, purely functional edifice—houses some of the Senate's most important committees, while the elegant Mansfield Room in the Capitol—a portrait of the majority leader looks down silently on the room, pipe in hand, as he was in life slightly removed and a bit above—is the location of weekly party caucus luncheons and receptions.[17]

The Senate of the 1960s under the leadership of Mansfield and Dirksen illustrates better than any other modern example what the Founders believed the institution of the Senate had to become: a legislative body where working across a political divide was not evidence of betrayal of your own party, but rather a mark of statesmanship, where the rights of the minority were respected, and where the nation's most important issues came to be litigated and, ultimately, legislated. By holding to the belief that the collective will of the Senate, empowered by good faith, candor, and civility would, even in the face of great social and cultural upheaval, move the nation forward, Mike Mansfield and Everett Dirksen deserve the reputations they enjoy decades after they left the Senate stage. At a time of great cynicism and worrisome concern about the direction of American politics, when significant numbers of Americans increasingly identify with authoritarian and antidemocratic leaders and methods, when national consensus about nearly everything seems beyond reach, and when the US Senate is often the most striking symbol of the nation's starkly partisan divides, the Senate of Mansfield and Dirksen reminds us of what political leadership can and should look like.[18]

They truly were giants of the Senate.

ACKNOWLEDGMENTS

This is my third book about the United States Senate, a trilogy of sorts written out of sequence, beginning in the 1920s and continuing through World War II with a biography of one of the Senate's true mavericks. A second book attempted to explain some of the reasons the Senate and the Republican Party began to change so much after the 1980 election. This book completes the trilogy by focusing on the Senate leadership in the 1960s. This Senate journey has been truly fascinating, and during the years spent researching and writing these books my debts to friends, scholars, librarians, and archivists have accumulated.

I owe an enormous debt of gratitude, one that I cannot possibly repay, to the great folks at the Maureen and Mike Mansfield Center at the University of Montana in Missoula and the Dirksen Congressional Center in Pekin, Illinois. Special thanks are owed to Deena Mansour, the director of the Mansfield Center, and to Tiffany White, who holds a similar position with the Dirksen Center. Both have been generous beyond measure in encouraging and supporting this book, and both centers provided financial support to further my research. Frank Mackaman, the former director of the Dirksen Center and a superb historian and fount of knowledge about all things Dirksen, spent countless hours responding to my questions and providing research materials. From the first moment I contacted Frank, he went out of his way to be helpful and encouraging.

The vast Mansfield Papers at the Maureen and Mike Mansfield Library at the University of Montana is without question one of the greatest collections of Senate papers in existence. Mansfield was, of course, a historian and he—thank goodness—apparently kept everything. The memos Mansfield wrote after important meetings, for example, are invaluable to understanding his approach to political leadership. The special collections at the Mansfield Library are ably presided over by Donna McRae, who was of enormous help. The same must be said for the collection's photo archivist, Mark Fritch, who cheerfully and immediately responded to all my inquiries and helped secure some of the great photos in this book.

Unlike Ev Dirksen, Mike Mansfield was publicity averse, but there are still many pictures of both senators. The superb photo collection at the Senate History

Office—the office was created when Mansfield was majority leader—has proved to be a great resource for all my Senate books. Photo archivist Heather Moore happily and always with insight went above and beyond to locate some wonderful images for the book, more photos than could be accommodated as it turned out. She is simply a joy to work with, as is Betty Koed, the current historian of the Senate.

My old friend Cheryl Oestreicher, head of special collections at the Albertson's Library at Boise State University, home to the papers of Idaho's Senator Frank Church and of my old boss, Governor Cecil Andrus, has never failed me. Often when I have tried and failed to locate a seemingly impossible-to-locate piece of research material, Cheryl has come through. I honestly do not know how she does it, but Cheryl never fails to amaze, and she helped me yet again with this book.

My friend Rob Saldin, a gifted political science scholar and the head of the Mansfield Center's Ethics and Public Policy Program at the University of Montana, applied his discerning eye to the entire manuscript and made numerous helpful suggestions. Rob has been a wonderful advocate for my telling of the Mansfield-Dirksen story. Rob was also instrumental in my appointment as a Mansfield Fellow, a great and unexpected honor that allowed me an ongoing relationship with the university where Mike Mansfield taught.

I am indebted as well to Professor Sean Theriault, a distinguished scholar of Congress who teaches at the University of Texas at Austin. Professor Theriault read the manuscript with great care and insight. His suggestions improved the work and for that I thank him.

Montanan Peggy Joki was kind enough to contact me after reading a piece I wrote about Mike Mansfield that appeared in the *Billings Gazette*. Peggy kindly sent me copies of her family's files about the tragic death in 1968 of her brother, Marine Lieutenant Thad Lesnick. The sadness of Thad's death was, one hopes, lessened at least a bit by Mansfield's outreach to the family, as well as by the remarkable political courage the majority leader demonstrated in advocating for gun-control measures when so many of his constituents clearly opposed them.

Teddy Roe, a former aide to both Mansfield and Montana Senator Lee Metcalf, kindly shared with me his written memories of the Senate when he worked there and answered my questions about Mansfield's brand of political leadership. It was a real pleasure getting to know him. John G. Stewart, once a top aide to Hubert Humphrey during the legislative struggle over the Civil Rights Act of 1964 and a direct participant in many of those historic events, was a source of great insight. John's dissertation on Senate leadership was invaluable.

No writer could ask for a better relationship than the one I have with the terrific people at the University of Oklahoma Press. A special acknowledgment to Kent Calder and Steven Baker at the Press, who have been generous and supportive of me through all three of my Senate books. Kirsteen E. Anderson did a superb job copyediting the manuscript and saved me from numerous errors.

Many historians and scholars of political science have studied and written about the tumultuous 1960s long before me. Their work, indispensable to this effort, is, I hope, generously and appropriately acknowledged in the notes and bibliography. One scholar in particularly has been an inspiration: political scientist Burdett Loomis, who read and favorably commented on my proposal for this book to the University of Oklahoma Press. "Bird" Loomis was a marvelous scholar, a teacher, and a truly nice fellow. I regret that his untimely death prevented him from seeing this book, which I dedicate to his memory and to that of another great scholar, Walter Nugent, who was also unfailingly generous to me. The third dedication is to the memory of the most accomplished politician I ever witnessed at close hand, Cece Andrus. Everyone needs a mentor and a role model. Andrus was mine.

Finally, and most importantly, I acknowledge the person who has always been my first and most constructive reader, my muse, and my best friend, Dr. Patricia Johnson. Trish has been my invaluable helper on every research project, my essential sounding board, and my eternal advocate. Thanks, Trish, for helping me always and in so many ways.

The Senate of Mike Mansfield and Everett Dirksen, while far from perfect, offers a remarkable contrast to what the institution has become in the twenty-first century. I have written this book, in part, to try and explain that the Senate was not always dysfunctional, and with better leaders—and better senators—it might again do much good for the nation. Errors of fact or interpretation are, of course, my responsibility.

NOTES

ABBREVIATIONS

DCC	Dirksen Congressional Center
EMD Papers	Everett McKinley Dirksen Papers, Dirksen Congressional Center, Pekin, IL
EMKI	Edward M. Kennedy Institute for the United States Senate, Boston, MA
FRUS	Foreign Relations of the United States
JFKL	John F. Kennedy Presidential Library and Museum, Boston, MA
LBJL	Lyndon B. Johnson Presidential Library, Austin, TX
Miller Center	Miller Center Presidential Recordings Program, University of Virginia, Charlottesville
MM Papers	Mike Mansfield Papers, Archives and Special Collections, Maureen and Mike Mansfield Library, University of Montana–Missoula
NMcN Papers	Neil MacNeil Papers, Dirksen Congressional Center, Pekin, IL
SHO	Senate Historical Office, Washington, DC

INTRODUCTION

Epigraph: *Congressional Record*, July 31, 1962, 15176.

1. Hart Research Associates and Public Opinion Strategies, "Americans Speak on the Senate," Edward M. Kennedy Institute, June 5–13, 2018, https://www.emkinstitute.org/resources/kennedyinstitute2018poll; "Congress and the Public," Gallup, accessed August 22, 2022, https://news.gallup.com/poll/1600/congress-public.aspx; Drolet, *Tocqueville, Democracy, and Social Reform*, 67–68.

2. Baker, "No Golden Age in the Senate." For two excellent general histories of the modern Senate, see Gould, *Most Exclusive Club*; and MacNeil and Baker, *American Senate*.

3. White, "Who Really Runs the Senate?"; White, *Citadel*, x.

4. Baker and Davidson, introduction to *First among Equals*, 3.

5. Walter J. Oleszek, "John Worth Kern," in Baker and Davidson, *First among Equals*, 24, 34.

6. Baker, "No Golden Age in the Senate"; Andrew J. Glass, "Mike Mansfield, Majority Leader," in Ornstein, *Congress in Change*, 143.

7. Ripley, *Power in the Senate*, 95.

8. Shapiro, *Last Great Senate*, xiii.

9. Mansfield interview, n.d., Collection 156, NM papers.

10. Reports, February 24, 1964, NM papers; Shapiro, *Last Great Senate*, 22.

11. *Congressional Quarterly Weekly Report*, December 1, 1984, 3024.

12. Bawer, "Other Sixties."

CHAPTER 1.   THE MANSFIELD-DIRKSEN WAY

Epigraph 2: Schlesinger, *Thousand Days*, 893.

1. Halberstam, *The Fifties*, 25–26; Bird and Sherwin, *American Prometheus*, 416–17; quotation from McCullough, *Truman*, 747.

2. Arms Control Association, "The Nuclear Testing Tally," reviewed August 2022, https://www.armscontrol.org/factsheets/nucleartesttally.

3. *New York Times*, September 22, 2017.

4. Ritchie, "Senate of Mike Mansfield"; MacNeil, *Dirksen*, 213; Oberdorfer, *Senator Mansfield*, 57.

5. Chernow, *Alexander Hamilton*, 259; Bradley, "Treaty Power and American Federalism," 411.

6. Kenneth C. Randall, "The Treaty Power," *Ohio State Law Journal* 51, no. 5 (1990), 1126.

7. *Washington Post*, November 27, 2015; Seaborg, *Kennedy, Khrushchev, and the Test Ban*, 3–8.

8. Mansfield, "H-bomb speech," June 14, 1957, MM Papers.

9. Ambrose, *Eisenhower*, 402; Seaborg, *Kennedy, Khrushchev, and the Test Ban*, 14–15.

10. Ambrose, *Eisenhower*, 576–77; Eisenhower, *White House Years*, 480–81.

11. *Los Angeles Times*, January 31, 1961; "State of the Union Message," January 30, 1961, JFKL; Huddle, "Limited Nuclear Test Ban Treaty," II-4; *New York Times*, January 31, 1961.

12. Andreas Wenger and Marcel Gerber, "John F. Kennedy and the Limited Test Ban Treaty: A Case Study of Presidential Leadership," *Presidential Studies Quarterly* 29, no. 2 (June 1999): 464.

13. Beschloss, *Crisis Years*, 292–93; Schlesinger, *Thousand Days*, 482–83, 892–93.

14. Wenger and Gerber, "John F. Kennedy and the Limited Test Ban Treaty," 469; Huddle, "Limited Nuclear Test Ban Treaty," VI-5. See also R. F. Kennedy, *Thirteen Days*; Sherwin, *Gambling with Armageddon*.

15. Kennedy to Khrushchev, October 28, 1962, Foreign Relations of the United States (hereafter FRUS), 1961–63, 6:187–88; Hulsey, *Everett Dirksen and His Presidents*, 173; Schlesinger, *Thousand Days*, 896.

16. Dallek, *Unfinished Life*, 619.

17. Dallek, *Unfinished Life*, 621; *Atlanta Constitution*, June 11, 1963; Hulsey, *Everett Dirksen and His Presidents*, 177.

18. Kennedy, Commencement Address at American University, Washington, DC, June 10, 1963, JFKL, https://www.jfklibrary.org/archives/other-resources/john-f-kennedy-speeches/american-university-19630610; Dallek, *Unfinished Life*, 621.

19. Thorpe, *Supermac*, 556; Dallek, *Unfinished Life*, 622; Wenger and Gerber, "John F. Kennedy and the Limited Test Ban Treaty," 479. See also Jacobson and Stein, *Diplomats, Scientists, and Politicians*.

20. Seaborg, *Kennedy, Khrushchev, and the Test Ban*, 238–57; Beschloss, *Crisis Years*, 621–25.

21. *New York Times*, July 27, 1963; *Sacramento Bee*, July 27, 1963.

22. Hulsey, *Everett Dirksen and His Presidents*, 178; MacNeil, *Dirksen*, 220.

23. Woods, *Fulbright*, 318–19; *New York Times*, August 13, 1963.

24. Woods, *Fulbright*, 319; Seaborg, *Kennedy, Khrushchev, and the Test Ban*, 269–72; Hulsey, *Everett Dirksen and His Presidents*, 179; *Chicago Tribune*, August 4 and 11, 1963. Senator John Stennis, the chairman of the Preparedness Subcommittee of the Armed Force Committee, held his own hearings on the treaty and issued a report with conclusions much different from those of the Foreign Relations Committee. The subcommittee warned that adopting the treaty would lead to "serious—perhaps even formidable—military and technical disadvantages to the U.S."

25. Mackaman, *Time Magazine's Neil MacNeil*, 77. MacNeil writes in his biography of Dirksen that Kennedy abruptly changed his mind about meeting with Dirksen after Senators Russell and Stennis announced their opposition to the treaty, which the president worried might stampede other senators. The two influential Southerners made their opposition known on Friday, and the White House meeting with Dirksen and Mansfield took place the following Monday. "The situation had changed," MacNeil wrote, "and the president needed Dirksen's support." Obviously, MacNeil did not have access to the tape recording of the White House meeting on September 9, 1963, and his account of the meeting, based almost certainly on Dirksen's telling of the story, suggests that Kennedy was less aware of the minority leader's desire to have the president send a scripted letter to the Senate than the recordings suggest.

26. Meeting on the Nuclear Test Ban Treaty with Senators Mansfield and Dirksen, September 9, 1963, Meetings, Tape 109, JFKL; *New York Times*, September 10, 1963.

27. Beschloss, *Crisis Years*, 632.

28. Ted Sorensen, oral history, JFKL.

29. Huddle, "Limited Nuclear Test Ban Treaty," VII-28; *New York Times*, September 12, 1963.

30. *New York Times*, September 12 and 25, 1963; *Congressional Record*, September 23, 1963, 16853; Seaborg, *Kennedy, Khrushchev, and the Test Ban*, 280–82; quotation from Reeves, *President Kennedy*, 594.

31. *New York Times*, September 12, 1963; *Christian Science Monitor*, September 14, 1963; *Washington Post*, September 24, 1963; *New Yorker*, October 5, 1963.

32. *Chicago Tribune*, September 25, 1963.

33. *New York Times*, October 28, 1986; Smith, *Eisenhower in War and Peace*, 738–40; Frank, *Ike and Dick*, 184–85.

34. Schlesinger, *Robert Kennedy and His Times*, 385–86; Beschloss, *Crisis Years*, 634–35.

35. Beschloss, *Crisis Years*, 635.

36. Baker with King, *Wheeling and Dealing*, 82–84; President's Daily Schedule, August 12, 1963, JFKL; *New York Times*, August 27, 1963; Beschloss, *Crisis Years*, 634–36.

37. *Charlotte Observer*, September 15, 2020. Then-vice president Joe Biden related Mansfield's advice about not questioning motives during a speech at Yale, White House, Office of the Vice President, "Remarks by the Vice President at Yale University Class Day," May, 17, 2015; https://obamawhitehouse.archives.gov/the-press-office/2015/05/17/remarks-vice-president-yale-university-class-day.

38. *New York Times*, September 8, 1963.

39. *Chicago Tribune*, October 7 and 8, 1963; *Billings Gazette*, October 8, 1963; *Helena Independent-Record*, October 9, 1963.

40. Fite, *Richard B. Russell, Jr*, 398; Goldberg, *Barry Goldwater*, 175; *Chicago Tribune*, September 25, 1963.

41. Sorensen, *Kennedy*, 740; Dallek, *Unfinished Life*, 629–30; Thorpe, *Supermac*, 556.

42. C. James DeLaet and James M. Scott, "Treaty-Making and Partisan Politics: Arms Control and the U.S. Senate, 1960–2001," paper presented at the Annual Meeting of the International Studies Association–Midwest, October 21–22, 2005.

43. Valeo, *Mike Mansfield*, 64–65.

CHAPTER 2.   BUTTE AND PEKIN

Epigraphs: Howard, *Montana*, 90; MacNeil, *Dirksen*, 23.

1. Schapsmeier and Schapsmeier, *Dirksen of Illinois*, 7; Oberdorfer, *Senator Mansfield*, 30.

2. Details of Dirksen's and Mansfield's early lives are drawn from Schapsmeier and Schapsmeier, *Dirksen of Illinois*, chap. 1; Hulsey, *Everett Dirksen and His Presidents*, chap. 1; and Oberdorfer, *Senator Mansfield*, chap. 2.

3. Hulsey, *Everett Dirksen and His Presidents*, 10–11; Burdett Loomis, "Everett McKinley Dirksen," in Baker and Davidson, *First among Equals*, 243.

4. Oberdorfer, *Senator Mansfield*, 22–28.

5. Schapsmeier and Schapsmeier, *Dirksen of Illinois*, 10–11: Hulsey, *Everett Dirksen and His Presidents*, 12; *Washington Post*, July 17, 1979; Dirksen, *Education of a Senator*, 55. See also Fonsino, "Everett McKinley Dirksen: The Roots of an American Statesman."

6. Oberdorfer, *Senator Mansfield*, 34–43; biography of Maureen Hayes Mansfield, Maureen and Mike Mansfield Foundation, https://mansfieldfdn.org/about/about-maureen-and-mike-mansfield/maureen-hayes-mansfield/. See also Mike Mansfield's commencement speech at Clarke College, May 29, 1965, MM Papers. In this speech, entitled "Women's Journey, USA," Mansfield said of Maureen, who had attended and later received an honorary degree from Clarke:

> All too often, the women who stand with public figures go unnoticed and unsung. But I know and I am delighted to acknowledge that if I had not had Maureen Mansfield by my side through the years, these years of public life would not have been possible. If I had not drawn strength from her patience, if I had not found courage in her understanding—if I had not had access to her wisdom, I would not be with you today. You would not have had occasion to invite me, for the simple reason that I would not have had anything very much to say to you.

7. Dave Eggers, "Illinois," in Weiland and Wilsey, *State by State*, 136; Dirksen, *Education of a Senator*, 82; *Woodford County Journal*, November 13, 1930.

8. Hulsey, *Everett Dirksen and His Presidents*, 13–14. The *Pekin Daily Times* published frequent stories about Klan activities, always portraying them in a favorable light. An example of typical coverage of the Klan was a brief account on December 20, 1923, in the *Gibson City Courier* in nearby Ford County: "The Ku Klux Klan burned a cross near the west end of Main Street last Saturday evening and it attracted a lot of attention. The cross is said to indicate that the Klan now has fifty or more members in this community."

9. MacNeil, *Dirksen*, 25, 41–46; Faver, "Analysis of Humor in Selected Speeches of Everett Dirksen."

10. Hulsey, *Everett Dirksen and His Presidents*, 15–16; *Chicago Tribune*, April 9, 1930; Schapsmeier and Schapsmeier, *Dirksen of Illinois*, 18.

11. Watkins, *Hungry Years*, 87; Hulsey, *Everett Dirksen and His Presidents*, 16–17; *Bureau County Tribune*, November 11, 1932.

12. Dirksen, *Education of a Senator*, 107–8; MacNeil, *Dirksen*, 41, 58–60.

13. *Rock Island Argus*, December 5, 1933; *DeKalb Daily Chronicle*, March 23, 1933.

14. Smith, *Colonel*, 380–92; *Chicago Tribune*, September 19 and 22, 1940.

15. Myron Brinig, excerpt from *Silver Bow*, in Kittredge and Smith, *Last Best Place*, 460; Emmons, *Butte Irish*, 13; Waldron and Wilson, *Atlas of Montana Elections*, 168, 175, 183, 189, 194, 202, 216, 232, 252.

16. Malone, Roeder, and Lang, *Montana*, 386; Oberdorfer, *Senator Mansfield*, 51; *Washington Post*, June 24, 1984.

17. Oberdorfer, *Senator Mansfield*, 62–63; Johnson, "Mike Mansfield, Burton K. Wheeler, and the Montana Senate Campaign."

18. *Great Falls Tribune*, July 11 and August 15, 1948.

19. *Missoulian*, October 25, 1949; *Santa Cruz Sentinel*, November 1, 1949; *Great Falls Tribune*, May 12 and November 2, 1949; *Montana Standard*, May 5, 1949; *Billings Gazette*, December 3, 1949.

20. *Kalispell, MT, Daily Inter Lake*, September 25, 1951.

21. *Fortune*, April 19, 1943; MacNeil, *Dirksen*, 70–74; *Decatur Herald*, January 15, 1946; *Decatur Daily Review*, November 16, 1946; Loomis, "Everett McKinley Dirksen: The Consummate Minority Leader," in Baker and Davidson, *First among Equals*, 236.

22. Penney, *Dirksen: The Golden Voice*, 7.

23. Faver, "Analysis of Humor in Selected Speeches of Everett Dirksen," 80.

24. MacNeil, *Dirksen*, 73–74; *Chicago Tribune*, December 3, 1943; March 17 and May 24, 1944; Loomis, "Everett McKinley Dirksen," 241–42.

25. MacNeil, *Dirksen*, 77–78; Schapsmeier and Schapsmeier, *Dirksen of Illinois*, 36; *DeKalb Daily Chronicle*, September 26, 1946; Galloway, "Operation of the Legislative Reorganization Act of 1946."

26. Faver, "Analysis of Humor in Selected Speeches of Everett Dirksen," 121.

27. Faver, "Analysis of Humor in Selected Speeches of Everett Dirksen," 126; Goodman, *Committee*, 494. In 1939, Dirksen delivered a humorous and savagely effective House speech against continued funding for the Federal Theatre Project, a government-funded New Deal effort that critics said amounted to nothing more than "sheer propaganda for Communism or the New Deal." Dirksen recounted the titles of several plays the project produced: "I have one here," he said, "*A New Deal for Mary*, which is a grand title. Then there is *The Mayor and the Manicure* and *Mother Goose Goes to Town*. Also, *A New Kind of Love*, I wonder what that can be. It smacks of something Soviet." The House subsequently voted overwhelmingly to reject the funding legislation. See Goodman, *Committee*, 42–46.

28. *Helena Independent-Record*, October 3, 1946; *Missoulian*, October 24, 1948; Oberdorfer, *Senator Mansfield*, 98.

29. MacNeil, *Dirksen*, 80–81; Schapsmeier and Schapsmeier, *Dirksen of Illinois*, 46–48; *Decatur Herald and Review*, January 4, 1948; *Washington Evening Star*, January 5, 1948; *Chicago Tribune*, January 7, 1948.

CHAPTER 3.   APPRENTICE TO LEADERSHIP

Epigraph: Matthews, *U.S. Senators and Their World*, 92.

1. Halberstam, *The Fifties*, 9; Schrecker, *Many Are the Crimes*, ix–xviii; Tye, *Demagogue*, 1–5. See also Murray, *Red Scare*, ix–xii.

2. MacNeil, *Dirksen*, 91; Senate Historical Office, "Scott Lucas: The 'Paper Majority' Leader," accessed September 4, 2022, https://www.senate.gov/about/origins-foundations/parties-leadership/lucas-scott.htm.

3. Evans and Novak, *Lyndon B. Johnson*, 40–41; Senate Historical Office, "Scott Lucas."

4. Reeves, *Life and Times of Joe McCarthy*, 222–23; Halberstam, *The Fifties*, 49–50, 54; Bagley, *Joe McCarthy and the Press*, 16–17; *Chicago Tribune*, February 10 and February 12, 1950. The *Chicago Tribune* and its sister newspaper, the *Washington Times-Herald*, both at the time under the firm control of Robert McCormick, were directly involved in both advancing McCarthy's allegations and supplying raw material for his speeches. See Smith, *Colonel*, 500; Bagley, *Joe McCarthy and the Press*, 54–55.

5. Deason, "Eye of the Storm," 248–49; Carbondale *Southern Illinoisan*, November 3, 1950. *Chicago Tribune*, July 24, 1950.

6. Deason, "Eye of the Storm," 244: Dirksen, *Education of a Senator*, xxiii; *St. Louis Post-Dispatch*, October 22, 1950.

7. *St. Louis Post-Dispatch*, October 22, 1950; Smith, *Colonel*, 504.

8. *Sun-Times*, November 2, 1950; *Pantagraph* (Bloomington, IL), November 2, 1950; Griffith, *Politics of Fear*, 125–26; Douglas, *In the Fullness of Time*, 562. See also Theodore Wilson, "The Kefauver Committee, 1950," in Schlesinger and Burns, *Congress Investigates, 1792–1974*, 353–82.

9. *Chicago Tribune*, November 8, 1950; *Alton Evening Telegraph*, November 10, 1950; *Chicago Tribune*, November 11, 1950.

10. Reeves, *Life and Times of Joe McCarthy*, 343–45; Wicker, *Shooting Star*, 88; Patterson, *Mr. Republican*, 470. Lucas laid the blame for his defeat on the corruption investigation conducted by fellow Democrat Estes Kefauver. Reportedly, Kefauver was distressed by the majority leader's defeat, but when he went to Lucas's office to express his regrets, Lucas rebuffed him. See Fontenay, *Estes Kefauver*, 179.

11. *Smithsonian Magazine*, September 2006; Johnson, "Mike Mansfield, Burton K. Wheeler and the Montana Senate Campaign of 1946"; Bloodworth, *Farewell to the Vital Center*, 11.

12. *Billings Gazette*, September 17, 21, 23, and 26, 1952; *Montana Standard*, October 26, 1952.

13. Oberdorfer, *Senator Mansfield*, 97–104; *Helena Independent-Record*, October 28, 1952; *Montana Standard*, November 2, 1952: *Missoulian*, October 25, 1952.

14. Oberdorfer, *Senator Mansfield*, 102; *Washington Post*, January 28, 2002.

15. *Montana Standard*, November 2, 1952; "Final Campaign Speech of Congressman Mike Mansfield, 1952," MM Papers. (Italicized words are underlined in the archive copy of the speech.)

16. Mansfield's campaign ran ads promoting the speech in several Montana newspapers, including the *Daily Inter Lake*, November 3, 1952; "Final Campaign Speech of Congressman Mike Mansfield, 1952," MM Papers.

17. Mansfield, "Gutter Politics," 1954," MM Papers.

18. Evans and Novak, *Lyndon B. Johnson*, 52; Caro, *Johnson: Master of the Senate*, 494.

19. *Montana Standard*, January 13, 1953; *Great Falls Tribune*, January 21 and 25, 1953; *Billings Gazette*, January 21, 1953.

20. Hulsey, *Everett Dirksen and His Presidents*, 46–47, 54; Patterson, *Mr. Republican*, 548–49; Halberstam, *The Fifties*, 212–13.

21. MacNeil, *Dirksen*, 100–1: Hulsey, *Everett Dirksen and His Presidents*, 50; *Chicago Tribune*, March 27, 1953; Smith, *Eisenhower in War and Peace*, 586–87; Eisenhower, *Mandate for Change*, 213. Mansfield developed a close working relationship with Minnesota senator Hubert Humphrey who, as biographer Albert Eisele has written, worked to organize "a liberal caucus in the Senate" with, among others in the Senate class of 1952, Mansfield, Washington's Henry Jackson, and Missouri's Stuart Symington. See Eisele, *Almost to the Presidency*, 97.

22. Grant, "The Bricker Amendment Controversy"; Cronin, "Minority Leadership," 244.

23. Mansfield statement, January 21, 1954, MM Papers.

24. Oberdorfer, *Senator Mansfield*, 146.

25. *Washington Post*, November 25, 1954.

26. Oberdorfer, *Senator Mansfield*, 111, 115–41; *Harper's*, January 1956.

27. Mansfield, "Establish a Joint Committee on Central Intelligence," March 10, 1954, MM Papers; Schlesinger, *Imperial Presidency*, 316–17; Mansfield memo to Kennedy, March 20, 1961, JFKL. Mansfield was dismissive of the occasional official briefings CIA leaders provided to Congress. Francis Valeo quoted him as saying, "You can get the same briefing by reading the *New York Times* and without having to remain silent about the source of what you learn." See Valeo, *Mike Mansfield*, 266–67. See also Weiner, *Legacy of Ashes*, 105.

28. Oberdorfer, *Senator Mansfield*, 104. Oberdorfer also recounts an incident where Harvey Matusow, the dirty-trick artist dispatched to Montana to smear Mansfield in 1952, attempted, a year later, to secure an appointment with Mansfield to apologize. Mansfield refused to see him.

29. Griffith, *Politics of Fear*, 116–17; Oshinsky, *Conspiracy So Immense*, 436–38; Cronin, "Minority Leadership," 298; MacNeil, *Dirksen*, 126–27.

30. *Meet The Press* transcript, November 7, 1954, EMD Papers; MacNeil, *Dirksen*, 128.

31. Oshinsky, *Conspiracy So Immense*, 484.

32. Dirksen, *Education of a Senator*, 225–26; Deason, "Eye of the Storm," 277.

ELEMENTS OF LEADERSHIP: ELOQUENCE, CORNPONE, SUBSTANCE, AND HUMOR

Epigraph: interview with Jack Valenti, "The Presidents: LBJ," *American Experience*, 2008, https://www.pbs.org/video/american-experience-the-presidents-lbj/.

1. Jennifer Mercieca, "We Are All Propagandists Now," *Texas A&M Today*, July 22, 2021, https://today.tamu.edu/2021/07/22/we-are-all-propagandists-now/.

2. Bagdikian, "Golden Voice of the Senate," *Saturday Evening Post*, October 6, 1962.

3. MacNeil, *Dirksen*, 5; Loomis, "Everett McKinley Dirksen: The Consummate Minority Leader," in Baker and Davidson, *First among Equals*, 236; Hulsey, *Everett Dirksen and His Presidents*, 2; *Esquire*, October 1, 1966.

4. MacNeil, *Dirksen*, 5, 62; *Time*, September 4, 1962. The *Time* article had no byline but was certainly written by MacNeil.

5. Mudd, *Place to Be*, 176–77.

6. "A Billion Here, A Billion There, "Dirksen Congressional Center, https://dirksencenter .org/research-collections/everett-m-dirksen/dirksen-record/billion-here-billion-there; "Everett Dirksen Said That?" EMD Papers.

7. *Life*, September 19, 1969; *Saturday Evening Post*, October 6, 1962.

8. *Meet the Press* transcript, November 7, 1954, EMD Papers; *Newsweek*, January 8, 1968.

9. Penney, *Dirksen: The Golden Voice*, 62; *Memorial Services Held in the Senate and House of Representatives* 159–60. Young Doug Frazer's tribute was originally printed in the *Moline Daily Dispatch*, September 23, 1969.

10. *St. Louis Globe-Democrat*, November 8, 1963.

11. Dirksen concluded his 1963 presentation of the marigold resolution, "Mr. President, I end where I began. I bring comfort to those who think that, perhaps, because of the unseasonable weather which we have had all over the country, there will be no spring. But Shelley wrote it beautifully when he said: 'If winter comes, can spring be far behind?' Mr. President, I introduce the joint resolution for appropriate reference." Faber, "Analysis of Humor in Selected Speeches of Everett Dirksen," 97–101. Dirksen's entire speech is printed in the appendix to Faber's thesis.

12. *Esquire*, October 1, 1966; *Dispatch* (Moline, IL), May 4, 1963; *Pantagraph* (Bloomington, IL), January 9, 1965.

13. *Time*, September 19, 1969.

14. Hulsey, *Everett Dirksen and His Presidents*, 148–49; Baker, *Friend and Foe*, 26.

15. Everett M. Dirksen, "Effective Speech," *Today's Speech*, April 2, 1967; MacNeil, *Dirksen*, 92.

16. Penney, *Dirksen: The Golden Voice*, 62, 64, 65; *New York Daily News*, January 15, 1967.

17. *Congressional Record*, December 15, 1967, 36175; *Meet the Press* transcript, November 7, 1954, EMD Papers.

18. Minutes of the Democratic Conference, August 17, 1964, MM Papers, Series 22, box 84, file 15;
Baldwin, *Hon. Politician*, 8; Olson, *Mansfield and Vietnam*, 2.

19. Oberdorfer, *Senator Mansfield*, 180; Schlesinger, *Thousand Days*, 374; Mansfield, "A Third Way on Berlin," June 14, 1961, *Mike Mansfield Speeches, Statements, and Interviews*, 437, https://scholarworks.umt.edu/mansfield_speeches/437.

20. *Billings Gazette*, June 25, 1961.

21. *Look*, July 26, 1966; *Life*, March 25, 1965; *Esquire*, October 1, 1966; Peggy DiMichele, oral history interview, MM Papers.

22. Francis Valeo, oral history interview, MM Papers; Oberdorfer, *Senator Mansfield*, 146.

23. "Senator Everett M. Dirksen," *What's My Line*, July 9, 1967, https://www.youtube .com/watch?v=Bw5pVjOfo5g.

CHAPTER 4.   HIGHEST ASPIRATIONS—MOVING TO SENATE LEADERSHIP

Epigraph: *Life*, March 26, 1965; Ross K. Baker, "Mike Mansfield and the Birth of the Modern Senate," in Baker and Davidson, *First among Equals*, 293.

1. *New York Times*, January 4, 1957.

2. Earle C. Clements, oral history interview, LBJL; Caro, *Johnson: Master of the Senate*, 855; Evans and Novak, *Lyndon B. Johnson*, 97–98; George A. Smathers oral history interview, SHO.

3. Oberdorfer, *Senator Mansfield*, 147; Baker, "Mike Mansfield and the Birth of the Modern Senate," in Baker and Davidson, *First among Equals*, 270; McPherson, *Political Education*, 183; Smathers, oral history interview, SHO.

4. McPherson, *Political Education*, 183; Smathers, oral history interview, SHO.

5. *New York Times*, January 4, 1957.

6. James A. Nelson to Mike Mansfield, November 27, 1957, MM Papers, Series 22, box 28; *Billings Gazette*, January 6, 1957.

7. *New York Times*, February 24, 1974; Montgomery and Johnson, *One Step from the White House*, 134; minutes of Senate Republican Conference, August 4, 1953, EMD Papers.

8. MacNeil, *Dirksen*, 120, 147; minutes of the Senate Republican Conference, January 3, 1957, EMD Papers; Schapsmeier and Schapsmeier, *Dirksen of Illinois*, 111–12.

9. *New York Times*, January 4, 1957.

10. *Face the Nation* transcript, January 9, 1955, EMD Papers; *Congressional Record*, May 22, 1957, 7358.

11. Jacob Javits and Carl Curtis, oral histories, Jean Torcom Interview Project, DCC.

12. White, *Taft Story*, 89; Montgomery and Johnson, *One Step from the White House*, 178–79; Burdett Loomis, "Everett McKinley Dirksen: The Consummate Minority Leader," in Baker and Davidson, *First among Equals*, 254; *Time*, February 11, 1957.

13. Helena *Independent-Record*, March 27, 1957.

14. Johnson to Mansfield, April 3, 1957, MM Papers, Series 18, box 18, folder 2; Steinberg, *Sam Johnson's Boy*, 456; Loomis, "Everett McKinley Dirksen: The Consummate Minority Leader," 272; *Saturday Evening Post*, October 1974.

15. MacNeil, *Dirksen*, 142.

16. Evans and Novak, *Lyndon B. Johnson*, 124–25.

17. *Time*, July 1, 1957; Caro, *Johnson: Master of the Senate*, 906–9. Others have taken issue with Caro's reading of these events. The historian Irwin F. Gellman, a biographer of Eisenhower, has written "Caro's account fights against a massive weight of evidence." His own research, Gellman says, finds no documentary evidence whatsoever to back Caro's account, and he also cites the denials of Idaho senator Frank Church and Oregon senators Wayne Morse and Richard Neuberger, as well as New Mexico's Clinton Anderson. See Gellman, *President and the Apprentice*, 380.

18. *New York Times*, June 22, 1957; *Anaconda Standard*, June 24, 1957; Evans and Novak, *Lyndon B. Johnson*, 130.

19. Frank Church, oral history interview, LBJL; Dallek, *Lone Star Rising*, 522; Mann, *Walls of Jericho*, 208–9.

20. *New York Times*, August 9, 1957; Mann, *Walls of Jericho*, 204–24; Crespino, *Strom Thurmond's America*, 114–15; White, *Citadel*, 71. Frank Church's biographers recount the Idaho senator's role in the jury trial amendment and note that a top Church aide, John Carver, said "Church saw the amendment as symbolic, a means by which to pass the bill." See Ashby and Gramer, *Fighting the Odds*, 82–91.

21. Hulsey, *Everett Dirksen and His Presidents*, 102.

22. *Meet the Press* transcript, May 19, 1957, EMD Papers.

23. *Meet the Press* transcript, May 19, 1957, EMD Papers.

24. Hulsey, *Everett Dirksen and His Presidents*, 112–14; MacNeil, *Dirksen*, 147–51; *Chicago Tribune*, December 9, 1958; *Herald and Review* (Decatur, IL), January 11, 1959.

25. MacNeil, oral history interview, EMKI; Cronin, "Minority Leadership," 356.

26. *Billings Gazette*, October 26, 1958; Waldron and Wilson, *Atlas of Montana Elections*, 216.

27. McPherson, *Political Education*, 130; Hulsey, *Everett Dirksen and His Presidents*, 119–20.

28. Mansfield-Johnson correspondence, MM Papers, Series 18, box 18, file 1.

29. Ambrose, *Eisenhower*, 596; Hulsey, *Everett Dirksen and His Presidents*, 124; Halberstam, *The Fifties*, 701; Beschloss, *Crisis Years*, 31–32; 97; Wicker, *Dwight D. Eisenhower*, 115.

30. *Evening Telegraph* (Alton, IL), July 25, 1960; *Chicago Tribune*, July 29, 1960; *Daily Dispatch* (Moline, IL), July 29, 1960; Schapsmeier and Schapsmeier, *Dirksen of Illinois*, 124; David Pietrusza, *1960: LBJ vs. JKF vs. Nixon*, 228–29. Nixon would not have won the election even if he had carried Illinois, which Kennedy won by a margin of 0.2 percent; he would have needed to capture Texas as well, which was not nearly as close a contest. Nonetheless, there persists a belief that the election in Illinois was stolen for Kennedy and with that theft so was the presidency. See *Washington Post*, August 8, 2017; and Cohen and Taylor, *American Pharaoh*, 270–79. Cohen and Taylor point to one Chicago ward where Kennedy polled 92 percent of the vote.

31. *Billings Gazette*, July 14, 1960; Baker, *Friend and Foe*; Shesol, *Mutual Contempt*, 45–52; O'Donnell and Powers with McCarthy, *Johnny, We Hardly Knew Ye*, 216–17.

32. Baker, "Mike Mansfield and the Birth of the Modern Senate," 264–65; *Independent-Record* (Helena, MT), July 16, 1960.

33. *New York Daily News*, August 20, 1960; *Chicago Tribune*, September 27, 1960.

34. *Billings Gazette*, July 26, 1960; *Congressional Record*, June 17, 1968, 7288.

35. *Montana Standard-Post* (Butte-Anaconda, MT), October 29, 1960; *Spokane Chronicle*, October 8, 1960; *Great Falls Tribune*, October 28, 1960.

36. *Mount Vernon Register-News*, September 15, 1960; *Belvidere Daily Republican*, September 23, 1960; *Chicago Tribune*, October 16, 1960; *Moline Dispatch*, November 8, 1960; *Chicago Tribune*, November 12 and November 20, 1960; Cohen and Taylor, *American Pharaoh*, 265. See also Kallina, "Was the 1960 Presidential Election Stolen?"

37. Mike Mansfield to John J. Walsh, July 20, 1960, MM Papers, Series 18, box 18, folder 1.

38. Mansfield, notes on a phone call from President-Elect John F. Kennedy, November 11, 1960, MM Papers, Series 22, box 103, folder 1; Mansfield, notes on a phone conversation with Bobby Baker, November 14, 1960, MM Papers, Series 22, box 103, folder 1; Olson, "Mike Mansfield's Ethos," 145.

39. Valeo, *Mike Mansfield*, 11. While researching his dissertation, Olson interviewed Reedy; see Olson, "Mike Mansfield's Ethos," 139–40; Stewart, "Independence and Control," 43.

40. White, "A Good Break," 108–11. In his *Harper's* article, White conveyed the conventional wisdom that replacing Johnson as Senate leader required not just the efforts of Mansfield, but those of Humphrey and Smathers as well. "Three pairs of feet have now been crowded into the boots heretofore worn by only Johnson," White wrote, "It will be profoundly interesting and instructive to see how they march" (111).

ELEMENTS OF LEADERSHIP: CARE AND FEEDING OF THE PRESS

Epigraph: Wicker, *JFK and LBJ*, 17.

1. C-Span "Weekend Public Affairs Shows," June 23, 1991, https://www.c-span.org/video/?18609-1/weekend-public-affairs-shows; *New York Times*, January 15, 1968; Transcript of *Issues and Answers, Congressional Record*, January 23, 1968, S269–271.

2. MacNeil, oral history interview, EMKI.

3. Mansfield, oral history interview by Don Oberdorfer, , MM Papers.

4. Oberdorfer, *Senator Mansfield*, photo insert.

5. Broder, *Behind the Front Page*, 218; Valeo, *Mike Mansfield*, 21; MacNeil, oral history interview, EMKI

6. Mudd, *Place to Be*, 175; *Chicago Tribune*, February 25, 1968.

7. *Chicago Tribune*, February 25, 1968.

8. *Chicago Tribune*, February 25, 1968; Drury, *Senate Journal*, 2; Hess, *Ultimate Insiders*, 47; transcript of ABC News *Issues and Answers*; January 29, 1961, EMD Papers; Vidal, "The Twenty-Ninth Republican Convention," in *United States*, 846.

9. *Longines Chronoscope*, February 16, 1955, https://www.youtube.com/watch?v=MTzNnpYg2G8; *Longines Chronoscope*, May 7, 1952, https://www.youtube.com/watch?v=VJnie5LLgEE.

10. Charles S. Johnson, correspondence with author, September 1, 2021; Oberdorfer, *Senator Mansfield*, 386.

11. Valeo oral history interview, SHO; Charles Ferris, oral history interview, SHO.

12. Halberstam, *Powers That Be*, 387; *Chicago Tribune*, October 8, 1961; MacNeil, *Dirksen*, 187–89; Schapsmeier and Schapsmeier, *Dirksen of Illinois*, 132–34; Dirksen, appearance on *Meet the Press*, 1963, featured in C-Span "Weekend Public Affairs Shows," June 23, 1991, https://www.c-span.org/video/?18609-1/weekend-public-affairs-shows. Barry Goldwater was another who complained about Ev and Charlie. "The image is all wrong," he said. "They should give the American people a picture of Republicanism that is something other than two elderly men who have had a hard life and look it." See Middendorf, *Glorious Disaster*, 25.

13. Mary McGrory, "The Show by Any Name . . . ," *Raleigh News and Observer*, March 3, 1963; UPI, "Senator Dirksen Comments on Cuban Matter," *Chicago Tribune*, February 4, 1963; Gwen Gibson, "D.C. Wash," *New York Daily News*, April 6, 1963.

14. *New York Times*, December 3, 1962; Halberstam, *Best and the Brightest*, 237; Oberdorfer, *Senator Mansfield*, 191–92; Mansfield, oral history interview by Don Oberdorfer, MM Papers.

15. Dallek, *Camelot's Court*, 337–39; Olson, *Mansfield and Vietnam*, 110–11; Valeo, *Mike Mansfield*, 24.

16. Hess, *Ultimate Insiders*, 120–24.

17. Mudd, *Place to Be*, 176; *New York Times*, April 24, 2004.

CHAPTER 5.   ONE BRIEF SHINING MOMENT

Epigraph: *Los Angeles Times*, December 21, 2020.

1. Mansfield memo to Lyndon Johnson, November 15, 1960, MM Papers, Series 22, box 100, folder 14.

2. *Austin American-Statesman*, November 18, 1960; *New York Times*, November 22 and 23, 1960.

3. Mansfield, memo on meetings with President-elect Kennedy, no date, MM Papers, Series 22, box 100, folder 1; *New York Times*, December 21, 1960. Mansfield suggested that Kennedy bring Dr. Arturo Morales Carrión and William B. Macomber into his administration. Carrión became deputy assistant secretary for Inter-American Affairs and Macomber, a top aide to Republican Senator John Sherman Cooper and a State Department official in the Eisenhower administration, became US ambassador to Jordan.

4. Oberdorfer, *Senator Mansfield*, 152; Guthman and Shulman, *Robert Kennedy in His Own Words*, 421.

5. Logevall, *JFK*, 637–40; Mansfield to John F. Kennedy, August 24, 1956, and Kennedy to Mansfield, undated but postmarked September 8, 1956, MM Papers, Series 18, box 18, file 7; Ambrose, *Eisenhower*, 299–301.

6. Mansfield, oral history interview, JFKL; Schlesinger, *Thousand Days*, 711.

7. MacNeil, *Dirksen*, 182–83; Hulsey, *Everett Dirksen and His Presidents*, 143–44.

8. *Atlanta Constitution*, December 16, 1960; *Indianapolis News*, November 18, 1960.

9. Evans and Novak, *Lyndon B. Johnson*, 307–8; Valeo, oral history interview, SHO; Byrd, *Senate*, 624; Shesol, *Mutual Contempt*, 62; Baker with King, *Wheeling and Dealing*, 135–36.

10. Oberdorfer, *Senator Mansfield*, 157–58; Caro, *Johnson: The Passage of Power*, 166. In their 1966 book on Johnson, Roland Evans and Robert Novak reflected the conventional wisdom about Mansfield being a weak leader, but also acknowledged that LBJ's domineering style left the Senate "a weaker institution than he found it." See *Johnsons The Exercise of Power*, 117.

11. Baker with King, *Wheeling and Dealing*, 140; McPherson, *Political Education*, 182; Loomis, "Everett McKinley Dirksen," in Baker and Davidson, *First among Equals*, 259; Baker, "Mike Mansfield," in *First among Equals*, 276. Johnson biographer Merle Miller claimed that Bobby Baker was mystified by Mansfield, the quiet scholar and solitary reader of books. Baker, Miller wrote, "could understand and deal with Senators who were hard drinkers, who were, to use a euphemism of the time 'skirt chasers,' who were anxious for bribes, begged for them even, accepted them almost without exception. But a book reader! Who could deal with a man like that?" Miller, *Lyndon*, 295.

12. Andrew J. Glass, "Mike Mansfield: Majority Leader," in Ornstein, *Congress in Change*, 154.

13. Humphrey, *Education of a Public Man*, 246.

14. Baker, *Friend and Foe*, 77–78.

15. Oberdorfer, *Senator Mansfield*, 174; Charles Ferris, oral history interview, EMKI; Sherman, *Political Legacy of George D. Aiken*, 66–67.

16. *Austin American-Statesman*, January 15, 1961; Mansfield, oral history interview by Oberdorfer, MM Papers.

17. Baker, *Friend and Foe*, 200.

18. Stewart, "Independence and Control," 54–55. See also Stewart, "Two Strategies of Leadership: Johnson and Mansfield," in Polsby, *Congressional Behavior*, 69–71.

19. Teddy Roe, interview by author, December 17, 2020; MacNeil, *Dirksen*, 230.

20. Dirksen to Mansfield, December 18, 1967, and January 15, 1966, MM Papers, Series 18, box 12, file 5.

21. Baker, *Friend and Foe*, 190, 197, 29.

22. "Everett Dirksen Said That?" 2nd ed., DCC; MacNeil, *Dirksen*, 305–6, 229–30.

23. Ferris, oral history interview, EMKI; Loomis, "Everett McKinley Dirksen," in Baker and Davidson, *First among Equals*, 253.

24. Matthews, *U.S. Senators and Their World*, 129; J. Stanley Kimmett, SHO Oral History Project, https://www.senate.gov/artandhistory/history/oral_history/Kimmitt_Stan.htm; Byron Hulsey, "Dirksen: Master Legislator," speech at the National Archives, January 11, 2001, https://dirksencenter.org/research-collections/everett-m-dirksen/dirksen-record/dirksen-master-legislator

25. Correspondence regarding Mansfield's elevation to majority leader, MM Papers, Series 15, box 59, files 1–5, December 27, 1960–January 28, 1961.

26. MacNeil, *Dirksen*, 52; Hulsey, "Dirksen: Master Legislator;" Valeo, *Mike Mansfield*, 19–21.

27. Mansfield, oral history interview by Oberdorfer, MM Papers.

28. Valeo, oral history interview, SHO.

29. *Eugene Register-Guard*, July 31, 1962; MacNeil, *Dirksen*, 230.

30. Reports, February 24, 1964, NMcN Papers.

31. Wicker, *JFK and LBJ*, 85; Dallek, *Unfinished Life*, 377–79. Dirksen tweaked Kennedy's reluctance to push a civil rights bill, suggesting that Senate Republicans would help pass the legislation if Democrats could "put their own ranks in order." See Republican Leaders' Press Statement, May 1, 1961, EMD Papers.

32. *Oakland Tribune*, May 1, 1961; Dirksen, speech to Republican Country Town Committeewomen, September 14, 1962, EMD Papers.

33. Hulsey, *Dirksen and His Presidents*, 149–51; Reeves, *President Kennedy*, 69; Schapsmeier and Schapsmeier, *Dirksen of Illinois*, 137. Ever attentive to how Washington, DC, issues played in Montana, Mansfield's office announced that a Butte resident, William M. Burke, would be among a group of Peace Corps volunteers heading to Nigeria early in 1963. See *Helena Independent-Record*, December 28, 1962.

34. "Communications Satellite Act of 1962"; Mann, *Legacy to Power*, 233. For more on Kerr and his influence in the Senate in this period, see Morgan, *Robert S. Kerr*.

35. Valeo, *Mike Mansfield*, 65–71.

36. Valeo, *Mike Mansfield*, 71.

37. *Congressional Record*, July 31, 1962, 15176.

38. *Great Falls Tribune*, August 24, 1962.

39. Schapsmeier and Schapsmeier, *Dirksen of Illinois*, 136; MacNeil oral history interview, EMKI.

40. Schlesinger, *Imperial Presidency*, 170.

41. Beschloss, *Crisis Years*, 211–24; *Lansing State Journal*, June 6, 1961; *New York Daily News*, June 7, 1961; Hulsey, *Everett Dirksen and His Presidents*, 155–57.

42. Hulsey, *Everett Dirksen and His Presidents*, 144; Dirksen, *Honorable Mr. Marigold*, 162–63.

43. *Rochester Democrat and Chronicle*, June 15, 1961; Mike Mansfield, oral history interview, JFKL; *New York Daily News*, June 16, 1961. In August 1961, Dirksen issued a joint statement with House Republican leader Charles Halleck: "We only wonder what the world thinks when President Kennedy correctly announces we are going to stand firm on our Berlin commitments only to have important Democratic spokesmen make statements which are at variance with that policy." See also Hulsey, *Everett Dirksen and His Presidents*, 156–57.

44. *Newsday*, February 8, 1962; *New York Times*, April 8, 1962; MacNeil, *Dirksen*, 195; *Des Moines Register*, April 11, 1962; Mansfield, oral history interview, JFKL; Mansfield, oral history interview by Oberdorfer, MM Papers.

45. Charles W. Eagles, "The Fight for Men's Minds: The Aftermath of the Ole Miss Riot of 1962," *Journal of Mississippi History* 71, no. 1 (Spring 2009): 1–53; Reeves, *President Kennedy*, 362.

46. *Sacramento Bee*, October 2, 1962.

47. Brinkley, *John F. Kennedy*, 111. See also Doyle, *American Insurrection*, for a history of the events in Mississippi in 1962.

48. *Tampa Bay Times*, December 3, 1961; Dorf and Van Dusen, *Clear It with Sid!*, 98; *Southern Illinoisian*, April 15, 1962.

49. *Chicago Tribune*, August 12, 1962.

50. *Daily Herald* (Chicago), August 30, 1962; Douglas, *In the Fullness of Time*, 574; Dorf and Van Dusen, *Clear It with Sid!*, 101–2; *Saturday Evening Post*, October 6, 1962; *Time*, September 14, 1962.

51. Telegram to Mansfield, August 28, 1962, and Dirksen to Mansfield, October 11, 1962, both in Series 18, file 12, MM Papers.

52. *Los Angeles Times*, August 5, 1962; *Helena Independent-Record*, August 5, 1962. The Senate Democratic Policy Committee conducted an analysis of GOP support for Kennedy during the first session of the Eighty-Seventh Congress. On 179 roll-call votes the most supportive Republican was New York liberal Jacob Javits, who voted against the White House position only 39 times. The least supportive Republican was Barry Goldwater, who opposed the administration 139 times. Dirksen was almost precisely in the middle of the Republican conference, opposing the administration 119 times and supporting it 60 times. See MM Papers, Series 22, box 83, folder 4.

53. Kennedy, "Soviet Arms Buildup in Cuba," speech delivered October 22, 1962, JFKL.

54. *Chicago Tribune*, October 21, 1962.

55. Plokhy, *Nuclear Folly*, 49; Beschloss, *Crisis Years*, 383.

56. Oberdorfer, *Senator Mansfield*, 180; Hulsey, *Everett Dirksen and His Presidents*, 170.

57. Reeves, *President Kennedy*, 392–93; Olson, "Mike Mansfield's Ethos," 221; Mansfield, oral history interview, JFKL.

58. Oberdorfer, *Senator Mansfield*, 180; Plokhy, *Nuclear Folly*, 359–60.

59. Oberdorfer, *Senator Mansfield*, 181; MacNeil, *Dirksen*, 207; *New York Times*, November 6, 1962; Hulsey, *Everett Dirksen and His Presidents*, 171.

60. Oberdorfer, *Senator Mansfield*, 190; *Montana Standard*, November 7, 1962. See also Donald A. Ritchie, "Advice and Dissent: Mike Mansfield and the Vietnam War," in Woods, *Vietnam and the American Political Tradition*.

61. Mann, *Grand Delusion*, 152–53.

62. Olson, *Mansfield and Vietnam*, 99–102; Oberdorfer, *Senator Mansfield*, 188; *Los Angeles Times*, June 11, 1962. Mansfield, "Interests and Policies in Southeast Asia," speech delivered at Michigan State University, MM Papers, Series 21, box 41, folder 44. Syndicated columnist Drew Pearson wrote after Mansfield's Michigan State speech that "aside from Mike Mansfield, who has warned that the United States cannot afford to get bogged down in Asian wars, there has been little debate in the halls of Congress." See Pearson column, *Santa Rosa Press Democrat*, June 17, 1962.

63. Ferris, oral history interview, JFKL; Mansfield, oral history interview, JFKL.

64. Clarke, *JFK's Last Hundred Days*, 62; Olson, *Mansfield and Vietnam*, 106–11.

65. Oberdorfer, *Senator Mansfield*, 194; O'Donnell related the story in an article several years later; see *Life*, August 7, 1970.

66. O'Donnell and Powers with McCarthy, *Johnny, We Hardly Knew Ye*, 16–17; Oberdorfer, *Senator Mansfield*, 195–97; Dallek, *Camelot's Court*, 350–51. At Mansfield's request, his Vietnam reports to Kennedy and Johnson were made public in 1973 by Richard Nixon's Secretary of State, William P. Rogers. As the *New York Times* reported on April 22, 1973, "The Senate majority leader, Mike Mansfield, secretly advised two Presidents in the nineteen-sixties to restrain, rather than extend, United States involvement in the Vietnam war."

67. Dirksen article for United Press International, printed in *Childress, Texas Index*, January 6, 1963; *Lincoln Star*, January 17, 1963; MacNeil, *Dirksen*, 217–18; Schlesinger, *Thousand Days*, 711.

68. Mann, *Walls of Jericho*, 365–66, 371; *Spokane Chronicle*, June 12, 1963; *Daily Oklahoman*, June 12, 1963. Leaders of the August 28, 1963, March on Washington met separately with Mansfield and Dirksen before the march. The delegation included Dr. Martin Luther King Jr., labor and civil rights icon A. Philip Randolph, the future Georgia congressman John Lewis, and United Auto Workers President Walter Reuther. Mansfield told the group there was no chance a civil rights bill would be considered in the Senate until the House of Representatives acted first. He said he could not promise there would be no filibuster. Dirksen told the same group that he remained opposed to legislation that would address desegregation of businesses serving the public. See *Austin American-Statesman* and *New York Times*, August 29, 1963.

69. *New York Times*, September 24, 1963; Schlesinger, *Thousand Days*, 979; *Billings Gazette*, September 26, 1963; *Great Falls Tribune*, September 27, 1963; Mansfield, oral history interview, JFKL; Clarke, *JFK's Last Hundred Days*, 198. According to one of Kennedy's advance staff,

Mansfield was moved nearly to tears when he was told the president planned to make the stop to visit Mansfield's father. See Bruno and Greenfield, *Advance Man*, 17.

70. Shesol, *Mutual Contempt*, 146; Valeo, *Mike Mansfield*, 77; Caro, *Johnson: The Passage of Power*, 164; *Montana Standard*, November 23, 1963.

71. *Akron Beacon Journal*, September 24, 1963; Valeo, *Mike Mansfield*, 77–78.

72. Valeo, *Mike Mansfield*, 77–78; *Minneapolis Tribune*, October 8, 1963.

73. *St. Louis Post-Dispatch*, October 9, 1963; *Billings Gazette*, November 4, 1963; Haines to Mansfield, no date, MM Papers, Series 19, box 552, folder 4; *Helena Independent-Record*, October 24, 1963.

74. *Billings Gazette*, November 5, 1963; *Washington Post*, November 17, 2017.

75. *Des Moines Register*, October 26, 1963; Oberdorfer, *Senator Mansfield*, 203–5; Dallek, *Unfinished Life*, 637–38.

76. Oberdorfer, *Senator Mansfield*, 204–5; Reeves, *President Kennedy*, 628; Thomas, *Robert Kennedy*, 267–68. Taylor Branch wrote that Mansfield was "badly shocked by what Hoover had laid out." Branch, *Parting the Waters*, 911–13.

77. Oberdorfer, *Senator Mansfield*, 205.

78. Oberdorfer, *Senator Mansfield*, 205.

79. Sabato, *Kennedy Half Century*, 129–30, 318; Clarke, *JFK's Last Hundred Days*, 79-87; Beschloss, *Crisis Years*, 616–17.

CHAPTER 6.   CAMELOT'S END

Epigraph: Allen Drury, *Advise and Consent*, 36.

1. Koskoff, *Senator from Central Casting*, 81.

2. *New York Times*, November 8, 1963; *Hartford Courant*, November 7, 1963; Koskoff, *Senator from Central Casting*, 89–90.

3. Valeo, *Mike Mansfield*, 80–81; Alsop's syndicated column appeared in three hundred newspapers, including the *Anniston Star*, November 2, 1963. McGrory's column appeared in, among other newspapers, the Hammond, IN, *Times*, November 13, 1963; *New York Times*, November 7, 1963.

4. *Hartford Courant*, November 8 and 17, 1963; *Chicago Tribune*, November 8, 1963; Mac-Neil, *Dirksen*, 230.

5. *Kansas City Star*, November 7, 1963; *Congressional Record*, November 27, 1963.

6. Ferris, oral history interview, SHO; Valeo, *Mike Mansfield*, 81; MacNeil, *Dirksen*, 230; Stewart, "Two Strategies of Leadership," in Polsby, *Congressional Behavior*, 71.

7. *Chicago Tribune*, October 9, 1963; *Indianapolis Star*, October 14, 1963.

8. *Los Angeles Times*, November 2, 1963; Mann, *Grand Delusion*, 285; Mansfield, "Observations on Viet Nam," memorandum to President Kennedy, August 19, 1963, in FRUS, 1961–63, vol. 3, Vietnam, January–August 1963; Oberdorfer, *Senator Mansfield*, 201.

9. *Idaho State Journal* (Pocatello), November 3, 1963; *Chicago Tribune*, November 1, 1963.

10. Bill Sanderson, "Merriman Smith's account of JFK's assassination," The Pulitzer Prizes, https://www.pulitzer.org/article/merriman-smiths-account-jfks-assassination; *Philadelphia Inquirer*, November 23, 1963; Ferris, oral history interview, EMKI; Oberdorfer, *Senator Mansfield*, 207–8.

11. *Daily Journal* (Franklin, IN), November 23, 1963; Oberdorfer, *Senator Mansfield*, 208.

12. *Boston Globe*, November 25, 1963; Manchester, *Death of a President*, 508. Mansfield biographer Don Oberdorfer wrote that he tried to resolve the confusion about who actually wrote the Kennedy eulogy but never "cleared up the contradiction." See Oberdorfer, *Senator Mansfield*, 541–42.

13. Johnson, *White House Diary*, 9; Steinberg, *Sam Johnson's Boy*, 620; Manchester, *Death of a President*, 541; Sabato, *Kennedy Half Century*, 31.

14. Manchester, *Death of a President,* 541.

15. Hulsey, *Everett Dirksen and His Presidents,* 144. Mansfield also spoke briefly in the Senate on November 25, saying, "We will find in his death some of his love and reverence for life, some of his humility, some of his patience and forbearance, some of his wisdom and some of his humor. And, so strengthened, we will join with the President in forging a new decency at home and a reasoned peace in the world. God willing, those things we shall find, or God help us all." Both the Mansfield and Dirksen statements were printed in the *New York Times,* November 26, 1963.

16. Transcript of Johnson phone call with Mansfield, November 29, 1963, Miller Center.

17. Mansfield, oral history interview, JFKL.

18. Transcript of Johnson phone call with Dirksen, November 23, 1963, Miller Center.

19. Jacqueline Kennedy to Mike Mansfield, MM Papers, Series 19, box 602, file 15, and Series 22, box 115, file 12.

CHAPTER 7.   AN IDEA WHOSE TIME HAS COME

Epigraph: Eastland quoted in Annis, *Big Jim Eastland*, 191.

1. Caro, *Johnson: The Passage of Power*, 429; *New York Times*, November 28, 1963.

2. *New York Daily News*, November 28, 1963.

3. Dallek, *Flawed Giant*; Sabato, *Kennedy Half Century*, 273.

4. Woods, *LBJ*, 461; Beschloss, *Taking Charge*, 85.

5. Mann, *Walls of Jericho*, 512–15; Risen, *Bill of the Century*, 257.

6. Purdum, *Idea Whose Time Has Come*, 6.

7. *Chicago Tribune*, February 17, 1964; MacNeil, *Dirksen*, 209–10; Mrs. Elmer Ratcliff, telegram to Mansfield, February 17, 1964, and Mansfield's response, February 19, 1964, MM Papers, Series 9, box 108, folder 8.

8. *New York Times*, February 18, 1964; MacNeil, *Dirksen*, 210; Fite, *Richard B. Russell, Jr.*, 124; Risen, *Bill of the Century*, 170.

9. Valeo, *Mike Mansfield*, 138; Risen, *Bill of the Century*, 174–75.

10. Risen, *Bill of the Century*, 173; Mansfield, "Civil Rights Act of 1964," February 17, 1964, MM Papers. "Mr. President" refers to the presiding officer of the Senate.

11. Mansfield, "Civil Rights Act of 1964," February 17, 1964, MM Papers.

12. *Los Angeles Times*, February 18, 1964.

13. *Spokesman-Review* (Spokane, WA), February 18, 1964.

14. Mansfield, "Minutes of Meeting with Senator Russell," MM Papers, Series 65, box 28, folder 12; Oberdorfer, *Senator Mansfield*, 232.

15. MacNeil, *Dirksen*, 232; *Chicago Tribune*, February 23, 1964.

16. *North Adams Transcript*, March 3, 1964; Mann, *Walls of Jericho*, 369; Evans and Novak column in the Elmira, NY, *Star-Gazette*, March 14, 1964.

17. Mrs. J. T. Tolberman to Mansfield, February 26, 1964; A. E. and Beverly Shaw to Mansfield, February 15, 1964; and Sarah C. Gerber to Mansfield, February 14, 1964; MM Papers, Series, 9, box 109, folder 2; "The Civil Rights Bill and Montana" no date, MM Papers. The heading on this explanation of the Civil Rights Bill indicates that at Mansfield's request, it was prepared by Congressman William McCullough, the Ohio Republican who was a key House supporter of the legislation.

18. *Billings Gazette*, February 22, 1964; Purdum, *Idea Whose Time Has Come*, 218; Ferris, oral history interview, SHO; Risen, *Bill of the Century*, 183.

19. Purdum, *Idea Whose Time Has Come*, 218–19; Offner, *Hubert Humphrey*, 183.

20. Mansfield, telephone call with Lyndon Johnson and Bill Moyers, February 20, 1964, Miller Center; McGrory's column appeared in the *Boston Globe*, February 27, 1964; Hulsey, *Dirksen and His Presidents*, 188–89.

21. Dirksen, telephone call with Johnson, February 3, 1964, Miller Center.

22. White column, *Austin American-Statesman*, February 21, 1964; Hulsey, *Everett Dirksen and His Presidents*, 188–89; *Billings Gazette*, February 22, 1964.

23. *New York Times*, February 27, 1964.

24. *Boston Globe*, February 27, 1964. In June 1963, Mansfield engineered the appointment of Montana's junior senator, Metcalf. as the "acting president pro tem" of the Senate. In his short time in the Senate, Metcalf had mastered Senate rules and he was a committed liberal. Columnist Mary McGrory wrote that Metcalf was "considered by the captain of the civil rights forces, [Humphrey] as a key figure in the present struggle." Presiding over the Senate and often ruling in Mansfield's favor was, Metcalf said, "my contribution to the filibuster." See McGrory column, *Boston Globe*, March 30, 1964.

25. Leuchtenburg, *The White House Looks South*, 304; *New York Times*, March 10, 1964; *Congressional Record*, March 9, 1964, 4585.

26. Senate vote tally dated April 8, 1964, MM Papers, Series 22, box 28, folder 11; Mann, *Walls of Jericho*, 398–99.

27. Branch, *Pillar of Fire*, 267; Risen, *Bill of the Century*, 188.

28. *Detroit Free Press*, March 27, 1964; Marble, *Malcolm X*, 301–2; *Pittsburgh Press*, March 27, 1964.

29. Stewart, "Independence and Control," 222, 184; *Louisville Courier-Journal*, April 14, 1964.

30. Mann, *Walls of Jericho*, 400–401.

31. Mackaman, *Long, Hard Furrow*, 49, 58; Mann, *Walls of Jericho*, 412.

32. Stewart, "Independence and Control, 225–28; Risen, *Bill of the Century*, 209–10.

33. *Boston Globe*, April 29, 1964.

34. Johnson, telephone call with Mansfield, April 29, 1964, Miller Center.

35. Kotz, *Judgment Days*, 138–39; Mackaman, *Long, Hard Furrow*, 59; Murray Kempton column, *Spectator*, April 24, 1964.

36. Eisele, *Almost to the Presidency*, 192–93; Kotz, *Judgment Days*, 138–39; Steinberg, *Sam Johnson's Boy*, 658.

37. Mansfield, "American Good Government Society," April 30, 1964, MM Papers; Humphrey, *Education of a Public Man*, 276–77.

38. *New York Times*, February 15, 1964; Goldberg, *Barry Goldwater*, 196–97; MacNeil, *Dirksen*, 238.

39. Mudd, *Place to Be*, 146–52.

40. Mann, *Walls of Jericho*, 412–14; Purdum, *Idea Whose Time Has Come*, 231.

41. *Reporter*, July 16, 1964.

42. Stewart, "Independence and Control," 255–56; minutes of the Senate Democratic Conference, January 8, 1964, MM Papers, Series 22, box 84, file 14.

43. *New York Times*, May 7, 1964. The contemporary observer was Stephen Horn, legislative assistant to Senator Thomas Kuchel, Horn's detailed log is archived at the DCC, available at https://dirksencenter.org/special-features/civil-rights/stephen-horns-notes-senate-civil-rights-meetings-1964, see Log 8, 181; Margolis, *Last Innocent Year*, 208; Hulsey, *Everett Dirksen and His Presidents*, 195.

44. Mackaman, *Long, Hard Furrow*, 77, 79. See also Stewart, "Independence and Control," 246–54, for a detailed discussion of Dirksen's approach to modifications of the House legislation.

45. Valeo, *Mike Mansfield*, 156–57. See also Stewart, "Independence and Control," 269–72.

46. Johnson, telephone call with Dirksen, May 13, 1964, Miller Center.

47. Valeo, *Mike Mansfield*, 153.

48. Loevy, *To End All Segregation*, 319–20: *Chicago Tribune*, May 31, 1964.

49. Purdum, *Idea Whose Time Has Come*, 300–2.

50. Purdum, *Idea Whose Time Has Come*, 300–2; *New York Times*, June 11, 1964.

51. Mackaman, *Long, Hard Furrow*, 83–84. Jon Margolis, in his cultural history of 1964, observed that in paraphrasing Victor Hugo "Dirksen relied on one of the few people in all of human history who might have been wordier than he." Dirksen told reporters that Hugo had kept a diary in which he had written that "no army is stronger than an idea whose time has come." In fact, Margolis wrote, Hugo did not keep a diary and his actual words were, "A stand can be made against invasion by an army; no stand can be made against invasion by an idea." Dirksen had, Margolis said, "edited Hugo and improved it." See Margolis, *Last Innocent Year*, 212.

52. Mann, *Walls of Jericho*, 426.

53. Purdum, *Idea Whose Time Has Come*, 303; Valeo, *Mike Mansfield*, 159–60; *New York Times*, June 11, 1964.

54. *New York Times*, June 20, 1964.

55. *Time*, June 19, 1964; *Chicago Defender*, June 22, 1964; *Daily Press* (Newport News), June 20, 1964; *Kansas City Star*, June 22, 1964; Mackaman, *Long, Hard Furrow*, 89, 85; Evans and Novak column in the *Daily Oklahoman*, June 20, 1964.

56. Mansfield, oral history interview by Oberdorfer, MM Papers.

57. Branch, *Pillar of Fire*, 387; *New York Times*, July 3, 1964. In searching dozens of photos of the signing ceremony, I found no picture that included Mansfield.

58. Clarke, *JFK's Last Hundred Days*, 356; Evans and Novak, *Lyndon B. Johnson*, 378–79; Woods, *LBJ*, 477.

59. Stewart, "Independence and Control," 274–75.

60. Stewart, "Independence and Control," 289–90.

61. Mansfield thank-you note to senators, June 22, 1964, MM Papers, Series 18, box 32, file 3.

62. Richard Russell to Mansfield, June 30, 1964; Herman Talmadge to Mansfield, June 25, 1964; Roman Hruska to Mansfield, June 22, 1964; all in MM Papers, Series 18, box 32, file 2.

63. Jacob Javits to Mansfield, July 8, 1964, MM Papers, Series 18, box 32, file 2.

64. Frank Lausche to Mansfield, June 24, 1964; Hubert Humphrey to Mansfield, July 3, 1964; both in Series 18, box 32, file 2.

65. Everett Dirksen to Mansfield, June 24, 1964, MM Papers, Series 18, box 32, file 2.

66. George Aiken to Mansfield, June 23, 1964, MM Papers, Series 18, box 32, file 2.

67. Orville E. Lanham to Mansfield, June 20, 1964, MM papers, Series 9, box 108, folder 9.

68. Risen, *Bill of the Century*, 257.

CHAPTER 8.   A GREAT SOCIETY AND A BITCH OF A WAR

Epigraph: Woods, *Prisoners of Hope*, 401.

1. *New York Times*, June 20, 1964; Hulsey, *Everett Dirksen and His Presidents*, 203; Perlstein, *Before the Storm*, 364–65. See also Middendorf, *Glorious Disaster*, 104.

2. *New York Times*, July 1 and 2, 1964; Dirksen, "Goldwater Nomination," July 15, 1964, EMD Papers; Perlstein, *Before the Storm*, 387–90; White, *Making of the President*, 213.

3. *Time*, June 19, 1964; MacNeil, *Dirksen*, 238; Mackaman, *Time Magazine's Neil MacNeil*, 86–87; White, *Making of the President*, 228–29; *New York Times*, July 18, 1964. For a contemporary account of the ultra-conservative nature of many of the Republican delegates to the 1964 convention, see Richard H. Rovere's column in *The New Yorker*, October 3, 1964.

4. White column in the *Daily Courier* (Bristol, PA), July 8, 1964; *New York Daily News*, August 14, 1964.

5. O'Donnell and Powers with McCarthy, *Johnny, We Hardly Knew Ye*, 454–55; Valeo, *Mike Mansfield*, 169–71.

6. Evans and Novak, *Lyndon B. Johnson*, 458–59; Offner, *Hubert Humphrey*, 197; Eisele, *Almost to the Presidency*, 215; Humphrey, *Education of a Public Man*, 297; Oberdorfer, *Senator Mansfield*, 249–50. For Johnson's determination to keep Robert Kennedy off the ticket, see Shesol, *Mutual Contempt*, 205–10.

7. *Billings Gazette*, October 29, 1964; *Great Falls Tribune*, September 12, 1964; Oberdorfer, *Senator Mansfield*, 251.

8. *Montana Standard*, October 13, 1964; *Great Falls Tribune*, October 13, 1964.

9. *Newsweek*, October 19, 1964; Olson, *Mansfield and Vietnam*, 136–7; Waldron and Wilson, *Atlas of Montana Elections*, 231–32.

10. *Missoulian*, October 11, 1964; *CQ Almanac, 1964*, 485–92.

11. *Missoulian*, September 4, 1964.

12. *Missoulian*, October 11, 1964.

13. Mansfield to Dirksen, November 1, 1964, and Dirksen to Mansfield, November 4, 1964, EMD Papers.

14. Dallek, *Flawed Giant*, 120; Margolis, *Last Innocent Year*, 359–60. Johnson's quotation about the impact of the Civil Rights Act on Democratic fortunes in the South was, according

to Bill Moyers: "I think we just delivered the South to the Republican party for a long time to come." Moyers, "What a Real President Was Like," *Washington Post*, November 13, 1988.

15. Mansfield speech to Democratic conference, January 4, 1965, MM Papers, Series 22, box 84, file 16. In the same period, Johnson had become steadily more dismissive of Mansfield, criticizing him to reporters and characterizing his advice on Vietnam as "spineless and weak." The level of presidential disrespect reached an ugly low when Johnson made a sexual pass at Mansfield's daughter, Anne, while she was visiting the White House. Anne apparently did not tell her father, but friends learned of the incident. See Oberdorfer, *Senator Mansfield*, 225.

16. Dallek, *Flawed Giant*, 131.

17. *Montana Standard*, December 26, 1963; *New York Times* News Service report in the *Chattanooga Daily Times*, December 26, 1962; Robert S. Allen and Paul Scott column, *Tampa Times*, January 2, 1963.

18. Transcript of Dirksen appearance on *Meet the Press*, January 24, 1965, EMD Papers; Hulsey, *Everett Dirksen and His Presidents*, 213. Mansfield also appeared on *Meet the Press* in January 1965. He warned against precisely what Johnson ultimately did—take the war to North Vietnam with a massive bombing campaign called Rolling Thunder. "I feel . . . strongly that we cannot carry the war into North Vietnam because if you carry the consequences of that action to its ultimate conclusion, it means war with Communist China, and a situation will be created which will be worse that it was in Korea." Olson, *Mansfield and Vietnam*, 141.

19. Oberdorfer, *Senator Mansfield*, 213–14. During a pivotal briefing for congressional leaders in July 1965 on the administration's plans to vastly increase troop levels in South Vietnam, Mansfield was the only person present to voice opposition, according to notes made by McGeorge Bundy, Johnson's national security advisor. See McMaster, *Dereliction of Duty*, 320.

20. *New York Times*, February 18, 1965; Knock, *Life and Times of George McGovern*, 326–27; Ashby and Gramer, *Fighting the Odds*, 193–94; Dirksen, telephone call with Johnson, February 17, 1965, Miller Center.

21. *Billings Gazette*, February 18, 1965; *Chicago Tribune*, February 18, 1965. Dirksen termed Church "a sunshine patriot." Branch, *Pillar of Fire*, 594.

22. Church, oral history interview, May 1, 1969, LBJL. J. William Fulbright, the chairman of the Foreign Relations Committee, lamented in 1966 that Dirksen (and Hickenlooper) were "in Johnson's pocket." See Robert G. Sherrill in *The Nation*, October 10, 1966.

23. Oberdorfer, *Senator Mansfield*, 241–45. Oberdorfer argues convincingly that presidential politics influenced the congressional reaction to the Tonkin Gulf situation, in that few Democrats wanted to respond in a way that would lend credence to Barry Goldwater's allegation that Johnson was displaying weakness in the face of communist aggression.

24. Stone, *Best of I. F. Stone*, 257.

25. Knock, *Life and Times of George McGovern*, 332; Oberdorfer, *Senator Mansfield*, 213–14; Olson, *Mansfield and Vietnam*, 196. See *The Nation*, October 10, 1966, for more on Johnson's use of leaks to, as Frank Church said, "make us afraid." Mansfield fought aggressively against the VA hospital closure in Montana, and eventually Johnson appointed a special commission to study which hospitals should be closed. The hospital in Miles City was not on the resulting list. See Oberdorfer, *Senator Mansfield*, 256–58. In his presidential memoir, published

in 1971, Johnson said nothing about his personal relationship with Mansfield or Mansfield's approach to Senate leadership. Most references are to Vietnam. On the other hand, Johnson praised Dirksen's loyalty and his "deep-rooted patriotism." Johnson, *Vantage Point*, 29–30, 158.

26. Oberdorfer, *Senator Mansfield*, 215.

27. Zelizer, *Fierce Urgency of Now*, 166; Dallek, "Lyndon Johnson and Vietnam."

28. *Nashville Tennessean, Great Falls Tribune*, and *Chicago Tribune*, March 8, 1965.

29. *New York Times*, March 8, 1965. Selma was selected as the focus of the voting rights battle because, as Byron Hulsey has noted, "In Selma's Dallas County only 335 of the 15,000 black citizens were registered to vote" in 1965, and Dr. Martin Luther King Jr. and other civil rights leaders "expected Sheriff Jim Clark to react to their peaceful protests with a viciousness and ferocity that would win the sympathy of the nation, the White House, and the Congress." Hulsey, *Everett Dirksen and His Presidents*, 210.

30. Aniko Bodroghkozy, "How the Images of John Lewis Being Beaten during 'Bloody Sunday' Went Viral," *The Conversation*, https://theconversation.com/how-the-images-of-john-lewis-being-beaten-during-bloody-sunday-went-viral-143080; Kotz, *Judgment Days*, 244, 260. See also Branch, *At Canaan's Edge*, 85. Johnson complained to Attorney General Nicholas Katzenbach that "Mansfield is huffy and mad and grumpy," which the president blamed on the proposed closure of the Miles City Veterans Administration hospital. Johnson, telephone call with Katzenbach, March 11, 1965, Miller Center.

31. *New York Times*, March 12, 13, 14, and 15, 1965; Updegrove, *Indomitable Will*, 140; Branch, *At Canaan's Edge*, 100.

32. Johnson, "The American Promise," Special Message to Congress, March 15, 1965, LBJL; Branch, *At Canaan's Edge*, 113.

33. Updegrove, *Indomitable Will*, 143; Goodwin, *Remembering America*, 334.

34. Kotz, *Judgment Days*, 317–26; *Washington Post*, December 15, 2017.

35. Ferris oral history interview, SHO.

36. Johnson, telephone call with Dirksen, April 5, 1965, Miller Center.

37. Loomis, "Everett McKinley Dirksen," in Baker and Davidson, *First among Equals*, 252; Mansfield, oral history interview by Don Oberdorfer, MM Papers. Journalist David Broder observed that Johnson "felt far more affinity for the cynical, showboating opposition leader—who was always ready to cut a deal—than he did for the prim, proper and painfully honest majority leader." Broder, *Party's Over*, 67.

38. Johnson, *White House Diary*, 237; Johnson, telephone call with Dirksen, March 18, 1965, Miller Center.

39. Loomis, "Everett McKinley Dirksen," in Baker and Davidson, *First among Equals*, 252; Ferris, oral history interview, SHO.

40. Kotz, *Judgment Days*, 329–30; Branch, *At Canaan's Edge*, 279. Zelizer, *Fierce Urgency of Now*, 219.

41. *New York Times*, August 7, 1965.

42. *Indianapolis Star*, August 7, 1965. In 2013—the case was *Shelby County, Alabama, v. Holder*—a sharply divided US Supreme Court ruled key provisions of the 1965 Voting Rights Act unconstitutional. Writing for the Court's five-justice majority, Chief Justice John Roberts stated, "The Voting Rights Act of 1965 employed extraordinary measures to address

an extraordinary problem," but he held that provisions of the act requiring federal "preclear-ance" before certain states with a history of voting discrimination could change their laws were outmoded. "There is no denying," Roberts wrote, "that the conditions that originally justified these measures no longer characterize voting in the covered jurisdictions." Critics pointed to the irony of a challenge to the Voting Rights Act coming from Alabama; contended the decision "gutted" Congress's work of fifty years earlier; and predicted, as has happened, wholesale efforts in many states to make voting more difficult. Despite having reauthorized the Voting Rights Act numerous times since its passage, Congress has not acted in the wake of the *Shelby* ruling. Writing in *The Atlantic*, Vann R. Newkirk II observed, "If the [VRA] represented a commitment by the federal government to ensure the true fulfillment of the Fourteenth Amendment's right to due process and the Fifteenth Amendment's erasure of race-based disenfranchisement, then Roberts's Court has all but dismantled that commit-ment." See, *Shelby County v. Holder*, June 25, 2013, *The Atlantic*, July 10, 2018.

43. *Life*, March 1965; *Cedar Rapids Gazette*, September 8, 1969; *New York Times*, March 14, 1965.

44. Dirksen, *Education of a Senator*, xxxviii; Zelizer, *Fierce Urgency of Now*, 220–21; *Chicago Tribune*, July 29, 1965.

45. *Life*, March 1965; *New York Times*, March 14, 1965.

46. Mansfield remarks to Democratic Conference, July 19, 1965, MM papers, Series 22, box 84, file 16.

47. Broder, *Party's Over*, 59; Dallek, *Flawed Giant*, 301.

48. Goodwin, *Lyndon Johnson and the American Dream*, 251–52.

49. *New York Times*, January 14, 1966; Dallek, *Flawed Giant*, 312; Hulsey, *Everett Dirksen and His Presidents*, 215–20; Mackaman, *Time Magazine's Neil MacNeil*, 153.

50. Lippmann column in the *Missoulian*, January 14, 1966; Starnes column in the *Raleigh News and Observer*, January 16, 1966.

51. Mansfield, "Vietnam: The Situation and Outlook," in "Two Reports on Vietnam and Southeast Asia to the President of the United States by Senator Mike Mansfield," December 17, 1965, 93 Cong., 1st Sess., 1973; Mansfield Vietnam Report, MM Papers, Series 13, box 70, file 4.

52. Mansfield, oral history interview by Oberdorfer, MM Papers. Johnson and Mans-field had a wide-ranging telephone conversation on June 25, 1965, that eventually turned to Vietnam. Johnson asked Mansfield for his latest thinking:

> *Mansfield:* I'm afraid, Mr. President, that eventually some government of Saigon is going to have to enter into negotiations with the Vietcong.
>
> *President Johnson:* Well, would that be the worst thing that could happen to us?
>
> *Mansfield:* No, sir!

Johnson, telephone conversation with Mansfield, Miller Center.

53. Oberdorfer, *Senator Mansfield*, 299; Hulsey, *Everett Dirksen and His Presidents*, 221.

54. *Nashville Tennessean*, November 9, 1966.

55. *Pittsburgh Press*, June 14, 1966; *New York Times*, August 31, 1966.

56. *Atlantic*, March 3, 2018; *Biloxi Sun Herald*, August 12, 1967; *Delta Democrat-Times*, August 12, 1967.

57. Kurlansky, *1968*, 41.

58. Evans and Novak, *Lyndon Johnson*, 499; *National Journal*, March 6, 1971.

59. S. M. Rowe Jr. to Dirksen, no date; Dirksen to E. J. Grede, May 31, 1967, both in EMD Papers; Dr. Paul Lauren, interview by author, November 12, 2021.

60. Dirksen to Mansfield, December 18, 1967, MM Papers, Series 18, box 12, file 5. Dirksen also lavished praise on Mansfield in a Senate speech on December 15, 1967. "He has brought to the leadership his sense of mission and responsibility and a tolerance and a humility that have never been equaled or exceeded, in my judgment," Dirksen said. "It is because of that rare understanding that he has, his slowness to anger, and his readiness to cooperate to the full, that has made it possible to go through this session when nerves were taut, when irritation was in the air, and when it could have exploded many times. And to him I express now my personal appreciation and that of my party." *Congressional Record*, December 15, 1967, CXIII, 36175.

CHAPTER 9.   END OF AN ERA

Epigraph: Mansfield, quoted in MacNeil, *Dirksen*, 230.

1. Oberdorfer, *Tet!* 34.

2. *Billings Gazette*, February 2, 1968: *New York Times*, January 15, 1968.

3. Kurlansky, *1968*, xvii.

4. Dallek, "Lyndon Johnson and Vietnam."

5. *Chicago Tribune*, February 27, 1968; Branch, *At Canaan's Edge*, 530.

6. MacNeil, *Dirksen*, 320–28; Douglas, *In the Fullness of Time*, 302–3; Hulsey, *Everett Dirksen and His Presidents*, 253–54.

7. *Chicago Tribune*, February 28, 1968; *New York Times*, February 27, 1968.

8. Zasloff, "Secret History of the Fair Housing Act"; *Life*, March 15, 1968. Zasloff challenges the general consensus that the act has been a failure. See also Cohen and Taylor, *American Pharoah*, 495–96, and Mackaman, *Time's Neil MacNeil*, 204–7.

9. *Chicago Tribune*, March 12, 1968; *Sacramento Bee*, March 12, 1968. Biographer Finley Lewis recounts Minnesota senator Walter Mondale's important role in the passage of the Fair Housing Act and contends that Dirksen's modifications to the bill were minor. One concession that was agreed to from the outset and not open for discussion, Lewis wrote, was that the "amendment would bear the name of the senior senator from Illinois." Lewis, *Mondale*, 170.

10. Woods, *LBJ*, 840; *Chicago Tribune*, April 12, 1968.

11. Woods, *LBJ*, 836–37; *Great Falls Tribune*, April 1, 1968; *Des Moines Tribune*, April 1, 1968. Mansfield spoke for the Democratic leadership during a White House session with Johnson late in 1968 when the group presented the president with a "new set of Florentine cufflinks, inscribed with 'LBJ.'" In a short tribute to Johnson, Mansfield noted that the former Senate majority leader had "never crossed the line of demarcation that divides the Executive from the Legislative but you have scrupulously observed the rights of your office as we have observed ours." Christian, *President Steps Down*, 25.

12. *New York Times*, June 27, 1968; Hulsey, *Everett Dirksen and His Presidents*, 264–65; *New York Times*, April 17, 2015.

13. Murphy, *Fortas*, 519–20; *Billings Gazette*, September 27, 1968. Fortas resigned from the court in 1969 under a cloud of even more ethical questions. Mansfield and Dirksen both said the Fortas experience would lead to more extensive investigation of Supreme Court nominees, and Mansfield—with Dirksen somewhat reluctantly agreeing—said it was time to enact public disclosure requirements for executive and judicial branch officials. See *Boston Globe*, May 19, 1969.

14. *New York Times*, September 19, 1968; Oberdorfer, *Senator Mansfield*, 344; *Great Falls Tribune*, June 6, 1968; *Quantico Sentry*, June 7, 1968; Mansfield to Mrs. Leo Lesnick, June 26, 1968, copy in author's collection.

15. *Billings Gazette*, June 30, 1968; *New York Times*, September 18, 1968; Valeo, *Mike Mansfield*, 264.

16. Mansfield to Mrs. Leo Lesnick, November 26, 1968, copy in author's collection; *Billings Gazette*, November 4, 1970.

17. Hulsey, *Everett Dirksen and His Presidents*, 271; Valeo, *Mike Mansfield*, 224–25; Wills, *Nixon Agonistes*, 275.

18. Mansfield, speech to Democratic Policy Committee, February 4, 1969, MM Papers; Oberdorfer, *Senator Mansfield*, 353–54.

19. Mansfield "Gutter Politics" speech, 1954, MM Papers; Farrell, *Richard Nixon*, 342–43.

20. *Los Angeles Times*, May 19, 1969; *New York Times*, April 30, 1969; *Philadelphia Inquirer*, June 28, 1969; Hulsey, *Everett Dirksen and His Presidents*, 271. The praised heaped on Dirksen for his leadership on civil rights vanished with a scathing *New York Times* editorial excoriating Dirksen for his obstruction of Nixon appointees and particularly for his ties to the American Medical Association. The newspapers called Dirksen "the most powerful spokesman for all the backward-looking forces on the reactionary side of the Republican Party." *New York Times*, April 30, 1969.

21. *Des Moines Register*, June 15, 1969.

22. *New York Times*, September 8 and 9, 1969; *Wisconsin State Journal*, September 11, 1969. Only ten senators (not counting those who later became president or vice president) have lain in state in the US Capitol Rotunda; in addition to Dirksen they are Henry Clay, Charles Sumner, John Logan, Robert A. Taft, Claude Pepper, Daniel Inouye, John McCain, Robert Dole, and Harry Reid.

23. Lawrence column in *Tacoma News Tribune*, September 10, 1969; Lisagor column in *San Francisco Chronicle*, September 8, 1969.

24. *Chicago Tribune*, September 8, 1969.

25. *New York Times*, September 25, 1969; Valeo, *Mike Mansfield*, 246, 250, 276; Beers, *Pennsylvania Politics*, 236; Oberdorfer, *Senator Mansfield*, 420–24; *New York Times*, May 4, 1972. See also Ferris, oral history interview, SHO.

26. *New York Times*, March 5, 1976; Valeo, *Mike Mansfield*, 276. *Times* columnist James Reston commented on Mansfield's retirement and long friendship with another Republican in a March 5, 1976, column headlined "Say It Ain't So, Mike!" "Mansfield of Montana, and

his old breakfast companion, George Aiken of Vermont, were special characters on Capitol Hill. Somehow they managed to be faithful to themselves, to their parties and to the nation, a combination few lawmakers could put together. They were models the Congress admired more than any other, and maybe the best of them all was Mike."

EPILOGUE

Epigraph: Journalist David Broder, oral history interview, EMKI; *New York Times*, September 10, 1969.

1. David E. Kyvig, "Redesigning Congress: The Seventeenth and Twentieth Amendments to the Constitution," in Zelizer, *American Congress*, 356.

2. Mansfield used the phrase "rock of the Republic" in the speech he prepared for delivery in November 1963 but instead was inserted in the *Congressional Record* due to John Kennedy's assassination. Mansfield eventually did deliver the speech to a Senate audience thirty-five years later. Mansfield, "The Senate and Its Leadership," speech to the Senate, MM Papers; *Washington Post*, March 25, 1996.

3. *New Yorker*, August 9, 2010.

4. *Washington Post*, November 19, 2020. See also B. Kal Munis and Robert P. Saldin, "Gone Country: Why Democrats Need to Play in Rural America and How They Can Do It Again," Niskanen Center, March 2021, for a discussion of how the rural state/urban state divide is affecting the Democratic Party, https://www.niskanencenter.org/gone-country -why-democrats-need-to-play-in-rural-america-and-how-they-can-do-it-again/.

5. Sinclair, *Unorthodox Lawmaking*.

6. *Baffler*, September 2020. John Dingell, the late Michigan Democrat who served in Congress longer than any other American, endorsed abolishing the Senate in 2018. Dingell wrote, "It has a nice ring to it, doesn't it? 'Abolish the Senate.' I'm having blue caps printed up with that slogan right now. They will be made in America." *Atlantic*, December 4, 2018.

7. Smith, *Senate Syndrome*, 19; Elie Mystal, "The Senate Cannot Be Reformed—It Can Only Be Abolished, *Nation*, November 12, 2021, https://www.thenation.com/article/politics /abolish-us-senate/; Mark Schmitt, review of *Closing of the Senate, Democracy Journal*, May 10, 2021, https://democracyjournal.org/magazine/the-closing-of-the-senate/; *New Republic*, April 13, 2021.

8. *Congressional Record*, August 31, 1976.

9. Mansfield, oral history interview by Oberdorfer, MM Papers.

10. Valeo, oral history interview, SHO.

11. *Congressional Record*, November 27, 1963.

12. Mansfield's speech was presented as part of the "Leader's Lecture Series" and is featured on the Senate website at https://www.senate.gov/artandhistory/history/video /LeaderLectureSeries_MansfieldMike.htm.

13. Mansfield, "The Senate and Its Leadership," speech, November 27, 1963, MM Papers.

14. *New York Times*, March 22, 1998.

15. Alan I. Abramowitz and Steven Webster, "'Negative Partisanship' Explains Everything," *Politico Magazine*, September–October 2017, https://www.politico.com/magazine /story/2017/09/05/negative-partisanship-explains-everything-215534/. Political scientists

Abramowitz and Webster write of negative partisanship, "In today's environment, rather than seeking to inspire voters around a cohesive and forward-looking vision, politicians need only incite fear and anger toward the opposing party to win and maintain power. Until that fundamental incentive goes away, expect politics to get even uglier." See also Abramowitz, *Great Alignment*.

16. *New York Times*, October 6, 2001; *Los Angeles Times*, October 6, 2001.

17. Charles Ferris compared Mansfield to the enigmatic Charles de Gaulle. "Someone once tried to categorize the ideology of Charles de Gaulle," Ferris said, "whether he was a rightist or a socialist, and a Frenchman said, 'Charles de Gaulle is neither left nor right. He is above.' Mansfield almost was treated that way." Ferris, oral history interview, SHO.

18. Hulsey, *Everett Dirksen and His Presidents*, 276–78.

BIBLIOGRAPHY

BOOKS AND ARTICLES

Abramowitz, Alan I. *The Great Alignment: Race, Party Transformation, and the Rise of Donald Trump*. New Haven, CT: Yale University Press, 2018.

Ambrose, Stephen. *Eisenhower: The President*. New York: Simon and Schuster, 1984.

Annis, J. Lee Jr. *Big Jim Eastland: The Godfather of Mississippi*. Jackson: University of Mississippi Press, 2016.

Ashby, LeRoy, and Rod Gramer. *Fighting the Odds: The Life of Senator Frank Church*. Pullman: Washington State University Press, 1994.

Bagdikian, Benjamin H. "Golden Voice of the Senate." *Saturday Evening Post*, October 6, 1962.

Bagley, Edwin R. *Joe McCarthy and the Press*. Madison: University of Wisconsin Press, 1981.

Baker, Bobby, with Larry King. *Wheeling and Dealing: Confessions of a Capitol Hill Operative*. New York: W. W. Norton, 1978.

Baker, Richard A., and Roger H. Davidson, eds. *First among Equals: Outstanding Senate Leaders of the Twentieth Century*. Washington, DC: Congressional Quarterly, 1991.

Baker, Ross K. *Friend and Foe in the U.S. Senate*. New York: Free Press, 1980.

———. "No Golden Age in the Senate," *Politico*, October 9, 2009.

Baldwin, Louis. *Hon. Politician, Mike Mansfield of Montana*. Missoula: Mountain Press, 1979.

Bawer, Bruce. "The Other Sixties." *Wilson Quarterly* (Spring 2004): 64–84.

Beers, Paul B. *Pennsylvania Politics: Today and Yesterday*. University Park: Pennsylvania State University Press, 1980.

Berman, Ari. *Give Us the Ballot: The Modern Struggle for Voting Rights in America*. New York: Farrar, Straus, and Giroux, 2015.

Beschloss, Michael R. *The Crisis Years: Kennedy and Khrushchev, 1960–1963*. New York: HarperCollins, 1991.

———. *Reaching for Glory: Lyndon Johnson's Secret White House Tapes, 1964–65*. New York: Simon and Schuster, 2001.

———. *Taking Charge: The Johnson White House Tapes, 1963–1964*. New York: Simon and Schuster, 1997.

Bird, Kai, and Martin J. Sherwin. *American Prometheus: The Triumph and Tragedy of J. Robert Oppenheimer*. New York: Knopf, 2005.

Bradley, Curtis A. "The Treaty Power and American Federalism." *Michigan Law Review* 97, no. 2 (2019), https://repository.law.umich.edu/mlr/vol97/iss2/3/.

Branch, Taylor. *At Canaan's Edge: America in the King Years, 1965–1968*. New York: Simon and Schuster, 2006.

———. *Parting the Waters: America in the King Years, 1954–1963*. New York: Simon and Schuster, 1988.

———. *Pillar of Fire: America in the King Years, 1963–1965*. New York: Simon and Schuster, 1998.

Brinkley, Alan. *John F. Kennedy*. New York: Henry Holt, 2012.

Broder, David. *Behind the Front Page: A Candid Look at How the News Is Made*. New York: Simon and Schuster, 1987.

———. *The Party's Over: The Failure of Politics in America*. New York: Harper & Row, 1971.

Bruno, Jerry, and Jeff Greenfield. *The Advance Man*. New York: William Morrow, 1971.

Byrd, Robert C. *The Senate, 1789–1989: Addresses on the History of the United States Senate*. Washington, DC: US Government Printing Office, 1988.

Caro, Robert A. *The Years of Lyndon Johnson: Master of the Senate*. New York: Knopf, 2002.

———. *The Years of Lyndon Johnson: The Passage of Power*. New York: Knopf, 2012.

Chernow, Ron. *Alexander Hamilton*. New York: Penguin, 2004.

Christian, George. *The President Steps Down: A Personal Memoir of the Transition of Power*. New York: Macmillan, 1970.

Clarke, Thurston. *JFK's Last Hundred Days: The Transformation of a Man and the Emergence of a Great President*. New York: Penguin Press, 2013.

Cohen, Adam, and Elizabeth Taylor. *American Pharoah: Mayor Richard J. Daley—His Battle for Chicago and the Nation*. Boston: Little, Brown, 2000.

"The Communications Satellite Act of 1962." *Harvard Law Review* 76, no. 2 (December 1962).

Crespino, Joseph. *Strom Thurmond's America*. New York: Hill and Wang, 2012.

Dallek, Robert. *Camelot's Court: Inside the Kennedy White House*. New York: HarperCollins, 2013.

———. *Flawed Giant: Lyndon Johnson and His Times, 1961–1973*. New York: Oxford University Press, 1998.

———. "Lyndon Johnson and Vietnam: The Making of a Tragedy." *Diplomatic History* 20, no. 2 (April 1996): 147–62.

———. *Lone Star Rising: Lyndon Johnson and His Times, 1908–1960*. New York: Oxford University Press, 1991.

———. *An Unfinished Life: John F. Kennedy, 1917–1963*. Boston: Little, Brown, 2003.

Dirksen, Everett McKinley. *The Education of a Senator*. Urbana: University of Illinois Press, 1998.

Dirksen, Louella. *The Honorable Mr. Marigold: My Life with Everett Dirksen*. Garden City, NY: Doubleday, 1972.

Dorf, Michael C., and George Van Dusen, *Clear It with Sid!—Sidney R. Yates and Fifty Years of Presidents, Pragmatism, and Public Service*. Urbana: University of Illinois Press, 2019.

Douglas, Paul H. *In the Fullness of Time: The Memoirs of Paul H. Douglas*. New York: Harcourt Brace, 1971.

Doyle, William. *An American Insurrection: James Meredith and the Battle of Oxford, Mississippi, 1962*. New York: Random House, 2001.

Drolet, Michael. *Tocqueville, Democracy, and Social Reform*. New York: Palgrave, 2003.

Drury, Allen. *Advise and Consent*. Garden City, NY: Doubleday, 1959.

———. *A Senate Journal: 1943–1945*. New York: McGraw-Hill, 1963.

Eisele, Albert. *Almost to the Presidency: A Biography of Two American Politicians*. Blue Earth, MN: Piper Co., 1972.

Eisenhower, Dwight D. *Mandate for Change*. Garden City, NY: Doubleday, 1963.

———. *The White House Years: Waging Peace*. Garden City, NY: Doubleday, 1965.

Emmons, David. *The Butte Irish: Class and Ethnicity in an American Mining Town, 1875–1925*. Champaign: University of Illinois Press, 1989.

Evans, Roland, and Robert Novak. *Lyndon B. Johnson: The Exercise of Power*. New York: New American Library, 1966.

Farrell, John A. *Richard Nixon: The Life*. New York: Doubleday, 2017.

Fite, Gilbert C. *Richard B. Russell, Jr., Senator from Georgia*. Chapel Hill: University of North Carolina Press, 1991.

Fonsino, Frank J. "Everett McKinley Dirksen: The Roots of an American Statesman." *Journal of the Illinois State Historical Society* (Spring 1983): 17–34.

Fontenay, Charles L. *Estes Kefauver: A Biography*. Knoxville: University of Tennessee Press, 1980.

Frank, Jeffrey. *Ike and Dick: Portrait of a Strange Political Marriage*. New York: Simon and Schuster, 2013.

Galloway, George B. "The Operation of the Legislative Reorganization Act of 1946." *American Political Science Review* 45, no. 1 (March 1951): 41–68.

Gellman, Irwin F. *The President and the Apprentice: Eisenhower and Nixon, 1952–1961*. New Haven, CT: Yale University Press, 2015.

Goldberg, Robert Alan. *Barry Goldwater*. New Haven, CT: Yale University Press, 1995.

Goodman, Walter. *The Committee: The Extraordinary Career of the House Committee on Un-American Activities*. New York: Farrar, Straus, and Giroux, 1968.

Goodwin, Doris Kearns. *Lyndon Johnson and the American Dream*. New York: Harper & Row, 1976.

Goodwin, Richard N. *Remembering America: A Voice from the Sixties*. Boston: Little, Brown, 1988

Gould, Lewis L. *The Most Exclusive Club: A History of the Modern United States Senate*. New York: Basic Books, 2005.

Grant, Philip A. "The Bricker Amendment Controversy." *Presidential Studies Quarterly* 15, no. 3 (Summer 1985): 572–82.

Griffith, Robert. *The Politics of Fear: Joseph R. McCarthy and the Senate*. Lexington: University Press of Kentucky, 1970.

Guthman, Edwin O., and Jeffrey Shulman, *Robert Kennedy in His Own Words*. New York: Bantam, 1988.

Halberstam, David. *The Best and the Brightest*. New York: Random House, 1969.

———. *The Fifties*. New York: Villard Books, 1993.

———. *The Powers That Be*. New York: Alfred A. Knopf, 1979.

Hess, Stephen. *The Ultimate Insiders: U.S. Senators in the National Media*. Washington, DC: Brookings Institution, 1986.

Howard, Joseph Kinsey. *Montana: High, Wide, and Handsome*. New Haven, CT: Yale University Press, 1959.

Hulsey, Byron C. *Everett Dirksen and His Presidents: How a Senate Giant Shaped American Politics*. Lawrence: University Press of Kansas, 2001.

Humphrey, Hubert H. *The Education of a Public Man: My Life in Politics*. Garden City, NY: Doubleday, 1976.

Jacobson, Harold Karan, and Eric Stein. *Diplomats, Scientists, and Politicians: The United States and the Nuclear Test Ban Negotiations*. Ann Arbor: University of Michigan Press, 1966.

Johnson, Lady Bird. *A White House Diary*. Austin: University of Texas Press, 1970.

Johnson, Lyndon B. *The Vantage Point: Perspectives of the Presidency, 1963–1969*. New York: Holt, Rinehart, and Winston, 1971.

Johnson, Marc C. "Mike Mansfield, Burton K. Wheeler, and the Montana Senate Campaign of 1946." *Montana: The Magazine of Western History* (Autumn 2020): 21–36.

Kallina, Edmund F. "Was the 1960 Presidential Election Stolen? The Case of Illinois." *Presidential Studies Quarterly* (Winter 1985): 113–18.

Kennedy, Robert F. *Thirteen Days: A Memoir of the Cuban Missile Crisis*. New York: W. W. Norton, 1969.

Kittredge, William, and Annick Smith. *The Last Best Place: A Montana Anthology*. Seattle: University of Washington Press, 1988.

Knock, Thomas J. *The Life and Times of George McGovern: The Rise of a Prairie Statesman*. Princeton, NJ: Princeton University Press, 2016.

Koskoff, David E. *The Senator from Central Casting: The Rise, Fall, and Resurrection of Thomas J. Dodd*. New Haven, CT: New American Political Press, 2011.

Kotz, Nick. *Judgment Days: Lyndon Baines Johnson, Martin Luther King, Jr., and the Laws That Changed America*. Boston: Houghton Mifflin, 2005.

Kurlansky, Mark. *1968: The Year That Rocked the World*. New York: Ballantine, 2004.

Leuchtenburg, William E. *The White House Looks South: Franklin Roosevelt, Harry Truman, Lyndon Johnson*. Baton Rouge: Louisiana State University Press, 2005.

Lewis, Finley. *Mondale: Portrait of an American Politician*. New York: Harper & Row, 1980.

Loevy, Robert D. *To End All Segregation: The Politics of the Passage of the Civil Rights Act of 1964*. Lanham, MD: University Press of America, 1990.

Logevall, Fredrik. *JFK: Coming of Age in the American Century, 1917–1956*. New York: Random House, 2020.

Mackaman, Frank H. *The Long, Hard Furrow: Everett Dirksen's Part in the Civil Rights Act of 1964*. Pekin, IL: Dirksen Congressional Center, 2014.

———. *Time Magazine's Neil MacNeil: Reporting on Senator Everett Dirksen, 1957–1969*. Pekin, IL: Dirksen Congressional Center, 2018.

MacNeil, Neil. *Dirksen: Portrait of a Public Man*. New York: World Publishing, 1970.

MacNeil, Neil, and Richard A. Baker. *The American Senate: An Insider's History*. New York: Oxford University Press, 2013.

Malone, Michael P., Richard B. Roeder, and William L. Lang. *Montana: A History of Two Centuries*. Seattle: University of Washington Press, 1991.

Manchester, William. *The Death of a President: November 20–November 25, 1963*. New York: Little, Brown, 2013.

Mann, Robert. *A Grand Delusion: America's Descent into Vietnam*. New York: Basic Books, 2001.

———. *Legacy to Power: Senator Russell Long of Louisiana*. New York: Paragon House, 1992.

———. *The Walls of Jericho: Lyndon Johnson, Herbert Humphrey, Richard Russell, and the Struggle for Civil Rights*. New York: Harcourt Brace, 1996.

Marble, Manning. *Malcolm X: A Life of Reinvention*. New York: Viking, 2011.

Margolis, Jon. *The Last Innocent Year: America in 1964—The Beginning of the "Sixties."* New York: William Morrow, 1999.

Matthews, Donald R. *U.S. Senators and Their World*. New York: Random House, 1960.

McCullough, David. *Truman*. New York: Simon and Schuster, 1992.

McMaster, H. R. *Dereliction of Duty: Lyndon Johnson, Robert McNamara, the Joint Chiefs of Staff, and the Lies That Led to Vietnam*. New York: HarperCollins, 1997.

McPherson, Harry. *A Political Education: A Journal with Senators, Generals, Cabinet Members, and Presidents*. Boston: Little, Brown, 1972.

Memorial Services Held in the Senate and House of Representatives of the United States, Together with Tributes Presented in Eulogy of Everett McKinley Dirksen. Washington, DC: US Government Printing Office, 1970.

Middendorf, J. William II. *A Glorious Disaster: Barry Goldwater's Presidential Campaign and the Origins of the Conservative Movement*. New York: Basic Books, 2006.

Miller, Merle. *Lyndon*. New York: Putnam, 1980.

Montgomery, Gayle B., and James W. Johnson, *One Step from the White House: The Rise and Fall of Senator William F. Knowland*. Berkeley: University of California Press, 1998.

Morgan, Anne Hodges. *Robert S. Kerr: The Senate Years*. Norman: University of Oklahoma Press, 1977.

Mudd, Roger. *The Place to Be: Washington, CBS, and the Glory Days of Television News*. New York: PublicAffairs, 2008.

Murphy, Bruce Allen. *Fortas: The Rise and Ruin of a Supreme Court Justice*. New York: William Morrow, 1988.

Murray, Robert K. *Red Scare: A Study in National Hysteria, 1919–1920*. Minneapolis: University of Minnesota Press, 1955.

Oberdorfer, Don. *Senator Mansfield: The Extraordinary Life of a Great American Statesman and Diplomat*. Washington: Smithsonian Books, 2003.

———. *Tet! The Story of a Battle and Its Historic Aftermath*. Garden City, NY: Doubleday, 1971.

O'Donnell, Kenneth P., and David F. Powers, with Joe McCarthy. *Johnny, We Hardly Knew Ye: Memoirs of John Fitzgerald Kennedy*. Boston: Little, Brown, 1970.

Offner, Arnold A. *Hubert Humphrey: The Conscience of the Country*. New Haven, CT: Yale University Press, 2018.

Olson, Gregory A. *Mansfield and Vietnam: A Study in Rhetorical Adaptation*. East Lansing: Michigan State University Press, 1995.

Ornstein, Norman J., ed. *Congress in Change: Evolution and Reform*. New York: Praeger, 1975.

Oshinsky, David M. *A Conspiracy So Immense: The World of Joe McCarthy.* New York: Free Press, 1983.

Patterson, James T. *Mr. Republican: A Biography of Robert A. Taft.* Boston: Houghton Mifflin, 1972.

Penney, Annette Culler. *Dirksen: The Golden Voice of the Senate.* Washington, DC: Acropolis Books, 1968.

Perlstein, Rick. *Before the Storm: Barry Goldwater and the Unmaking of the American Consensus.* New York: Hill and Wang, 2001.

Pietrusza, David. *1960: LBJ vs. JFK vs. Nixon: The Epic Campaign That Forged Three Presidencies.* New York: Union Square Press, 2008.

Plokhy, Serhii. *Nuclear Folly: A History of the Cuban Missile Crisis.* New York: Norton, 2021.

Polsby, Nelson W., ed. *Congressional Behavior.* New York: Random House, 1971.

Purdum, Todd S. *An Idea Whose Time Has Come: Two Presidents, Two Parties, and the Battle for the Civil Rights Act of 1964.* New York: Henry Holt, 2014.

Randall, Kenneth C. "The Treaty Power." *Ohio State Law Journal* 51, no. 5 (1990): 1089–1126.

Reeves, Richard. *President Kennedy: Profile of Power.* New York: Simon and Schuster, 1993.

Reeves, Thomas C. *The Life and Times of Joe McCarthy.* London: Blond and Briggs, 1982.

Ripley, Randall B. *Power in the Senate.* New York: St. Martin's Press, 1969.

Risen, Clay. *The Bill of the Century: The Epic Battle for the Civil Rights Act.* New York: Bloomsbury, 2014.

Ritchie, Donald A. "The Senate of Mike Mansfield." *Montana: The Magazine of Western History* 48, no. 4 (1998): 50–62.

Sabato, Larry J. *The Kennedy Half Century: The Presidency, Assassination, and Lasting Legacy of John F. Kennedy.* New York: Bloomsbury, 2013.

Schapsmeier, Edward L., and Frederick H. Schapsmeier. *Dirksen of Illinois: Senatorial Statesman.* Urbana: University of Illinois Press, 1985.

Schlesinger, Arthur M. Jr. *The Imperial Presidency.* Boston: Houghton Mifflin, 1973.

———. *Robert Kennedy and His Times.* Boston: Houghton Mifflin, 1978.

———. *A Thousand Days: John F. Kennedy in the White House.* Boston: Houghton Mifflin, 1965.

Schlesinger, Arthur M. Jr., and Roger Burns. *Congress Investigates, 1792–1974.* New York: Chelsea House, 1975.

Schrecker, Ellen. *Many Are the Crimes: McCarthyism in America.* Princeton, NJ: Princeton University Press, 1998.

Seaborg, Glenn T. *Kennedy, Khrushchev, and the Test Ban.* Berkeley: University of California Press, 1981.

Shapiro, Ira. *The Last Great Senate: Courage and Statesmanship in Times of Crisis.* New York: PublicAffairs, 2012.

Sherman, Michael, ed. *The Political Legacy of George D. Aiken: Wise Old Owl of the Senate.* Montpelier: Vermont Historical Society, 1995.

Sherwin, Martin J. *Gambling with Armageddon: Nuclear Roulette from Hiroshima to the Cuban Missile Crisis.* New York: Knopf, 2020.

Shesol, Jeff. *Mutual Contempt: Lyndon Johnson, Robert Kennedy, and the Feud That Defined a Decade.* New York: W. W. Norton, 1997.

Sinclair, Barbara. *Unorthodox Lawmaking: New Legislative Processes in the U.S. Congress.* Washington, DC: CQ Press, 2012.

Smith, Jean Edward. *Eisenhower in War and Peace.* New York: Random House, 2012.

Smith, Richard Norton. *The Colonel: The Life and Legend of Robert E. McCormick.* Boston: Houghton Mifflin, 1997.

Smith, Steven S. *The Senate Syndrome: The Evolution of Procedural Warfare in the Modern U.S. Senate.* Norman: University of Oklahoma Press, 2014.

Sorensen, Theodore C. *Kennedy.* New York: Harper & Row, 1965.

Steinberg, Alfred. *Sam Johnson's Boy: A Close-up of the President from Texas.* New York: Macmillan, 1968.

Stone, Gary. *Elites for Peace: The Senate and the Vietnam War.* Knoxville: University of Tennessee Press, 2007.

Stone, I. F. *The Best of I. F. Stone.* New York: PublicAffairs, 2006.

Thomas, Evan. *Robert Kennedy: His Life.* New York: Simon and Schuster, 2000.

Thorpe, D. R. *Supermac: The Life of Harold Macmillan.* London: Chatto & Windus, 2010.

Tye, Larry. *Demagogue: The Life and Long Shadow of Senator Joe McCarthy.* Boston: Houghton Mifflin Harcourt, 2020.

Updegrove, Mark K. *Indomitable Will: LBJ in the Presidency.* New York: Crown, 2012.

Valeo, Francis R. *Mike Mansfield, Majority Leader: A Different Kind of Senate, 1961–1976.* Armonk, NY: M. E. Sharpe, 1999.

Vidal, Gore. *United States: Essays 1952–1992.* New York: Random House, 1993.

Waldron, Ellis, and Paul B. Wilson. *Atlas of Montana Elections: 1889–1976.* Missoula: University of Montana Publications in History, 1978.

Watkins, T. H. *The Hungry Years: A Narrative History of the Great Depression in America.* New York: Henry Holt, 2000.

Weiland, Matt, and Sean Wilsey. *State by State: A Panoramic Portrait of America.* New York: HarperCollins, 2008.

Weiner, Tim. *A Legacy of Ashes.* New York: Anchor Books, 2007.

Wenger, Andreas, and Marcel Gerber, "John F. Kennedy and the Limited Test Ban Treaty: A Case Study of Presidential Leadership." *Presidential Studies Quarterly* 29, no. 2 (June 1999): 460–87.

White, Theodore. *The Making of the President, 1964.* New York: Atheneum, 1965.

White, William Smith. *Citadel: The Story of the U.S. Senate.* New York: Harper and Brothers, 1956.

———. "A Good Break." *Harper's*, March 1961, 108–11.

———. *The Taft Story.* New York: Harper and Brothers, 1954.

———. "Who Really Runs the Senate?" *Harper's*, December 1956.

Wicker, Tom. *Dwight D. Eisenhower.* New York: Henry Holt, 2002.

———. *JFK and LBJ: The Influence of Personality upon Politics.* New York: William Morrow, 1968.

———. *Shooting Star: The Brief Arc of Joe McCarthy.* New York: Harcourt, 2006.

Wills, Garry. *Nixon Agonistes: The Crisis of the Self-Made Man.* Boston: Houghton Mifflin, 1969.

Woods, Randall Bennett. *Fulbright: A Biography*. New York: Cambridge University Press, 1995.

————. *LBJ: Architect of American Ambition*. New York: Free Press, 2006.

————. *Prisoners of Hope: Lyndon B. Johnson, the Great Society, and the Limits of Liberalism*. New York: Basic Books, 2016.

————. *Vietnam and the American Political Tradition: The Politics of Dissent*. New York: Cambridge University Press, 2003.

Zasloff, Jonathan. "The Secret History of the Fair Housing Act." *Harvard Journal of Legislation* 53 (January 20, 2016): 247–78.

Zelizer, Julian E., ed. *The American Congress: The Building of Democracy*. Boston: Houghton Mifflin, 2004.

————. *The Fierce Urgency of Now: Lyndon Johnson, Congress, and the Battle for the Great Society*. New York: Penguin, 2015.

DISSERTATIONS AND THESES

Bloodworth, Jeff. "Farewell to the Vital Center: A History of American Liberalism, 1968–1980." PhD diss., Ohio University, 2006.

Cronin, Jean Torcom. "Minority Leadership in the United States Senate: The Role and Style of Everett Dirksen." PhD diss., Johns Hopkins University, 1973.

Deason, Brian S. "Eye of the Storm: A Political Biography of Senator Scott W. Lucas of Illinois." PhD diss,, Southern Illinois University, 2000.

Faver, Frankie Bozeman. "An Analysis of Humor in Selected Speeches of Everett Dirksen." MA thesis, Texas Tech University, 1970.

Huddle, Franklin Pierce. "The Limited Nuclear Test Ban Treaty and the United States Senate." PhD diss., American University, 1965.

Olson, Gregory Allen, "Mike Mansfield's Ethos in the Evolution of United States Policy in Indochina." PhD diss., University of Minnesota, 1988.

Stewart, John G. "Independence and Control: The Challenge of Senatorial Party Leadership." PhD diss., University of Chicago, 1968.

Stone, Gary Steven. "The Senate and the Vietnam War, 1964–1968." PhD diss., Columbia University, 2000.

INDEX